D1617531

WRITING
THE VOICE
OF PLEASURE

WRITING
THE VOICE
OF PLEASURE

Heterosexuality Without Women

ANNE CALLAHAN

palgrave

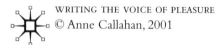

WRITING THE VOICE OF PLEASURE
© Anne Callahan, 2001

First published 2001 by
PALGRAVE
175 Fifth Avenue, New York, N.Y. 10010 and
Houndmills, Basingstoke, Hampshire RG21 6XS.
Companies and representatives throughout the world

PALGRAVE™ is the new global publishing imprint of St. Martin's Press LLC Scholarly and Reference Division and Palgrave Publishers Ltd (formerly Macmillan Press Ltd).

ISBN 0-312-23937-8 hardback

Library of Congress Cataloging-in-Publication Data

Callahan, Anne.
      Writing the voice of pleasure : heterosexuality without women / by Anne Callahan.
          p. cm.
      Includes bibliographical references and index.
      ISBN 0-312-23937-8
      1. Sex role in literature. 2. Man-woman relationships in literature. 3. European literature—History and criticism. 4. French literature—History and criticism. I. Title.

PN56 .S52 C35 2001
809'.93353—dc21

                                                                    2001036146

A catalogue record for this book is available from the British Library.

Design by Westchester Book Composition

First edition: October 2001
10 9 8 7 6 5 4 3 2 1

Printed in the United States of America.

Contents

CONTENTS

Acknowledgments

$\mathcal{T}$his book has been a collaborative effort from the moment it began to take shape—and before. Hardly a day has gone by in the past decade that an interested student, colleague, or friend hasn't made a suggestion, provided a remarkable example, or thoughtfully commented on a sentence, a page, a chapter, or in some cases a lengthy draft. I have tried to acknowledge individual contributions throughout the text and in the notes, but some are so great and so personal as to merit special mention here.

Janis Glasgow's invitation to present a paper at a conference on George Sand in 1982 was the beginning of what has become for me a habit of reading and rethinking the writer who is the inspiration for this book. For their warm reception and support, I am grateful to the George Sand Association, a group of scholars and artists whose intellectual and social companionship has been indispensable to the conceptualization of the chapters on Sand. Special thanks to Pierrette Daly, Thelma Jurgrau, Isabelle Naginski, Annabelle Rea, Eve Sourian, and Dorothy Zimmerman.

The staff and researchers of the Centre René Nelli des Études Cathares in Carcassonne, France gave me access to invaluable documents on the culture of Occitania and shared with me the pleasure of daily conversations about their work. Special thanks to Nicholas Gouzy and Anne Brenon for their warm collegial welcome. I must also thank Loyola University Chicago for the paid leave of absence which allowed me to travel to Carcassonne to do the necessary research for the book's first chapter. I am grateful to the many colleagues and staff members in Loyola University Chicago's Department of Modern Languages & Literatures, whose interest in my work has been a great support. Special thanks to Ann Bugliani, Patricia Clemente, Wiley Feinstein, Paolo Giordano, Deni Heyck, Jeffrey Librett, David Pankratz, Gilbert Pestureau, and Cynthia Rudolph.

Several other friends, colleagues, and collaborators should be mentioned by name. Andrew McKenna's Faculty Seminar in Theory provided the impetus for me to make the connections between my work and contemporary theoretical debates. Andrew has also read and commented on the manuscript, and our conversations over the years have played a vital role in my commitment to writing. Mary Lydon's patient, attentive reading of an early draft helped clarify the book's focus. Florine Bruneau's persistent questions about my use of the term "androgynous fusion" resulted in an indispensable breakthrough. Sanford Ames's gentle persuasion to submit a piece to a volume on Duras would turn out to be more significant in the evolution of the concept of "vagabondage" than either of us could have known at the time. Elaine Marks offered support and encouragement of the project in its critical early stages. I want to take this opportunity to acknowledge the importance of the wisdom and integrity of her work to feminist scholarship. My debt to Louise J. Kaplan is enormous. Her willingness to take time from a full professional schedule to read this book and the wise advice she offered so generously came at a crucial time in its preparation for publication. The ideas generated during almost-weekly conversations with Tom Cox appear in the pages of this book—and breathe life into them—in ways he alone will recognize. Discussions with Glenn Morocco about the Spanish women writers of the group *versos con faldas* (verses with skirts) brought a fresh perspective to my thinking about linguistic transvestism. The energy, loyalty, intelligence, research skill and knowledge of popular culture brought to this project by my research assistant, Gina Zupsich, merits very special mention.

I thank Kristi Long of Palgrave for her vision as editor and as scholar. Her knowledge of culture led her to an inspired choice of readers, for whose recommendations I am most grateful. I thank Kristi for her warm and always prompt attention during the editing process.

The realization of this book owes more than I can ever adequately describe to C/Zinc, an informal writing group of five women including myself. I have relied on the loving friendship, the quick wit, the collective wisdom, and the individual professional expertise of Pamela Caughie, Susan Cavallo, Janice Mouton, and Eleanor Honig Skoller, whom I call the "paramedics" of writing—always on call to resuscitate not only the writing, but the writer. This book has been realized in great part due to their individual contributions as well as to their collective support. Eleanor has been the first reader of each of the chapters of this final version of the book. I am grateful for her enlightened and elegant editing.

My husband, historian Walter Gray, has been involved in the making of this book every step of the way. His involvement goes far beyond reading the manuscript several times to check the accuracy and relevance of historical material. His knowledge and love of languages, international travel, music, art, and his genius for integrating serious academic work and the good life have provided a balance without which a project of this scope would not have been imaginable. For the pleasure of his company on this voyage of the spirit and the mind, I dedicate this book to him.

Introduction

Dans tout homme qui parle de l'absence de l'autre, du féminin se déclare: cet homme qui attend et qui en souffre, est miraculeusement féminisé. Un homme n'est pas féminisé parce qu'il est inverti, mais parce qu'il est amoureux.

(In any man who utters the other's absence something feminine is declared: this man who waits and who suffers from his waiting is miraculously feminized. A man is not feminized because he is inverted but because he is in love.)

—*Roland Barthes,* Fragments d'un discours amoureux
(Fragments of a Lover's Discourse)

When Mme de Chartres admonished her daughter, La Princesse de Clèves, about the dangers of believing in the illusions of courtly love, "while minimizing none of its charm,"[1] she herself firmly believed in the existence of the heterosexual couple in Western representation. I would like to suggest, however, that by the time of the French Renaissance, during the reign of Henry II (1547–1559), the historical setting for Madame de Lafayette's 1678 novel, Mme de Chartres' belief was already based on an illusion, whose charms I should not like to minimize either. For some four centuries before Mme de Chartres' warnings, the heterosexual couple in Western narrative had become and still is a literary device to represent the inevitable feminization of one who writes the absence of the other, one who writes desire. The fate of the Princesse de Clèves, celibacy and withdrawal from desire, points to author Mme de Lafayette's sense of the unavailability, in this written tradition, of a place from which a heterosexual woman can write her desire—and desire writing.

The tradition of this literary device, the creation of a fusionary heterosexual couple to represent a male writer's feminization, can be found at least as far back as the medieval French poets who are credited with the invention of *Fin'Amors,* the original name of the literary philosophy which has come to be known as courtly love and touted by some cultural and literary historians as a revolutionary relationship between the sexes.[2] Each of the words of the phrase "relationship between the sexes" has been problematized in contemporary theoretical discourse. For example, Jacques Lacan's pithy dismissal of the possibility of a sexual relationship when he states, "il n'y a pas de rapport sexuel" (there is no sexual relationship) (*Le seminaire XX* [1975] 17). Or, Judith Butler's extravagant move in raising the possibility that if gender is not natural but constructed, the same might also be true of sex (*Gender Trouble* [1990] 7). Philippe Sollers concludes that heterosexual love is an unnatural cultural arrangement in his novel, *Passion fixe* (2000), when he writes: "Un homme et une femme qui s'aiment sont les plus grands pervers de la terre" (A man and a woman who love each other are the most perverse beings on earth) (119).[3] Yet the assumption of a tradition of heterosexual desire in literature persists as an undisputed and necessary ground from which to make a case for the absence of alternative voices and subject positions in Western representations of sexual desire.[4] While I do not question the ethical imperative to undermine assumptions that shore up a politics of exclusion, I do question the assumption of conventional heterosexuality in the case of literary models of romantic love.[5] In a well-known essay, Adrienne Rich attributes a significant role to romantic love narratives in the construction of "compulsory heterosexuality."[6] Such an attribution assumes that in the narratives the lovers are of opposite sexes. It is my contention that in this literary tradition the sexuality is not heterosexual, nor is it homosexual, as Eve Kosovsky Sedgwick has suggested in *Between Men.*[7] It is, rather, an effect of the writing—what I call the *troubadour effect.*

It was the troubadours of twelfth-century France who introduced into our literary heritage the ideals of heterosexual courtly love based on a complicated philosophy of sexual exchanges which developed into a poetics.[8] Prior to the troubadours and their philosophy of *Fin'Amors,* ideal love in the court was the preserve of *compagnonnage,* or male friendship. René Nelli, author of 78 books on Occitania and well-known, especially in France, as an expert on troubadour eroticism, has described *Fin'Amors* as the homoeroticization of heterosexuality.[9] Although I do not agree with Nelli's assessment of the value of *Fin'Amors* for women, it was his recognition that this poetry is not clearly heterosexual that moved me to further pursue the sexuality idealized in the conventions of courtly love poetry. Because Nelli understands that the eroticism of troubadour poetry is not heterosexual, his impulse is to place it within the only other existing model for ritualized ideal love at the time, that of *compagnonnage*—the service of male friendship often called *affrèrement,* or brotherhood (*L'Érotique des troubadours* [1963] 214). According to Nelli, in one of the rituals of *Fin'Amors,* an *asag* or love test that takes place when the lovers lie in bed, partially or fully unclothed, separated by a sword, the two exchange sexes. The woman is symbolically raised to the status of a man in order to be worthy of the quality of love reserved for male friendship, or, in other words, to be loved unto death as expressed in the following typical formulation of *affrèrement:* "prius se velle cum Bertearid mori quam usquam alibi in summis deliciis vivere" (I prefer to die with my friend Bertarid than to live in delight with another) (Nelli, *ET* 14). The man becomes a woman by giving up his natural aggression, both sexual and social. Lancelot, in Chrétien de Troyes' *Chevalier de la charrette* (1170), is a good example of this behavior in a knight who loves with *Fin'Amors.* According to the romance, when the other knights of the Round Table go rushing off to tournaments, Lancelot prefers to stay behind, dallying with the queen and her ladies. In Chrétien's story, he does not linger because he is in love with Queen Guinevere, but he falls in love with her because he prefers to spend time with women rather than compete in knightly tournaments. Likewise, in several versions of the romance of Tristan and Iseut, Tristan is a harpist and singer. The romantic hero's penchant for creativity, associated with music and with the feminine, makes him vulnerable to the power of the love potion.[10] With troubadour poetry, the figure of the romantic lover enters literature; together with the illusory woman created by the voice of his pleasure, they constitute the spurious heterosexual couple of medieval romance.

The exchange of sex roles is presented in the poetry as mutual and lasting. Textual analysis, however, shows that the woman's transformation is brief and illusory. Georges Duby, the dean of historians of medieval culture in France, titles his book, *Mâle Moyen Âge* (1988), indicating that it was indeed so—a very "male middle ages."[11] All of the courtly love rituals associated with the medieval class system called chivalry are about changing male behavior.[12] In the case of the *asag,* it is the man who is changed. One of the best known of the troubadours, Bernart de Ventadorn, for example, writes that his former self disappears through service to the *dame:*

Miralhs, pus me mirei en te,
M'an mort li sospir de prëon,
C'aissi.m perdei com perdet se
Lo bels Narcisus en la fon. (Press 77)

*(Mirror, since I mirrored myself in you
sighs from deep down have slain me*

3

and thus I was lost as, in the pool
the fair Narcissus was lost)

The *joi* which is the goal of troubadour poetry is defined by the first known troubadour, Guillaume IX, as *une sortie de soi* (moving out of oneself), and *le passage à l'autre* (passing into the other) (Nelli, *Le roman de Flamenca* [1989] 98).[13] It is significant that the use of the term "dame" to describe the idealized woman derives from the masculine "don" and in some of the earliest Provençal poetry the designation remains in the masculine form.[14] This masculine appellation signifies the woman's worthiness to be loved as much as a man, and evokes the poet's desire to conceive of her as his master in the love relationship. Her social status is not changed by this (Duby, Nelli, Brenon). That she is female, however, is never far from the poet's consciousness, and one of the most troubling aspects of the troubadour love lyrics is the confusion between the woman in her masculine and worthy guise, and her femaleness and "abominable" correspondence to Nature, to paraphrase the nineteenth-century poet Baudelaire ("Mon coeur mis à nu," III 406).[15] Her natural sex provides the poet with the source of his own femininity in two ways: one, as a source of identification with the other sex (rather than with the same sex as in *compagnonnage*); and two, paradoxically, because women are "by nature" incapable of the loyalty and devotion required of male *compagnonnage,* it furnishes him with reasons to bemoan his fate as a slave to the love of a woman whom he has transformed into a master only in his imagination, placing him in the traditional feminine position in the structure of desire. Barthes' words, quoted in my epigraph, sum up the structure of desire and the language of love in Western representation since the troubadours: "un homme n'est pas féminisé parce qu'il est inverti, mais parce qu'il est amoureux" (a man is not feminized because he is inverted, but because he is in love). The man in love, and who speaks or writes it, is not homosexual, nor is he in the masculine position; one writes desire from the position of the feminized male.[16] In spite of the male writer's feminization, the absent Other in narratives of desire is represented as a woman. This representation—structurally a double femininity—creates the illusion of a heterosexual couple. For example, in both the medieval and Wagnerian versions of Tristan and Iseut, Iseut literally evaporates after Tristan's death.[17] In both versions, Tristan dies from a physical injury. There is no cause given for the death of Iseut, the character who lives on for a short time after his death to embody the voice of his pleasure. In Wagner's opera, Isolde (Iseut) expires when—actually, *because*—the song ends. The couple in the romance is a chimera. There is no couple. There is only the feminized male and his idealization of an imaginary Other.

It is in Rousseau that I first found the writing effect that I later traced to the troubadours. In all my readings of him, I never found him, or his fictional characters, to be the heterosexual lovers one would expect from the philosopher who moved a generation of writers and readers to forsake cynical libertinage for ideal love. The reason, I discovered, was that Rousseau's lovers brought back into fashion the structural dynamics of *Fin'Amors*— a feminized man, slave to his *dame-don* (lady-lord). In the *Confessions* (1782–1789) he describes his dominant trait as *un coeur sensible* (a sensitive heart) (*Oeuvres Complètes* I: 7); his only desire is to kneel at the feet of an imperious mistress without possessing her (*OC*, I: 17). Like the troubadour poets, for Rousseau the consummation of love for the lady is accomplished in the writing. He shows this explicitly in *Julie, ou la nouvelle Héloïse* (1761) when Saint Preux, waiting expectantly in her closet surrounded by her clothes and *odeur de femme* (scent of a woman), but foiled by the unexpected arrival of her father, exclaims: "Quel bonheur d'avoir trouvé de l'encre et du papier!" (Thank God, I found paper and ink!) (*OC*, II: 147).

I became aware of the extremely knotty and slippery problem of a woman who desires to write narratives of romantic love in the troubadour tradition while reading George Sand. In her autobiographical and fictional writings, Sand explicitly evokes Rousseau's writing as important to her own. In *Histoire de ma vie* (*Story of My Life*) (1854–1855) she describes how Rousseau's sublime language affects her: "le langage de Jean-Jacques s'emparait de moi comme de la musique" (Jean-Jacques' language took possession of me like music) (*Oeuvres autobiographiques*, I: 1060). In the same work she takes leave of her male predecessor when she writes, "tu me pardonneras, Jean-Jacques, si je laisse tes adorables pages pour reprendre les miennes" (Forgive me, Jean-Jacques, if I close your pages that I adore to take up my own) (*OA*, I: 13).[18]

Sand's apology is not meant for Rousseau, but offered ironically to a society for which the male is entrenched as the writer, occluding women, who must not only apologize for desiring to write, but must choose between art and love. In *Elle et lui* (1859), she describes the problem of Thérèse-Jacques, a woman artist, as having to choose between the pleasure of painting and an erotic relationship with another artist, Laurent. Like the Princesse de Clèves, Thérèse-Jacques chooses celibacy in order to exercise her subjectivity. In the modernist period, Colette makes this kind of choice the subject of her novel, *La vagabonde* (*The Vagabond*) (1911). Her protagonist, Renée Néré, is a woman of letters who feels forced to choose between writing and heterosexual love. The pleasure of writing, unavailable to her when she is in love with a man, ultimately prevails. She extols the pleasures that she gets from the writing itself:

Écrire. C'est le regard accroché, hypnotisé par le reflet de la fenêtre dans l'encrier d'argent, la fièvre divine qui monte aux joues, au front, tandis qu'une bienheureuse mort glace sur la papier la main qui écrit. Cela veut dire aussi l'oubli de l'heure, la paresse aux creux du divan, la débauche d'invention d'où l'on sort courbatu, abêti mais déjà récompensé, et porteur de trésors qu'on décharge lentement sur la feuille vierge, dans le petit cirque de lumière qui s'abrite sous la lampe. (*Oeuvres*, I: 1074)

(To write is to sit and stare, hypnotized by the reflection of the window in the silver inkstand, the divine fever mounting to one's cheeks and forehead while a blissful numbness freezes the hand that writes on the paper. It also means forgetting time, lazily curled up in the hollow of the divan, and then the orgy of inspiration from which one emerges stupefied and aching all over, but already recompensed and laden with treasures that one unloads slowly on to the virgin page in the little circle of light under the lamp.)

Virginia Woolf, a contemporary of Colette, has the chimeric eponymous man-woman protagonist of *Orlando* (1928), who travels through English literary history from the Elizabethan age to the 1920s, say ecstatically as she writes in her final, modern female incarnation:

And she plunged her pen neck deep in the ink. To her enormous surprise there was no explosion. She drew the nib out. It was wet, but not dripping. She wrote. The words were a little long in coming, but come they did. . . . Now, therefore, she could write, and write she did. She wrote. She wrote. She wrote. (265–66)

Because they are and remain women, Sand, Colette, and Woolf, try to own their positions as writers without the qualifying appellation of "woman" writer. But this is not a simple move from the position of object of the male writer's desire into a subject position. Although for centuries the woman has been the object of the male writers' desire, as a result of the *troubadour effect* there really is no heterosexual couple in this structure. A woman writer cannot, then, reverse the ground, and represent the man as object of her desire. As Barthes reminds us, the man who writes is in the feminine position, leaving the heterosexual woman who wants to write in the narrative tradition of romantic love with neither an object of desire nor a subject position. Without a position or a place to reside, the woman writer is, in effect, a vagabond. As Colette so aptly puts it:

J'écris sur les guéridons boiteux, assise de biais des chaises trop hautes, j'écris, un pied chaussé et l'autre nu, mon papier logé entre le plateau du petit déjeuner et mon sac à main ouvert, parmi les brosses, le flacon d'odeur et le tire-bouton; j'écris devant la fenêtre qui encadre un fond de cour, ou les plus délicieux jardins, ou des montagnes vaporeuses. . . . Je me sens chez moi, parmi ce désordre de campement, ce n'importe où et ce n'importe comment, et plus légère qu'en mes meubles hantés. (*Oeuvres*, I: 1222)

(I write on wobbly pedestal tables, sitting sideways on chairs that are too high, I write with one foot shod and one bare, the paper lodged between the breakfast tray and my open handbag, all among the brushes, the bottle of scent and the button-hook; I write sitting at a window that frames part of a courtyard, or the most delicious gardens, or misty mountains. I feel myself at home amid this disorder of a camp, this no matter where and no matter how, and freer than among my haunted furniture.)

Colette's vagabond writer is at the same time still in bondage to her woman's body. In one of her weaker moments, Renée explains:

Tout est contre moi. Le premier obstacle où je bute, c'est ce corps de femme allongé qui me barre la route, un voluptueux corps aux yeux fermés, volontairement aveugle, étiré, prêt à périr plutôt que de quitter le lieu de sa joie. (*Oeuvres*, I: 1217)

(Everything is against me. The first obstacle I run into is the female body lying there, which bars my way, a voluptuous body with closed eyes, deliberately blind, stretched out and ready to perish rather than leave the place where its joy lies.)

Still tied to the traditional feminine role as object of desire, taught by literature to want to be loved, and ultimately consumed by a man, a woman writer has to choose between the bondage of being the vagabond or the object of male desire. One of the aims of my study is to suggest that another slip of the knot in the structure of the romantic love narrative is the connection between the *vagabondage* of the woman writer and the misrecognition that there is a heterosexual couple in that tradition. *Vagabondage* is the situation of the woman writer condemned to shift subject positions between masculine subjectivity and identification with the feminine object of desire (and of writing). The voice of pleasure, which for the male writer is achieved in the splitting of the subject into masculine and feminine with the result that both genders are contained within masculinity, is not accessible to women. Women who write in this tradition are forced to choose between sexual pleasure and literary expression.

I introduced the term *vagabondage* in an article on Marguerite Duras's *L'Amant* (1984) in which for the first time in my own writing I formulated a question which had haunted my work on women and writing. In that article, I asked why women writers identified with the female body as object in their own writing. Women writers as prolific as Duras and Colette seemed unable, even disinclined, to move into the position of the writing subject without advocating either identification with the written feminine body or withdrawal from desire itself. In my usage as it has since developed, the term *vagabondage* combines the words vagabond, from Colette's title, and bondage, a masochistic pleasure associated with femininity in the construction of gender in eroticism. The connection between the *troubadour effect* and *vagabondage* did not come until later when I put together two questions which kept arising in my work. The question that triggered the writing of my first book, *Erotic Love in Literature,* was "why is the heterosexual male romantic lover effeminate?" In the article on Duras, a second question emerged: "If writing produces language and subjectivity, why does the act of writing narratives of heterosexual desire not move women into a subject position?" It took years of dealing with the two questions as separate issues before I realized that not only were they related, but that the answer to the first was also the answer to the second. The woman writer is in bondage to a representation which involves both the illusion of the heterosexual woman, and female impersonation on the part of male writers.

Barbara Johnson calls the literary device of the male writer's feminization "male self-difference," and describes Baudelaire's poetic depiction of himself as both the wound and the knife (*la plaie et le couteau*) as the "male privilege to play femininity" ("Gender and Poetry" [1991] 178). The *troubadour effect,* or the way in which the poet assumes femininity as a source of both subjectivity and subjection, is an abiding and defining phenomenon in fictions of heterosexual desire since the twelfth century; the phenomenon Johnson calls attention to in the love poetry of the latter half of the nineteenth century is also present at the incipience of love poetry and romantic love narratives seven centuries earlier. The illusion of sexual difference of romantic lovers from these first fictions of heterosexual desire has derived from the poet's difference from other men, and from himself. Simply put, male femininity is what constitutes sexual difference in heterosexual fictions. If there is no female subjectivity in these fictions, it is not because the woman is an object of desire. This may be the case in social practice, and that practice may in fact derive from the seductive power of literature, and the illusions it creates. In her critically acclaimed biography of Colette *Secrets of the Flesh: A Life of Colette* (1999), Judith Thurman muses about the "fascinating and baroque form of transvestism" which she sees in Colette's early writing (85). She describes the gender positions Colette assumes in her writing as a puzzle, one which corresponds coincidentally to a writing problem I have undertaken to work through in this book:

She is a woman writing as a man, Willy, who poses as a boyish girl, Claudine, who marries a "feminized" man, the aging Renaud, who pushes her into the arms of a female lover, Rézi, with whom she takes the virile role. (85)

The *troubadour effect* is a *supplément* (to invoke Derrida), neither a troubadour, nor a lady, but a representation of the pleasure of giving voice to the troubadour's creative impulse. The role of the supplement in representations of desire in Western metaphysics has been described by Jacques Derrida in *De la grammatologie* (*Of Grammatology* [1967]). The supplement, according to Derrida, "comes in place of a lapse, a nonsignified or a nonrepresented, a nonpresence. There is no present before, it is not preceded by anything but itself, that is to say by another supplement" (*Of Grammatology* 303–4). The human quest for origins and for wholeness creates the need to compensate for this nonpresence. As Josué Harari puts it, "The Derridean demonstration consists of showing that the whole edifice of Western metaphysics rests on the possibility of compensating for a primordial nonpresence by way of the supplement" (*Textual Strategies* [1979] 34). Significantly for my argument, Paul de Man considers the logic of the supplement a paradox because it represents an excess that is also a lack, "there is no escape from the pressure of a differentiation that never allows for a totalizing integrity" (*Allegories of Reading* [1979] 180). To come full circle to my argument, writing is the expression of the supplement, the excess which is at the same time a lack. Andrew McKenna specifies, "writing represents the 'supplement of origin,' the mark or excluded member in which language originates" (*Violence and Difference* [1992] 75). The "lady" of troubadour narratives, then, would be—in Derridean terms—in the position of the supplement, a nonpresence. Nonpresence, I argue, continues to be the role of the woman in Western narratives of heterosexual romance.

Derrida replicates the *troubadour effect* in his own effort at writing heterosexual romance, *La carte postale* (*The Post Card*) (1980), a pastiche of an epistolary novel, in which the romantic heroine is squarely placed in the position of the "supplement of origin." The voice of the mistress to whom the letters are addressed is absent from the text; the male lover, Derrida himself, composes both parts of the correspondence. Moreover, the main theme of the book is a deconstruction of a drawing on the post card which serves as a pretext for the series of letters. The drawing depicts Socrates seated at a table, engaged in writing. Plato stands behind his mentor, telling him what to write but pretending that the writing is produced by Socrates. The position of Plato behind Socrates, in addition to the unfortunate positioning of a large sword-like object, makes it appear—to Derrida's amusement—that Plato is sodomizing Socrates while the latter writes. All of the

9

actors in this erotic text supposedly addressed to a woman, are men—Derrida, Plato and Socrates. There is no space on Derrida's post card for the woman's pleasure as writer or as lover.

Although the implications of supplementarity for women's desire and women's writing are not within the purview of McKenna's book, he provides insight into the problem by relating Derrida's theory of language and Girard's theory of violence:

> We must locate the origin of language not in the mark itself, which means nothing, but in its exclusion as the exclusion of nonmeaning, of nondifference. This is where Girard locates the victim, from whose exclusion meaning is thereafter free to proliferate. (75–76)

Western representation excludes women from writing desire when, in search of a nonexistent original wholeness, it marks Woman as the representation of that search, forever excluded from language and subjectivity while always present as its mark, what I call the voice of pleasure—a so-called feminine voice signifying male desire for language. For the male artist, the voice's pleasure is derived from the search itself, from composing; the name "troubadour" comes from the verb "trobar" meaning to find, "trouver," in modern French. In the language of the medieval poets, "to find" is synonymous with "to compose" and the pleasure expressed by the feminine voice of the troubadours can best be described as the pleasure of finding the voice: that is to say, the voice's pleasure is inseparable from its production.[19] Through the composition of songs of love, the troubadours achieve that state of ecstasy called *joi,* or as Guillaume IX has it, the "moving out of oneself." This state of bliss resembles the state of perfection aspired to by the Cathars, the heretical Christian sect which flourished in the same area at the time of the troubadours. This coincidence of time, place, and the desire to achieve *joi* through love (human love for the troubadours, divine love for the Cathars) has led to a number of historical and critical commentaries linking the two, among which the most widely read in our time, both in France and elsewhere, is Denis de Rougemont's *L'Amour et l'occident* (*Love in the Western World*) published in 1939.

In spite of the error of his conviction that troubadour love poetry is the secret incantation of the precepts of the Cathar heresy, it is to De Rougemont's credit to have focused the attention of international literary studies on medieval Occitania and on its importance to the structure of desire in Western representation. An interest in the forgotten civilization of Occitania had already been created in France in the nineteenth century with the publication of two influential works: Fabre d'Olivet's *Le troubadour* (1803) and Napoléon Peyrat's five-volume book, *L'Histoire des Albigeois* (1870–72), which told a story rife with sentimentality beginning with the reconstruction of Montségur in 1204, and ending in the fourteenth century with the death of Bernard Délicieux, a Franciscan monk condemned for protesting the Inquisition in Carcassonne in 1319. Together, d'Olivet's celebration of troubadour love songs and Peyrat's description of the glorification of women in Catharism created an image of Occitania as a culture of love. Krystel Maurin, author of a 1995 study of women and femininity in the Cathar imagination, *Les Esclarmonde,* writes, "Catharisme et courtoisie se fondent pour générer l'illusion d'une 'civilisation romane' où l'amour, qu'il fût humain ou divin, était le ciment de l'unité et le secret de la liberté. En ce sens, les femmes incarnent l'Occitanie d'avant la croisade" (Catharism and *courtoisie* merged to generate the illusion of a 'romanesque civilization' in which love, whether human or divine, was the cement of the unity {of Catharism and *courtoisie*} and the secret of freedom) (39). Peyrat declared both the poetry and the religion of Occitania, *brigande* (outlaw) and designated femininity as the sign of this outlaw culture (*Les Albigeois et l'Inquisition* t.I, 37). Maurin insists, however, that one not confuse this glorification of "femininity" as evidence of even the slightest hint of "feminism." On the contrary, she writes: "La féminité se confond déjà avec la langue" (femininity is already confused with language) (40).

In the early nineteenth century after the publication of d'Olivet's *Le troubadour,* manuscripts were found and some of the poetry itself was published. Ossian and the Count of Arlincourt made the designation "troubadour" fashionable for poets (Maurin 30).[20] Although research since the 1970s—when much new material on the Cathars was brought to light by scholars like Le Roy Ladurie, Jean Duvernoy and Michel Roquebert—shows that previous theories about the relationship between troubadours and Cathars were mainly erroneous, Peyrat's work is still revered while it is also proscribed, called "un mythe magnifique" (a magnificent myth) (Maurin 37). It is, perhaps, due to the continuing seduction of Peyrat's magnificent myth that certain affinities between the troubadours and the Cathars, especially surrounding representations of femininity and masculinity, still come up in the recent revisionist scholarship (Brenon, Maurin).

A discussion of the intersection of troubadours and Cathars, including the debates in current research, constitutes a part of the first chapter of this book, which is devoted to the culture of Occitania, an area of southern France that has yet to yield its mysteries, especially in regard to its reputation as the birthplace of love between the sexes in literature. The fascination it still holds for historians, sociologists, theologians, and literary scholars is attested to by the enormous production of scholarly articles and books since the 1970s. I also discuss the problem of defining *joi* and the reasons why scholars like De Rougemont have confused mystical ecstasy with erotic bliss and how the substitution of one for the other produces the illusion of a woman as the representation of male self-difference. Because this structure is present even in writing where there can be no confusion with heterosexual romantic love, namely poetry by male mystics, it becomes clear that the object of the desire expressed is not a woman, but the writer's self-difference figured as Woman. For example, the Spanish mystic and poet San Juan de la Cruz (Saint John of the Cross) (1542–1591), explicitly refers to himself as a bride when writing of his desire for Christ.[21]

The illusion that the desire represented in the Occitanian tradition is heterosexual gives the male writer access to the split subjectivity necessary to experience the specific pleasure of writing. The question I develop in this study is: "How does a woman gain access to the same pleasure of subjectivity, to writing, to desire?" The voice of pleasure seduces on at least two levels: it expresses a desire for creative expression, and an equally powerful desire for sexual pleasure.

In *The Queen's Throat* (1995) Wayne Koestenbaum associates identification with the diva's voice with the pleasure of gay male subjectivity: identification with the diva's voice often gives the gay man the first experience of his difference from other men. However, it is an experience that creates the illusion of heterosexuality: "Opera makes me feel two-gendered, the idea of heterosexuality blooming inside my head. Violetta and Alfredo are making love in my bloodstream and thus my body isn't just one body; two formerly thwarting rivers meet" (40). His pleasure derives from both listening to the voice of pleasure and from creating yet another version of it by writing about the effect the music has on him. In spite of the fact that Koestenbaum's book is a celebration of a specifically homosexual pleasure, he represents this voice as an imaginary *heterosexual* experience of pleasure. The illusion of the sexual difference of two voices produced by a single troubadour passes into Western narrative and into culture as conventional heterosexuality; the figure of the feminine voice emanating from the male body does not appear perverse or even contrived because it seems to mirror a conventional social category in a direct and simple way. Both De Rougemont and Nelli discuss the feminine characters in narrative as if they were actual women, and as if the way in which they are loved in the fictions of desire were somehow noble. For De Rougemont, this noble sentiment that is necessarily chaste (due, in De Rougemont's view, to the Cathar influence) is perverted as the representation changes down through history—the woman ultimately reverting to the role of temptress and adulteress. While it is true that Nelli elaborates a theory of "the homoeroticization of heterosexuality," whereby the woman in the narrative is conceived of as a man to be worthy of a knight's love based on the model of *compagnonnage,* it is also true that he mistakenly reads this sex-change as a promotion in rank for the woman, confusing a literary representation with a social sexual category.

Women should not be compelled to turn away from the pleasures provided by canonical literature and art, such as listening to the magnificent voice of Jessye Norman or Jean Eaglen sing the role of Wagner's Isolde. What is imperative, however, is to renounce the pleasure of identification with an illusory woman born of a poet's transports; this is the subject of Flaubert's novel, *Madame Bovary* (1859). Because she mistakes the adulterous heroines of literary convention as women whose pleasure she can reproduce for herself by imitating their voices, Emma bores one lover and frightens another. Rodolphe is bored with her reproductions of feminine desire, which sound counterfeit to him. The *troubadour effect* reveals its presence in Flaubert's novel when Léon expresses the fear that he is becoming more Emma's mistress than she is his. Flaubert makes it clear that Léon's malaise is not caused by simple role reversal. On the contrary, Emma is the essence of femininity for Léon:

> Il savourait pour la première fois l'inexprimable délicatesse des élégances féminines. . . . Par la diversité de son humeur, tour à tour mystique ou joyeuse, babillarde, taciturne, emportée, nonchalante, elle allait rappeler en lui mille désirs, évoquant des instincts ou des réminiscences. Elle était l'amoureuse de tous les romans, l'héroïne de tous les drames, le vague elle de tous les volumes de vers. (342)

> *(He now savored for the first time the ineffable delicacies of feminine refinements. . . . With the diversity of her moods—by turns mystic, joyous, loquacious, taciturn, passionate, or nonchalant—she awakened a thousand desires in him, aroused his instincts and memories. She was the amorous heroine of all novels and plays, the vague she of all poetry.)*

What is it about the scenario of desire conceived for them by Emma that does not conform to Leon's notions of conventional heterosexuality? The answer is to be found in literature—Emma's model—in which erotic desire is far from conventional. The fact that Léon is confused points to the subtle nature of the *troubadour effect.* Writing from the point of view of a male reader of Flaubert's novel, cultural anthropologist Eric Gans has characterized the confusion about "what women want," in this way: "in the modern world, only the woman can be 'masculine'" (*Madame Bovary: The End of Romance* [1989] 34). Likewise, in his essay on Flaubert, Sartre raises the question of Flaubert's "femininity" and suggests that what emerges at first as an effect of style can be mistaken for sexual perversity if a writing effect is mistaken for lived sexual experience. Both Gans and Sartre, however (and even Flaubert himself) stop short of discerning the complex operations of the *troubadour effect*.

The source of Léon's confusion about Emma's femininity is his failure to fully understand the literary tradition that has mediated his desire for Emma, making her the woman of his dreams. He has fallen in love with a female impersonator; Emma's model for the ideal woman is the feminized male writer. Léon's description of Emma's femininity is ironically borrowed from the "lady" of the troubadour tradition:

> Jamais il n'avait rencontré cette grâce de langage, cette réserve du vêtement, ces poses de colombe assoupie. Il admirait l'exaltation de son âme et les dentelles de sa jupe. D'ailleurs, n'était-ce pas *une femme du monde,* et une femme mariée! une vraie maîtresse enfin? (342)

> *(Never before had he encountered this grace of language, this modesty of attire, these languid, dovelike poses. He admired the exaltation of her soul and the lace on her petticoat. Furthermore, was she not a "lady" and a married woman—in short, a real mistress?)*

With the ironic juxtaposition of graceful language and dovelike poses, soul and petticoat, fictional "lady" and "real" mistress, Flaubert's writing itself is an ironic performance of the crisis of representation which produces the *troubadour effect* and, in its wake, *vagabondage.* Poetic language and mystical transcendence masquerade as women posing in petticoats: Emma poses in petticoats to resemble the counterfeit women of troubadour poetry.

The *troubadour effect* creates many chimeras of erotic bliss as it appears in literature, art and music; the feminine voice emanating from a male body is the basic figure which gives rise to a succession of cultural representations that, although ostensibly different, all share a structure. My material for the most part is drawn from the classics of Western culture, but I also show that there is a historical continuum of the *troubadour effect* in a variety of cultural forms including music, film, and television. The illusion of sexual difference created by the *troubadour effect* is not female impersonation in any conventional sense of the term, that is to say, the male artist does not disappear behind a feminine masquerade, which can subsequently be dropped to reveal the "real thing." My purpose in naming this phenomenon is not unrelated, however, to the work of theorists who point to conventional masquerades to reveal "that gender is a kind of persistent impersonation that passes as the real" (Butler, *Gender Trouble* x). The examples Butler uses to make her point are female impersonators—Divine, for example—whose performances do not involve the production of sexual identity, but are rather conspicuous appropriations of an identity already established as a social sexual category. Similarly, in *Vested Interests* (1993), Marjorie Garber asks us to see the constructedness of gender (9). As she puts it, "The parodic repetition of the original reveals the original to be nothing other than a parody of the idea of the natural and the original" (42). While the literary representation that I am naming the *troubadour effect* involves male appropriation of the feminine voice, the representation is not parodic; it is rather a performance that produces the very sexual identity that it seems to appropriate.

Koestenbaum makes a similar point about the invention of the phonograph when he writes:

> The phonograph could captivate sounds with or without the knowledge or consent of the source of their origin. These captivated voices were often women's; but the wish to captivate was male. . . . the phonograph, like psychoanalysis or the telephone or Cubism or Surrealism, was a male collaborative invention that played with the boundaries of voice and identity (often female or materna), and made voice seem an emanation of male will. (49)

Koestenbaum's subject is a very specific one: the queen's throat (a double entendre, which encompasses both the diva and the gay man) liberates the expression of repressed sexual longing when it expands the throat of the homosexual man to the point that he experiences the production of sound as if it were he himself singing. "Am I listening to Leontyne Price or am I incorporating her, swallowing her, mesmerizing her? . . . And I begin to believe—sheer illusion!—that she spins out *my* self, not hers", he writes seductively (43).

An example of how literal female impersonation serves to place the literary tradition I call the *troubadour effect* in relief is the performance art of French male transvestite, Frédériche, who makes up half of his body to look like a well-known and often impersonated female singer, Diana Ross for one example, and half to resemble a male singer who is and is not himself. The garment he wears has a long slit skirt on one leg, trousers on the other; the skirted half wears a beaded top, the trousered half a man's jacket; the hair is short and sleek on one side, and long and full on the other. He entertains by singing duets, presenting alternatively one side and then the other to the audience, changing the register of the voice to match the persona facing out. The two halves of the chimera join in a romantic love duet, singing of their desire for each other, and creating an illusion of lovers of different sexes. One of the jokes of the performance is of course that its creator gets to imagine not only singing with, but actually being Diana Ross. The illusion brings down the house when he turns full front, forcing the audience to look at the divided self who sings the romantic duets and to come face to face with its fascination with the fiction of heterosexual desire created by his virtuosity.

This playful gesture recalls Rosalind's epilogue in *As You Like It* (1599) in which Shakespeare's comic heroine appears as a woman—in love with Orlando—for a very brief time at the beginning of the play. She quickly discards her feminine garb and spends the major part of the play's action disguised as Ganymede, a name which recalls the Ephebe of Greek mythology. When Ganymede tricks Orlando into a make-believe marriage by way of rehearsal for a marriage to his beloved Rosalind, the gods intervene and Rosalind's feminine costume reappears to cover the figure of Ganymede-Rosalind. In the epilogue, the boy actor who plays the role of Ganymede-Rosalind, still costumed as the feminine avatar, reminds the men in the audience who have fallen in love with the character, Rosalind, that "she" was an illusion, that Ganymede's sex is closer to the physical sex of the actor on stage.

In one form or another, this figure of desire dominates Western representation. Whether it appears in an explicit, unified image of a feminine voice emanating from a male body (for example, castrati, the first "divas" of Western culture, who—if we are to believe the recent film portrait of the eighteenth-century castrato Farinelli—excited women to orgasm and drove men mad with desire) or as the illusion of the presence of both a man and a woman in canonical narratives of romantic love (for example, *Tristan and Iseut*), the representation of erotic pleasure is not heterosexual. This is not to say that erotic pleasure as represented in art and literature is homosexual; it is not my intention here to "out" the canon, but, on the contrary, to question the very terms that such a project entails by challenging the assumption of a heterosexual tradition in literature. While it may be true that conventional, compulsory categories govern sexual behavior in society, there can be no such presumption about erotic pleasure as represented in literature.

This book explores the relationship between the fiction that there is a heterosexual couple in Western literature and women's writing. The first chapter, "Occitania: The Culture of Love," presents the history of the *troubadour effect* by discussing the culture of Occitania which produced the troubadours, including *Fin'Amors,* the troubadour philosophy of love, which established both the language of poetry and the language of love in Western literature. In the second chapter, "Vagabondage in the Age of Chivalry," I discuss early examples of *vagabondage* in the writing of the women troubadours, called *trobairitz,* in the *lais* of Marie de France, who wrote a version of the story of Tristan and Iseut; in the sonnets of Louise Labé, who questions the possibility of a male object of desire for a woman writing in the Petrarchan mode, in the tales of Marguerite de Navarre, whose *L'Heptaméron* (1559) is in essence a critique of *Fin'Amors,* and in the fiction of Madame de Lafayette, whose *Princesse de Clèves* marks the end of courtly love as such, written at the end of that period of modern history defined by chivalry and its heroes.[22] The third chapter, "She and He: The Myth of Androgynous Fusion Defused" shows the persistence of the *troubadour effect* in the fiction and theory of heterosexual desire in the Romantic era, when romantic love was again a major literary theme. The crystallization of the *troubadour effect* in the creation of an explicitly feminine male hero by Rousseau, and further developed in the German philosopher Johann Gottlieb Fichte's theory of the *Ich* and *Nicht Ich* (I and Not I), is the focus of this chapter, which concludes with George Sand's critique of male femininity in Rousseau and in the generation of writers influenced by him. The fourth chapter, "The Old Troubadour: George Sand," is the book's most extensive treatment of an individual writer. It is devoted to Sand's critique of the Romantic myth of male self-difference *qua* sexual-difference in two of her major novels, *Indiana* (1832) and *Lélia* (1833). Two chapters follow my treatment of Sand. The first of these, chapter five, "The Vagabond: A Modern Heroine," deals with various treatments of *vagabondage* in fiction by women since the Modernist era, including Colette's *La vagabonde* (1911), Virginia Woolf's *Orlando* (1928), works by Marguerite Duras (1914–1995), and Toni Morrison's *Jazz* (1992). The sixth and final chapter, "The Voice of Pleasure: The Troubadour Continuum," demonstrates the continuing presence of the *troubadour effect* in cultural landmarks such as *Johnny Guitar* (1954), *Some Like It Hot* (1959), *Kiss of the Spider Woman* (1985), *The Crying Game* (1992), *Chasing Amy* (1997), and *Seinfeld* (1991 to 1998). In this final chapter, I relate the material in previous chapters to contemporary popular culture, arguing that in spite of an apparent openness to creative exploration of non-traditional sexual relationships, our narratives of desire still conform to an age-old tradition of heterosexuality without women.[23] The chapter provides new ways to read the insistence of the illusion of the romantic couple at the dawn of a new millennium.

The history of the *troubadour effect* becomes imbricated with *vagabondage.* In the seventeenth century, Madame de Lafayette conveys the absence in

Western culture of a place for women to experience the pleasures associated in the troubadour tradition with *joi,* through the metaphor of the
Princesse de Clèves's renunciation of erotic pleasure, disappearance from
court, and her quiet death. During the Romantic era, George Sand's heroines are exiled from society and from the happiness associated with heterosexual love because they desire to express themselves as artists. In the
twentieth century, Colette reminds us that nothing has changed; Renée
Néré, Colette's vagabond writer, predicts a similar fate for herself in a letter
to the lover she must leave in order to write:

> Je laisse, à chaque lieu de mes désirs errants, mille et mille ombres à ma
> ressemblance, effeuillées de moi, celle-ci sur la pierre chaude et bleue des
> combes de mon pays, celle-là au creux moite d'un vallon sans soleil, et cette
> autre qui suit l'oiseau, la voile, le vent et la vague. Tu gardes la plus tenace:
> une ombre nue, onduleuse, que le plaisir agite comme une herbe dans le
> ruisseau. . . . Mais le temps la dissoudra comme les autres, et tu ne sauras plus
> rien de moi, jusqu'au jour où mes pas s'arrêtront et où s'envolera de moi une
> dernière petite ombre. (*Oeuvres,* I: 1232)

> *(In each place where my desires have strayed, I leave thousands and thousands of
> shadows in my own shape, shed from me: one lies on the warm blue rocks of the ledges
> in my own country, another in the damp hollow of a sunless valley, and a third follows
> a bird, a sail, the wind and the wave. You keep the most enduring of them: a naked,
> undulating shadow, trembling with pleasure like a plant in the stream. But time will
> dissolve it like the others, and you will no longer know anything of me until the day
> when my steps finally halt and there will fly from me a last small shadow.)*

Colette's exquisite description of the places visited by the restless
vagabond in search of peace associated with death involves a process of forgetting; it is not a physical death, but the passing away shadow by shadow, of
a prevalent feminine persona, the heroine of heterosexual romance. Renée
has played this role before; it attracts her as strongly as it repels her. By the
time she is ready to give up the last small shadow of that character, she will
have been already forgotten by the man she loves. Her fantasy of forgetting
becomes writing, as Marguerite Duras also came to understand (see Chapter 5).

The plight of the Princesse de Clèves, of Sand's heroines, and of Renée
Néré is described by their creators in the same terms: to have no place to
be. I read this as a metaphor for the situation of the woman writer who has
no space to write in; the narrative situation of no place to be is a metaphor
for *vagabondage.* Ironically, the feminine persona which represents the
chronic obstacle to writing for women begins as a literary figure which

does not represent a woman at all, but rather the male writer's desire to free himself from the assumption that he writes from the secure position of the conventional masculine subject. The romantic hero, mirroring the male writer's feminization, is a man whose sexual identity is marginalized because he is in love. The appeal of the romantic hero persists in novels by women. In *La vagabonde,* Renée Néré is able to resist Max until the moment in the narrative when he begins to speak of his mother. In this crucial scene—crucial because it marks the moment when Renée falls in love with Max—Max deviates from the representation of an unambiguous masculine character bent on possession of the object of his desire. He is on a nostalgic trip to what he calls "his maternal forest" (*sa forêt maternelle*) (*Oeuvres,* I: 1145). His intimate connection to the maternal is what finally seduces Renée; this feminization, however, is only an illusion. Max quickly gets back on track, but Renée is already in love. Fighting her way back to the freedom of the vagabond means not only deciding to write, but deciding to forget her bondage to the body represented as the feminine in romantic love narratives.

For the women discussed in this book, coming to writing involves forgetting the very writing to which they are addicted without losing or repressing the desire to write itself. The difficulty that this poses has to do with the convention that makes writing a representation of male self-difference, blocking women's access to writing, not because of gender, but because of sex. What passes for male self-difference is a subject position and, as such, is not necessarily reserved for men. But because femininity has been constructed as a writing position that women, because of their sex, have been considered unworthy to assume, there is confusion about the availability of the feminine, as a writing effect, to women. This structure is similar to the ambivalence of the exchange of hearts in *Fin'Amors* where a man becomes feminine in order to become the perfect lover—and poet. A woman, on the other hand, assumes the masculine position for only the briefest moment, and then at the discretion of her lover. A woman in this tradition cannot be trusted to adhere to the model of the ideal feminine; it takes a man to be a "real" woman. It is a great irony that if *vagabondage* is ever to disappear as a punishment for women who dare to write, women must appropriate a position that has been marked feminine. It is this paradox that creates *vagabondage.*

This is what Virginia Woolf means when she says in *A Room of One's Own* (1929) that women must forget their sex to write, "she wrote as a woman, but as a woman who has forgotten that she is a woman" (93). To bring Woolf's realization into my purview, one can paraphrase her by saying that she wrote, but as a woman who has assumed the position of the writer for whom femininity is an effect of the writing, having forgotten that she is a woman—and unworthy. There are three important things here: sex, gender, and a writing position. What has become clear to me is that there is not merely sex and gender, but a third position created by the writing which because of the *troubadour effect* has been marked as feminine, but which has historically been occupied only by men. The writing position is marked as feminine only because it is a position of difference for men; femininity associated with writing is not congruent with an actual woman. In this sense, femininity can be assumed as self-difference by women as well as by men, which is the case with the writers discussed in chapter five. There is, however, a price to be paid. The small shadow left by Colette's woman of letters, Renée Néré, will be cast by a woman who has forgotten her desire to be desired, having chosen subjectivity, and the desire to write. As she puts it, "Oui, de l'oublier, comme s'il n'y avait d'urgent au monde que mon désir de posséder par les yeux les merveilles de la terre!" (Yes, forgotten him, as if the only urgent thing in the world were my desire to possess through my eyes the marvels of the earth) (*Oeuvres*, I: 1221).[24] To voice the urgency of Renée's choice, Colette creates an "insidious spirit" that whispers, "'Et s'il n'y avait d'urgent, en effet, que cela? Si tout, hormis cela, n'était que cendres? . . .'" (And if indeed that were the only urgent thing? If everything, save that, were merely ashes?) (*Oeuvres*, I: 1221).

Colette's vagabond spends her nights miming an array of feminine types in the music hall. In Colette's fictional world, the performance of femininity in a woman does not enable writing, but rather it is an obstacle to writing. In fact, the performance of femininity is Renée's default position as a "femme de lettres qui a mal tourné" (a woman of letters gone wrong) (*Oeuvres*, I: 1075). It is precisely because she performs femininity as a woman in love that she cannot write. By calling into question the heterosexuality of fictions of desire in canonical narratives dating back at least eight centuries, the analyses in this book provide a historical perspective for poststructuralist and postmodernist creative and theoretical works that challenge categories of sexual identity.[25]

In his still provocative essay on writing and subjectivity, "La mort de l'auteur" (The Death of the Author [1968]), Roland Barthes articulates a concept of writing as the performance of identity. He contends that in literary writing the concept of the author (a subject who uses language as an instrument to convey a reality which preexists it) yields to the concept of the writer (a subject whose very being is bound up in the act of writing or as with Proust's narrator, with wanting to write and not being able to). Proust's *A la recherche du temps perdu* (1927–29) ends when writing becomes possible. The author, represented by the narrator's model for his desire to be a novelist, Bergotte, dies in order to give birth to a writer, a new being. The writer is neither the narrator who cannot write, nor an author who writes what he already knows, but an identity in process, specifically a writing performance in process. For Proust's writer protagonist, language is both the quest and its object. Barthes writes, "au lieu de mettre sa vie dans son roman . . . il fit de sa vie même une oeuvre dont son propre livre fut comme le modèle" (instead of putting his life into his novel . . . he made his life itself a work of which his own book was the model) (492, 51). Thus, Barthes articulates the theory that makes the concluding meaning of Colette's novel explicit. In pursuit of subjectivity, writing is the only urgent thing; the novel ends when writing finally becomes possible, "l'auteur entre dans sa propre mort, l'écriture commence" (the author enters into his own death, writing begins) (491, 49).

Both versions of the birth of the writer, Colette's and Barthes', involve the metaphor of forgetting as a necessary prelude to the beginning of writing. There is a critical difference, however, between the two writers, which can only be described in terms of sex. Simply put, the author is a man, the vagabond is a woman. The performance of subjectivity made possible for the writer by forgetting the sex of "the author" is described by Barthes as a performance of femininity or, as I prefer to say, a performance of male self-difference. Barthes' essay begins:

> Dans sa nouvelle, Sarrasine, Balzac, parlant d'un castrat déguisé en femme, écrit cette phrase: "C'était la femme, avec ses peurs soudaines, ses caprices sans raison, ses troubles instinctifs, ses audaces sans cause, ses bravades et sa délicieuse finesse de sentiments." Qui parle ainsi? Est-ce le héros de sa nouvelle, intéressé à ignorer le castrat qui se cache sous la femme? Est-ce l'individu Balzac, pourvu par son expérience personnelle d'une philosophie de la femme? Est-ce l'auteur Balzac, professant des idées "littéraires" sur la féminité? Est-ce la sagesse universelle? La psychologie romantique? Il sera à tout jamais impossible de le savoir, pour la bonne raison que l'écriture est destruction de toute voix, de toute origine. L'écriture est ce neutre, ce composite, cet oblique où fuit notre sujet, le noir-et-blanc où vient se perdre toute identité, à commencer par celle-là même du corps qui écrit. (491, 49)

> (In his tale Sarrasine, Balzac, speaking of a castrato disguised as a woman, writes this sentence: "She was a Woman, with her sudden fears, her inexplicable whims, her instinctive fears, her meaningless bravado, her defiance, and her delicious delicacy of feeling." Who speaks in this way? Is it the hero of the tale, who would prefer not to recognize the castrato hidden beneath the "woman"? Is it Balzac the man, whose

personal experience has provided him with a philosophy of Woman? Is it Balzac the author, professing certain "literary" ideas about femininity? Is it universal wisdom? Romantic psychology? We can never know, for the good reason that writing is the destruction of every voice, every origin. Writing is that neuter, that composite, that obliquity into which our subject flees, the black-and-white where all identity is lost, beginning with the very identity of the body that writes.)

The reference to Zambinella, Balzac's fascinating, richly erotic figure whose composite body signifies the new character born in Barthes' essay—the writer—prepares the reader for the subtle and seductive moves the essayist makes as he moves towards the climactic phrase, "the author enters into his own death, writing begins" (49). The presence of Zambinella marks the performance of the writer's identity, a performance of sexual identity, female impersonation to be exact. Contrary to what Barthes says, writing here is not neuter, it is feminine. *Neutre* in French means both neuter and neutral. One would be tempted to say that Richard Howard's translation is inaccurate here and that *neutre* should be translated as neutral, which does not have sexual connotations, whereas neuter is a sexual term. Given Barthes' clearly sexual description of *neutre* as the position of the feminized male, however, the translation is correct.[26] By calling the feminine "neuter," Barthes excludes women from the performance in question in his essay. In Barthes, the feminine is conflated with the neuter to designate a position available to male writers desiring freedom from the clearly and conventionally defined masculine position reserved for the author. The space designated as neuter is then a space available only to men: the space of the male who accepts symbolic castration—the loss of the identity of the body that writes—as a *sine qua non* for the subject writing itself into being.

It is important to recognize that the argument of Barthes' essay is compatible with feminist critiques of concepts of subjectivity that bolster the prestige of the "author." Barthes makes powerful and influential arguments for writing as producing subjectivity, rather than being produced by a knowing subject. Like Barthes, feminist theorists strive to make the writer's position available to subjects who are not identified with the universal masculine. Barthes exploits the availability of the non-authorial terms *feminine* and *neuter* to define the position of male writers who willingly move out of the role of author. Richard Rorty has similar theoretical reasons for using the feminine pronoun *she* to describe himself when he assumes the position of the liberal ironist, in *Contingency, Irony and Solidarity* (1989). The move from *he* to *she* signifies his openness to redescription. Barthes does not exploit the possibilities afforded by his own theory of writing, which would be to open up a neutral—not neuter—space to both men and women who desire to write.

Neither Barthes, nor theorists like Rorty who share the desire to reinvent the language of subjectivity, can designate the writer's position as neutral. The neutral position is not neutral at all in a culture in which universal, unmarked subjectivity is registered as masculine. Nonetheless, Barthes' move to the neuter position is useful because it eliminates the reference to a real male or female body, but he does not really eliminate the problem because he has relegated the neuter position to male self-difference, leaving us in nearly the same predicament.

Barthes' preoccupation with Balzac's *Sarrasine* is one of his signatures as a critic. In his *S/Z* (1968), Barthes' reading of *Sarrasine* shows how the eroticism of this strange story is grasped by the reader in spite of the fact that it is not readily available to the conscious mind—that the eroticism is in the language rather than in the story's erotic content. The signifying letters, *s* and *z,* which traverse the text in characters' names, in descriptions of places, and in situations can be read as feminine and masculine versions of the same letter. In the play of these letters, desire writes itself as self-difference. In Balzac's narrative, however, the body in question, which eludes sexual definition, is described in a way that places the tale in the tradition of the *troubadour effect.* Heralding the birth of the writer is the body of a castrato who masquerades as the soprano, Zambinella. The castrato is, in turn, the model for a statue of a beautiful woman created by the sculptor Sarrasine, a man fatally in love with the female impersonator. Later in Balzac's story, Sarrasine's statue of a beautiful woman is used as the model for a sensuous painting of the beautiful boy, Adonis. The figure of eroticism first appears in the text as a man—the castrato Zambinella. There is no female model for the statue of the beautiful woman. Balzac, in fact, makes it clear that in the fictional world of the *Comédie Humaine* (*The Human Comedy*) (1842–50), ideal beauty is always found in a feminine man, never in a woman. It is also true that since sexual desire and beauty in narrative are very often metaphors for the desire to write, Balzac's poets and writers are *hommes-filles,* (girl-men) like Balzac's Lucien de Rubempré, who is at once a Romantic poet, the heterosexual romantic hero of several novels, and, at the same time the object of desire of the homosexual Vautrin, whose personality dominates the *Comédie.*[27]

The transformed identity of the newly-born writer of Barthes' "La mort de l'auteur" and of subsequent essays on language, subjectivity, and the pleasure of the text is that of a feminine man. For Colette, the beginning of writing for the vagabond involves forgetting the performance of the feminine; for Barthes, the birth of the writer depends on the availability of the performance of the feminine to signify writing and desire. If writing is "the only urgent thing," then describing and defining the conditions that contribute to *vagabondage*—one of which is the *troubadour effect*—and exploring ways to refigure sexual difference in writing is a matter of life and death for women who desire to write.

CHAPTER 1

Occitania: The Culture of Love

Le Joi représente, en effet, l'union de la virilité et de la féminité
en l'homme, dans le seul désir.

*(In truth, joi represents the union of virility and femininity in man, in
complete desire.)*

—*René Nelli*, L'Érotique des troubadours
(Troubadour Eroticism)

The modern Western notion of heterosexual romantic love emerges
as a literary theme in the troubadour love songs of twelfth- and
thirteenth-century Occitania. In an area in the south of France,
now generally called Languedoc, lyric poets revolutionized the representation of ideal love by suggesting that the love of a man for a woman might
be as intensely passionate, loyal, and ennobling as male homosexual love. In
antiquity, Platonic love and Aristotelian friendship provided personal relationships whose worth could not be matched by heterosexual love. In the
Christian world, the medieval institution of *compagnonnage* (classical male
friendship) intimately bonded two knights in a symbolic fusion of souls
(*ET,* 16–17).[1] In the fifteenth-century romance based on the life of the
chivalric hero Jean de Beuil, *Le jouvencel,* we find a typical description of a
knight's love for his *compagnon:*

> You love your comrade so in war. When you see that your quarrel is just and
> your blood is fighting well, tears rise to your eye. A great sweet feeling of loy-
> alty and pity fills your heart on seeing your friend so valiantly exposing his
> body to execute and accomplish the command of our Creator. And then you
> prepare to go and die or live with him, and for love not to abandon him. And
> out of that there arises such a delectation, that he who has not tasted it is not
> fit to say what a delight it is. Do you think that a man who does that fears
> death? Not at all; for he feels so strengthened, he is so elated, that he does not
> know where he is. Truly he is afraid of nothing. (in Huizinga 76–77)

As recently as 1997, in *The Invention of Love,* Tom Stoppard portrays the love of his main character, poet A. E. Housman, for his friend, Moses Jackson, as an example of classical friendship. Housman confesses his feelings to the unsuspecting, rather naïve Jackson using the following analogy:

> Theseus was never so happy as when he was with his friend. They weren't sweet on each other. They loved each other, as men loved each other in the heroic age, in virtue, paired together in legend and poetry as the pattern of comradeship, the chivalric ideal of virtue in the ancient world. Virtue! What happened to it? It had a good run—centuries!— . . . . Well, not any more, eh, Mo? Virtue is what women have to lose, the rest is vice. (76)

According to the Program Notes of Chicago's Court Theater's Fall 2000 production of *The Invention of Love,* Stoppard recently said of his play: "It's easy to misperceive *The Invention of Love.* I do it myself. I start talking about Latin scholarship and poetry and . . . almost miss the central axis, which is: it's a love story" (20). At a telling moment in the play itself, the Housman character relates an anecdote: "In the translation of Tibullus in my College library, the *he* loved by the poet is turned into a *she:* and then when you come to the bit where 'she' goes off with somebody's wife, the translator is equal to the crisis—he leaves it out" (40). It seems that poets and playwrights are still trying to figure out how perfect love ever became associated with women. For Stoppard's Housman, modern sensibilities dictated a pronoun change—a simple case of linguistic transvestism.

According to René Nelli, the process was far more complicated. *Compagnonnage* was the model for the androgynous fusion of souls (*communion animique*), the source of *joi* for the heterosexual lovers of troubadour poetry.[2] Because the troubadour's notion of ideal heterosexual love was based on the model of *compagnonnage* and its rites and rituals derived from the cult of brotherhood called *affrèrement,* Nelli characterizes *Fin'Amors,* the troubadour philosophy of refined mutual erotic love, as "the homosexualization of heterosexuality" (*AMC* 217–227).[3] While Nelli's recognition that *Fin'Amors* is not clearly heterosexual represents a step towards a reconsideration of the gender composition of the romantic couple of Western culture, his redescription of the couple as "homosexualized" is an oversimplification of troubadour poetics and its role in defining heterosexual eroticism.

The first western lyric poets to write in the vernacular, the troubadours entertained the aristocracy in courts in Languedoc, where the *langue d'oc,* or Provençal—which Dante called "the mother tongue" of all vernacular

26

poetry—was spoken (*Purgatorio,* Canto XXVI: line 117).[4] The troubadours and their influence traveled rapidly to both the north and the south, making it difficult to distinguish between poems whose geographical provenance was Occitania and those that came from other areas.[5] What is indisputable, however, is that the movement began in the South and that the first reference to *Fin'Amors* occurred in Occitania, where troubadours were at the center of a culture that developed around love poetry. Unlike the *jongleurs* who intoned *chansons de geste,* epic poems originating in monasteries and abbeys for the purpose of praising the mythical heroes of Christendom, the troubadours performed their own compositions, words and music in praise of a (mythical) woman.[6] The language of the troubadours was established as both the language of poetry and the language of love in Western literature—therein lies a problem, the conflation of a poetics with sexual behavior.[7] As Huchet puts it: "La femme et la poésie deviennent un même objet proposé au désir masculin" (Woman and poetry become a single object of masculine desire) (*L'Amour discourtois* 14).

Guillaume IX (1071–1127), ninth duke of Aquitaine, the richest, most powerful aristocrat in Western Europe at the time and grandfather of Eleanor of Aquitaine, is generally considered to be the first lyric poet to write in the vernacular—in his case, the *langue d'oc.* His first poems are in the naturalist tradition, in which women are either reviled or described as easily accessible objects of male lust; their presence in the poetry is a pretext for an expression of a banal *joie de vivre* (Nelli, *ET* 85). After 1100, however, Guillaume's poetry has an entirely different orientation, and at the core of the change is a shift in the notion of *joi.* The banal pleasure connoted by the expression *joie de vivre* is left behind by the new generation of poets for whom *joi* takes on a transformed meaning, linked more to the desire to sing and to compose poetry than to simple sexual pleasure or lust. This change is due to Guillaume's invention of a new genre that fused music with poetry. According to Stephen Nichols, specialist in Provençal lyric poetry, "In this new form the human voice played a crucial role. For the first time the singer was not simply lending his voice to perform a narrative, but took on a poetic identity: the speaking subject was also the subject of the poem" (Hollier 31). Nichols succinctly documents how the splitting of a writer's subjectivity into both subject and object of writing came about in literary history. When this split occurs, the subject who writes is assumed to be masculine, and that part of the writer's subjectivity that is transformed into the object of the writer's desire, the part of the self that expresses the exalted pleasure of creativity, is—based on textual signs—assumed to be feminine. Medieval scholar Robin Hass says this about a change that occurs in the late twelfth and early thirteenth century: "The poet as *artifex*, imagination and linguistic rejuvenation as the site of invention . . . are integrated in the creation of a feminized text" (16).

In early troubadour lyrics, the designation of the split subject of the male poet into masculine and feminine gives rise to what I describe as the *troubadour effect,* the phenomenon whereby the voice that expresses the pleasure a man takes from writing is designated as feminine. Guillaume calls this pleasure *joi,* which Nelli describes as follows: "C'est une joie 'pure' parce qu'elle dépend d'un bien que l'on voudrait avoir mais que l'on n'a pas. C'est tout simplement le désir, mais valorisé: la joie de désirer" (It is a "pure" joy because it depends on a good that one wants to have, but which one does not have. It is very simply desire, but valorized: *the joy of desiring*) (*ET* 85).[8] The joy of desiring, or desire having no object other than itself, and valorized by its association with the conception of poetry is evoked by Guillaume when he writes, "Fari un vers de dreyt nien" (I will write a poem about nothing at all.) (Jeanroy, *les chansons de Guillaume IX* [1913] iv). Describing *joi,* or the pleasure he takes in writing about nothing, Guillaume writes:

> Anc mais no oc hom faissonar
> Co's en voler ni en dezir
> Ni en pensar ni en cossir'
> Aitals joi no ot par trobar
> Pus hom gensor no'n pot trobar
> Ni huelhs vezer ni boca dir,
> A mos ops la vuelh retenir
> Per lo cor dedins refrescar
> E per la carn renovellar,
> Que no pesca envellezir (in Topsfield, *Troubadours and Love* 50)

> *(Never could a man find a way to express* (trobar) *what* joi *is; it is neither longing, nor desire, nor thought nor meditation. It has no equal.*
> *Since one cannot find* (trobar) *a more gracious lady nor eyes see, nor lips tell, I desire to retain her for my very own, to refresh the heart within me and renew my flesh so that it may not grow old)[9]*

Note the play on the word *trobar,* the origin of the word *troubadour.* The first use of *trobar* encompasses the phrase "to find a way to express." The second use means simply "to find (a lady)." The word *troubadour* depicts this combination of finding and inventing: Finding a way to express *joi* drifts almost unnoticed into the invention of a lady. The poem goes on to evoke the *Fin'Amors* ritual of the exchange of hearts. Here, the poet is

metamorphosed into "her," the "nothing" about which the poem is written, and as long as the *joi* continues, he holds within himself a feminine
heart which does not come from an actual woman, but from singing in the
voice of an absent presence to which he gives the name lady.[10]

Nichols describes the advent of lyric poetry in the vernacular as a
moment when the relationship between writing and acquiring subjectivity
is explicit. He writes:

> They [the poems] are rather a vehicle, the first in a modern European lan-
> guage, for showing how poetic voice, the articulated language of a speaking
> subject, situates itself between an inherited culture in flux and a particular
> unconscious, expressed in lyrics as individual consciousness finding or ques-
> tioning its identity. (Hollier 32)[11]

In *L'Amour discourtois* (*Discourteous Love*)—the title is a pun, playing on
the French *discours* (discourse), so "discursive love,"—Jean-Charles Huchet
makes a strong argument to the effect that the troubadours did not invent
heterosexual love, but "a new way to speak it so as not to have to do it"
(une nouvelle façon de le dire pour ne pas le faire) (16–17). In the years
following Guillaume IX, between 1130 and 1150, the voice of Occitania is
best represented by the poets Cercamon, Marcabru, Bernart Marti, and
Jaufré Rudel, who created what Nelli calls "une érotique de transition" (a
transitional erotics)(*ET* 105). It was during this period that sexual abstinence became a part of the representation of ideal love between the sexes.
A transition between Platonic idealization of the beloved and a fully developed philosophy of intersexual love, the eroticism of the poetry of this
period was a realistic depiction of the physical frustration involved in elevating a woman to the level of friend, an elevation which involved the
deferral of the sex act (*le fait*) (Nelli, *ET* 106).[12] With these transitional
erotics, suffering is commingled with *joi,* and from this time on it is inseparable from the "joy of desiring." At the same time, suffering becomes associated in the erotic imagination with the inaccessible "feminine," both its
cause and its expression.[13] In a study devoted to the Provençal notion of *joi,*
Belperron (1948) writes that it was in "la femme" as a source of suffering
that the troubadours realized one of the goals of *Fin'Amors,* the "joy of
desiring," in which pleasure and suffering are inextricably linked (88).

It is also during this crucial transitional period of troubadour history,
specifically in a poem by Marcabru, that *joi* is explicitly linked to a new
philosophy of love, *Fin'Amors,* "Canto per joi de Fin'Amors" (I sing from
the *joi* of *Fin'Amors*)(De Jeanne [1909], XIII 7–8).[14] In addition to *joi,* suffering and singing emerge during this period as necessary components of

the new literature. Bernart Marti writes of how he accepts suffering in love as the way to greater happiness in singing, "Non es meravelha s'eu chan melhs de nul autre chantador, que plus me tra'l cors vas amor e melhs sui faihz a so coman" (It is no wonder if I sing better than any other singer, for my heart draws me more to love and I am better suited to do its bidding) (Hoepffner [1929],VI).

Although *joi* originally describes a feeling that cannot be willed, or even imagined (as we have seen from Guillaume's poem above), in ordinary poetic usage it often means either the woman loved or an exaltation of the senses. Beginning with Guillaume's poetry, then, in the troubadour lexicon, *joi* was identified with the poetic invention of a voice of pleasure, of writing pleasure. Because its properties are related to excess, to transcendence of the limits of the self, and to otherness, this voice appeared to be distinct from the writing subject.[15] The voice of self-difference, essential to writing pleasure, was given the name *domna,* marking *joi* as feminine.[16] This representation of femininity, as I will show, eventually became associated with actual women during the period from 1130 to 1150, and the first of the so-called feminine qualities to appear in troubadour poetics is the enjoyment of suffering. In the poem quoted above Marti makes it clear that "having no desire for love" means having no desire to sing, which would eliminate the need for an actual woman. A cultural phenomenon occurs during this period, however, which creates the misconception that the woman of the poetry is an actual woman. The vocabulary of the poetry composed during these years to express poetic striving is translated into a code of social behavior known as *courtoisie* (courtesy). The term first appears in Cercamon, but it is Marcabru who defines it simply, "E cortezia es d'amar" (Courtesy is love) (De Jeanne, XV 20). *Courtoisie* is identified in turn with *mezura,* a term introduced by Marcabru, which means one thing for the poet and another for the courtly lover. To describe a poet, *mezura* means "sensibilité épurée" (purified sensibility); for a courtly lover, it is good behavior (Nelli, *ET* 69). Cercamon makes the connection between poetic sensibility and courtly behavior explicit as well. Both Marcabru and Cercamon use the term *mezura* simultaneously with *joi,* retaining the notion that the prolonging of desire by sexual abstinence purifies a poet's perception and elevates his song. Sexual abstinence is proof of a lover's requisite humility and patience.

For the poet, then, *mezura* is connected with transcendent desire; for the run of the mill lover whose relationship in the real, social world might be with an actual woman, the meaning of *mezura* is less than transcendent, and resembles sexual repression rather than sublimation in art. The troubadour Bernart Marti goes so far as to thank the lady for the torture she inflicts,

"Ges per zo nan ai en talan, Si tot mon coratge masel, Dels mals no.m puesc partir un dorn" (Even though she kills my heart, I can not pull back an inch from the wrongs she inflicts on me) (Hoepffner, VIIII 35). The lady has now become the agent of the self-inflicted suffering necessary to poetic invention and *joi*. Marcabru substitutes the term "love" for the lady. Just how easy it is for both poet and reader to confuse the representation of "the joy of desiring" with love, with the presence in the poetry of a flesh and blood woman is seen in these verses, "On plus n'ay meilhor coratge D'amor, meilhs m'es deslonhada" (The more my heart is inclined towards love, the further away love moves from me) (De Jeanne, XXVIII 3). Although these words seem to indicate the existence of an object of desire who withdraws affection, Nelli assures us that in all of Cercamon's work there is not one single erotic evocation which corresponds to a real act, past or present (*ET* 135). Love is poetic invention, and it is poetry that eludes the poet, not a woman.

It is during the next period of troubadour poetry (1150–1250), which Nelli calls "the classical age of the troubadours," that *Fin'Amors* can be seen as a comprehensive myth. The best known poets of this period are Bernart de Ventadorn, Raimon de Miraval, Bertran de Born, Bertran d'Alamanon, Arnaut de Mareuil, Arnaut Daniel, and Peire Vidal. During this time, poetic invention becomes commingled and confused with heterosexual eroticism, prompting Nelli to now define *joi* as "the union of virility and femininity in man in complete desire" (Nelli, *ET* 172). In other words the move from poetics to sexual behavior has taken place. The masculine and feminine selves of the poet's split subjectivity are heterosexual lovers.

The story of the invention of heterosexual romantic love in Occitania takes at least two more turns before we see the component parts woven together into a myth. The rituals of *Fin'Amors*—the *asag* and the exchange of hearts—further complicate the severing of one into two, by modeling the new heterosexual eroticism on male friendship. Two powerful cultural influences coexisted in Occitania, the one literary, the other religious. The poets of love shared a very specific and limited geographical region in a very specific and limited historical period with the church of love, Catharism. According to recent scholarship, it was primarily because the Cathars caught the interest of nineteenth-century Romantics that the troubadour philosophy of love became fashionable during that period.[17]

From the thirteenth to the nineteenth centuries, Occitania was a forgotten civilization due to the virtual destruction of the area by the Albigensian Crusades and the Inquisition, both of which were directed against the Cathars, a medieval Christian neo-manichaean sect whose origins can be traced to the Bogomil churches of Dalmatia and Bulgaria. The Cathars are better known to readers of European history as Albigensians from the French city, Albi, where there was a strong local movement in the twelfth and thirteenth centuries. Catharism was above all a reform movement—one of many at the time when there was a general sentiment of need for reform in the Church—which called for the return to Christ's message of poverty and preaching (Duby, *Mâle Moyen Âge* 26–27). Catharism was named "the church of love" because divine love and forgiveness characterized the movement. Rejecting the Old Testament, which depicts a vengeful God, in favor of the New Testament, which depicts God as good, forgiveness replaced revenge as the Cathar interpretation of the Christian message. There is no hell in the Cathar religion.[18] Certain Cathar beliefs were considered by orthodox Christians to be pernicious and subversive and resulted in the Cathars' condemnation as heretics, especially the "Two Principles" that claim the existence of two separate divinities, Good and Evil.

The tenet that the physical world, including the human body, is the creation of the evil principle, or Satan, motivated them to prohibit procreation and to prescribe sexual abstinence even in marriage. Although the love preached by the Cathars was not sexual love, it was largely due to their emphasis on love combined with the rule of sexual abstinence, that their association with the troubadours is often misinterpreted. One of these misconceptions revolves around the fact that both Cathars and troubadours exalted sexual abstinence as a goal. There were major differences, however, in the reasons each had for their belief in this practice. For the Cathars, sexual abstinence was intended to deny the value of the body and its appetites, ultimately bringing an end to the human race and allowing for the possibility of the fusion of human souls with God in a state of love. For the troubadours, such abstinence was intended as a tribute of respect for the body and was practiced only in a state of *Fin'Amors,* pure passionate love which could only exist when the lovers share intense physical as well as spiritual desire.[19]

Denis de Rougemont's *Love in the Western World* (1939) is largely responsible for having promulgated the misconception that the troubadours wrote their poetry to spread the Cathar heresy. His theory is that the hermetic language of one of the poetic forms of troubadour poetry, the "trobar clus" (closed verse), was really two different languages, the language of courtly love and a coded language understood only by Cathar initiates.[20] For scholars of Catharism, this misconception goes to the heart of misunderstandings about Cathar beliefs. The reforms promulgated by the Cathars were aimed at rendering Christ's message simpler, closer to its original purpose of teaching the poor. Hence, the idea of a complicated coded language to represent Cathar beliefs is inconsistent with the movement toward a simple message.

In spite of the errors in his account of the nature of the relationship between Cathars and troubadours, Rougemont is not wrong about the existence of a connection. Knowing where the two groups converge and diverge helps to distinguish the components of the pattern of sexual relations that, as the commonplace would have it, revolutionized love in the Western world.[21]

Love in the Western World is the history of what Rougemont sees as a fatal confusion between love and desire in troubadour poetry, creating "an inescapable conflict in the West between passion and marriage, a conflict which he predicts will destroy Western society unless it recognizes that marriage is more serious than the love which it cultivates, and that marriage cannot be founded on a fine ardor" (8). For the moralist Rougemont, the conflict grew out of a confusion between *Agape,* which he equates with Christian love (67), and *Eros.* Rougemont's own seductive and surfeited prose deployed in the cause of redressing the error, gives testimony to how the confusion arose in the first place and has contributed more to an increase of interest in the "fine ardor" he condemns rather than to Rougemont's stated goal. To define *Eros* he writes, "complete Desire, luminous Aspiration, the primitive religious soaring carried to its loftiest pitch, to the extreme exigency of purity which is also the extreme exigency of Unity" (61). The primitive religion that inspired the extreme exigency of Unity is, in Rougemont's view, Catharism. *Eros* can only be satisfied in death because its demand is for union, or fusion with the All, and not for the communion of *Agape.* For Rougemont, the dangerous ideal named romantic love comes from "a degenerate Platonism" which "sends us in pursuit of chimeras that only exist inside ourselves" (74).

Rougemont's critique of the chimeric nature of fusionary love is appropriate. However, my sense of the problem it creates differs from his in an important way. Whereas Rougemont sees adultery resulting from the disappointment experienced when human love does not live up to the expectation of fusion, I see the exclusion of women from the so-called fusionary sexual "relation" as the real danger. In a passing remark on man's quest for a transcendent unified self and its relation to *Eros* in Western poetry, Rougemont inadvertently points to the *troubadour effect* when he quotes Goethe's assertion that "Woman is man's goal" (64). For the Romantics to say that "Woman is man's goal" does not mean that man desires to possess a woman, but that the ideal of transcendent unity for a man is achieved by "becoming Woman." The term "becoming Woman" is an intentional reference to Gilles Deleuze and Félix Guattari's *Mille plateaux* (1980) in which they argue that in modernist writing, the only way to get away from dualisms, "to pass in-between," is to become Woman. For them, there is no "becoming Man." To be man is simply to be. If a man taps into the indiscernible, into "becoming," which is identified in *Mille plateaux* with the act of writing, he becomes Woman. I see this process, whereby Woman figures the male writer, as existing (at least) since the troubadours. I call this writing effect the *troubadour effect*.

Fifty years after Rougemont's study, we are still sorting out the complicated sexual revolution of Occitania. While no one pursues this question with the passion and conviction of René Nelli, the value of understanding troubadour eroticism in order to understand contemporary issues surrounding desire and representation is strongly suggested by several theorists, including the psychoanalyst Jacques Lacan. Citing Nelli's *L'Amour et les mythes du coeur* as a source for his own understanding of the conventions of courtly love, Lacan evokes the cultural revolution of Occitania as a "decisive" moment in determining the terms of sexual relations and the experience of desire (*L'Amour courtois* [1964], 177, 183). For Lacan, Occitania is the cultural moment when the object of desire is transformed into a symbolic function in a process called sublimation and he is intrigued by the question of how an activity of poetic creation had such an enormous and determining influence on sexual relations. He makes the point that in twelfth-century Occitania a poetics became an erotics—a transfer that he characterizes as having been made with startling ease. This erotics, which began as a poetics of sublimation in which the beloved woman is an empty object whose only value is symbolic, continues to influence "l'organisation sentimentale de l'homme contemporain, et y perpétuent leur marche" (the organization of contemporary man's sentimental attachments, and continues its forward march) (178).[22]

For a long time, it was thought that all documents of the historical Cathars had been destroyed by the ravages of the Crusades, but the religion had spread throughout much of Europe from the tenth to the fifteenth centuries, making it possible for twentieth-century scholars to recover documents such as *The Book of the Two Principles,* Inquisition registers, and chronicles from places outside of Occitania, allowing them to revise misconceptions about the Cathars' beliefs and practices.[23]

In addition to their association with love and sexual abstinence, the Cathars and troubadours intersect on another point that comes up in more recent studies; both would seem to support a new social role for women. The Cathars allowed women to preach and to perform sacred rites; the songs of the troubadours elevated the *dame* to the role of "master" vis-à-vis a subservient male lover, a change that was reflected in the court hierarchy. The so-called revolution in the status of women, however, is deceptive. Cathar women preachers were allowed to preach only to other women

(Brenon, *VVC* 195) and the last male Cathar preacher, Bélibaste, is reported to have said that even though the body is only a material envelope for the soul, which has no sex, before entering paradise, women had to become men.[24] In other words, those to whom the word was addressed—by both men and women preachers—were inevitably women, and although a man had to become feminine in order to enter paradise, being a woman was not being worthy enough. As for the elevation of women to the title of "monseigneur" in troubadour love lyrics, it is the very existence of the lady as a flesh and blood woman that this study challenges. Repeatedly, we see in historical documents and scholarship on the tradition a confusion between poetic figures and the social realities of women.

As historical social phenomena, Cathars and troubadours were very different; this is not the case with their cultural residues that persist in representations of sexual relations in the West. If some historians have misrepresented the similarities of Cathars and troubadours, their misrepresentations are now part of Occitania's history and have to be taken into consideration when assessing Occitania's legacy. This much is certainly true, it was inevitable that troubadours and Cathars would have met at certain courts in the south of France, where "the one preached in the afternoon, the other sang in the evening" (Brenon 200). But more important than actual contacts between individuals is the intersection of ideas. Brenon writes:

> Il ne s'agit plus en effet de débattre une fois de plus des influences réciproques et des accords secrets qui ont pu manifester entre des hommes qui parlaient de Dieu et d'autres qui parlaient d'amour, mais de situer à juste place, dans cette grande période de mutation des mentalités . . . tous les personnages qui parlaient un langage neuf. (198)

> *(It is no longer a question of debating yet again the reciprocal influences and secret pacts which could have appeared between men who spoke of God, and others who spoke of love, but to situate in their proper place all those who spoke a new language in this great period of change in mentalities)*[25]

Boswell asserts, "Apart from the monastic clergy, love does not appear to have been a concern to tenth-century Europeans in any context—theological, moral, sexual, or emotional. Twelfth-century Europeans, especially in urban areas, do not seem to have been able to think of much else" (208).[26] By all accounts, it appears that despite Rougemont's errors, he was right to credit Occitania with the invention of modern romantic love.

The culture of Occitania, with both its troubadours and its Cathars, was resurrected in the nineteenth century because it seduced those Romantics who found affinities and precedents in its philosophy for their quest for fusion with the Infinite. The palpable heterosexual eroticism of representations of the quest for a mystical Infinite is clearly expressed in Balzac's *La fille aux yeux d'or* (The Girl with the Golden Eyes, 1834) whose narrator observes:

> Paquita semblait avoir été créée pour l'amour, avec un soin spécial de la nature, son génie de femme avait fait les plus rapides progrès. Quelle que fût la puissance de ce jeune homme, et son insouciance en fait de plaisirs, malgré sa satiété de la veille, il trouva dans la *Fille aux yeux d'or* ce sérail que sait créer la femme aimante et à laquelle un homme ne renonce jamais. Paquita répondait à cette passion que sentent tous les hommes vraiment grands pour l'infini, passion mystérieuse si dramatiquement exprimée dans Faust, si poétiquement traduite dans Manfred, et qui poussait Don Juan à fouiller le coeur des femmes, en espérant y trouver cette pensée sans bornes à la recherche de laquelle se mettent tant de chasseurs de spectres, que les savants croient entrevoir dans la science, et que les mystiques trouvent en Dieu seul. (438)

> *(Nature seemed to have taken special care to form Paquita for love. From one night to the next her feminine genius had made the most rapid progress. Great as was this young man's prowess and his blasé attitude to pleasure, in spite of the fact that he had reached satiety on the previous occasion, he found in his golden-eyed girl the complete seraglio which a loving woman knows how to create and which a man can never refuse. Paquita responded to the craving which all truly great men feel for the infinite, that mysterious passion so dramatically expressed in* Faust, *so poetically translated in* Manfred, *which urged Don Juan to probe deep into the heart of women, hoping to find in them that infinite ideal for which so many pursuers of phantoms have searched; scientists believe they can find it in science, mystics find it in God alone.)*

This is a clear example in Romantic literature of the confusion between a man's search for transcendence and an actual woman's sexuality.

Nowhere is the pattern of poetics and sexual relations that characterizes the romantic legacy of Occitania present in a more complete form than in the writings of Nelli. His theory that the "homosexualization of heterosexuality" is the "finality of erotic love," (*AMC* 217–227) is inspired by both troubadour eroticism and a personal devotion to Catharism.[27] In all of his writings it is the ritual of the exchange of hearts to which he returns as the most revolutionary aspect of troubadour eroticism. The following passage from Nelli's "L'Amour courtois" describes the exchange of hearts as it exists in male friendship:

> Le guerrier a toujours eu besoin d'un *alter ego*, d'un auxiliaire qui lui fût plus fidèlement dévoué que les autres membres de son clan et même de sa famille.

C'est pourquoi, chez presque tous les peuples, l'amitié entre hommes s'est idéalisée en se cérémonialisant: des rites d'échange des sangs par incision ou par potion, accompagnés de serments solennels devant témoins, lui ont donné très tôt un caractère sacré et presque magique. Les deux amis étaient censés ne former qu'une seule et même personne. Le moyen âge a connu de telles unions amicales reposant sur la symbolique de l'échange des coeurs (signifant métaphoriquement l'échange des sangs): le compagnonnage chevaleresque n'a été qu'une variété de cet affrèrement viril par lequel l'amitié réalisait la communion fraternelle de deux consciences, et le dépassement de chacune au profit de l'autre.

Ces amitiés—sans se confondre d'ailleur absolument avec l'homosexualité—ont toujours revêtu un aspect *misogyne* accentué. (104–105)

(The warrior has always needed an alter ego, *an aide who was more loyal to him than the other members of his clan, or even his family. This is why, in almost every nation, male friendship was idealized and ritualized. Rites of exchange of blood by cuts or by drinking, accompanied by solemn oaths sworn before witnesses, gave them very early on a sacred, almost magical character. The two friends were supposed to form one single person. Such unions of friends formed by a symbolic exchange of hearts (symbolizing the exchange of blood) existed in the middle ages: chivalric* compagnonnage *was one version of viril* affrèrement *by which friendship realized the fraternal communion of two consciences and the transcending of each for the good of the other. These friendships, without being confused absolutely with homosexuality, always bore a marked element of misogyny).*[28]

The original exchange of hearts, which admittedly "bears a marked element of misogyny," is the model for the androgynous fusion assumed by generations of romantic writers to be the goal of heterosexual lovers. It is preceded in by an *asag* or love test that tests the woman's worthiness to participate in the male ritual. In principle, the lovers exchange sexes, the woman becoming a man; the man becoming a woman. Ideally, the exchange of sexual identities would be reciprocal, "Les temps étaient venus où la femme allait affirmer sa volonté de devenir homme (symboliquement) pour que l'homme devînt femme (sur le plan symbolique)" (The time had come for the woman to affirm her will to become man (symbolically) so that the man might become woman (on the symbolic plane) (63). As Nelli goes on to explain, however, the masculinization of the woman does not outlast the time of the ritual *asag,* "once she has shown herself to be worthy of sincere love, she has nothing else to do" (196). The femininity gained by the man in the exchange of hearts, however, becomes a permanent part of his transformed identity.[29]

These thirteenth-century lovers are models of the type of man who would be able to participate fully in what, for Nelli, is the ideal intersexual erotic relationship with a woman. He goes so far as to call the "finality of erotic love" bisexuality, a term he misuses. The most obvious misuse is that he is concerned only with heterosexual eroticism. More important, however, in terms of his own stated goal of intersexual mutuality—renamed bisexuality in the article "L'Amour courtois" for the purpose, I suppose, of exhorting contemporary men to seek the pleasures of *Fin'Amors*—is his misconception that what he is describing is a man and a woman in love. Actually, what he is describing is the union of two feminine beings, a man in love and a woman who conforms to his mirror image. Nelli writes:

> Cet amour . . . apparaît comme un greffon féminin enté sur la virilité et revigorant la part féminine qui est naturellement dans l'homme, mais qu'il a si longtemps refoulée (86)

> *(This love . . . appears as a feminine shoot grafted onto virility and reviving the feminine part that is naturally in man, but which he has so long repressed.)*

Nelli sees the best examples in the modern era of the persistence of troubadour eroticism in surrealist poetry. He maintains:

> Tous les surréalistes ont affirmé que l'amour n'avait point d'autre objet que lui-même (comme la poésie); que cet objet n'était ni sur la terre ni dans les cieux, ni même tout à fait dans l'être aimé, mais dans la passion comme "vouloir aimer," comme source de l'imaginaire, comme l'explosion de la nature dans le monde transparent des images auxquelles la matière donne poids, mais aussi notre esprit. S'ils valorisent la femme et l'amour, c'est seulement au nom du destin inconscient qui se cherche à la fois dans l'ami et l'amie, et pour faire la preuve que l'on ne peut aimer qu'un être capable d'incarner, de symboliser notre sort terrestre, ou, tout au moins, de passer par lui. On voit comment ils retrouvent sur le plan poétique l'un des mythes qui nous ont paru inhérents à la passion, et peut-être la première érotique des troubadours. (115)

> *(All the surrealists affirmed that love has no other object than itself (like poetry), that object exists neither on earth nor in heaven, nor even entirely in the loved one, but in passion as "to wish to love," as a source of the imaginary, as the explosion of nature in the transparent world of images, to which matter, but also our mind, has given weight. If they valorize women and love, it is only in the name of an unconscious destiny that seeks itself in the lover and the beloved in order to prove that one can only love a being capable of incarnating, of symbolizing our earthly fate, or at least passing through it. One sees how they discover on a poetic level one of the myths which seem to us to be intrinsic to passion, or to the first eroticism, that of the troubadours.)*

There are a several places in this passage where the language merits attention. Nelli begins by saying that love exists for itself; yet he brings a love object into the picture, hedging about its real presence by saying that love does not exist "entirely in the loved one." It is important for Nelli—and herein lies the problem—to allow for the possibility that although love does not exist on earth, that it might possibly exist in a woman. This paradoxical representation sustains the illusion of a female presence in heterosexual passion. And although he clearly says that it is woman—l'amour ou la femme—that gives the surrealist poet access to his destiny, he then refers to the loved one in both the masculine and the feminine forms of the word ami(e) (friend), creating the illusion of intersexual mutuality. His highest praise for surrealist poetry comes in the form of a tribute to, as he puts it, "the circumstances that the surrealists bring to light." Nelli describes surrealist poetics as follows, "elles génèrent le vrai par la stupeur du beau, et non point par accord avec la raison. Autrement dit, elles sont *féminisées*" (They generate truth through the daze of beauty, not at all through reason. In other words, they are *feminized*) (114).

Although Nelli's analysis of surrealist love is insightful, he seems blind to the fact that the description of coming into subjectivity—"nous mettre au monde, nous faire assister à notre propre apparition" (giving birth to the self, assisting in our own arrival into the world)—through writing depends on the metamorphosis of the male poet into a woman. When the major surrealist poet André Breton writes, "Et je ne sais plus tant je t'aime/Lequel de nous deux est absent" (And I love you so much that I no longer know/which one of us is absent), my response is that I *do* know: one of us was never there in the first place (in Nelli, *AMC*, 113). For a woman, the *asag* inevitably leads to a double bind. In principle, it tests her masculine strength and virtue, but as we have seen, the exchange is far from mutual. The man assumes his feminine side, the mirror image of her, and she fades away. Any vestige of manly virtue that remains in the woman is negative: her strength resides in her resistance to sexual passion.

Nelli is not alone among modern critics and theorists who suggest that at the time of its emergence as a clearly observable literary phenomenon, love between the sexes is not clearly heterosexual. In *Love in the Western World,* Rougemont establishes troubadour poetry as the source of the tradition and, with a passing remark, he raises the question of its conventional heterosexuality, "And once more small fact is that in the twenty-sixth Canto of the *Purgatorio* two of the troubadours most ardent in praising the beauty of their Ladies, the Provençal Arnaut Daniel and the Tuscan Guido Guinicelli are found in the sodomites circle" (98).[30] Other writers observe in passing the ambiguity of the sexuality in troubadour poetry, among them the critic C. S. Lewis, the poet T. S. Eliot, the psychoanalyst Julia Kristeva, and the medieval historian George Duby.[31] To question the heterosexuality of troubadour poetry comes down to seeing that the troubadours were less interested in the lady than in developing new refined poetic forms in the vernacular to express a writer's subjectivity. This is not to say that the troubadours or their successors wrote homosexual lyrics. Joë Bousquet (1897–1950), the surrealist poet and Nelli's great friend, leaves a striking modern poetic expression of this ambiguity in his unpublished *Cahier noir* (*Black Notebook*), "Sur le corps de la femme, je caresse l'inexistence des autres hommes" (On the woman's body, I caress the absence of other men) (in Nelli, *ET,* 344).

Around 1250, the period of the composition of the anonymous romance, *Le roman de Flamenca,* the most complete narrative of *Fin'Amors* and the last major work emanating from the medieval culture of Occitania, a new fashion in literature, the romance, had already been around for almost a century in the north. Lovers such as Tristan and Iseut, Erec and Enide, and Lancelot and Guinevere became the heroes and heroines of the new genre, precursor to the modern novel. While we remember the names of the heterosexual lovers of romance literature, the names of the troubadours whose voices embody both the masculine and the feminine roles are forgotten. Called "romances" because they were written in the vernacular—*li romans*—instead of in Latin; in French the modern novel is still called *le roman.*

The rapid spread of Occitanian poetic forms and themes to the north was due to the marriage of Eleanor to Henry Plantagenet: "The rise of *romance* coincided with a divorce and subsequent remarriage that made history seem like a romantic novel," writes Jean-Charles Huchet (Hollier 36). In 1152, Eleanor's marriage to Capetian king Louis VII was declared void for reasons of consanguinity, and two months later Eleanor married Henry Plantagenet, who ascended the English throne as Henry II in 1154. Eleanor's dowry to Henry included Aquitaine, Limousin, Poitou, and Berry. Her dowry went beyond real estate—it included the love poetry of the troubadours, several of whom accompanied her from the south of France to the court of England. Their presence at Henry's coronation is a matter of historical record (Marrou 47). So, while the first romances to have endured in the literary canon come from the north of France, their language and the core motif of courtly love came from the south with the troubadours who accompanied Eleanor on her journey from Aquitaine to England. Two centuries later, Dante, who had not yet forgotten the provenance of romance, proclaims the importance of this influence in *The Divine Comedy:*

Fu miglior fabbro del parlar materno.
Versi d'amore e prose di romanzi
soverchiò tutti; e lascia dir li stolti
che que di Lemosì credon ch'avanzi. ("Purgatorio," Canto XXVI: 117–120)

(He was a better artisan of the mother tongue, surpassing all those who wrote their
poems of love or prose romances—let the stupid ones contend, who think that from
Limoges there came the best) (tr. Mandelbaum)

Although the myth of Tristan and Iseut, reputed to be the first romantic lovers in Western literature, had enjoyed a long oral tradition dating from at least as far back as ninth-century Celtic legends, its romance version by the English troubadour Thomas dates from around 1170.[32] This is also the date assigned to the composition of the first known romance, *Érec et Énide* (Erec and Enide) by the northern French troubadour (called trouvères in the *langue d'oui,* spoken in the north), Chrétien de Troyes.[33] Chrétien's name comes from the location of the court of the countess Marie, Eleanor of Aquitaine's daughter, where the first romances were composed. More important than the chronology of their composition, however, is the fact that the romance of Tristan and Iseut and the Arthurian romances of Chrétien de Troyes—all of which have had an enormous influence on the representation of romantic love in Western literature and culture—show in their turn evidence of the influence of the poetics and the sexual codes and rituals that govern heterosexual behavior in *Fin'Amors.*[34]

One of the most important elements that comes into the tradition with *Tristan and Iseut* is that of the love potion, or *philtre.* These heterosexual lovers do not fall in love because of a natural inclination, or because intersexual mutuality has the social value of male friendship, but because they drink a love potion. The *philtre* begins as a love potion in *Tristan and Iseut* and reappears in romantic love narratives in many forms. It is a literary device that represents the fact that heterosexual desire is mediated and not only is it not "natural," but it is not even a readily acceptable social convention, due to the basic mistrust of women by the inventors of heterosexual love.[35]

One of the most explicit narrative explanations for the necessity of the *philtre* is that from the twelfth century until the present, heterosexual romantic love is anti-social. Indeed, in the year 2000, at the dawn of the millennium, Philippe Sollers calls it "the most perverse relationship on earth" (119). In spite of the fact that *Fin'Amors* is modeled on male friendship, and is considered necessary for the knight's transformation into a gentleman, the idea of recognizing a woman as a friend is in fact inconceivable.

A man who loves a woman with *Fin'Amors* is in the ambivalent position of needing the association with the feminine in order to prove his superiority to other men. Paradoxically, the woman who represents ideal femininity is, at the same time, unworthy of love because of her sex—a precursor of the *femme fatale*.

With the creation of the heterosexual couple in the romance genre comes the necessity to describe the physical characteristics of the lovers. As I will show in the following discussion, ideal beauty in romantic love narratives is *feminine beauty found in a man*. This ideal of beauty comes about because of the convergence in twelfth-century romance of many elements, some, such as the exchange of hearts, come directly from *Fin'Amors* and troubadour lyric poetry. Others, such as the man's feminine beauty, are incarnations of what in the poetry were intangible qualities in the poet-lover. It is not difficult, then, to imagine how the myth of androgynous fusion that was the goal of the exchange of hearts in *Fin'Amors* produced the romantic hero as a man possessing feminine beauty.

The feminine quality of Tristan's beauty is established in an early reference to his striking resemblance to his mother, Blanchefleur. This reference is decisive because it is Tristan's feminine beauty that fixes King Mark's gaze on his nephew, a narrative moment in all of the versions of the legend that places Tristan squarely in the feminine position vis-à-vis Mark, who occupies the position of the patriarch in the romance. In the Bédier version (1900), the first meeting of the two is described as follows:

> Mais surtout il admirait le bel enfant étranger, et ses yeux ne pouvaient se détacher de lui. D'où lui venait cette première tendresse? Le roi interrogait son coeur et ne pouvait le comprendre. Seigneurs, c'était son sang qui s'émouvait et parlait en lui, et l'amour qu'il avait jadis porté à sa soeur Blanchefleur. (9–10)

> *(Yet most he wondered at the stranger boy, and still gazed at him, troubled and wondering whence came his tenderness, and his heart would answer him nothing; but my lords it was blood that spoke, and the love he had long since borne his sister Blanchefleur.)* (9)

From this moment on, Mark loves Tristan exclusively, to the point of proclaiming to his court that "aussi longtemps que vivrait son cher neveu, nulle fille de roi n'entrerait en sa couche" (so long as his dear nephew lived no king's daughter should come to his bed) (26, 27). For Tristan's part, he vows to give his body to King Mark (20).

Iseut enters the story as Tristan's double: she is the body he gives to

Mark, and at the same time she is the mirror image of Tristan's mother, the lost self, the other half he seeks. The identification of Iseut with Blanchefleur, Mark's beloved sister and Tristan's double is made through two scenes in the romance. After giving birth to Tristan, Blanchefleur kisses her newborn son, lies down beside him and dies of grief for her husband, Rivalen, Tristan's father. In all of the versions, in the *Liebestod* scene (love-death) Iseut's death doubles Blanchefleur's. This is how it is depicted by Bédier:

> Elle se tourna vers l'orient et pria Dieu. Puis elle découvrit un peu le corps, s'étendit près de lui, tout le long de son ami, lui baisa la bouche et la face, et le serra étroitement: corps contre corps, bouche contre bouche, elle rend ainsi son âme; elle mourut auprès de lui pour la douleur de son ami. (219, 202)
>
> *(And when she had turned to the east and prayed God, she moved the body a little and lay down by the dead man, beside her friend. She kissed his mouth and his face, and clasped him closely; and so gave up her soul, and died beside him of grief for her lover.)*

By marrying Iseut, Mark is able to please his court by marrying a king's daughter, and to keep his promise to love Tristan exclusively, for Iseut has exchanged hearts with Tristan. From the moment Tristan and Iseut drink a love potion prepared by Iseut's mother meant for Iseut and Mark on their wedding night, they are one. Iseut's servant, Brangien, to whom the potion was entrusted by Iseut's mother, comes upon the two unsuspecting victims of the *philtre* immediately after they have drunk the love potion. Her reaction to the sight of them echoes the image of a single being split into two from Plato's myth of the androgyne, "Brangien entra et les vit qui se regardaient en silence, comme égarés et comme ravis" (Brangien came upon them and saw them gazing at each other as though ravished and apart) (46, 43). Their fusion, both fatal and idealized in keeping with the ambivalence towards heterosexual fusion in *Fin'Amors,* is symbolized by the leafy briar that joins their twin tombs after their death.[36] The *philtre* is a literary device used to make explicit a sexual identification that has already been established by descriptions of the lovers' equal beauty and equal desirability. If one were to remove the *philtre,* to refuse the illusion of the lovers' sexual difference fusing into one erotic angel, we would find that we had already been prepared to accept the illusion. In fact, the true purpose of the *philtre* is not to deceive the lovers and to relieve them of the moral responsibility for their act, but to convince the reader that the identification of the heterosexual lovers is a miracle of fusion of sexual difference when in fact that difference has already been attenuated prior to the operation of the *philtre*. The *philtre* desymbolizes by simultaneously creating and collapsing difference between the lovers.

As represented on anything from medieval casket reliefs to a Metropolitan Opera poster advertising a production of Wagner's operatic version of their romance, Tristan and Iseut are as physically alike as twins. On the cover of the Vintage paperback version of *The Romance of Tristan and Iseut* as retold by Bédier, both have long hair and flowing robes; Tristan wears an over-sized sword and Iseut carries a large cup. The illustrator's choice of differentiating signs, the sword and the cup, is the only—not so subtle—suggestion that the lovers are not of the same sex. These overt and blatant signs are necessary, it seems, because the legendary status of Tristan and Iseut as the first heterosexual romantic lovers in Western literature is based—in the text—not on conventional notions of sexual difference, but on a shared femininity.[37] Tristan and Iseut are equally beautiful and that beauty is feminine; both are desired by King Mark, a figure of traditional masculinity.[38]

Chrétien de Troyes wrote courtly romances based on the legend of King Arthur and the Knights of the Round Table. The legend of Arthur is as old, or older than the Celtic sources of the Tristan story.[39] This does not prevent Chrétien from making Tristan a knight of the Round Table in several tales, including his first romance, *Érec et Énide*, in which Enide's beauty is compared to Queen Iseut's (6). This reference in a romance thought to be written as early as 1170 (Owen, *Arthurian Romances,* xviii) would seem to indicate that troubadours were familiar with versions of the story that predated Thomas's twelfth-century version of the romance. By 1178, when he wrote *Cligès,* Chrétien is clearly preoccupied with the romance version. *Cligès* is Chrétien's anti-Tristan. In *Cligès* Chrétien repudiates the lesson of Tristan and Iseut that love is a sinful, destructive force in human sexuality and attempts to show how happiness and harmony can result through the institution of Christian marriage. This does not change the fact, however, that several structures of *Fin'Amors*—always adulterous—persist in this story: the equal beauty of the lovers, their exchange of sexual identities, and the love test. Because Chrétien's stories share structural similarities with the stories of fatal adulterous love, they also share its dangers and problems. In *Érec et Énide,* Érec spends so much time in bed with Énide that his masculinity is questioned by his fellow knights and others at the court. Tristan's virility was also affected by his love for Iseut, making him impotent with his beautiful and desirable new wife, Iseut of the White Hands. The consequences for each lover are different: it is Tristan's sexual performance that is affected, whereas in Érec's case, it is his prowess on the battlefield that is doubted by the others. In both narratives, however, the masculinity of a man who loves a woman too much is in jeopardy.

The story of *Érec et Énide* is that of the conflict between private eroticism and public image for a man who loves a woman with *Fin'Amors*. In romantic love narratives, the lovers are able to maintain equality—what Nelli calls intersexual mutuality—with relative ease in a private erotic space. When the same couple appears in public, however, they are expected to resume the traditional masculine and feminine sex roles. This is one of the places in the tradition in which we see the confusion of a poetics with social sexual relations.

The power that a woman has to be a desiring subject is an arbitrary power given to her by a man who, according to the code of chivalry, becomes her slave for the purposes of the erotic relationship. This servitude does not, however, go beyond the private space of eroticism where the man can play the role of Narcissus who seeks the ideal self in the mirror of representation. What is represented—as a man's ideal self—is the woman, the *dame*, the lady. The confusion of a mirror image of the male self with a fictional woman is expressed in an unambiguous description of Énide's function in the structure of desire:

> Grande était la beauté de la jeune fille. Nature, qui l'avait façonée, y avait mis tous ses soins; elle-même s'était plus de cinq cents fois émerveillée de ce qu'elle avait pu, une seule fois, former une si belle créature, car, depuis lors, en dépit de toute la peine qu'elle avait prise, elle n'avait pu en aucune manière en produire un nouvel exemplaire. De celle-ci, Nature porte témoignage: jamais plus belle créature n'a été vue de par le monde. Je vous dis en vérité que les cheveux d'Iseut la Blonde, si blonds et dorés qu'ils fussent, n'étaient rien auprès de celle-ci. Elle avait le front et le visage plus lumineux et plus blancs que n'est la fleur de lys; son teint était merveilleusement rehaussé par une fraîche couleur vermeille dont Nature lui avait fait don pour relever l'éclat de son visage. Ses yeux rayonnaient d'une si vive clarté qu'ils semblaient deux étoiles; jamais Dieu n'avait si bien réussi le nez, la bouche, et les yeux. Que dirais-je de sa beauté? Elle était faite, en vérité, pour être regardée, si bien qu'on aurait pu se mirer en elle comme en un miroir. (11–12)

> *(The maiden was extremely attractive; for Nature, who had created her, had put all her care into the work and had herself marveled times without number that just this once she had contrived to make so lovely a person; and afterwards, try as she might, she was never able to reproduce her original model. Nature bears witness that never was so exquisite a creature seen in the whole world. I tell you truly that the hair of the blonde Iseut did not shine so fair that she could stand comparison with her. Her brow and face were more pure and white than the lily. Her features were tinted with a fresh rosy hue*

wondrously painted by Nature upon her whiteness. Her eyes shone with such radiance that they seemed like two stars. Never was God able to form finer nose, mouth and eyes. What could I say of her beauty? It was truly such as was made to be gazed upon, for in it one might have looked at oneself as in a mirror.) (6)

The number of swift moves from nature to culture and from the object of the gaze to the one who gazes indicates that this passage has more to do with the problem of representation than with a woman's natural beauty. Here, as elsewhere in the romances, Chrétien makes conscious ironic allusions to the absence of an original female beauty, making its construction as a male attribute, not belonging to women at all, as clear as it can possibly be in a fiction that involves the assumption of heterosexual desire. In the passage itself, Nature is described as an artist who has problems with representation, unable to reproduce the "original." This original, imagined in the figure of Énide, cannot be represented without reference to another representation, the blonde Iseut. The hair of one "original" beauty outshines that of another "original" in a sentence that closes the text on itself, showing that its depiction of female beauty does not exist outside of the text. Couched in the description of Énide's complexion, however, with "its fresh rosy hue wondrously painted by Nature upon the whiteness," is another text, this one by Ovid. Énide's beauty replicates the beauty of Narcissus, the original beautiful young man, the feminine hero who falls in love with his own self-difference in *Metamorphoses,* ". . . he gazed at the twin stars that were his eyes, at his flowing locks, worthy of Bacchus or Apollo, his smooth cheeks, his ivory neck, his lovely face where a rosy flush stained the snowy whiteness of his complexion, admiring all the features for which he himself was admired" (85).

That Chrétien is thinking of Ovid's model for ideal male beauty is confirmed in the final line of the passage when the reader is asked to identify with Érec's gaze, "It was truly such as was made to be gazed upon, for in it one might have looked at oneself as in a mirror." The references to Nature, and then to Iseut as a model for beauty are erased when the passage evolves towards Érec's own subjectivity as the model for Énide's beauty. When Érec first lays eyes on Énide, she is dressed in a white shift—symbolic of her status as a screen onto which Érec projects his desire to transcend the limits of the self. Érec wins Énide as a prize when he triumphs in the sparrow-hawk contest. The value in the romances of such tournaments is significant for an understanding of how the construction of feminine beauty is transferred from a poetic abstraction to the dramatic interest of the narrative form. In the sparrow-hawk contest, as in most other similar tournaments, the victor chooses the lady he will take as his prize by announcing that she is the most beautiful lady present. Her beauty is not recognized as such prior to a powerful—and beautiful—knight's representation, "à tort ou à raison , que celle qui lui plaît est la plus belle et la plus noble" (rightly or wrongly, the one he favors is the most attractive and beautiful) (*Érec et Énide*, 2, 1). It is not until the process of constructing feminine beauty as determined by the subject, whose desire is a mirror image in the feminine, that the gaze becomes reciprocal and a heterosexual couple emerges as a figure in the text:

Plus il la regarde, plus elle lui plaît. Il ne peut se retenir de l'embrasser; il prend plaisir à s'approcher d'elle et se sent en repos rien qu'à la regarder. Il ne cesse d'admirer sa tête blonde, ses yeux riants et son front clair, le nez, le visage, et la bouche, et ce spectacle est pour lui d'une douceur qui touche son coeur. Il admire tout jusqu'à la hanche: le menton et la gorge blanche, les flancs et les côtés, les bras et les mains. Mais la demoiselle, pour sa part, admire le jeune homme avec non moins d'intérêt, et d'un coeur aussi loyal qu'il la contemple elle-même sans se lasser. Certes, il n'auraient pas payé rançon pour être dispensés de se regarder mutuellement. Ils étaient égaux et pairs en courtoisie, en beauté et en générosité. Il se ressemblaient à tel point par la manière d'être, l'éducation et le caractère que nul homme résolu à dire la vérité n'aurait pu décider quel était le meilleur, ni le plus beau, ni le plus sage. (39)

(The more he gazes, the more she pleases him. He cannot help kissing her. He delights in drawing close and keeping his eyes fixed on her. His gaze lingers over her fair hair, her laughing eyes and pure brow, her nose, face, and mouth; and he is touched to the heart by a great tenderness. He gazes at everything down to her hips; the chin and white throat, the waist and sides, arms and hands. But no less intent than the knight, the maiden vies in gazing at him with fond eye and true heart. For no reward would they have stopped looking at one another! They were a perfect match in courtliness, beauty and great nobility of character; and they were so much of a kind and equal in conduct and bearing that no one wishing to tell the truth could have chosen the better or fairer or wiser of them.) (20)

Clothes do make the woman. Érec insists that she accompany him to King Arthur's court dressed in her simple white shift, so that she can be made in an image he will choose for her, with the queen's help. One of the first moments, then, in the making of the couple, is the construction of Énide into the perfect woman, equal in beauty and grace to the perfect man, Érec. The theme of the story involves the changes she must then undergo in order to become his equal in valor and courage, as well as in grace and beauty. Énide's love for Érec will be tested by a love test which shares this similarity with the *asag* of *Fin'Amors*: the woman's ability to play the same role as the knight's male *compagnon* is tested; in other words, in both the *asag* and the love test to which Érec subjects Énide, a woman is raised from her weak, feminine state (which had to be first invented, in Énide's case) to a state of masculinity, because only then can a man truly love her without risking his own masculinity.

As the story progresses, Énide is disturbed by public opinion which accused Érec of being recreant, a criticism that could destroy his public image as a knight. Énide lies in Érec's arms as he sleeps, but she herself remains awake and talks to herself about Érec's misfortune: her fatal attraction to him that is destroying his reputation. Here again, we see the woman, no matter how lovely and in love she is, as a *femme fatale*. She sees herself as such, and society sees her as deadly to Érec's masculinity. When Érec is awakened by the sound of her voice, she denies that she has been speaking aloud and tells her husband that he must have been dreaming. But Érec persists and she is compelled to tell him the truth. Érec, infuriated, immediately resolves to prove that his prowess and strength are not diminished. He orders Énide to prepare herself for a journey in search of adventure, and further orders that she ride ahead of him, where she will be constantly exposed to danger and to hardship. She must also remain silent and speak only if and when he speaks to her. The love test has begun. As with all love trials, it tests the woman and it involves a double bind. She is damned if she does and damned it she doesn't. If she does not speak when her husband is in danger, then she does not love him. If she does speak when he's in danger, she does not respect him.

When he orders Énide to ride ahead of him in their adventures, imposing upon her an order of silence, Érec places Énide in a very ambiguous position. She is first the woman who must obey the man and who is completely dependent on his strength and leadership. She must also become manly and virile to prove that she is a fit *compagnon,* or fellow knight, to be worthy of being loved with *Fin'Amors*. As they set off for their adventures which will test Énide's love and trust, Érec brutally imposes his will upon her. When she has met every test, he will once again swear obedience and devotion to her, his beloved *dame,* and his proven *compagnon.* Énide is terrified, of course, during their many encounters with danger, most of which include the threat of rape.[40] The only way in which Énide can prove her valor as a knight is to resist the sexual advances of the villains they meet during their adventure. A male knight has many adventures through which he can prove his virility, a woman's sexuality is both her weapon and the enemy—the obstacle and the prize! Énide is strong, however, according to the poetic ideal of *Fin'Amors*. She courageously endures any violence:

Ah! peu m'importe ce que tu peux me dire ou me faire: je ne crains ni tes coups ni tes menaces. Bats-moi, frappe-moi tant que tu voudras: tu auras beau te montrer féroce, je ne ferai pour toi ni plus ni moins, même si tu devais à l'instant m'arracher les yeux de tes propres mains ou m'écorcher toute vive.

(Ah, she cried, I do not care what you say or do to me. I am not afraid of your blows or your threats. I have struck myself and have wounded myself quite enough. You will never be too brutal for me, and I will do nothing for you, even if you pluck out my eyes with your hands, or chop me up alive.) (127, 65)

To prove that she has now acquired the virtue of a true *compagnon*, that the transformation is now complete, she plays the role of a squire and carries Érec's lance, "Érec courut prendre son écu, il le pendit à son col par la guiche. Énide prit la lance . . ." (Érec runs to pick up his sword and hangs it around his neck by its strap. And Énide takes the lance . . .) (128, 64).

Énide has met the final test. Érec accords his full pardon and reaffirms his obedience to her every command:

Ma douce soeur, je vous ai bien éprouvée en toute chose. Cessez désormais de vous inquiéter, car je vous aime maintenant plus que jamais et je suis à nouveau sûr et certain que vous m'aimez parfaitement. Je veux être dorénavant tout à vos ordres, comme je l'étais précédemment. (129)

(Sweet sister, I have put you completely to the proof! Don't be at all fearful, for now I love you more than ever, and I am again wholly certain that you love me perfectly. From now on I wish to be entirely ours to command, as I was before.) (65)

By a love test modeled on the ritual *asag*, Énide has become, symbolically, her lover's male friend. She displays the male characteristics of fidelity and moral courage. Her power, however, is artificial and arbitrary, whereas his capacity to love is real, because of what he has to give up for it, namely his masculine public persona. Moreover, a woman's power can be withdrawn at any moment by a man. Another aspect of the double bind is that only when a woman has proven her manliness can she be loved as a woman. In *Tristan and Iseut,* however, the exchange of hearts allows Tristan to maintain characteristics of both masculinity and femininity simultaneously. He dies from a hero's wound and for the love of the queen. She dies in a passive way, linking her to one aspect of femininity and excluding her from the agency of masculinity. She dies because her heart has died. Iseut is "the Fair" and "of the Golden Hair." Tristan is an individual, described for his attributes: his heroism, his abilities. Like Énide, Iseut is a prize won by Tristan for heroic acts.

In spite of the *asag,* a woman's moral character is consistently called into question in romances. For example, when Tristan marries Iseut of the White Hands, he is unable to consummate his marriage because he cannot break his vow to Iseut and sleep with his wife. He is in control of his sexual destiny and in control of his "vow," of his "honor." Iseut must sleep with Mark and so is forced to break her vow to Tristan. In spite of the presence of narrative devices meant to establish the romantic heroine's worthiness to be loved by the hero, her honor is never as sure as is his. The feminine means tenderness and the ability to love when it is found in the male; when it is found in the woman it always involves moral weakness. The woman is poison; a man who loves a woman will die of that love, and it is not a worthy thing to die for. This brings up the problem of *compagnonnage* vs. heterosexual erotic love; a man cannot love a woman and still maintain his power and honor as a knight, although in order to maintain his knightly status, he must be capable of *Fin'Amors.*

This paradox is evident in *Cligès,* a work intended by Chrétien to counter a tale of adulterous love (*Tristan and Iseut*) with a tale of married love that included the same narrative elements: Cligès, like Tristan, lost his mother and father at an early age, his mother, Soredamor (her name evokes both sister and love) died of a broken heart after his father, Alexander's death; his uncle Alis is the king, and like Mark does not wish to take a wife, because he had made a vow to his brother Alexander to have no heir so that Cligès would have the throne upon his uncle's death. But, like Mark, Alis is urged by his vassals to take a wife and so goes to Germany to seek the emperor's daughter. Like Tristan, Cligès falls in love with his uncle's betrothed, the Iseut figure, Fénice. A magic potion, or *philtre* is also employed in this story, not to cause unlawful love between Cligès and Fénice, but to prevent Fénice from losing her virginity to her legitimate husband because it is Cligès whom she loves and should rightly have married, had Alis kept his pledge. It is with this twist in the convention of the *philtre* that Chrétien establishes that Cligès and Fénice's love is not adulterous, since Fénice's marriage to Alis is based on a broken vow. In this story, there is a love test that is the reverse of the traditional one: that is, here the abstinence is in the lawful marriage. In this story, there is a love-death that is the reverse of the traditional love-death: here the lovers do not die so that they can join together in perfect fusion in eternity, but death is feigned so that the lovers may enjoy sexual fusion here on earth in the symbolic garden. Despite a happy ending, the marriage of Cligès and Fénice, who reign as emperor and empress of Greece, the moral of this story maintains the constant distrust of women that runs through these romances. Fénice is allowed to enjoy happiness with Cligès, but no empress after her is ever allowed to leave Constantinople, and none is ever permitted to be in the company of any male who is not a eunuch. One cannot truly say that Iseut is rehabilitated in Chrétien's story. The distrust of the idealized woman, friend and *compagnon,* is inherent to this tradition.[41]

The descriptions of the lovers' physical beauty shows once again the way in which the question of the origin of feminine beauty is sidestepped. Fénice is not compared to Iseut, as Énide is, because Fénice is an original, "il ne peut y avoir qu'un Phénix à la fois, ainsi Fénice, ce me semble, n'avait nulle pareille en beauté" (peerless in beauty. Nature was never able to create her like again) (102, 129). Cligès's beauty, however, does exist in representation. Like Érec, he is explicitly compared to Narcissus:

> Il était plus beau et avenant que Narcisse qui dessous l'orne vit en la fontaine sa forme et l'aima tant qu'il la vit qu'il mourut, à ce que l'on dit, parce qu'il ne l'avait pu atteindre. C'est qu'il avait plus de beauté que de sagesse. Mais Cligès en avait tant plus que l'or fin passe le cuivre. (103)

> (He was more handsome and charming than Narcissus, who saw his reflection in the spring beneath the elm tree, and, on seeing it, fell so much in love with it that they say it caused his death, as he was unable to possess it. Whereas he had much beauty, if little sense, Cligès had far more, just as pure gold surpasses copper) (129).

Chrétien tries to escape the influence of the Tristan model. Fénice's beauty defies representation—except in the pages of this romance, where her beauty is *not* described. As for Cligès, his beauty surpasses that of Narcissus. If the reader holds the image of Narcissus in mind as the most perfect beauty imaginable, then, like Fénice's, the beauty of Cligès cannot be represented except as more beautiful than the most beautiful boy of representation. Moreover, not only is Cligès beautiful, he possesses all good qualities, both physical and moral, in abundance. Compared to King Mark's nephew, Cligès "mieux connaissait l'escrime et l'arc que Tristan, et mieux aussi chasse à l'oiseau et chasse aux chiens." (knew more of swordsmanship and archery than Tristan, and more than he of birds and dogs) (103, 130) Since, as Chrétien tells us, "nulle qualité ne lui manquait" (he lacks nothing), Cligès possesses all the qualities that the male desiring subject desires in a woman (103, 130). Therefore, Fénice cannot be the opposite, or what the desiring male subject lacks. She is, rather, that which exists in him and must be manifested to him in a form outside of himself in order to be his pleasure. The reason she must exist is also clearly stated in the text, "Mais nul coeur n'est en deux endroits. . . . Chacun d'eux garde son coeur de même que plusieurs voix peuvent chanter même chanson à unisson" (But one heart cannot be in two places . . . each one keeps his own heart just as several voices are able to sing together in unison) (104, 131). The analogy with singing in unison is significant; it allows the poet, Chrétien, to express his own desire to split into two in order to enjoy the pleasure of singing, while knowing that he retains his singular identity. Here again it is Balzac, in *The Girl with the Golden Eyes,* who best expresses the implications of the role of the Narcissus myth in the confusion between the physical reality of a female sex partner and a poetic representation of male self-difference:

> Veux-tu? s'écria-t-elle. Ai-je une volonté? Je ne suis quelque chose hors de toi qu'afin d'être un plaisir pour toi. (439)

> *(Need you ever say "Will you? to me?" she exclaimed. "Have I a will? I exist outside of you only in order to be a pleasure for you.")*

Chrétien considers the problems with the goal of androgynous fusion in a critique of *Fin'Amors*—first, the idea of two hearts in one body as a "real" experience of fusion is ridiculous, "Je ne parlerai pas comme ceux qui unissent deux coeurs en un seul corps puissent loger deux coeurs." (I shall not follow those who say there are two hearts united in one body, for it neither is true nor seems to be that there should be two hearts in a single body) (104, 130). Moments later, however, Fénice thinks of the one who has smuggled away her heart and wonders why their bodies are not close enough for her to retrieve it (131). Cligès, too, is aware of having exchanged hearts, "J'ai aimé là-bas. Mais rien n'ai aimé qui fût de là-bas. Comme l'écorce sans aubier mon corps sans coeur fut en Bretagne" (I was in love over there, but not with anyone who came from here. Like bark without wood, my body was without its heart in Britain) (119, 163). In other words, although the writer is aware that the literary convention is absurd, his characters are already under the influence of the power of literature as a *philtre* and the language of love determines its nature in spite of the writer's desire to change its representation, or to make explicit the fact that heterosexual desire is a metaphor for writing.

The direct influence of troubadour poetry, northern romances and the conventions of *Fin'Amors* continued in explicit ways throughout medieval literature well into the thirteenth century, creating courtly love, a code of love based on *Fin'Amors,* but in an adulterated form, available to all courtiers and not limited to the perfect lover and hero. A second trend in literature had also grown up alongside courtly love by 1270. This trend, epitomized by Jean de Meun's *Le roman de la rose* (*The Romance of the Rose*) (ca. 1275), satirized the ideals of courtly love. If *Fin'Amors* was dying out with Occitania, its legacy lived on in courtly love.

The intersection of the two contradictory currents are evidenced in the two versions of *Le roman de la rose*. In the first part, Guillaume de Lorris writes a manual of refined seduction that adheres to the courtly tradition, whereas in the second part, completed by Jean de Meun, *Le roman de la rose* becomes a satire of all courtly ideals and repudiates the notion that sexual instincts can be sublimated for the cause of intersexual mutuality.

While I agree with Nelli that *Fin'Amors* and its flawed successor courtly love have defined heterosexual romantic love in literature since the twelfth century, I take issue with his belief that the structure of desire in trouba-dour poetics represents an ideal of mutuality between the sexes. Lacan, too, sees troubadour poetics as a continuing presence and a problem that reveals and obscures its own solution. Lacan's focus is on the origins of sublima-tion in Western culture: "La création de la poésie consiste à poser, selon le mode de la sublimation propre à l'art, un objet que j'appellerai affolant, un partenaire inhumain" (By means of a form of sublimation specific to art, poetic creation consists in positing an object I can only describe as terrify-ing, an inhuman partner) (*Le séminaire VII* 180).

Lacan's depiction of the process of sublimation supports my contention that the woman exists in courtly love poetry as signifier (215). The point I would make is that to say the poetic process of sublimation involves the repression of the feminine is not an exact description of what is involved. In troubadour poetics, male subjectivity is split into masculine and femi-nine; the feminine becomes less terrifyingly "other" because it is subli-mated and contained within masculinity. The romantic lovers of literature, whose coupled names are as well known today as they were at the time of their creation, sprang from the split of the single subject of troubadour poetry into himself—as the romantic lover—and a lady who for the most part is unnamed, or simply called *domna* (lady). The ambiguity of the lady's presence is underscored by the fact that *domna* is often replaced by the grammatically masculine for *mi dons*.[42] Both the absence of a model for heterosexual desire for women writers and cultural blindness to that absence are due to the presence of a spurious heterosexual couple in narra-tives of desire.

CHAPTER 2

Vagabondage in the Age of Chivalry

Marie de France is the first woman novelist of our era. If I cannot quite simply call her the first woman novelist, that is only because I believe the writer of the Odyssey was also a woman.

—*John Fowles*[1]

$\mathcal{M}$arie de France, known today as the first woman poet in the history of French literature, is recognized as having written at least three of the major extant works of the twelfth-century Renaissance, the *Lais,* the *Fables* and the *Espurgatoire seint Patriz (The Purgatory of Saint Patrick).* Yet, unlike Chrétien de Troyes, the only other writer of the period credited with so many works, Marie was compelled to justify her desire to write. The Preface to the *Lais,* her best known work, is a public act of defiance of the social codes that dictated women's silence, couched in the language of an *exordium:*[2]

> Celui à qui Dieu a donné du savoir et un talent de conteur n'a pas le droit de garder le silence ni de demeurer caché et il ne doit pas hésiter à se montrer. (1)
>
> *(Anyone who has received from God the gift of knowledge and a talent for storytelling has no right to remain silent, nor to remain hidden, and he must not hesitate to make himself known.)*

The problem with a woman making herself known is a serious one in medieval poetics because breaking silence is tantamount to destroying *Fin'Amors,* and, more important, its system of poetic expression. Women's silence in this period is not due exclusively to what Tillie Olsen, in *Silences* (1978) characterizes as "the age-old denial of enabling circumstances—because of one's class, color, sex—which has stunted (not extinguished) most of humanity's creativity" (261). Silence, for women of the nobility like Marie de France, is bound up with heterosexual desire as well, making it more difficult to break than if it were solely an issue of human rights. Fear that speaking out makes a woman undesirable to men was—and still is—a cause of anti-feminism among otherwise privileged and enlightened women. Nowhere is this more true than in France, the least feminist, most "feminine" country in Europe. Paradoxically, the arbitrary and illusory power that women have wielded in French culture since the invention of courtly love in the twelfth century is an obstacle to a strong feminist movement in France. I say illusory because in France there is a correlation between the veneration of the feminine and the resistance by both women and men to feminism.

The history of women's rights in France is unique in the West.[3] In the Middle Ages noble women enjoyed more (but not equal) rights than after the French Revolution (1789) when they lost the right to express themselves in the public realm. Aristocratic women of the *ancien régime* possessed some power and public status that the male leaders of the French Revolution rescinded and then refused to extend to any other women. Before 1789, women who inherited noble estates could not only administer them in their own names, but in some regions enjoyed the right to vote in local and regional assemblies that such property conferred. As late as 1661, aristocratic women could still receive titles of nobility in their own right, and they exercised the prerogatives of their rank by sitting as members of the *parlements* until the eve of the French Revolution itself. Such privileges accrued, it is true, to only a tiny minority, but a considerably larger group of prominent women enjoyed extensive informal power and influence in French society of the late seventeenth and eighteenth centuries. This sphere consisted largely of urban *salons* organized and animated by aristocratic women in which intellectual figures, writers, nobles, high government officials, and other members of the urban elite came together for conversation and conviviality in a setting distinct from the much more restricted and hierarchic life of the royal court. While the hostesses made themselves the cultural arbiters of an emerging polite society of cultivation and taste, the men who forged the Revolution thought that these women exercised undue power, and emasculated the nation (see chapter 3).[4] Critiques of women's cultural and political power shaped some of the discourse of the Revolution because it became a critique of the *ancien régime* itself. After 1789, revolutionaries set out to eliminate all remnants of an aristocratic culture they believed to be decadent and corrupt. They resolved to replace an effeminate monarchy of artifice and ornament with a virile republic of virtue and reason. Women were banished from all public life. The Napoleonic code, named for a man reputed throughout the

Romantic era that began during his Empire as a man who "loved women," institutionalized the anti-feminism of the Revolution. But feminine power, associated with aristocratic women prior to the Revolution, did not leave the French imagination with the abolition of women's rights nor with the relegation of women to the civil status of a minor child under the Napoleonic Code. French culture is still "feminine." The major French exports are cuisine, fashion, and perfume, and France has always been a sexually mixed society; Frenchmen enjoy women's company and the *salon* culture has never disappeared from French social life. Unlike English gentlemen, who traditionally prefer the hunt and exclusive men's clubs to mixed society, or Italian men whose leisure time is spent at the café on the public square in all male company, French men socialize in mixed company and that company is dominated by the feminine arts. President Jacques Chirac's eulogy for Pamela Harriman, American ambassador to France (1993–97), reminds us of the persistence in contemporary France of the notion that a beautiful, well-dressed, well-educated woman with the special skills of a good hostess wields power in the political arena:

> She was elegance itself; she was grace. . . . This great lady was also a peerless diplomat. In the impassioned debates that regularly pepper our friendship, she was, for President Clinton as well as for me, an irreplaceable interlocutor, perfectly attuned to our thoughts and expectations as well as to the respective constraints on us, which she always faithfully interpreted. (New York Times 2/9/97)

For the American president Clinton, it was the money she raised for his election campaign in her Washington, D.C. *salon* that won her the ambassadorial post, but for the French president Chirac, her success in that post was due to her ability to be "attuned to" the thoughts of powerful men. The illusion of feminine power, which blinds French women to sexism, misogyny and anti-feminism, dates back to the age of chivalry when a lady's power resided in her capacity to reflect, as in a mirror—"faithfully interpret"—a man's self-expression. This is not to say that the desire to please is a reason for anti-feminism only in France; this phenomenon is found among women everywhere. The importance of the predominance of this attitude in France is particularly relevant to this study because the legacy of courtly love, a French phenomenon, affects heterosexual women's relationships to feminism throughout the West. The focus of this study is the implications of this cultural reality for women's writing.

For men, the desire to write and erotic desire are, as I have shown in the previous chapter, fused into a single desire in the notion of *joi,* the "joy of desiring."[5] A woman's passive and silent presence in lyric poetry and courtly romance is structurally identical to a composer's desire to transcend the limits of the self through composition (*trobar*), represented in the writing as love for a lady. Consequently, a woman who writes in this period transgresses the laws of two cultural systems. First, she destroys erotic desire by breaking the courtly code of secrecy, which demands silence. Second, and more important than the damage she has done to courtly love by breaking the silence, is that by speaking, she gives voice to the unrepresentable. For example, by giving voice to Érec's loss of masculinity, Chrétien de Troyes' Énide represents the unrepresentable, Érec's split subjectivity (see chapter 1). Énide exposes Érec's difference from other men, and from himself, thereby revealing the secret masked by the *troubadour effect,* that the femininity of the lady in troubadour lyrics is a masquerade.

In her classic article, "Womanliness as Masquerade" (1986), Joan Rivière makes the point that it is impossible to separate "womanliness" from masquerade, "The reader may now ask how I define womanliness or where I draw the line between genuine womanliness and the 'masquerade.' My suggestion is not, however, that there is any such difference; whether radical or superficial, they are the same thing" (38). Interpreting Rivière's theory in *Vested Interests,* Marjorie Garber writes, "The woman constructed by culture is, then, according to Rivière, already an impersonation. Womanliness *is* mimicry, *is* masquerade" (355). When a woman writes, she quite literally reveals the male masquerade of femininity by representing herself, a woman, as the voice of femininity. R. Howard Bloch identifies one of the major themes of the *lais* of medieval France as "the telling of a tale of love which should remain hidden" (123).[6] Toril Moi provides an apt description of the conflation of a woman's voice with the unrepresentable—poetic expression itself, when she says of Andreas Capellanus, author of *The Art of Courtly Love,* "he has unmasked a problem of general linguistic and epistemological importance (how can language convey truth), and blames it all on the deviousness of women instead" (29).

Marie's *lais* are of great interest in this regard in that each of them tells two stories at once, a love story and a story of writing. Generally speaking, a *lai* is a narrative lyric poem dealing predominantly with a love story, shorter than a romance, but written in the same verse form for the same audience. Because the love stories are already known to her audience from earlier versions, Marie is able to draw attention to issues of representation. She does this explicitly, as she writes in the Preface:

Je me suis mise à former le projet d'écrire quelque belle histoire et de la traduire du latin en langue commune. Mais ce travail ne m'aurait pas valu grande estime car tant d'autres l'avaient déjà fait! Alors j'ai songé aux lais que j'avais entendus. Je ne doutais pas, et même j'étais certaine, que leurs premiers auteurs et propagateurs les avaient composés pour perpétuer le souvenir des aventures qu'ils avaient entendu raconter. J'ai entendu le récit d'un certain nombre et je ne veux pas les laisser perdre dans l'oubli. J'en ai donc fait des contes en vers, ce qui m'a coûté bien des veilles. (2)

(I began to form the project of writing a beautiful story and translating it from Latin into the vernacular. But this work would not have been worth much since so many others had already done it. Then I thought about the lais that I had heard. I thought, in fact I was sure, that their first authors and propagators had composed them to perpetuate the memory of adventures that they had heard about. I had heard a certain number of them recited and I do not want to see them lost from memory. I have thus composed tales in verse, which have cost me many a sleepless night.)

This explanation of how the project of writing the *lais* evolved serves to convey several messages. Marie first establishes her identity as a talented writer by breaking the silence imposed on women by tradition, if not by law. The *lais* break with another tradition as well, this one having to do with the transformation of a literary genre, tantamount to creating a new one. She will not do a translation from the Latin, as many have done, but something new—the creation of a new genre: narrative *lais* in written form, based on Breton songs. But these are not simple transcriptions; Marie's *lais* are unveilings rather than reproductions. According to Bloch, her conscious goal in writing is to reveal each text as "a series of rewritings" (Bloch, *Medieval Misogyny* [1991] 134). Consequently, the layers of textual secrets in Marie's *lais* are even more dense than the convention of the hidden tale requires. A reason for this is that a woman who assumes the subject position of the writer of heterosexual desire is compelled to write two stories, a love story and with it—enfolded in it, and essential to its structure—the story of the virtual unavailability to women of the position she has assumed. This is what I call *vagabondage*.

In each of her revisions of Breton *lais,* Marie refers in some way to elements of the Tristan legend, especially in *Chèvrefeuille,* the best known of all her *lais,* in which she develops a specific episode.[7] Unhappy after more than a year in exile on the coast of Brittany, Tristan steals back to Cornwall, determined to see Iseut. Iseut now lives at Mark's court, having been reinstated as its queen, thanks to lies she told to convince Mark and the courtiers that she and Tristan were not lovers. Learning that the court will travel to the castle of Tintagel for Pentecost, Tristan has carved his name and a message on a branch of hazelwood and placed it in the path of the courtly procession. Iseut's desperate lover hides in bushes by the roadside, lying in wait for her to pass. The hazelwood branch establishes the influence of *Fin'Amors* on Marie's *lai* by symbolizing androgynous fusion. Iseut had once told Tristan that if a honeysuckle vine wraps itself around a branch of hazelwood, the two could not be separated without killing them both. The message carved on the branch repeats Iseut's words, "Belle amie, il en est ainsi de nous: ni vous sans moi, ni moi sans vous" (Beautiful friend, so it is with us: neither you without me, or me without you" (*Tristan et Yseut: les premières versions européennes* 215). As Tristan had hoped, Iseut sees the branch, reads the message and orders her entourage to stop. Iseut seeks Tristan in the woods alongside the path of the procession where—hidden from sight in keeping with *Fin'Amors*—the lovers take joy in each others' arms for a brief moment. Marie's version moves from the love story to a story that interests her more, that of the composition of the *lai*. When Iseut departs Tristan takes up his harp and composes a *lai* called *Chèvrefeuille* in order to preserve the beauty of the words carved on the branch.

> par désir de se rappeler les paroles de la reine qu'il avait mises par écrit, Tristan, qui savait bien jouer de la harpe, en avait fait un nouveau lai. D'un seul mot, je vous indiquerai son titre: "Gotelef" pour les Anglais, "Chèvrefeuille" pour les Français. Je viens de vous dire la véritable histoire du lai que j'ai raconté ici. (*Tristan et Yseut* 216)

> *(To remember the queen's words Tristan, who played the harp well, composed a new lai. In a word, I will give you the title, gotelef in English, chèvrefeuille in French. This is the true story of the lai, which I have just narrated.)*

In an ironic twist, Marie credits Tristan with having written *Chèvrefeuille*. The attribution of the composition of *Chèvrefeuille,* unique among versions of the Tristan myth because it is called by a name other than that of the lovers, to someone other than herself (one of her own characters) serves to place the question of authorship in relief. Furthermore, she insists on giving us her title "in a word"—*chèvrefeuille,* calling attention to herself as the writer of the *lai* with this unique name, "this is the *true* story of the *lai,* which *I* have just narrated" (emphasis added). Several layers of textual appropriation are unveiled in the story of the honeysuckle and the branch of hazelwood, which according to the *lai,* is first told by Iseut. It is the queen, not Tristan, who first used the metaphor of the two trees to represent the love between Tristan and herself. Tristan then carves Iseut's exact words into the hazelwood branch. What Tristan actually wrote on the branch changes as the *lai* unfolds. The opening lines of the *lai* say that he carved only his name. In the closing lines, however, Marie indicates that an entire *lai* appears on the branch—the same *lai* that she has just written and we have just read. The conflation of Marie's writing and Iseut's words (Tristan is only relaying "the queen's words") deconstruct the assumption that the writing position is masculine despite the fact that the single name inscribed on the branch is Tristan. By changing the familiar name of the legend from *Tristan and Iseut* to *Chèvrefeuille,* a poetic figure for fusion of two into one, Marie insists on the *Fin'Amors* goal of androgynous fusion as the primary focus of her version of the love story. Her critique of *Fin'Amors* reveals that the goal of writing, however, is far removed from any notion of *two.* This critique is ironically inscribed with the single name carved into the branch; "Tristan" replaces "Tristan and Iseut" as the (single) identity of the subject of desire. When Marie writes, "This is the true story of the *lai,* which I have just narrated," the "I" refers to Marie. She claims authorship in several of the *lais* by attributing them to herself simply and directly as "Marie." At the end of the *Fables,* we find the best known assertion of her identity as the writer: "I am Marie, I am from France." Read in the context of all her writings, the "I" in *Chèvrefeuille* is "Marie." By substituting "I" for "Tristan," the poet of the *lais* reclaims for herself the femininity associated with writing. Although the writing position has been reserved for men, paradoxically, it has been marked as feminine since the Middle Ages.

In an article called "Nom de femme et écriture féminine au moyen âge" (The Name of the Woman and Feminine Writing in the Middle Ages) (1981), the critic Jean-Charles Huchet, discussing the attribution of the *lais* of Marie de France, makes some very telling remarks in an attempt to get at the problem not only of the identity of the author of the *lais* but of writing and sexual difference when he asks:

> Est-ce là, pour autant, affirmer que cette écriture est féminine? Peut-être! A la condition toutefois de ne pas réduire la féminité aux attributs biologiques du sexe authentifié par un nom de femme. Car ce nom moins que jamais nous paraît sûr. N'est-il pas venu, lors de la mise en manuscrit par le copiste de H, revendiquer une écriture dont l'habileté à produire la fiction du "un" était ressentie comme le signe d'une différence, tant il est vrai qu'il vaut mieux, en cette fin du XIIe siècle, entamer le privilège masculin de l'écriture que de laisser croire qu'un homme a pu franchir, dans la langue, la barre qui clive les sexes et se ranger sous la bannière de la féminité. (429)

> *(Is this [the feminine signature Marie] as much as to affirm that this writing is feminine? Maybe! On the condition that one does not at the same time reduce femininity to the biological attributes of the sex authenticated by a woman's name. For that name is less sure than ever. Didn't it happen, during the copying of a manuscript by the*

copyist of H, that writing with the ability to produce the fiction of a "one" was claimed as the sign of a difference, because it was so much better at the end of the twelfth century to broach the masculine privilege of writing than to let it be believed that a man was able to broach—in language—the barrier that divides the sexes and to fall in line behind the banner of femininity.)

Whether one is convinced that Marie is the author of the *lais,* Huchet's reasons for placing in doubt the absolute certainty of such an assumption gives pause. For Huchet, it would have been better—in the twelfth century—to accept the unlikely idea that a woman wrote than to consider the even more improbable idea that a man's writing bore the mark of femininity. I contend that both ideas are equally possible, and that the very nature of the writing of the *lais* attributed to Marie could prove to be either a woman writer's playful, ironic reappropriation of the feminine signature, or an equally playful admission on a man's part that writing, when linked to desire, is always feminine. A more serious concern I have with Huchet's remarks is that they reinforce tendencies by canon makers to question a woman's authorship of a classic as in the case of Madame de Lafayette and *La Princesse de Clèves,* or to question the femininity of women who write classics, as in the case of George Sand. The seemingly inevitable observations about Sand being either too masculine ("Il fallait la connaître comme je l'ai connue pour savoir tout ce qu'il y avait de féminin dans ce grand homme" [One had to know her as I did to know how much of the feminine was to be found in this great man] writes Flaubert at Sand's death [*Correspondance Flaubert/Sand* 535), or too feminine (Nietzsche's characterization of Sand as a "writing cow" [in Naginski 222] provide innumerable and sometimes humorous examples of how women writers baffle even the brightest men.[8] Huchet hits the nail on the head when he unwittingly attributes the suspicion of the sexuality of women who write to anxiety about confronting the sexual personae of men who write fictions of heterosexual desire.[9] The epigraph from John Fowles at the start of this chapter indicates an identification between femininity as a writing effect and the sex of a writer. If, as Fowles seems to playfully suggest, Marie was not the first woman novelist, it is because a woman can't be the first *anything.* A man has already occupied the position marked as feminine.

Marie's attention to the feminine signature moves the focus from the social and sexual realities of a writer's life to writing as representation. Representations of self and self-difference resist social/sexual categories that are in fact antithetical to the poetics of the period, especially, as Bloch argues in *Medieval Misogyny* (1991), to the form of the *lai* (134–35) about which he writes, "An excess (surplus) that cannot be said, the presence of the body is excluded from the text" (134). That is, the bodies of the lovers are displaced by language. In the case of *Chèvrefeuille,* the deferral is infinite: the coupling takes place in Iseut's description of the metaphorical embrace of the honeysuckle and the hazelwood, then in the words carved by Tristan, then in the *lai* written by Tristan, but which bears Marie's signature, making the text a "series of rewritings, which no matter how perfect, always leave a 'surplus of meaning'"(Bloch, 134). The voice of pleasure is precisely what is left over, the excess that defines desire, and which has been designated as feminine. Furthermore, in an odd reversal of the Tristan story, *Les deus amants (The Two Lovers)*, Marie uses the familiar device of a *philtre,* which in her *lai* is never consumed—an anti-*philtre,* as it were—to emphasize the necessity for deferral. A similar pattern of displacement, deferral, and textual density characterizes the entire collection of *lais* and points to writing as a form of desire.

Marie is the first woman to have written in the *langue d'oui.* The *trobairitz,* women troubadours (approximately twenty) who lived at roughly the same time, wrote in the *langue d'oc.*[10] Scholars have advanced several possible historical factors to account for the existence of women poets in Occitania, all of which support my contention that women's silence was—and is—bound up with eroticism at least as much as it is with oppression when the women in question enjoy privileged social status. Women's power during this period is attributed to inheritance laws that were favorable to them, to the absence of men from their fiefdoms during the Crusades, to the education and high degree of literacy of women of nobility, and to the relatively privileged position of women of aristocratic birth (all of the *trobairitz* were aristocrats, three of them countesses).[11]

The writing of Marie and of her Occitanian contemporaries reveals a preoccupation on the part of women writers of the period with the relationship of writing to desire. Marie's approach resembles linguistic theory; she rewrites familiar love stories, drawing attention to issues of representation. The poetic forms used by the *trobairitz* fall into two general categories: love poetry in a single voice and poetic dialogues. Verses in a single voice are called either *cansos* (love poems or songs) or *sirventes* (moralizing poems, political, personal, or didactic in tone, dealing with subjects other than love); the most common form of poetic dialogue is the *tenso,* a dialogue or debate poem in which two speakers express their points of view on one subject in alternating strophes of identical rhyme-schemes. Because they write either lyric poems (*cansos*), or engage in dialogue and debate (*tensos*), the writing of the *trobairitz* is more personal than Marie's; many of the poems speak frankly about sexual matters.

Both Marie and the women troubadours question—albeit in different forms—the representations of desire that traditionally have been the products of the male imagination. Both write within a system that they are compelled—as they write—to critique. *Trobairitz* writing brings a different perspective to our understanding of the art of courtly love, which until the appearance of Meg Bogin's book in 1976, was always considered from the point of view of the troubadours. The *trobairitz* call into question the notion that *Fin'Amors* gave women sexual power over men. As described in their poetry, this power was artificial and arbitrary; its rituals lifted a woman to the position of absolute sovereign, when in reality she was the slave to a master who sometimes agreed to reverse the roles in order to play the chivalric game.

The lady was always socially superior to the knight; this social superiority was exchanged against a "natural" sexual inferiority. Equality was symbolically established through this exchange. The *tenson* between Marie de Ventadorn and Gui d'Ussel, for instance, clearly indicates that for her, while the man has everything to gain by insisting on equality in love, for the woman this equality is a regression, "ieu lo jutge per dreich a trahitor, si.s rend pariers ei.s det per servidor" (I call him a traitor who wishes to be her equal, being her servant) (Bogin 124). Also, the reasons for the elevation, empowerment, and equality of women in *Fin'Amors* undermine the benefits an individual woman might derive from the new code of love. In *Fin'Amors,* a woman is represented as a sovereign only so that she might become an object worthy of a man's love and a worthy subject for his songs—a means to a higher good. This representation is complicated by the fact that by virtue of her sex, a woman was considered naturally inferior even to a socially inferior lover. In order to give her the value that her rank would command if she were a man, the rituals of *Fin'Amors* transform her symbolically into a man. In order to be celebrated in heterosexual love lyrics, a woman had to be conceived of in the male imagination as the equal of his male lord or companion.

It is important to keep this ambiguity in mind when trying to understand the anguish and confusion—the *vagabondage*—expressed in *trobairitz* poetry.[12] The verses of Castelloza, for example, are representative of the consistent complaint that although in theory *Fin'Amors* celebrates female sexuality and grants women a power they have not previously enjoyed, their sexual relationships were far from satisfying, and their power arbitrary and fleeting:

Bels amics, de fin coratge
vos amei, pois m'abellitz,
e sai que faich ai follatge
que plus m'en etz escaritz. (Bogin 150)

(Handsome friend, as a lover true
I loved you for you pleased me
but now I see I was a fool
for I've barely seen you since)

Garenda states the case of the real woman turned into an idol in explicit terms:

Vos que.m semblatz dels corals amadors,
ja non volgra que fossetz tan doptanz;
. . . que ges dompna non ausa descobrir
tot so qu'il vol per paor de faillir. (Bogin 132)

(You're so well-suited as a lover, I wish you wouldn't be so hesitant. . . . For a lady
doesn't dare uncover her true will for fear of failing [losing her reputation for virtue].)

That the truth of the lady's will is sexual desire is revealed by Tibors:

Bels dous amics, ben vos posc en ver dir
que anc no fo qu'ieu estes ses desir
pos vos conven que.us tenc per fin aman. (Bogin 105)

(Handsome, sweet friend, I can tell you truly that I've never been without desire since
it pleased you to become my courtly lover.)

Domna H. complains quite frankly about lovers who take the *asag* too seriously. She poses the situation of a lady who has asked her two lovers each to swear that he would do no more than hug or kiss her. One immediately breaks his oath; the other doesn't dare. The lady prefers the lover who is so blinded by sexual passion "that he can't hear or see or know if he does wrong or right" (qu'ab jazer et ab remirar l'amors corals recaliva tan fort que non au ni non ve ni conois quan fai mal o be) (Bogin 162). The confusion created by the rituals of *Fin'Amors* is expressed by the best known of the *trobairitz*, the Countess of Die when she "breaks the silence," by writing:

A chantar m'er de so qu'ieu non volria,
tant me rancur de lui cui sui amia,

65

car l'am mais que nuilla ren que sia'
vas lui no.m val merces ni cortesia,
ni ma beltatz ni mos pretz ni mos sens,
c'atressi.m sui enganad' e trahia
com degr'esser, s'ieu fos desavinens. (Bogin 108)

(I am so angry at he who is supposed to be my lover, and whom I love, that I am singing about what I should keep silent. What good are my good manners, my beauty, my reputation and my understanding: I have been as abused and betrayed as if I were guilty.)

Judging from the poetry as a whole, the erotic pleasure celebrated by *Fin'Amors* comes into direct conflict with rituals such as the *asag;* the women of the period are consequently confused and frustrated.

Fin'Amors is not only a celebration of the joy of love, it also celebrates the joy of singing (*trobar*) and the pleasure of composing. Although the lines cited above show that the poetic content of *Fin'Amors* is not wholly suitable to women poets, they want to participate in the pleasure of writing. But with writing pleasure, "the joy of desiring," they also want to love and be loved as flesh and blood women. They want to have real relationships with men, both as sex partners and as valued friends. Their common desire to be acknowledged as individuals, to enjoy real, not merely symbolic, equality with men is articulated in Guillelma's *tenson* with Lanfrancs Cigala (Bogin 159–60). And although some of the *trobairitz* demand the ritualistic authority and power over the lover that is accorded to a woman in the rules of *Fin'Amors* (Marie de Ventadorn and the Countess of Die), this is not the dominant attitude (Bogin 122, 106).

For the most part, they refuse the role of an imperious mistress who commands a humble slave with the artificial and arbitrary power bestowed on women by the codes of courtly love. For them, the capacity to love and to suffer, roles traditionally assigned to the male in courtly lyrics, is not tied to one's sex, but to one's position as a lover and as a singer. Castelloza writes, "Ja de chantar non degr' aver talan, /quar on mais chan /e pietz me vai d'amor" (I should have had my fill of song/for the more I sing/the worse I fare in love) (Bogin 146). Thus, the gender assignments of the roles of sovereign and subject are exchanged when the woman becomes the lover by assuming the position of writer. Azalais writes, "I'd gladly stay forever in your service" (Bogin 120).

Evidence that the *trobairitz* were aware of the importance of writing to subjectivity is found in the poem by Lombarda called "I'm Glad I Wasn't Called Bernarda for Bernart." In this poem, Lombarda rejoices in the fact that she did not take the name of her husband, but has her own name and her own identity. If she were represented merely as the feminine version of a man's name (his reflection in a mirror, so to speak), she herself would have no image when she looked in the mirror. The poem recognizes the power of representation and celebrates a woman's right to represent herself:

Car lo mirailz e no veser descorda
tan mon acord c'ab pauc no.l desacorda,
mas can record so qu'l meus noms recorda,
en bon acord totz mons pensars s'acorda. (Bogin 140)

(For the mirror with no image so disrupts my rhyme that it almost interrupts it; but then when I remember what my name records, all my thoughts unite in one accord.)

Like Marie de France, Lombarda insists on the right to her name. Neither poet is content with representing a male lover's self-difference, with being his reflection in a mirror. The idea that a woman's identity is separate from her lover's comes into conflict with the poetics of *Fin'Amors* and with the deferral and frustration that are the source of *joi*. In *A History of Their Own* (1988), Bonnie Anderson and Judith Zinsser describe the difference between the troubadours and the *trobairitz* in the following way:

Men's lyrics and chansons praised discretion and delighted in the anguish of anticipation. The women, in contrast, called for forthright declarations, railed at missed opportunities, and delighted in thoughts of the consummation of passion. (107)

Joan Ferrante has compared the use of direct address, of the second person as compared to the first or third, in troubadour and *trobairitz* poetry, and concludes that "women are more given to the direct approach. They address the object of their feelings, while the male poets are as likely to address their fellow men as their ladies" ("Notes" [1992] 65). The *trobairitz* exhibit a much greater tendency to address the lover directly, which is to say that the invention of an ideal other with whom the poet identifies to such an extent that he achieves a lost wholeness, is not typical of their writing. Lise Wicky-Ouaknine (1987) writes in this regard:

Dans ce temple aux idoles de l'imaginaire masculin, les femmes troubadours (les trobairitz) renverseront quant à elles les statues glacées et parfaites, pour des femmes de chair et de sang. (35)

(In this temple of idols of the masculine imaginary, the women troubadours for their part turned over the perfect, frozen statues for flesh and blood women.)

This is not to say that women writers of the period, like their male counterparts, do not affirm the eroticism of writing. For women, it is not just a substitute for a relationship with an actual lover. While it is true that the writing often describes suffering due to the loss of a lover, that loss is not the purpose of the writing itself. The desire to write sometimes results in suffering, due to the fact that a woman who writes does not conform to the fiction of femininity as it is elaborated in the complex poetics of sexual difference which constitutes *Fin'Amors,* and thereby risks losing her lover. The essential paradox of *Fin'Amors* in this regard is that, as Marianne Shapiro puts it, "a lady's desire must express itself as the wish to be possessed. . . . The desiring subject would be, *in potentia,* the desired object" (562). Self-difference, or the split subjectivity essential to the writing process, can be seen then as a major structural problem for women who write of heterosexual desire.[13] According to Shapiro:

> As long as lover and lady are felt to be related as aspirant and ideal, respectively, the lady may even grant the lover all he prays for and still retain her dignity, enclosed in the anonymity of the *senhal* (or pseudonymic sign) that represents her in the poem. But concern or desire on the lady's part would transform her into a mortal and desiring creature, like a man, but otherwise automatically relegated to inferior status. (563)

Since love in *Fin'Amors* is virtually identical to the poem itself, a woman—by writing—breaks with the pattern of the "asymmetrical relationship a poem projects between the courting man and the courting woman" (Shapiro 564). Castelloza's verses, "the more I sing, the worse I fare in love," are quite different from the general sentiment of troubadour poetry, which says that the worse I fare in love, the better I sing.[14] Wicky-Ouaknine contrasts the suffering found in *trobairitz* lyrics with what she calls "the literary artifices, idols and sublimations" of their male counterparts (36). She concludes her comments on the difference between the men and the women poets of the period with these words:

> Car si l'amour courtois est chanté et magnifié, les trobairitz nous rappellent que dans la vie, il perd souvent son éclat et ses convictions. Elles révèlent, sans rien cacher, ce que sont les sentiments de ces femmes, en ces temps de fin'amor. (36)

(For if courtly love is sung and glorified, the trobairitz remind us that in life, it often loses its lustre and its convictions. They reveal, hiding nothing, the feelings of women at the era of Fin'Amors.)

In other words, one might say, with Shapiro, that "the poetic content, forms, and the motifs of the system of *Fin'Amors* were clearly not wholly suitable or applicable to women lyricists" (561).[15] I read *vagabondage* in women's writing throughout this study as a conflict between dominant philosophies of heterosexual love, for example Romantic love in the nineteenth century, and women's desire to write. Shapiro's conclusion points to the structural problem of self-difference for a woman writer:

> Since the beloved lady was the apex of value for the male, her transposition to activity does not imply a concomitant transposition of the passive male to perfection. In none of the women's poems therefore, does the masculine beloved appear to incarnate or substitute, as she had, for a total scheme of ideals (565).

Women writers are inevitably involved, as I have said in the previous discussion of Marie de France, with a critique of the system that governs writing and desire at the same time that they avail themselves of that system. Shapiro argues that the poems of the *trobairitz* make constant reference to a preceding story of amatory discourse:

> Whereas troubadour lyric as a whole proceeds from a negative stance on the part of the poet, it is still held to the tenet of harmony between intention and accomplishment. The women's poems in their problematic relationship to external societal norms cannot lay claim to such an accomplishment. (565)

In the case of Castelloza's verses cited previously, for example, the identification of desire and singing is evoked by reversing the troubadour structure. In general, women who assume the writing position do so against the system which structures heterosexual eroticism and supports antifeminism. Their unconventionality becomes part of the story they write.

A work that has been called "the most illustrious prose work in the short story genre to appear during the Renaissance" (Winn [1991] 318) was written by a woman who, like Marie de France and the *trobairitz* occupied a privileged place in French society. *L'Heptaméron,* written by Marguerite de Navarre (1492–1549), queen of Navarre and the sister of the French king, was published posthumously in 1559. So impressive was Marguerite's intelligence that at her funeral Charles of Sainte-Marthe was moved to describe her as "one who had a manly heart in her woman's body" (L. M. Richardson [1929] 112), foreshadowing by three centuries Flaubert's eulogy for George Sand—Sand was characterized as a feminized man, Marguerite as a manly woman. Like Marie de France and the *trobairitz* before her, Marguerite situates her work within a tradition. The *Heptameron* is a response to Boccaccio's *Decameron* (1353), whose translation into French was commissioned by Marguerite herself.[16]

In the Epilogue to the *Decameron,* Boccaccio claims that the stories he writes are women's own stories, told to him by women whose voices he is transcribing faithfully:

> Saranno similmente de quelle che diranno, qui esserne alcune che, non essendoci, sarebbe stato assai meglio. Concedasi: ma io non poteva né doveva scrivere se non le raccontate, e per ciò esse che le dissero le dovevan dir belle, ed io l'avrei scritte belle. (1241)

> *(There will likewise be those who will say that it would have been better to omit some of the stories. That may be true: but I could only transcribe the stories as they were told, that is to say that if they had been told beautifully, I should have written them beautifully.)*

Boccaccio's apology for writing the feminine is very much in keeping with Huchet's speculations about feminine writing in the twelfth century. Boccaccio takes credit for telling women's stories and builds a handy disclaimer into his work for any tell-tale signs of "femininity" in the writing. Boccaccio's expressed opinion in the Epilogue is that women are incapable of lengthy discourse. Marguerite subverts his theory by assigning the name of Parlamente—she who speaks—to one of the narrators of her collection of stories; Parlamente is clearly Marguerite's *porte-parole*. Ironically, of the five men and women narrators, it is almost always Parlamente who tells the longest stories, and who gives the lengthiest speeches in the discussions that follow the tales.

In the *Decameron* there are ten narrators: seven men and three women. According to critic Carla Freccero , "the equal division of the sexes" in the *Heptameron,* "emphasizes the thematic importance of gender difference and signals *l'Heptaméron*'s polemical relationship to Boccaccio's model" (Hollier 145). Marguerite imitates the technique used by Boccaccio, to have one person tell a tale and the others discuss its implications. Unlike the discussions in Boccaccio, those in the *Heptameron* represent diverse points of view. They are diverse, subjective, and often contradictory; the major point being that no single interpretation can be given to sexual behavior derived from the rituals and codes of courtly love.[17]

Marguerite's critiques of the *asag* in Tales XLVII and XVIII are fairly humorous satires of the love test. Tale X, on the other hand, is a serious work that could be characterized as a performative fiction. It plays out the inevitable and fatal consequences of the ritual, and moves its reader to reflect on theoretical issues surrounding the ways in which *Fin'Amors* can be seen as a "malady of death," to borrow Marguerite Duras's title (1982) which plays on the homonymic affinity of the French "maladie de l'amour," (malady of love) and "maladie de la mort" (malady of death).

Tale XLVII involves two men who are best friends. When one of them marries, the two friends who live "non seulement comme deux frères, mais comme un homme tout seul" (not only as if they were two brothers but as one single man), and sleep together in the same bed with the new wife (312). The married man sleeps in the middle. Marguerite turns *Fin'Amors* around in such a way as to reveal its homoerotic model. The fusion created by the exchange of hearts takes place between the two men, not between the husband and wife. Marguerite moves the woman from her traditional position in the triangular structure of desire to reveal a more accurate configuration: The husband's place in bed situates him as the object of both the friend's and the wife's desire. In spite of sleeping in the position of the sword, the obstacle to sex, and in spite of the fact that he himself has made the sleeping arrangements, the husband imagines his best friend as his rival and accuses him of desiring his wife. Marguerite draws a picture, in other words, of the triangular structure of desire, making the male rivalry/friendship that rules male eroticism not only explicit but intentional.

The roles of Catherine (Jeanne Moreau) in François Truffaut's 1962 film *Jules et Jim* (based on Henri-Pierre Roché's novel of the same name) and of Julia, Sebastian's sister and double in Evelyn Waugh's *Brideshead Revisited* (1945) are two familiar examples of the structure of Tale XLVII in modern literature. A more recent example is the triangle in Kevin Smith's 1997 film *Chasing Amy*. The leading character's desire to share a sexual experience with his best friend and his girlfriend is by no means new or experimental (see chapter 6); it is as old as *Fin'Amors*.[18] Even though the wife's virtue has nothing really to do with the desire in Tale XLVII, it becomes the issue. The married man does not believe that his wife has not betrayed him with his best friend and only worthy rival. The structure creates the inevitable double bind: If the wife is not desired by her husband's friend, then she must not be worthy of his own desire either. She innocently becomes the source of conflict between the men, and she is their scapegoat as well.

In Tale XVIII, a young nobleman of exemplary courtly virtue falls in love with the most beautiful woman of the countryside. Because of the youth's incomparable beauty and grace, the lady finds herself in love with him even before he himself is aware of his own feelings for her. She insists, however, on testing the virtue and sincerity of the young man and forces him to undergo a classic love test before she will agree to satisfy his desire. They lie in bed together, partially disrobed, and the young man is desperately frustrated, but his control is perfect because his aspiration for an enduring and perfect love—*Fin'Amors*—is the strongest of physical restraints. The woman, however, is astonished by his chastity. She believes, in fact, that he could not really be attracted to her and even suspects that he had spent his sexual energies elsewhere before he entered her bed. She devises a second test. She asks him to declare his love to her young and beautiful servant, pretending that her reputation would be protected if people thought he was courting the maid rather than the mistress. He is again obedient. When the lady is sure that her maid has fallen in love with her ersatz suitor, she tells him that she is ready to reward him for his patience. In reality, it is the tempting and desirable maid who is waiting in her mistress's bed. The young man is immediately aware of the substitution and leaps out of bed in a rage, cursing both the maid and her mistress. The lady, deeply impressed by this new evidence of the strength of the young man's love for her, begs his forgiveness, which he grants. The significance of Tale XVIII lies in the parody of the traditional love test. Especially interesting is the discussion following the tale in which Saffredent, a member of the group shows the basic contradiction in the test by asserting that if a man is willing to undergo the love test, he will be called "*de frigidis et maleficiatis*" (frigid and impotent), i.e. his virility comes under suspicion (141). The love test proves a woman's virtue and discredits a man's virility. The fact that the double bind is intrinsic to *Fin'Amors* becomes clear in all of Marguerite's tales involving its codes and rituals. The double bind here involves both the man and the woman. If a man conforms to the rules of *Fin'Amors,* his masculinity—like Chrétien's Érec—falls under suspicion. If a woman rewards a man's constancy with sex—which they both desire, she has lost her power and the story of desire is ended.

Tale XVIII is a benign example of the double bind of the *asag.* Tale X, on the other hand, shows how the logic of the *asag* leads ultimately and inevitably to violence. The lovers' names, Amadour and Floride, represent their functions in the tale, the lover and the flower remind us of Jean de Meun's *Roman de la Rose* (*Romance of the Rose*); the lover's function is to penetrate the fortress guarding the rose, the rose's function (with her entourage) is to resist penetration. The lover and the rose of Jean de Meun's romance are allegorical, not so Amadour and Floride. In Marguerite de Navarre's story, confusion as to the meaning and goal of the love test leads to attempted rape. That the fault lies in the courtly ritual is made clear when Amadour defends himself for having tried to force himself on Floride by saying:

Ma dame, j'ay toute ma vie desiré d'aymer une femme de bien; et pour ce que j'en ay trouvé si peu, j'ay bien voulu vous experimenter, pour veoir si vous estiez, par vostre vertu, digne d'estre autant estimée que aymée. Ce que maintenant je sçay certainement. . . . (75)

(My lady, for my entire life I have desired to love a good woman. But I have found so few of them that I wanted to test you, to see if you were as worthy to be respected for your virtue as you are to be loved. I now know for certain that you are. . . .)

When Floride resolves that she can only pass the love test by giving no further sign of her love to Amadour, he sees this as a challenge to become more aggressive sexually, even cruel and abusive. When the lovers meet for the last time it is as mortal enemies:

(il) imagina une invention très grande, non pour gaingner le cueur de Floride, car il le tenoit pour perdu, mais pour avoir la victoire de son ennemye, puis que telle se faisoit contre luy. (77)

(he devised a grand scheme, not to win back Floride's heart, for he firmly believed it lost, but to gain a victory over his enemy, as she had done over him.)

Amadour predicts his own death in a later scene when, carrying out his vow to conquer Floride—the woman he once loved and now sees as his enemy—he attempts to rape her. Before her mother hears her screams and prevents the rape, Amadour has vowed that his fight with Floride will be a fight unto the death. Later in the story, he reiterates his desire for death:

Mais combien que la mort me fuye, si la chercheray-je tant, que je la trouveray; car en ce jour-là, seullement, j'auray repos. (81)

(No matter how death flees from me, I shall seek it and find it, for only on that day shall I have peace.)

Amadour's desire for the obstacle ends finally with his own death; Floride finds peace in the Convent of Jesus. Floride is in the classic double bind of the woman who is desired for her virtue, which can only be maintained if she refuses to satisfy the desire it inspires in her lover. When Floride refuses his aggressive and brutal sexual advances, Amadour claims to be testing her virtue. When we remember that chivalry is a military code and that courtly love is one of its tenets, it appears logical that a woman who resists will inevitably be in the position of a man's mortal enemy. In an essay on Tale X called "A Severe and Militant Charity," (1988) Sanford S. Ames, citing Lacan's reference to Marguerite de Navarre, makes the point that the desire for the impossible ideal, Floride in Tale X, is desire for an absence.[19] He writes, "this absence was, as well, an effect of writing, of that which offered the present trace of absent divine presence or of a missing, adored body." "Love's trope," for Ames, is "relation where none existed" (89). The lady in courtly love narratives is, as I have shown, an absent presence. Ames makes the connection between the so-called woman of courtly love and the scene of writing when he writes:

> Woman became the place onto which lack, magnified by writing, was projected. Absence and inaccessibility are thus there at the beginning of a text as the "no place" of the other, the absence of the loved one. (89)

Desire for writing represented as heterosexual desire leads, in my analysis, to the conflation of desire for the obstacle, the "nothing," a space in which to write, with desire for a woman. Furthermore, in its most romantic renderings, desire for the obstacle is represented as the desire for death. The inaccessibility of the absent "lady" of courtly love is advanced as the cause of the romantic lover's death when it is actually death that he desires and deliberately seeks.

The *troubadour effect,* then, involves not only the appropriation of the feminine as the writing position for male writers, but the identification of Woman with writing itself. By writing, women materialize into individuals, occupying the space reserved for the projection of male self-difference. By writing themselves, women make it impossible to maintain the illusion of heterosexual desire in courtly love. Because of this, it is consistently the case that in spite of their education and privileged status, women writing in the age of chivalry are compelled to justify their desire to write.

Louise Labé (1512–1566) belonged to the rising bourgeoisie of Lyons, a cosmopolitan center. Like the aristocracy, families of Louise's social class valued education for their daughters. The author of 24 sonnets, Louise writes from much the same position as the *trobairitz,* frankly admitting sexual desire and skeptical of the convention of the inaccessible lady. The 24 sonnets tell the story of *Fin'Amors* from what François Rigolot characterizes as an "ironic perspective" (Hollier 267); the lover offers to be the lady's servant, but loses interest in her as soon as he has aroused her passion for him. I read Sonnet XXI as particularly relevant to the consequences of the *troubadour effect* for women's writing. In this sonnet, Labé wonders about how to represent masculine beauty in the Renaissance when the courtly love tradition continues in the Petrarchan mode popular at the time:

Quelle grandeur rend l'homme venerable?
Quelle grosseur? quel poil? quelle couleur?
Qui est des yeux le plus emmieleur?
Qui fait plus tot une playe incurable?
Quel chant est plus à l'homme convenable? (OC, Sonnet XXI: 132–133)

(What height makes a man worthy of adoration?
What build? what hair? what color?
What kind of eyes are the sweetest?
Who inflicts the most incurable wound?
What song is the most suitable for men?)

The problem that Labé sees—the absence of male objects of desire as models for women—is a real one, made more difficult to surmount than even her pointed sonnet suggests because the beauty of the ideal lady in *Fin'Amors,* as I have demonstrated, is based on the ideal of masculine beauty of Greek and Roman antiquity, Narcissus, or the beautiful boy. At least as far back as the twelfth century, ideal beauty—in women as well as in men—is represented as a specific kind of male beauty, as found in statues of David by Donatello or Michelangelo. Representations of what might be called "masculine" men, such as Michelangelo's Moses, lack erotic appeal. Ideal beauty in a woman reflects, as in a mirror, an image of the feminized male's self-difference, and his difference from conventional images of masculinity.[20]

This paradox becomes explicit in the ideals of beauty advanced by fifteenth-century Florentine neoplatonists, artists, poets, and theoreticians who had developed Plato's notion of love between men and the cult of adolescent male beauty as a means of spiritual fusion in love into a philosophy of ideal love between men and women. In spite of its so-called heterosexuality, however, the ideal of beauty in Neoplatonism remained a curious form of transvestism in which feminine beauty in a woman was identical to the beauty of a beautiful boy, and masculine beauty in a man was identical to the beauty of an ephebe (or a pre-pubescent female). A woman who described male beauty in this tradition was in fact describing ideal beauty in both sexes. A more difficult obstacle to the heterosexual desire expressed by a woman poet who followed the convention that the only available model for male beauty was that of a beautiful boy, is that her own *persona* would resemble the Venus of Shakespeare's *Venus and Adonis,* a sexually voracious Goddess of Love who "murders" the tender boy "with a kiss."[21]

As the tradition evolves, the beautiful boy eventually becomes an erotic figure for both men and women—a convention that continues into contemporary representations of women who dare to express sexual desire. In sixteenth-century theater and poetry, the beautiful boy becomes an explicit object of women's desire, in and for himself, not by way of veiled references to Narcissus such as in the descriptions of Énide and Fénice (see chapter 1). Shakespeare's Adonis, for instance, can be read as a representation of the beautiful boy who is the common object of desire of both men and those exceptional women who assert their desire. Like Narcissus, Adonis was loved by one goddess and by many gods. Shakespeare's plays exploit the convention of boy actors playing women's roles to similar ends, attested to by Olivia's desire for Cesario and Phoebe's for Ganymede. Richard Barbour makes a relevant point (1995) with reference to a later work written during the general period under consideration here—Ben Jonson's *Epicoene; or the Silent Woman* (1609)—when he suggests that one of the charms of boy actors is that the figure of the pretty youth allows for the convergence of "homo-and heteroerotic desire." Barbour identifies women's heterosexual desire with male homosexual desire, but specifically pederastic desire. This identification is in keeping with a tendency in contemporary theory since Barthes to reserve the feminine writing position for anyone but a woman.[22] Barbour's argument, that "women could enjoy the boys, and the female roles the boys played, without disturbing men's territorial enjoyment," is well constructed and points to the multiple possibilities of what he calls "one's sexual repertory" (1007). But I would take issue with his conclusion that "this attraction to boys argues for erotic mutuality in the playhouse for men and women" (1017). Barbour's notion of "mutuality" poses a problem similar to that posed by Nelli's conclusion that the exchange of hearts creates "intersexual mutuality." The "sexual repertory" of Barbour's vision of a more open eroticism boils down to a sexual repertory open only to men, appealing to a fantasy of female impersonation. Indeed, Barbour exposes the spurious nature of the mutuality he sees in Jonsonian theater when he writes,

> If in men's eyes boys are women with agreeable pluck, then for women boys are a more companionable and pliable version of men. As a sexual partner, the youth may allow a woman to initiate, to assume strength without fear of retaliation. On stage, the youth in skirts represented for women a publicly active version of their proscribed selves. That the object of female desire

beneath the gown was in fact a boy deflected the threat to insecure men of tribadism and of serious procreative rivalry; women could openly enjoy the woman the boy performed. (1018)

In similar fashion to the woman writer confronted with the structural problem described above, that of being both the subject who writes and the written body, the women in Jonson's audience identify—in Barbour's view—with the female impersonator, the object of desire constructed as a conventional representation of male self-difference.

Although Neoplatonism was pervasive in Western literature in Italy, France, and England during the period of Louise Labé's production, her writing, while demonstrating control of Neoplatonic conventions, calls into question its assumption that the poet is a man. In Sonnet XXIII, Labé resorts—in a subversive way—to describing her own beauty as the object of desire of her own poem. Writing about the impossibility of identifying the writing subject in some of Labé's most provocative verses, Rigolot says that poetic language is by its nature ambiguous:

> La confusion n'est pas attribuable à quelque échec esthéthique mais au désir de traduire, dès le seuil des sonnets français, le chaos intérieur de la *persona* lyrique. L'Amour et la Folie affirment leur co-présence antagoniste en cette évocation double de l'objet et sujet du désir. (*OC* 23)

> *(The confusion cannot be attributed to a failure of aesthetics but to the desire to trans-late, from the inception of the French sonnet form, the interior chaos of the lyric per-sona. Love and Madness affirm their antagonistic co-presence in this double evocation of the object and subject of desire.)*

Rigolot's description of the co-existence of the subject and object of desire in the sonnets as "antagonistic," adds an important dimension to the discussion of the split subject in lyric poetry by helping to explain why heterosexual lovers in the literary tradition that begins with troubadour lyric poetry are doomed to be enemies. Furthermore, it sheds light on the writing problem of *vagabondage*. A woman writer confronted with this problem is divided into two, she is both the subject who writes and the written body; she is the representor who identifies with the represented, the writer and the written, the self and the conventional representation of a writer's self-difference. Reproaching her lover for his conventional praise, Labé nonetheless repeats it when she writes:

Las! que me sert, que si parfaitement
Louas jadis et ma tresse doree

Et de mes yeus la beauté comparee
A deus Soleils, dont Amour finement

Tira les trets causez de son tourment?
Ou estes vous, pleurs de peu de duree?
Et Mort par qui devoit estre honoree
Ta ferme amour et iteré serment? *(OC, Sonnet XXIII: 134)*

(Alas! of what use are my golden tresses and my eyes whose beauty has been compared to two Suns, so perfectly praised by my lover who draws them as the traits which caused his torment? Where are you, tears of such short duration, and Death on which you swore your undying love and spoken oath?)

In the rhetoric of courtly love, feminine beauty is not an object of desire, but an object—an artifact—of writing, and as such is of use to neither a woman poet, nor to an actual woman who might possess conventional beauty (as did Labé herself).

Shakespeare reflects wittily on the nature of this paradox in Sonnet XX, addressed to a man, not to a woman. The women described in the sonnet are not the heroines of literature; it is the fair young man for whom the poem is written, the Master-Mistress of Shakespeare's passion, whom the poet casts in the role of the feminine heroine. Shakespeare brings the paradox of sexual difference in romantic love to light by means of a sexual pun:

A woman's face, with nature's own hand painted,
Hast thou, the master-mistress of my passion;
A woman's gentle heart, but not acquainted
With shifting change, as is false woman's fashion:
An eye more bright than theirs, less false in rolling,
Gilding the object whereupon it gazeth;
A man in hue, all hues in his controlling,
Which steals men's eyes, and women's souls amazeth
And for a woman wert thou first created;
Till Nature, as she wrought thee, fell a-doting,
And by adding one thing to my purpose nothing.
But since she prick'd thee out for women's pleasure,
Mine be thy love, and thy love's use their treasure.

The poem is rife with double entendres, including the one "thing which is nothing." In the sonnet, the fact that both poet and beloved feminine hero have, through the power of representation, become women is explicit: The phallic "thing" has been replaced by "nothing," a word used here to represent both the absence and the presence of sexual difference. The absence of the phallus is represented as a symbolic presence of female sexuality, the "nothing," is a powerful evocation of the control that representation exercises in the determination of sexual difference. The language play that interests me more, however, because of its critical relevance to the dilemma created for a woman writer such as George Sand by female impersonation, is the play on the term "false woman." At first reading, we see its meaning as a woman who is unfaithful. But, in the context of the poem, the young man to whom the poem is addressed represents both masculinity and femininity: he is the "master-mistress," the words have been rhythmically and phonetically joined to form an entity. There is no doubt that "false" is meant to signify bogus as well as inconstant. The false women of the poem are impersonators, the master-mistress, the real woman. False women are incapable of love, according to the poet; they are satisfied with the pleasure provided by the "no-thing" which Nature added to the young man to prick them out for false woman's pleasure. The poet alone is capable of love, a sexually ambiguous definition of love, heavily coded in terms of sexual difference, and in which sexual difference is to no purpose.

The Neoplatonic ideal of beauty and the resulting confusion between homoeroticism and heteroeroticism continued to dominate romance narratives and was the central theme of the most important fictional work in early seventeenth-century France, Honoré d'Urfé's long pastoral novel, *L'Astrée* (1619). *L'Astrée* has two claims to fame in literary history: It was the most widely read novel in pre-classical France despite its length (3 parts of several hundred pages each) and, according to the *Confessions,* it was Rousseau's *livre de chevet* (bedside book). *L'Astrée* recounts the story of an *asag* that involves the hero passing as a woman—his lady's best friend—for nearly the entire novel. The femininity of the courtly lover was so explicit by the 1600s that today's reader has a hard time believing its enormous appeal to seventeenth-century readers who responded to the pastoral romance, a popular genre at the time, as a story of heterosexual desire.

In the story, Astrée, the heroine, forbids her lover, Céladon, to appear before her until she has given permission. Céladon tries to commit suicide by throwing himself into a river. He is rescued by a nymph and comforted by an old druid who proposes that he return to society disguised as a woman—the druid's own daughter, Alexis, who is cloistered in a druid convent and not likely to reappear in public to expose Céladon's masquerade. Once his womanly appearance has been perfected, Céladon is able to deceive even his own brother. Alexis/Céladon returns to Forez, and is soon known as the most beautiful woman in the land. When Alexis and Astrée meet, they praise each other's perfect beauty and, within a short time, Astrée has fallen deeply in love with Alexis, declaring that she will follow

Alexis wherever she goes. When the relationship between Alexis and Astrée becomes more physical, they exchange such long passionate kisses that some of their companions wonder aloud whether the two young women may indeed be lesbian lovers. D'Urfé's Alexis is not an actual woman, but rather a man different from other men—passive and obedient to a woman's power—the courtly lover. Ideal love exists between Alexis and Astrée, but if Céladon continues in his disguise, they cannot reach a state of intersexual mutuality, the goal of *Fin'Amors*.

An arbitrary dénouement occurs when the nymph who had rescued Céladon from the river at the beginning of the story insists that Céladon and Astrée incarnate Beauty and form the perfect androgynous couple who have been fused by love into one being. They wear different clothes, of course, and that is the only way to identify Céladon as a man and Astrée as a woman. This union of souls does not characterize the heterosexual couple's social reality, however, because when Céladon finally wins Astrée by imposing his kiss upon her—although they both accept what love has ordered—he reacts with pleasure as a man should, and she reacts with modest shame, as a woman feels she must. Astrée's pleasure is short lived in this love story that makes explicit the implications of male femininity in *Fin'Amors*. The point of d'Urfé's novel is that a man disguised as a woman will always be more beautiful than any woman ever could be. The enjoyment of the double pleasure of femininity and heterosexual love belongs to Céladon/Alexis alone. Astrée finds pleasure in loving another woman, who is actually a man. She loses her object of desire as soon as Céladon reclaims his socially superior masculine identity.

In a letter to her friend Clémence de Bourges (1555), Labé counsels women to seek not those pleasures that accrue to women as objects of desire, but the far more satisfying pleasures associated with the activity of writing:

> Et si quelcune parvient en tel degré, que de pouvoir mettre ses concepcions par escrit, le faire soigneusement et non dédaigner la gloire, et s'en parer plustot que de chaines, anneaus, et somptueus habits: lesquels ne pouvons vrayement etimer notres, que par usage. (OC 41)

> (And if some women do reach the point of being able to put their thoughts into writing, let them do this carefully, not disdaining glory, and thereby adorn themselves with their writings rather than with gold chains, rings, and sumptuous clothing: which we can truly call our own only by custom.)

In the same letter, Labé prefigures what Barthes has called *un incessant apprentissage* (an unceasing apprenticeship [of a writer]) in Proust's *Recherche*

(*Le degré zéro de l'écriture* 135), comparing the pleasures of writing, or representation, to the pleasure of (so-called) lived experience:

> Quand il avient que mettons par escrit nos concepcions, combien que puis apres notre cerveau coure par une infinité d'afaires et incessamment remue, si est ce que long temps apres, reprenans nos escrits, nous revenons au mesme point, et à la mesme disposicion ou nous estions. Lors nous redouble notre aise: car nous retrouvons le plaisir passé qu'avons ù ou en la matiere dont escrivions, ou en l'intelligence des sciences ou lors estions adonnez. Et outre ce, le jugement que font nos fecondes concepcions des premieres, nous rend un singulier contentement. (OC 42–43)

> *(When we put down our thoughts in writing, no matter how much our minds race about in numberless occupations and incessant turmoil, nevertheless we come back to the same point even after picking up our writings after a long period, and in the same frame of mind in which we originally were. Then our pleasure doubles, for we find again the past pleasure that we had in the subject matter about which we were writing or in the knowledge of the sciences which we were studying, and then the judgments which we subsequently make upon our first ideas give us a unique contentment.)*

Pleasure, for Labé, resides not in lived experience, but in memory and specifically in the representation of a remembered experience. If women are excluded from mediating erotic experience through representation, they are virtually excluded from erotic pleasure itself. To obey the rule of courtly love and to remain silent for fear of losing one's sexual desirability, then, is to renounce the very pleasure which the silence is supposed to insure.

Such is the case for the heroine of Madame de Lafayette's novel, *La Princesse de Clèves.* The narrative tells a familiar story of a married woman's passion for a romantic hero and her struggle to avoid adultery and maintain her virtue. The psychology of the heroine of Madame de Lafayette's novel, however, is far from conventional. When her husband dies, making it possible for her to finally consummate her passion for a man whom she has desired chastely, without betraying her husband whom she also loves, she goes against all conventional expectations and unconditionally rejects the possibility of their sexual union—forever. For this and other reasons, the novel represents the end of the age of chivalry and heralds the advent of modernity in fictions of heterosexual desire.[23] The eponymous heroine is modern in her complexity; she is a fully-drawn fictional character who represents all of the goals and obstacles that characterize the double desire for subjectivity and for erotic pleasure of the women writers discussed so far in this chapter. Like the poets Marie de France, the *trobairitz,* and Louise

Labé, Madame de Lafayette's princess breaks the silence imposed on women by the courtly code of secrecy when she reveals her desire for the Duc de Nemours to her husband, the Prince de Clèves. The princess's story exposes the hypocrisy of courtly love in a way unlike any narrative before it, including *L'Astrée,* which lacks psychological realism. There is no *deus ex machina* in *La Princesse de Clèves* to restore the illusion of heterosexual romance. Equally as important, *La Princesse de Clèves* also differs from another major vogue in the literature of the period, the novel of gallantry. Written only twenty years after Madeleine de Scudéry published *Clélie* (1759), which included the most celebrated document in *salon* literature, the "Carte de Tendre" (the map of the Land of Tenderness), a "course in gallantry" (de Jean, *NHFL* 301)—*La Princesse de Clèves* endures as a scathing critique of gallantry.[24]

Beginning with the marquise de Rambouillet's *chambre bleue* (blue room) created in 1610, the *salon* emerged as an alternative court where conversation became a "fine art" (de Jean, *NHFL* 301). Until the waning of the influence of the *salons* in the 1660s, women presided over the game of gallantry. The "Carte de Tendre" was the guide to the rules of gallantry in the same way that Andreas Capellanus's *The Art of Courtly Love* provided the precepts of courtly love that dominated in the era of *Fin'Amors.* The period of the social dominance of the *salons* contributes to persistent misconceptions about the nature of women's power in French society. The arbitrary nature of women's power during this period of *salon* activity is seen in the dénouement of *L'Astrée,* which was extremely popular among the *précieuses,* women who presided over the *salons.* Called "precious" because of their brilliant, refined, and affected conversational style, this power did not protect them from being satirized in Molière's *Les précieuses ridicules (The Ridiculous Précieuses).* The deceptive nature of women's apparent power in the age of chivalry is attested to by theatre audiences who still enjoy laughing at the pretentiousness of Molière's *précieuses,* while the women of this early feminist literary movement have long been forgotten. Indeed, Madame de Lafayette is the only woman intellectual of the period whose writing is still read. Interestingly, not only is *La Princesse de Clèves* still read, it is considered to be the best work of fiction written in seventeenth-century Europe, and "a milestone in the history of the novel" (Hollier 354).

One of the most brilliant features of *La Princesse de Clèves* is that its action turns on the impossibility for either characters or reader to distinguish between representation and "the real thing." "Gallantry" is the term used by Madame de Lafayette to describe the code of behavior in love affairs that were spreading during the last years of Henry II's reign and pandemic in the court of Louis XIV. Gallantry in *La Princesse de Clèves* can perhaps best be understood as the "performance" of courtly love, in the same way that *sprezzatura* describes the affectation of chivalric behavior among gentlemen of the aristocracy in Castiglione's *Courtier.* By the sixteenth century, the period in which the novel is set, chivalry had evolved into gallantry. The roles and rituals of *Fin'Amors* had lost all connection to their original ideals—as dubious as they might have been—and were now enacted as in a game of chess. Since chivalry itself was originally an elaborate system of representation, highly coded and ritualistic, we might say that gallantry is a performance of a performance.

Madame de Lafayette's introduction to the novel's setting resembles the panoramic shots found in films such as *Ridicule* (Laconte 1995), one dazzling beauty and handsome courtier after another engaged in animated conversation about romantic intrigues, appropriately called "gallantries." A reputation for gallantry is easy to acquire, one has only to learn how to make artificial, contrived, and self-interested social behavior appear to be natural and sincere. It was easy to recognize Tristan or Érec as heroes. They were unequalled in beauty and knightly courage. But at a court where all of the men have learned to model themselves on Tristan, how does a woman distinguish between a vile seducer and a sincere lover?

Madame de Lafayette's critique of gallantry is complicated by the often sympathetic portrayal of the novel's principal *galant* and romantic hero, the Duc de Nemours. By thematizing the heroine's doubt of her lover's motives, Madame de Lafayette questions the clichéd characterization of the literary figure of the romantic hero as a "lover of women." His motives are suspect, and his love of women is debatable at the very least. Madame de Lafayette can be said to be a visionary in this regard; this type of feminine male hero reappears in the next century as the rake, typified by Laclos' Valmont. The manner in which the femininity of the heterosexual lover is criticized in eighteenth-century literature is evoked by the very name of Richardson's Lovelace, a play on the seducer's major appeal, his love of the feminine. To recast love of the feminine as love of lace places in relief the transvestism of the seducer. Eighteenth-century French society was intolerant of the femininity of characters like Tristan, Érec, Amadour, and Nemours, seeing their affinity with the feminine as a metaphor for the weak moral fiber of the *ancien régime.* After the Revolution decimated the social class to which rakes like Valmont belonged, the feminine hero did not disappear from Western culture, he was reborn as the sensitive artist of the Romantic era (see chapter 3).

Nemours' literary lineage as a descendant of Tristan is established at his first mention in the novel. His extraordinary beauty distinguishes him from his fellow *galants* and makes him, like Narcissus, attractive to both men and to women, "Un chef d'oeuvre de la nature . . . il avait un enjouement qui plaisait également aux hommes et aux femmes. . . ." (Nature's master-piece . . . he had a lively quality that pleased men and women alike) (71–72). Like Tristan, he was the strongest and the most handsome ("le mieux fait et le plus beau") (72). It is natural that he be the object of the gaze, "on ne pouvait regarder que lui dans tous les lieux où il paraissait" (it was impossible to look at anyone else when he was present) (72). His beauty is rivaled only by that of the heroine, whose name is Mademoiselle de Chartres, when she first appears at court as a very young and unmarried woman. Neither the Duc de Nemours or Mademoiselle de Chartres are described as individuals; each represents a certain type of beauty. The hero and heroine do not fall in love until after she is married to the Prince de Clèves, a man who, like the prototype King Mark in the Tristan myth, is worthy of her love and esteem.

The first meeting between the Duc de Nemours and the Princesse de Clèves is a romantic cliché complete with a *philtre* effect, creating the illu-sion of the fusion of two into one. Since *The Romance of Tristan and Iseut,* the *philtre* has been the single most important sign of the role played by representation in the operation of romantic love. The *philtre* represents representation, as it were. It is through the mediation of a *philtre* that lovers fall in love—the *philtre* transforms self into other, other into self: in one magical moment individual personal and sexual identities are con-fused.[25] The *philtre* would seem to eradicate sexual difference; if this were so, its power would indeed be magical. In the most explicit cases of the operation of the *philtre* in literature, however, the sexual identification of the lovers has already been suggested; the *philtre* is a literary device used to make explicit a sexual identification that has already been established by descriptions of the lovers' equal beauty and equal desirability.[26] If one were to eliminate the *philtre,* to remove the illusion of the fusion of the lovers' sexual difference into one erotic being, we would find that we had already been prepared to accept the illusion. The purpose of this literary device is not only to deceive the lovers and to relieve them of the moral responsibility for their act, but to convince the reader that the identifica-tion of the heterosexual lovers is a miracle of fusion. The *philtre,* I would argue, is a *trompe l'oeil* that creates and collapses sexual difference between two characters who have both been previously described as feminine, both in appearance and in cultural position and behavior. In much the same way that it mediates the lovers' desire for each other, it symbolizes as well the way in which the reader's desire to experience the lovers' joy is mediated by certain standard narrative structures, among them the *philtre* itself.

In *La Princesse de Clèves,* the spell is cast when the Duc de Nemours and the princess dance together under the gaze of the entire court, including the King. The dancing couple is a figure of androgynous fusion, their individual bodies transformed by the imagination into one figure of artistic movement. The mediation of the lovers' desire for one another and of the crowd's desire for romantic love is echoed in the reaction of the Chevalier de Guise, who witnessed the scene as if it were the operation of the *philtre,* always related to sight in romantic narratives:

> ce qui venait de passait lui avait donné une douleur sensible. Il le prit comme un présage que la fortune destinait M. de Nemours à être amoureux de Mme de Clèves; et, soit qu'en effet il eût paru quelque trouble sur son visage ou que la jalousie fît voir au chevalier de Guise au-delà de la vérité, il crut qu'elle avait été touchée de la vue de ce prince. . . . (48)

> *(what had just taken place caused him to feel pain. He took it as an omen that fate meant M. de Nemours to fall in love with Mme de Clèves. Whether her face had really betrayed some inner turmoil or whether jealousy had caused the Chevalier de Guise to see more than was there, he believed she had been affected by the sight of the prince. . . .)*

In this novel, which is a classic example of various forms of what Girard calls "mediated desire" (*Deceit, Desire and the Novel*), it is not only social pressure that determines what the lovers see in each other. The princess's mother, Madame de Chartres, had already mediated her daughter's desire to fall in love by representing its fatal attraction. When Madame de Chartres tells her daughter of the dangers of romantic love, "minimizing none of its charm," she prepares a love potion as potent as the one prepared by Iseut's mother.

The only *philtre* more powerful than the mother's pedagogy is writing. The heroine's claim that "there could be no other story like mine," is at once a statement about her character's difference from other women at the court of Henry II where the novel is set, and the metaphoric designation of herself as a writer. As Joan de Jean has argued so convincingly, there is textual evidence to warrant describing the heroine as a writer, namely, references to her "story," the circulation of letters central to the plot, and an explicit scene of writing, which makes the connection between writing and eroticism ("Lafayette's Ellipses" [1984]). The novel's dénouement, the princess's withdrawal from the world of courtly love and her renunciation of sexual pleasure, is inevitable. When Madame de Lafayette places her heroine in the position in which she is forced to choose between heterosexual love and her desire for "a higher and more detached vision," she shows that she is caught in *vagabondage* (241). A woman in love—in *Fin'Amors*—is not free to possess the world with her own eyes, since her eyes are the mirror of male self-difference. She is, therefore, forced to choose between sexual pleasure and the pleasure of subjectivity. The hypocrisy inherent in the philosophy of *Fin'Amors* is that the woman is not desirable unless she is distinguished from all other women by her "manly virtue." Any mark of distinction and autonomy is relinquished, however, to form the heterosexual couple of *Fin'Amors.*

Madame de Lafayette does not give up easily on the possibility that her heroine might have it both ways, that she might enjoy both subjectivity and an erotic relationship with Nemours. But this cannot be. As Colette puts it three centuries later, the woman writer is, in effect, a vagabond. Still tied to her traditional feminine role as object of desire, the woman writer is in bondage to the choice of possessing the world with her own eyes and seeing the world through the eyes of a woman who is the object of male desire. The Princesse de Clèves is the heroine of two stories, and is ultimately forced to choose between the two roles. The princess's split subjectivity is apparent in the description of her life after she breaks with Nemours: she spends her few remaining years between the convent (also the only choice for Marguerite de Navarre's Floride) and home which, in the novel, is a place associated with the free reign of her erotic imagination. Each of the novel's two explicitly erotic scenes takes place in the setting of one of the princess's residences; one of the scenes involves writing, the other fetishism.

The writing scene takes place at a moment in the narrative when the heroine has become acutely aware that her feelings for Nemours resemble the dangerous sensations that her mother had warned her against. Mistaken in her belief that a letter, which has been lost by his friend the Vidame de Chartres, is addressed to Nemours, the princess is sick with jealousy and with the recognition that this could be her story. The letter has been written to the Vidame by a woman in a state of despair over his unfaithfulness. The words the Princesse de Clèves reads in the letter, "Jamais douleur n'a été pareille à la mienne" (nobody has ever suffered as I do) and "cette résolution que j'ai prise de ne vous voir jamais" (this resolution never to see you again) (145) foreshadow the evolution of her own story including the very words she will use to describe her own situation later in the novel, "il n'y a pas dans le monde une autre aventure pareille à la mienne" (there could be no other story like mine") (187) as well as the words used to describe her renunciation of the duke, "la résolution . . . de ne voir jamais Monsieur de Nemours" (the resolution never to see Nemours again) (235).

The letter functions as a catalyst to bring the lovers together. This powerful *philtre* works its magic. For many reasons having to do with court intrigue, a copy of the letter requested by the queen, which, after a series of peripeties has been returned to its author, must be made to satisfy her curiosity. This turn of events serves to bring Nemours and the princess together to copy the letter. The Prince de Clèves sends for Nemours to help his wife recreate the letter, which she knows by heart, because she thought it was addressed to Nemours—a reason her husband cannot guess. The eroticism of the writing in this scene is created by its triangular structure, reminiscent—mimetic in fact—of the classic courtly triangle of lord, lady, and knight. The classical triangle has been redescribed in contemporary criticism as two men whose rivalry is represented by their mutual desire for a woman in which homosexual identification is the key (Sedgwick, *Between Men* 47). I have described the prototype in *The Romance of Tristan and Iseut* as a woman and a man who form a single figure of romantic love under the masculine gaze of the husband, who represents traditional masculinity. In this novel, the actors in the triangle shut themselves up to copy the lost letter. The eroticism of the scene is depicted in the following words:

> Cet air de mystère et de confidence n'était pas d'un médiocre charme pour ce prince et même pour Mme de Clèves. La présence de son mari . . . la rassurait en quelque sorte sur ses scrupules. Elle ne sentait que le plaisir de voir M. de Nemours, elle en avait une joie pure et sans mélange qu'elle n'avait jamais sentie: cette joie lui donnait une liberté et un enjouement dans l'esprit. . . . (144)

> *(This atmosphere of mystery and secrecy had no ordinary charm for Nemours and even for Madame de Clèves. The presence of her husband . . . calmed her scruples. She felt only the pleasure of seeing M. de Nemours, a pure, unmitigated joy that she had never felt before: this joy brought a feeling of freedom and gaiety to her spirit. . . .)*

Madame de Lafayette disrupts the conventional structure of triangular desire in this scene. The princess is transformed from a passive object of desire of both husband and lover, and from a mere copyist into a writer (once rewritten by the princess, the letter no longer resembles the original) who is empowered by the novelist to take pleasure in the process—which Madame de Lafayette names joy—resonating *joi,* the double pleasure of writing and desire.

Only the pavilion scene in the novel is more erotic. Here, as in the writing scene, desire is mediated through representation. The Princesse de Clèves is so tormented by the conflict between her love for her husband and her desire for Nemours that she has withdrawn from the court to spend time at their country home. Nemours follows her there, and hidden from her sight he spies on her through the wide open windows of a little summer house. Madame de Lafayette describes the scene in these words, "elle était seule; mais il la vit d'une si admirable beauté qu'à peine fut-il maître du transport que lui donna cette vue" (she was alone, but he saw in her such a marvelous beauty that he was barely able to control the transports he felt at the sight) (201). The erotic allure of the scene is intended to seduce the reader along with Nemours, "Il faisait chaud, et elle n'avait rien, sur sa tête et sa gorge, que ses cheveux confusément rattachés" (It was hot, and she wore nothing on her head and breast but her loosely gathered hair) (201). Once again, the conventional structure of a man as desiring subject and a woman as object of his desire is disrupted. Nemours' voyeuristic pleasure is doubled in this scene by the fetishism of the Princesse de Clèves. Alone and in a state of *déshabillé,* she is not, however, passive but involved in her own erotic fantasy:

> Elle était sur un lit de repos, avec une table devant elle, où il y avait plusieurs corbeilles pleines de rubans; elle en choisit quelques-uns, et M. de Nemours remarqua que c'étaient des mêmes couleurs qu'il avait portées au tournoi. Il vit qu'elle en faisait des noeuds à une canne des Indes, fort extraordinaire, qu'il avait portée quelque temps et qu'il avait donnée à sa soeur. (202)

> *(She was lying on a day bed, with a table before her, on which were placed several baskets filled with ribbons; she had chosen several of them and M. de Nemours noticed that they were the same colors he had worn in the tournament. He saw that she was tying bows onto an extraordinary cane from India, which he used to use and that he had given to his sister.)*

In addition to playing with fetishes the princess gazes at an image of the duke while he looks at her.[27]

> Elle prit un flambeau et s'en alla, proche d'une grande table, vis-à-vis du tableau du siège de Metz, où était le portrait de M. de Nemours; elle s'assit et se mit à regarder ce portrait avec une attention et une rêverie que la passion seule peut donner. (202)

> *(She took a torch and went over to a large table in front of the painting of the siege of Metz that contained the likeness of M. de Nemours. She sat down and began to gaze at it with a fascination and reverie that could only have been inspired by true passion.)*

There is a certain *quid pro quo* going on here. Early in the novel, the Duc de Nemours steals a portrait of the Princesse de Clèves that had been commissioned by her husband. In a moment of complicity, the princess sees him stealing it and says nothing; he sees that she sees him stealing it. This play on the gender of the object of the gaze is repeated in the pavilion scene: he watches her watching him. Even when a woman assumes the position of what John Berger calls "the surveyor" (*Ways of Seeing* [1972] 46), she is never entirely delivered from the position of the surveyed. It could be argued that this is why magazines with photos of nude men are successful with homosexual men, but not with women. Women prefer to look at pictures of nude women, to see themselves as objects. A painting called "The Reclining Baccante" by Trutat (1824–1848) prefaces Berger's chapter on this subject. In the painting, a nude woman reclines on a day bed while a man looks at her through an open window. Berger writes:

> Men look at women. Women watch themselves being looked at. This determines not only most relations between men and women but also the relation of women to themselves. The surveyor of woman in herself is male: the surveyed female. Thus she turns herself into an object—and most particularly into an object of vision: a sight. (47)

The woman's body is the object of a desire that is shared by both lovers; her body is viewed as the site of erotic pleasure. The woman writing heterosexual desire becomes a split subject in the same way that the troubadour split himself into the male writer, the desiring subject, and the feminine other. What Nemours sees as he watches the princess is not only her own, but his own feminized and fetishized image in the gaze she directs at his portrait:

> On ne peut exprimer ce que sentit M. de Nemours dans ce moment. Voir . . . une personne qu'il adorait . . . tout occupée de choses qui avaient du rapport à lui et à la passion qu'elle lui cachait. . . . (201)
>
> *(It would be impossible to express what M. de Nemours felt at this moment. To see a woman he adored . . . entirely absorbed in things connected with him and with the passion she was hiding from him. . . .)*

The requirement of self-difference, or split subjectivity for writing, is staged in this scene.

Equally in evidence is the problem this represents for the woman writer. The difference is that she identifies with the women in the tradition while the very act of writing moves her into the subject position traditionally associated with the masculine. There is an inevitable double bind for the woman writing in a tradition where the surveyor, or the writer, occupies the masculine position. In order for the woman to represent the sexual difference, or the feminine difference that allows for the illusion of heterosexuality in romantic love, she has to make a double structural move. She first moves into the masculine position of the writer, or the lover: hence, the princess is depicted as a desiring subject, fetishizing Nemours, and gazing at his portrait. The site of eroticism in this novel, however, as in every novel in the tradition, is the woman's body. There is no possibility of a "sexual relation" if the scene continues with the woman in the position of desiring subject who gazes at an object of desire; hence, Nemours' menacing presence in the pavilion scene.

Taken as a story of writing, *La Princesse de Clèves* is as ironic as *Madame Bovary*. In both novels, the heroine falls prey to the representation of her role in heterosexual romance. In the case of the princess, her creator gives her an awareness of the seduction of representation and mimesis and prepares the reader for her canny choice of refusing to play the role written for her in the narrative tradition, in spite of her strong desire to do so, a desire mediated by the very representations that she refuses. Emma Bovary's tragedy, on the other hand, is her lack of awareness of the dangers of representation and her desire to identify with the adulterous heroines in romantic love narratives.[28] The difference between Emma Bovary and the Princesse de Clèves is the latter's awareness that it is impossible to believe a lover who plays his role so expertly. Each internal narrative replicates the princess's story in spite of her insistence that it is original: "il n'y a pas dans le monde une autre aventure pareille à la mienne" (there could be no other story like mine in the world) (175). Each tale of gallantry becomes a mirror that reflects the story we are reading, and which the Princesse de Clèves is reading right along with us via the circulation of letters and court gossip. The heroine's ultimate insight, which leads her to refuse Nemours, is prefigured when she sees him steal her portrait. She knows that he in turn has seen her seeing him steal her image, "Mme de Clèves aperçut par un des rideaux, qui n'était qu'à demi fermé, M. de Nemours. . . ."(Through one of the curtains, which was only half drawn, Mme de Clèves caught sight of M. de Nemours) (106). In this play, their gaze is never mutual, neither in the stolen portrait scene nor in the pavilion scene; androgynous fusion is an illusion created by the *philtre*. At the novel's conclusion, the curtain is drawn open, and the princess decides to withdraw from the prisonhouse of representation to become one of those individuals who have "des vues plus grandes et plus éloignées" (who have a higher and more detached vision) (241).

The Princesse de Clèves is not at the convent full time. She also goes back home, where the most erotic scenes in the novel have taken place. Home, for the Princesse de Clèves, generates the language of desire.[29] The femininity of the language of desire is underscored by Madame de Lafayette insomuch as the letter copied was written by a woman, and Nemours' reaction to the sight of the princess gazing at his image and playing with fetishes leaves no doubt that his role here is feminine. His subjectivity is split. As he gazes at her, he is forced to see himself as the object of her desire, as the object of representation. Naomi Schor has characterized Nemours' position in the pavilion scene as the "spectator of his own desirability" ("Portrait of a Gentleman" [1987] 118). Nemours' position in the scene links his character to Narcissus, affirming his place in a lineage that dates back to Fin'Amors and courtly romance. Nemours is both subject and object of his own gaze, whereas the princess is only the subject of hers. This scene is an exemplar par excellence of the split subjectivity of the feminized male (romantic) hero—or of male self-difference.

It is not without significance that Nemours' desire is associated throughout the novel with purloined images, and that the Princesse de Clèves is in the position of having to steal them back. Exhausted with the struggle for identity, she composes an unexpected ending to the love story, she has the last word—followed by silence. The seventeenth-century precursor of Colette's vagabond refuses the role of heroine in a tale of gallantry. The price of dissent is celibacy and silence; those representations of desire available to her in the course of the narrative, masochistic love letters and fetishes, are relinquished when she renounces romance, choosing to live in a state of *vagabondage*.

CHAPTER 3

She and He:
The Myth of Androgynous Fusion Defused

Il n'y a plus qu'un sex, et nous sommes tous femmes par
l'esprit.

(There is only one sex remaining, and we are all women in spirit.)

—*Montesquieu, "Mes Pensées"*[1]

The Princesse de Clèves became, paradoxically, the prototype of the
heroine of the novels of seduction that dominated European fiction during the eighteenth century, but with a difference. The virtuous heroines of novels by Samuel Richardson (1689–1761) and
Choderlos de Laclos (1741–1803), for example, were not endowed by their
creators with the power to choose how their stories would end—or, more
accurately, how they would not end. The princess's distrust of Nemours'
motives marks the beginning of a major change in the representation of the
romantic couple. Nemours is a transitional figure in the genealogy of Tristan's literary descendants. After using all of the arguments available to him
from the language of courtly love, he conforms to the convention of the
lady's power and accepts the princess's decision not to see him again; the
next generation of libertines have lost all respect for the rules of courtly
love in spite of their cunning and self-interested use of its language. The
Princesse de Clèves's literary descendants, the virtuous heroines of the
novels of the next generation, do not get away with such resistance. The
princess's decision to renounce her passion for Nemours is informed by
the knowledge that the power of the lady in courtly love is nothing but a
convention, and a dying one at that. Because she possesses this knowledge,
the Princesse de Clèves is able to view Nemours' performance of the role
of romantic lover with skepticism, freeing her from unconditional identification with the role of (his) romantic heroine. The Princesse de Clèves's
decisions, her honesty with her husband, and the choice to honor his mem-

ory rather than yield to her passion for Nemours were viewed by many contemporary readers as examples of self-love, attesting to the change in what was considered to be correct courtly behavior.

A man's valor did not fare much better than a woman's virtue in the twilight of the age of chivalry. There are several prototypes of the eighteenth-century European literary type known in English as the libertine or rake and in French as the "libertin," or "le séducteur" (the seducer). The trajectory of the character of Don Juan is a useful example to show the link between the medieval type, the *galant,* and the libertine. The historical Don Juan Tenorio was a fourteenth-century Spanish aristocrat whose reputation for erotic conquests was fictionalized first by Tirso de Molina's *El burlador de Sevilla* (1634), and later in France by Molière's *Dom Juan* (1665). The fact that for contemporary cultural historians Don Juanism has come to mean not only womanizing but male femininity is due in large part to the appropriation of the character by Byron in his poem, *Don Juan* (1819–24). Byron's Don Juan is a "most beauteous boy," "slight and slim," "blushing, and beardless." He is sold as a slave in Constantinople, forced into female clothing by a eunuch, and smuggled into the Sultana Gulbeyaz's harem for her pleasure. Language plays a significant role in calling into question Don Juan's heterosexuality: in the harem, he is referred to only as "she" and "her."

Lovelace, the heroine's nemesis in Samuel Richardson's *Clarissa* (1747–48), is another name associated with the prototype of the seducer. The genre of the epistolary novel allows for the possibility of a multiple, variously gendered, first-person narrative voice. When Lovelace writes to his friend Jack, "And now Belford, I can go no further. The affair is over. Clarissa lives," the reader senses that his words should be taken both literally and metaphorically: Clarissa has physically survived being drugged and raped, and the narrative feminine poetic persona has survived a battle with vile masculinity (V: 314). Lovelace explains to Jack why female psychology holds no secrets for him; he understands women so perfectly because he shares so many of the emotions and feelings of their sex. Comparing himself to Tiresias, he writes:

> One argument let me plead in proof of my assertion; that even we rakes love modesty in a woman, as they are accounted (that is to say, the slyest) love, and generally prefer, an impudent man. Whence can this be, but from a *likeness in nature?* (IV: 114–115)[2]

Clarissa remains faithful to her strong moral code and religious beliefs. Like the Princesse de Clèves, Clarissa wants nothing to do with romantic love, as she makes clear in a letter to her friend and confidante, Anne Howe,

"But as to the word LOVE—justifiable as it is in some cases . . . it has methinks, no pretty sound with it" (I: 197). The fate of the middle class English virgin differs, however, from that of her aristocratic French precursor. Lovelace holds the real power and imposes his will on Clarissa. Richardson does not grant his heroine control of her story.

The Présidente de Tourvel, the heroine of Chaderlos de Laclos' *Les liaisons dangereuses* (1782) is doomed as well. Like Clarissa, she is destroyed by a man who, in the tradition of Marguerite de Navarre's Amadour and Richardson's Lovelace, establishes her as "a worthy enemy" (Letter IV), and adopts the feminized persona of a courtly lover to win her confidence:

Cependant, qui fut jamais plus respectueux et plus soumis que moi? . . . c'est l'accusé devant son juge, l'esclave devant son maître . . . ordonnez et j'obéis encore. (Lettre XCI)

(And yet who was ever more respectful and more submissive than I? . . . I am the prisoner before his judge, the slave before his master . . . command and I will still obey.)

In a campaign resembling a Hegelian battle for mastery, Valmont schemes to drive Tourvel to surrender herself to him in the same way in which she has until now surrendered herself to God. She will become his "slave" (Letter LXX). Unable to deny her attraction to Valmont or to confide her feelings to anyone but him (he has insinuated himself into the role of confidant, a role usually played by a woman, the *confidante,* in novels of the period), she ends up in a face-to-face struggle that she is destined to lose (her defeat and destruction are analyzed in Letter XCVI). Armed only with religious faith and virtue, she does not possess the resolve of the Princesse de Clèves.

By an interesting coincidence, the role of Valmont in Stephen Frears' 1988 film based on Laclos' novel is played by John Malkovich, who is both a character and an actor in Spike Jonze's 1999 film, *Being John Malkovich.* In Jonze's highly imaginative and hilarious film, a puppeteer, Craig (John Cusack), finds a secret passage in the office where he works, which leads into the head of John Malkovich (who plays himself). Anyone entering the slippery tunnel leading to Malkovich's head is able not only to feel what the curiously seductive actor is feeling, but to control what he feels as well. When Craig's plain wife, Lottie (Cameron Diaz), enters Malkovich's head while he makes love to Maxine (Catherine Keener)—a sexy woman desired by both Craig and Malkovich—the women fall in love with one another. Part of the joke of this iconoclastic comedy is the implication that Malkovich is a better lover when a woman has taken over his brain. The great romance of the film is lesbian; it looks heterosexual, however, because at the moment of *jouissance*—which leads to a pregnancy—one of the women is inhabiting a man's body. The film's appeal turns on how its subject (John Malkovich) sends up the ambiguous erotic persona he projects as an actor, the very quality that he brings to his portrayal of Valmont.

In Laclos' *Les liaisons dangereuses,* the Vicomte de Valmont's sexual type is placed in relief when he plays the role of surrogate and seduces a beautiful young virgin, Cécile Volanges, for Madame de Merteuil. Prior to the seduction, Merteuil mediates Valmont's desire for Cécile's body by describing how delicious the young virgin is and lamenting the fact that she cannot have the pleasure of deflowering her herself. In a sinister rendition of *Fin'Amors* rituals of the *asag* and the exchange of hearts, the relationship between Valmont and Merteuil is based on the false premise of intersexual equality. Former lovers, Merteuil and Valmont's relationship now resembles that of two *compagnons* in pursuit of erotic conquests, intent on seducing and corrupting innocent and virtuous victims of both sexes. The same factors that destabilize the mutuality of *Fin'Amors* are at work in Laclos' sinister version. Confronted with the dilemma of finding a prize to offer Valmont for Tourvel's seduction, Merteuil offers herself as a trophy, perpetuating the scenario of a chivalric tournament.

The double bind of courtly love persists in the eighteenth-century novel; a woman's body represents both the challenge and the prize, the obstacle and the object desired. The power of a woman like Merteuil, who has consciously and ingeniously fashioned a persona calculated to liberate her from the restraints placed on women's sexuality, is nonetheless arbitrary power. When Merteuil refuses to pay off their bet, Valmont retaliates and in the end she is publicly humiliated and driven from France.

In spite of the fact that Valmont is just as guilty of corrupt morals as Merteuil, he is redeemed by the tradition of the hero when he dies an honorable death in a duel with a true *compagnon*—another man. There is no metanarrative in which Merteuil can be redeemed, no way out of the double bind for a woman in the courtly tradition. She must be punished for her "masculine" promiscuity. Valmont, on the other hand, is redeemed—paradoxically—because of his "feminine" nature; his love of women, especially his relationship with Merteuil, is blamed for his depravity. There can be no doubt that Valmont is Tristan's descendant in the sense that for both hero and villain in the literature of the age of chivalry, close association with a woman is poison, fatal to a man with otherwise heroic qualities.

At this time in literary history, the behavior of aristocratic men who loved women rapidly evolves into a dissolute Don Juanism. By the middle of the next century, in the post-classical, pre-revolutionary age, effeminacy is blamed for the decimation of the social class that had cultivated courtly love. This view is reflected in this chapter's epigraph from Montesquieu in which language reveals the paradox of male femininity. The juxtaposition in French of the masculine pronoun meaning all (*tous*) and the noun meaning women (*femmes*) in the phrase that translates as "we are all women," renders visible in language the principle that playing "femininity" is a male privilege engendered by the processes of language acquisition and identity formation. These synchronous processes depend on the recognition of the difference from the (masculine) self which the existence of the (feminine) other represents (to the self).

Published midway between Richardson's *Clarissa* and Laclos' *Les liaisons dangereuses,* Jean-Jacques Rousseau's epistolary novel, *Julie, ou la nouvelle Héloïse* (*Julie, or the new Heloise*) (1761), created a revolution in the depiction of the romantic lover. Like the others, Rousseau's novel is a story of the conflict between a woman's virtue and her lover's tenacity. Its aim, however, is not to depict the degradation of a society in moral decline, but to offer—as do Rousseau's political works—a program for change.[3] While the name Héloïse recalls the medieval lovers Heloise and Abelard, the modernity of Rousseau's lovers, Julie and Saint-Preux, is evoked by the title's claim of newness. At the height of the popularity of a mode of fiction depicting romance as degenerate and the romantic lover as the emblem of a society in need of revolutionary change, Saint-Preux takes us back to the beginning of a tradition that in spite of having engendered the likes of Valmont, began with valorous knights like Tristan and Érec. The name Saint-Preux summons up the courage of medieval knights, called "preux" in the old French language, fashioning a Romantic, utopic myth of the innocence of the age of chivalry.[4] The symbolic exchange of hearts with its companion myth of the fusion of the lovers' identities remains central to the structure of love in the Romantic era.

Rousseau's ideas for a renewal of faith in the individual's ability to transcend the limits of the self and self-love (*amour propre*) developed into a Romantic theory in Germany, not in France. Like the troubadours of twelfth-century Occitania, the poets of nineteenth-century Europe were extolled as heroes uniquely endowed with the ability to imagine the full potential of individual subjectivity. The creation of the figure of the artist as the new hero of the post-Revolutionary age was spearheaded by Johann Gottlieb Fichte (1762–1814). Fichte's theory of the "I" and the "Not I" (the *Ich* and the *Nicht Ich*) set forth in his *Wissenschaftslehre* (*The Science of Knowledge*) (1794) and in the lectures he gave at the University of Jena in the period of the French Revolution (1794–1799), inspired the German and English poets—Novalis, Coleridge, Wordsworth among others—who

attended his lectures. Fichte's philosophy was that the "I" achieved autonomy by positing the "Not I," recognizing it as such, and assimilating it back
into the Self to which it belongs. He wrote:

> Both self and not-self alike are products of an original act of the self, and
> consciousness itself is merely a product of the self's first original act, its own
> positing of self. The opposed self and not-self are to be unified thereby, to be
> posited together, without mutual elimination. The opposites in question
> must be taken up into the identity of the one consciousness. (I: 459)

The "Not I" is *not* to be mistaken for the "other." The "Not I" is not
"other," it belongs to the self in the same way that the halves of the mythical androgyne belong to each other. The "Not I" is only revealed to the
self, however, in manifestations which exist outside of the self—the creation
of the beloved. Fichte concludes:

> Hence, what is required is the conformity of the object with the self; and it
> is the absolute self which demands this, precisely in the name of its absolute
> being. In relation to a possible object, the pure self-reverting activity of the
> self is a *striving;* and as shown earlier, *an infinite striving* at that. This boundless
> striving, carried to infinity, is the *condition of the possibility of any object whatso-*
> *ever:* no striving, no object. (emphasis added) (I: 459)

For Fichte, in order to achieve wholeness, an individual must find a way
to represent the "Not I" to the self, and subsequently to fuse "I" and "Not
I" in an integrated consciousness. Artistic creation and romantic love are
the primary means to this fusion. For purposes of philosophical speculation, one of the examples Fichte uses to represent the nature of the "Not I"
to an all male student body is that of a woman who both is and is not the
poet himself. The poetic expression of Fichte's philosophy includes works
such as Novalis's (1772–1801) *Heinrich von Ofterdingen* (published posthumously) in which the poet known as "the prophet of Romanticism" identifies his poet hero as falling in love with a woman's face in a blue flower,
which appears to him in a dream. The face, as it turns out, is his own—
unrecognizable to him until he understands his poetic vocation. In *The
Blue Flower,* her 1995 Booker Prize novel based on Novalis's life, Penelope
Fitzerald takes up the theme of the "Not I". The hero Fritz relates Fichte's
theory of triads to masculinity and femininity when he says to one of the
female characters:

> You might look at them (Fichte's triads)as representing the two of us. You are
> the thesis, tranquil, pale, finite, self-contained. I am the antithesis, uneasy,

contradictory, passionate, reaching out beyond myself. Now we must question whether the synthesis will be harmony between us or whether it will lead to a new impossibility which we have never dreamed of. (56)

Later, when Fitzgerald's poet falls in love with Sophie, he finds her to be the perfect likeness of Italian Renaissance painter Raphael. Sophie's resemblance to Raphael makes her the perfect mirror for Fritz's own artistic ambition. He says:

That is my Söphgen to the life. It is Raphael's self-portrait of course. . . . But how can a girl of twelve look like a genius of twenty-five? (87)

Another of Fichte's disciples, Friedrich Wilhelm Joseph von Schelling (1775–1854) is credited with the Romantic idea that consciousness is the only immediate object of knowledge and that only in art does the mind become fully aware of itself. The Romantic artist (in search of self-realization) and the lover (in search of the "Not I" represented as a woman) merge in the marriage of philosophy and literature in the Romantic era. The Romantic theories of the self, which gave rise to Romantic love, shatter any illusions that the myth of fusion—what René Nelli calls *communion animique* referring to *Fin'Amors*—is a philosophy of heterosexual love.

At the height of the Romantic movement, Balzac satirized the femininity of the stereotypical Romantic poet in the character of Lucien de Rubempré in his *Illusions perdues* (*Lost Illusions*) (1843). In a poem that the youthful Lucien writes to his mistress, Louise de Bargeton, Balzac parodies the absence of an actual woman in Romantic poetry. The poem's title is "*A Elle*" (To Her). Balzac exploits the possibilities offered by French grammar in which a pronoun agrees with the noun it replaces. In the poem, "*elle*" appears only in the title, replaced in the body of the poem by the pronoun "*il*," meaning "he" or "him." The gender shift is effected by a writing trick. In the first line of the poem, a masculine noun, "*chérubin*," is used to describe the "Elle" of the poem's title.[5] This allows the poet to call the poem's beautiful object of desire, the *elle* of its title, *il* (for *chérubin*) throughout the poem:

A Elle

Souvent un chérubin à chevelure blonde
Voilant l'éclat de Dieu sur son front arrêté,
Laisse aux parvis des cieux son plumage argenté,
Et descend sur le monde.

Il a compris de Dieu le bienfaisant regard:
Du génie aux abois il endort la souffrance;
Jeune fille adorée, il berce le vieillard
Dans les fleurs de l'enfance (93–94)

(Oft a blonde haired cherubin
Veiling the brilliance of God's light on his distinctive
forehead
Leaves his silvered plumage at the entrance to heaven
And comes down to earth

He has understood God's benevolent wish
That he calm the grief of genius
Adored young girl, he cradles the old man
In the flowers of youth) (My translation)

The blond-haired angel is none other than Lucien himself, often described in the novel in precisely these terms by adoring women and men alike. Like Narcissus, Lucien possesses beauty that inspires genius; its attribution to a young girl in the poem's last stanza is a case of easily detected linguistic transvestism. In the Penguin edition of *Lost Illusions* (1971), the translator (Herbert Hunt) makes an arbitrary choice to translate "*il*" as "she" thereby heterosexualizing a poem, which, read in the context of the novel, is clearly meant as a parody. The translation reads as follows:

Often an Angel, lily-tressed, takes flight
From Heaven's courts all radiant with glory
Where to Jehovah seraph choirs recite
Humanity's sad story.

Leaving the cohort of celestial legions
She lays aside her golden sistrum, yields
Her silver wings, and droops through starry fields
To this world's darker regions.

Divine compassion moves her to assuage
The grief of genius; or, as winsome maid
In childhood's bloom bewitchingly arrayed,
Dispel the gloom of age. (91)

The femininity of the male poet, as well as many of the Romantic ideas and ideals of Fichte's lectures at Jena were inspired by the writings of

Rousseau. The hero of *Julie,* Saint-Preux, is so feminine that he is confused in the novel's structure with his beloved Julie's best friend, Claire, who asks a critical question, "l'âme a-t-elle un sexe?" (Does the soul have a sex?) (*OC,* II: 206). The triangular relationship between Julie, Saint-Preux, and Claire represents a deviation from the usual structure of Rousseau's *ménage à trois* in which the third character is an unambiguously masculine man, the feminine hero's rival for the love of a woman.

In the novel, the feminine homoeroticism of the lovers is highlighted by Rousseau's invention of a supplement to the classic *ménage à trois* of the *Confessions* (1782–89) in which, for example, the intimacy between Rousseau and Sophie d'Houdetot—the woman whom Rousseau says was the greatest love of his life and in whom he saw his Julie, "l'idole de mon coeur" (the idol of my heart)—is described as "une intimité presque sans exemple entre deux amis de différens sexes" (an intimacy almost without example between two friends of different sexes) (*OC,* I: 440–3). In the novel, this structure is doubled in the *ménage* of Saint-Preux, Julie, and Claire. Whereas the central triangle in the novel is a classic *ménage à trois* (Saint-Preux, Wolmar, and Julie), the triangle formed by the lovers and Claire is a more interesting—and revealing—variation. I would go so far as to argue that, in the final scene of the novel, the Jean-Jacques figure of the *Confessions* is transformed through the *philtre* of fiction into a woman— Claire d'Orbe—who is, in my view, the most original creation in all of Rousseau's writing. Claire comes the closest of all his creations, fictional and autobiographical, to Rousseau's own sexuality as represented in his autobiography. Claire loves Julie in the same way that Jean-Jacques loves Madame de Warens and Sophie d'Houdetot. Saint-Preux's presence in this *ménage* is illusory; the designation "*à trois*" is actually misleading in this instance. The translucent Claire, whose name is identical with her function, is a feminine figure superimposed on the feminine hero, Saint-Preux.[6] It is not a coincidence that in addition to meaning clarity, Claire's name closely resembles Clarens, the name of the fictional estate that represents a cultural utopia in the novel. In *Origines* (1988), Annie Leclerc's memoir on the books which inspired her own desire to write, Claire stands out as a figure of the generic "writer."[7] Leclerc makes the homophonic connection between her own name (Leclerc) and Claire's identification with the writing itself in a poetic reflection:

> Serait-ce maintenant l'occasion de te dire tout ce qui m'unit au prénom Claire, tenant de si près à clarté? . . . Sache seulement qu'en toute fiction qu'il me prend d'écrire je veux une Claire. Une toute claire par qui s'ouvrirait la voie de la clarté. Claire, la transparente. (Leclerc 49)

(Is now a good time to tell you of all that unites me with the name Claire, so close to clarity? . . . I will say only that in each work of fiction that I might write, I want there to be a Claire. A toute claire *(very* claire/clear*) who shows the way to clarity. Claire, the transparent one.)*

It is Claire who explains Julie's function in the novel. If Saint-Preux is the feminine man, Julie is the illusory woman, a figure of self-difference, the Not-I of the Romantic hero. Claire explains Julie's special nature:

> une de ses âmes d'une certaine trempe qui transforment pour ainsi dire les autres en elles-mêmes; elles ont une sphère d'activité dans laquelle rien ne leur résiste: on ne peut les connoître sans les vouloir imiter. (*OC*, II: 204)

> *(one of those souls of a certain stamp that in a manner of speaking transform others into themselves; they have a sphere of influence within which nothing can resist them: one cannot know them without wanting to imitate them)*

Rousseau renders the meaning of Claire's words explicit in his *Entretien sur les romans* (*Discussion of novels*) in which he writes, "Cette Julie, telle qu'elle est, doit être une créature enchanteresse; tout ce qui l'approche doit lui ressembler; tout doit devenir Julie autour d'elle" (This Julie, such as she is, must be an enchantress; everything that approaches her has to resemble her; everything around her has to become Julie) (*OC*, II: 28).[8]

Like his prototype Abelard, Heloise's tutor, Saint-Preux, is emasculated. In the case of Saint-Preux, however, the castration is symbolic: since the lovers cannot and will not have sex, his sex represents both a pretext and an obstacle to their love story. After their initial surrender to physical desire, which results in a pregnancy and its miscarriage, their relationship is transformed into passionate friendship. This transformed relationship constitutes Rousseau's cultural experiment. The new romantic lovers live together as two children who look to Julie's husband, Wolmar, for moral, spiritual, and physical support—a representation that doubles the autobiographical relationships of Madame de Warens (Wolmar's double), Rousseau, and Claude Anet with one another. By means of a writing effect resembling a series of mirror images, the passionate friendship of the heterosexual lovers, Saint-Preux and Julie, is, in its turn, doubled in the novel: the reflection of the same-sex friendship of Claire and Julie corresponds more faithfully to the sexuality of the heterosexual couple as it exists in Rousseau's imagination. Claire explains her feelings in a letter to Julie explaining why she plans to leave her husband to live with Julie and Wolmar at Clarens; Claire's candid expression of her feelings is typical of her character:

il ne m'est rien auprès de ma Julie. Di-moi, mon enfant, l'âme a-t-elle un sexe? En vérité, je ne le sens guère à la mienne. Je puis avoir des fantaisies, mais fort peu d'amour. Une invincible et douce habitude m'attache à toi dès mon enfance; je n'aime parfaitement que toi seule. (*OC*, II: 206–07)

(He is nothing to me compared to my Julie. Tell me, my child, does the soul have a sex? In truth, I hardly feel one in my own. I am capable of fantasies, but very little of love. An invincible and sweet habit has attached me to you since our childhood. I have perfect love for you alone.)

Julie's response to Claire's question, "does the soul have a sex?" is "Non, mon enfant, l'âme n'a point de sexe, mais ses affections les distinguent" (No, my child, the soul has no sex, but its affections distinguish between them) (*OC*, V: 629). Julie's words provide some insight into the problem; the soul has no sex, but when it is a question of romantic love, sexual difference is an issue; the language of love represents difference in terms of sexual difference, even when the relationship between lovers does not correspond to these terms. Claire's interpretation of perfect love and spiritual affinity is different from Julie's. Although Claire can conjure up images of sexual love between herself and a man, her heart will never fuse with a man's heart. For Claire, perfect spiritual fusion with another woman presents no such psychological dilemma.

The character of Saint-Preux is tormented by virtually all of the problems inherent in the heterosexual model of *Fin'Amors*. His desire for Julie is complicated by the fact that he also wants to be her friend, that his friendship for Claire is complicated by sexual attraction, and that friendship for Wolmar (Julie's husband) can never be isolated from a feeling of guilt since the older man has given him access to his wife, the woman Saint-Preux loves. The ideal *ménage* as conceived by Claire would be for her and Julie to live together "*à deux*"; any sexual expression of their perfect friendship in the physical sense would be irrelevant since the soul, according to Claire, does not have a sex. Like her creator, Rousseau, the expression of her own sexual desires would be reserved for erotic fantasy and Julie would have the memory of the great passion she once shared with Saint-Preux. What Claire imagines as perfect love is same-sex friendship imbued with heterosexual fantasy. This is precisely the love that the Rousseau of the autobiography shared with Sophie d'Houdetot, the "idol of his heart." During the time they spent together like two friends of the same sex, Sophie spoke to Rousseau of her love for his friend, Saint-Lambert:

elle me parla de St. Lambert en amante passionnée. Force contagieuse de l'amour! . . . j'étois saisi d'un frémissement délicieux que je n'avois éprouvé jamais auprès de personne. Elle parloit et je me sentois émus; je croyois ne faire que m'intéresser à ses sentimens quand j'en prenois de semblables; j'avalois à longs traits la coupe empoisonnée dont je ne sentois encore que la douceur. (*OC*, I: 440)

(she spoke to me of St. Lambert as a passionate lover. Contagious power of love! . . . I felt a sudden delicious shiver that I had never felt in the presence of anyone else. She spoke and it was I who was moved; I thought that I was only interested in her feelings when I began to feel similar ones; I swallowed the poisoned cup in long drafts, tasting only its sweetness.)

Through the agency of representation, the *philtre* symbolized in literature as the poisoned cup since Tristan and Iseut, Rousseau begins to experience the same feelings as the woman who is telling her story. He becomes Sophie and shares in her desire: desire for her absent lover that is commingled in Rousseau's erotic imagination with his own desire. Nowhere in his writing does Rousseau ever clearly distinguish between his desire for a woman and his desire to be that woman. One of Rousseau's most persistent and baffling formulas is used here to describe his relationship with Sophie:

Mais j'ai tort de dire un amour non partagé; le mien l'étoit en quelque sorte; il était égal des deux côtés, quoiqu'il ne fut pas réciproque. Nous étions ivres d'amour l'un et l'autre; elle pour son amant, moi pour elle . . . si quelquefois égaré par mes sens j'ai tenté de la rendre infidelle, jamais je ne l'ai véritablement désirée. . . . Je l'amois trop pour vouloir la posséder. (*OC*, I: 443–44)

(But I am wrong to say a love not shared, mine was in some way. It was equal on both sides, although it was not reciprocal. We were both intoxicated with love, she for her lover, me for her. . . . if I was sometimes led astray by my senses and tried to make her unfaithful, I never really desired that. . . . I loved her too much to want to possess her.)

The fictional relationship between Saint-Preux, Claire, and Julie in *Julie* is a more faithful representation of Rousseau's sexuality as depicted in the *Confessions:* Claire represents Rousseau, Julie is Sophie, and Saint-Preux is the absent lover, Saint-Lambert. The romantic lover's identification with a woman is so close that physical possession is no longer possible. The sexual difference that is fundamental to the heterosexual notion of possession and submission—to the masculine and feminine roles in sex—is eradicated, and no alternative is suggested by the narrative. The reader of both the autobiography and the novel is seduced by the male narrator's refusal to possess the woman he loves and frustrated by the impossibility of sexual pleasure for lovers who share love as two women. Claire's solution would eliminate the need for the male partner in romantic love to ever have to consider "possessing" the woman he loves: the variation on the distribution of the sexes represented by the character Claire's inclusion in the *ménage à trois* liberates the romantic lover, the feminine hero, from the physical burden of the masculinity which he has already surrendered figuratively by falling in love.

Although Rousseau begins his autobiography with the word "I," he immediately places into question the referential value of the first person pronoun by declaring, "Je suis autre," (I am other) a formulation which later resonates in Rimbaud's "Je est un autre" (I is an other). The "I" of the *Confessions* is constructed in relationship to Rousseau's difference from himself, a difference sometimes represented as sexual ambiguity, more often as unambiguous femininity:

> Ainsi commençoit à se former ou à se montrer en moi ce coeur à la fois si fier et si tendre, ce caractère efféminé mais pourtant indomptable, qui . . . m'a jusqu'au bout mis en contradiction avec moi-même, et a fait que l'abstinence et la jouissance . . . m'ont également échappé. (*OC*, I: 12)

> *(And so in this heart, at once so proud and so tender this effeminate yet indomitable character began to form and to show itself. . . . I was in contradiction with myself to the very end, so that both abstinence and sexual satisfaction . . . equally eluded me.)*

Rousseau's femininity requires constant adjustments in the distribution of the sexes in scenarios of love and friendship in his writing.

As recounted in *Confessions,* Rousseau's most important relationships with women were ambivalent to say the least: Madame de Warens, "Maman," whom he loved but with whom he did not want to have sex;[9] Thérèse, with whom he had sex but did not love; Sophie d'Houdetot, whom he declared to be the love of his life but with whom he enjoyed a relationship that resembled a friendship between two women (*OC,* I: 444). His encounter with a woman named Giuletta in Venice reads like a microcosmic narrative of his ambivalence towards women. At first he sees Giuletta as an angel, but when the possibility presents itself to have sex with her, he sees her as a deformed monster. Rousseau's predilection was for relationships conforming structurally to a *ménage à trois.* By sharing Madame de Warens with Claude Anet, and Sophie with Saint-Lambert, Rousseau is able to have an intimate, albeit non-sexual, relationship with a woman while avoiding the conventional structure of the couple. There is an exception to this proclivity, however, in his relationship with Thérèse Lavasseur, Rousseau's common-law wife and the mother of five children— probably his—given up for adoption. Because his love for Thérèse was not romantic, he had no fear that his imagination would become involved. He describes their relationship as one that had to do with sex: "sans avoir rien de propre à l'individu" (having nothing to do with the individual) (*OC,* I: 414). When living with Thérèse he was really alone, like a man in the state of nature who needed a woman from time to time for sex, with no desire for an *intimate* union. For Rousseau, romantic love—a feminine plot—has placed civilized man in chains.[10] The first great Romantic, then, and the writer credited with the renaissance of the romantic tradition in the age of libertinage, despised romantic love because of its compulsory and, I argue, spurious, heterosexuality. The romantic hero desires to be all things in him- self. "I have thought as a man; I have written as a man and I have been called bad. Well, now I shall be a woman," Rousseau wrote to Madame Boy in the 1760s (in Cranston, II 33–4). Furthermore, in a letter to Mme de Verdelin written during the same period, he wrote: "I wear a long robe; I weave ribbons. *Me voilà,* more than half a woman. If only I had always been one!" (in Cranston, II 34).

The exchange of sexual identities is not reciprocal; Rousseau is repulsed by women with masculine qualities. The flat chest of his blue-stocking patron Madame d'Épinay is reason enough to preclude sexual desire; on the other hand, he is captivated by the sight of her cousin Sophie d'Houdetot in a riding habit, which suggests transvestism. He describes his reaction, "Quoique je n'aime guères ces sortes de mascarades, je fus pris à l'air romanesque de celle-là, et pour cette fois ce fut de l'amour." (Although I hardly like these sorts of masquerades, I was taken by the romanesque nature of this one, and this time it was love) (*OC,* I: 439).[11] The masculin- ity of Sophie is an illusion, along the lines of a hallucination, a poetic dream, whereas Madame d'Épinay's flat chest, in combination with her role in Rousseau's life as his financial benefactor, is all too real. The effect cre- ated by Sophie's transvestism is related to the ritual of the exchange of hearts in troubadour eroticism. In *Fin'Amors,* ideally, the exchange of sex- ual identities which the exchange of hearts involves is reciprocal. The mas- culinization of the woman is symbolic and fleeting, not intended to outlast the duration of the ritual *asag* scene; the femininity gained by the man in the exchange of hearts, however, becomes a permanent part of his new identity. The reasons for this are related to the conflation of the myth of the androgyne with the myth of Narcissus in *Fin'Amors* poetics in which a man seeks his ideal self in the mirror of representation; he falls in love with his own self-difference as represented by a woman who appears to him in the form of the "Not I," the part of the self that has been lost—or forgotten. The goal of art in Romanticism, like troubadour poetics, is the reunion of the separated halves of a mythical originary person. Paraphrasing the words of Marcel Proust, true paradises are always already lost.

Rousseau's depiction of love between the sexes leads to one conclusion: it is impossible. Nevertheless, his representation of the desire for subjectivity and of the role played by romantic love in the search for a unified self became the model for Romantic art and for the depiction of heterosexual love for the next several generations of writers. George Sand, whose grandmother instilled in her a love of Rousseau's prose at an early age, had a passionate, yet ambivalent, attachment to her precursor's writing. Explicit references to Rousseau are for the most part reverent, such as the following nostalgic sentiment:

> La langue de J.-Jacques . . . s'emparèrent de moi comme une musique superbe éclairée d'un grand soleil. Je le comparais à Mozart; je comprenais tout. (OA, I: 1060)

> *(The language of Jean-Jacques . . . took hold of me like superb music illuminated by a great sun. I compared him to Mozart; I understood everything.)*

The importance of Rousseau to Sand's early education, and her continuing preoccupation with every aspect of his life and work are well documented by the writer herself in numerous passages scattered throughout her autobiography, *Histoire de ma vie* (*Story of My Life*) (1848–1854), and elsewhere.[12] Sand's sexual difference from Rousseau complicates the traditional oedipal pattern of the "anxiety of influence," which, according to Harold Bloom, involves a male writer's desire to both identify with and move beyond the literary father. My focus is the anxiety of writing as a woman when the father already occupies the position of "the feminine." A good part of the first chapter of *Histoire de ma vie,* called "Pourquoi ce livre?" (Why this book), is devoted to explaining how her autobiography is different from Rousseau's *Confessions.* Her major argument is that women should not write confessional literature that humiliates, shames, and accuses its author. Whereas assuming the position of a guilty, masochistic genius serves the purposes of male writers desiring to be perceived as suffering for art and for love, for a woman to assume such a position merely confirms received notions of the baseness of female nature. According to Sand, women's writing is always read as confessional, because the public refuses to distinguish between the woman writer and the female characters she invents. Critic Barbara Johnson reiterates Sand's point when she writes that "when men employ the rhetoric of self-torture, it is *read* as rhetoric. When women employ it, it is confession. Men are read rhetorically, women, literally" ("Gender and Poetry" 176).[13]

The strategies to subvert male appropriation of femininity as a writing effect abound in Sand's fiction. As for Rousseau in particular, her critique is clearly in evidence in *Consuelo;* explicit and implicit references to Rousseau traverse its fifteen hundred pages from beginning to end. In the first pages of this novel Sand writes:

> Lecteur, tu ne te rappelles que trop ces détails et un épisode charmant raconté par lui à propos dans le Livre VIII des *Confessions.* Je n'aurai garde de transcrire ici ces adorables pages, après lesquelles tu ne pourrais certainement pas te résoudre à reprendre les miennes. (I: 45)

> *(Reader, you remember only too well these details and a charming episode on the subject recounted by him [Rousseau] in Book VIII of the* Confessions. *I will be on my guard against transcribing these adorable pages here, after having read them you would certainly not want to take up mine again.)*

The episode alluded to in this passage takes place in Book VII, not Book VIII of the *Confessions.* Sand leads the reader to the wrong book in Rousseau's autobiography—for good reason. When *Consuelo* begins, the heroine is a young girl who has lost her mother to an early death; she sings like an angel; she is in love with a tenor named Anzoleto. In Book VII (not Book VIII) of the *Confessions,* Rousseau meets a young soprano named Anzoletta in Venice. Anzoletta's mother is willing to sell her to the highest bidder and because Rousseau is naturally attracted to a creature abandoned by maternal love, he forms what he calls "un attachement paternel" (a paternal attachment) for the young woman. Sand reassigns the genders of the situation by having Consuelo characterize her attachment for Anzoleto as that of a mother, not a father, for "le fils de mon âme" (the son of my soul).

Consuelo has made a vow to her mother that she would never allow Anzoleto to take her (her mother's) place in Consuelo's bed, where the mother and daughter slept together before the mother's death. (Isaac Rousseau and his son often shared the same bed after the mother's death, according to the *Confessions.*) One night when Anzoleto must spend the night at Consuelo's, she works out this plan, "Mais en te laissant dormir ici pour la première fois, ce n'est pas la place de ma mère que je te donne, c'est la mienne" (When you sleep in this bed, I will be giving you my place, not my mother's) (I: 72). The gender-bending switch of letters in the name

Anzoletta/Anzoleto and the displacement of the male lover from the mother's place in the bed combine in Sand's subtle but nonetheless explicit subversion of Rousseau's code of love and writing.

When Consuelo coquettishly offers Anzoleto her own place in bed and moves herself into what was her mother's place in that bed, she demonstrates how it is possible for both lovers to have access to the feminine as difference. Anzoleto is not the novel's quintessential romantic hero, however. That role belongs to Albert de Rudolstadt, a Romantic type in the tradition of Rousseau, whom she meets in Bohemia. The narrator describes him in the following way:

> Dès sa première enfance, il eut l'esprit frappé d'idées bizarres. . . . À l'âge de quatre ans, ils prétendait voir souvent sa mère auprès de son berceau, bien qu'elle fut morte . . . il voyait sa petite mère. . . . Il passait pour fou, et unissait à une âme sublime, une maladie de l'imagination. (I: 207)

> *(From early childhood, his mind was filled with bizarre ideas. . . . At four years of age he thought he saw his mother by his crib, although she was dead . . . he saw his little mother . . . he was considered to be mad, in him a sublime soul existed together with a sickness of the imagination.)*

Albert mistakes Consuelo for his deceased mother and has forgotten his own name, believing it to be Jean. In an attempt to wake him from his illusions, Consuelo says, "Ton nom n'est plus Jean" (Your name is no longer Jean) (I: 330). Her efforts to save him from a mental disorder associated with confused and mistaken identity is central to their love story. Confused identity, however, continues to haunt their romance in the service of narrative experimentation. Consuelo marries Albert on his death bed, but the marriage cannot be consummated because of Albert's failing physical health, which is caused by mental delusions—we recall that Jean-Jacques Rousseau was unable to possess any woman he loved for similar reasons. Albert dies shortly after the marriage, at which moment Consuelo swears eternal fidelity to her husband and returns to Venice, the city of music, to pursue her career as a singer. In Venice, she has a romantic encounter with a masked stranger named Liverani, who bears an uncanny resemblance to Albert, her dead husband. The resemblance is so strong, in fact, that her desire for Liverani sends her running back to Bohemia to renew her marriage vows to her deceased husband. When Consuelo renews her vow to Albert in the cave where they first met, the mysterious stranger known as Liverani miraculously appears, removes his mask, and reveals himself to be Albert. The man Consuelo married on his deathbed resembled Jean-

Jacques of the *Confessions*. The creation of the mysterious stranger, Liverani, frees Albert from being arrested in a travesty of sexual impotence *qua* femininity such as the one that imprisons the tortured subject of the *Confessions*. Consuelo and Albert marry a second time according to the rites of the "Invisibles," a Romantic cult whose rituals resemble the rituals of *Fin'Amors* in their goal of androgynous fusion.

The fusion in Sand's novel, however, is an illusion. When Consuelo looks into her husband's eyes she says, "Oh, Liverani," an anagram for the rival who is not a rival (le rival, ni rival), a parody of triangular desire which also questions the notion that the object of desire has an actual identity outside the imagination of its creator (III: 416). The success of Sand's creation, Liverani, as a figure of the liberation of desire from association with death and with the feminine as its exclusive, and inaccessible object, is attested to by Flaubert, a writer passionately consumed by the question of the relation between representation and desire. In 1867 he wrote to Sand, "Pourquoi suis-je 'amoureuse' de Liverani? c'est que j'ai les deux sexes, peut-être" (Why am I a woman in love with Liverani? maybe I possess both sexes) (*Correspondance Flaubert-Sand* 118). Like Claire, Liverani is a figure whose narrative function is to preclude an essentialist resolution into "the other sex" of a writer's self-difference. For although Rousseau's self-difference takes on a feminine representation in Claire and Sand's a masculine one in Liverani, both Claire and Liverani are translucent figures of the illusion of sexual identity, superimposed on characters who already have ambiguous sexual identities.[14] Flaubert has fallen in love with a writing effect. Consuelo escapes the fate of the Princesse de Clèves—a celibate widow—thanks to a writing trick performed by Sand in the fantastic setting of a fictional cave.

No such *deus ex machina* saves the heroine of Sand's *Elle et lui,* a fictional account of her affair with the Romantic poet Alfred de Musset, from the celibacy associated in women's writing with *vagabondage*. In this *roman à clef,* Sand confronts the dilemma of a woman writing in the age of Romanticism by showing the impossibility of heterosexual romance when both lovers are artists, in which case the woman's subjectivity resists dissolving into male self-difference. Laurent, the hero of the novel, is a painter who sees Thérèse, the woman he loves and also a painter, as a rival. His desire to be more of a woman than she destroys their love. Although the hero and heroine are depicted at the beginning of the novel as individuals who do not conform to stereotypical socially constructed images of masculinity and femininity, they do eventually fall into the standard sex roles of heterosexual romantic love narratives when their relationship becomes sexual. When they become lovers, the individuals Thérèse and Laurent become the "she" and "he" of heterosexual romance, with all that these categories imply. As first represented, the differences between Laurent and Thérèse are not related to binary opposition between the sexes. The differences that do exist between the two, as represented by Laurent in the novel's first pages, are artistic. His painting is impressionistic, making him unable to accept commissions, since he depends on inspiration, and cannot produce on command. The most important difference between them, according to Laurent, is that creation causes him great suffering. She, on the other hand, paints realistic likenesses of her models, and earns her living as a portrait artist. Although these differences are not categorically sexual, Sand casts them in terms of sexual difference, echoing the prevailing Romantic theory. Thérèse, the "she" of the novel, is more masculine than "he" since her painting, according to Laurent, is the work of a competent and productive copyist, not the creation of an anguished visionary.

Beginning with a series of letters, *Elle et lui* mimics an epistolary novel—the first of many evocations of Rousseau's *Julie*. The heroine's name is Thérèse-Jacques, a designation that fuses the names of Rousseau and Thérèse, the woman he married shortly before his death and to whom he referred as "le supplément dont j'avois besoin" (the supplement I needed) (*OC,* I: 332). Derrida has brought Rousseau's notion of the supplement into the discourse of literary theory, where it now has common currency. In a discussion of the supplement's place in the representation of desire in Western literature, Derrida writes that it is a substitute, but that "as substitute, it is not simply added to the positivity of a presence, it produces no relief, its place is assigned in the structure by the mark of an emptiness" (*Of Grammatology* 144–145). The supplement can never be adequate to the lack, writes Josué Harari, "since it is always in excess" (*Textual Strategies* 34). Sand's Thérèse represents, for Laurent "un ami [sic] sérieux, et intelligent" (a serious and intelligent [male] friend) (56). Laurent describes the differences between their work as one of sexual difference. He writes:

> vous savez que pour moi *vous n'êtes pas Mlle Jacques,* qui fait des portraits ressemblants très en vogue, *mais un homme supérieur qui s'est déguisé en femme,* et qui, sans avoir jamais fait l'académie, devine et sait faire deviner tout un corps et toute une âme dans un buste, à la manière des grands sculpteurs de l'antiquité et des grands peintres de la renaissance. (41) (emphasis added)

> *(you know that in my eyes* you are not Mlle. Jacques, *who paints life-like portraits very much in vogue,* but a superior man disguised as a woman, *who although he has never studied in the Academy, divines and has the art of making others divine a whole body and a whole soul from a bust, in the manner of the great sculptors of antiquity and the great painters of the Renaissance.)*

If Thérèse (Mademoiselle) Jacques is only disguised as a woman, it is Laurent who is truly feminine; he describes his own work in the following way:

L'invention me trouble et me fait trembler: l'exécution, toujours trop lente à mon grè, me donne d'effroyables battements de coeur, et c'est en pleurant et en me retenant de crier que j'accouche d'une idée qui m'enivre, mais dont je suis mortellement honteux et dégoûté le lendemain matin. Si je la transforme, c'est pire, elle me quitte: mieux vaut l'oublier et en attendre une autre: mais cette autre m'arrive si confuse et si énorme, que mon pauvre être ne peut pas la contenir. Elle m'oppresse et me torture jusqu'à ce qu'elle ait pris des proportions réalisables, et que revienne l'autre souffrance, celle de l'enfantement, une vraie souffrance physique que je ne peux pas définir. Et voilà comment ma vie se passe quand je me laisse dominer par ce géant d'artiste qui est en moi, et dont le pauvre homme qui vous parle arrache une à une, par le forceps de sa volonté, de maigres souris à demi mortes! (53–54)

(Creation disturbs me and makes me tremble: the execution, always too slow to suit me, makes my heart beat horribly, and I weep and have to control myself to keep from crying out when I give birth to an idea which intoxicates me—but which I am ashamed of and disgusted with the next morning. If I change it, it is worse, because then I lose it: then it is better to forget it and wait for another; but that one comes to me in such confusion and it is so enormous that my poor being cannot hold it. It weighs me down and tortures me until it has assumed full-grown proportions, and then the other pain comes on me, the pain of childbirth, a real physical pain, which I cannot describe. And that is how my life is when I allow myself to be dominated by the giant artist who dwells in me, and from whom the poor man who is speaking to you tears out, with the forceps of his will, pitiful half-dead mice.)

Sand's humorous and ironic intent is clear. Laurent ignores the sex (and the maternity—we later discover that Thérèse has a son) of the person to whom he is speaking. According to Fichte, qualities associated with the feminine have value to the Romantic artist only if acquired through transformation and fusion.[15] These same feminine qualities of intuitiveness, submissiveness, and passivity do not constitute genius when found in a biological woman where they are "natural," and therefore, as Baudelaire would later remark, "abominable." For a woman to undergo an analogous transformation and acquire masculine qualities, on the other hand, would not produce the same result. The move must be from "I" to "Not I", from (masculine) subjectivity to identification with the (feminine) object as "other." A woman would first have to achieve subjectivity, a structural position associated with men in Fichte's system, and then posit the feminine as different from the self. This is the sense of Felix Guattari's provoca-

tive remark about Virginia Woolf in which there is a gratuitous mentic
George Sand:

> Well, Virginia Woolf herself was a woman, but one sees that in order to
> become a woman writer, she had to follow a certain trajectory of becoming
> as woman, and for that she had to begin by being a man. One could certainly
> find in George Sand things perhaps more remarkable than this. ("Liberation
> of Desire" 62)

Guattari does not elaborate on his intuition that one might find remarkable
subject position moves in Sand's writing. Along with the strategic moves in
subject position in *Elle et lui,* there are explicit passages in the novel that
show Sand's awareness of the problem of *vagabondage*. In Laurent's letter
quoted above, for example, we sense that Sand understands that in the creative act, a woman writer's femininity will be seen as impersonation ("a
superior man disguised as a woman"), while a man's impersonation will be
interpreted as the real thing. In narratives of romantic love, the object of a
man's desire for fusion with the feminine is represented as sexual desire for
a woman. A fictional, and spurious, "she" becomes the object of his desire,
allowing the writer as "he" to resume the masculine position of desiring
subject. This paradox structures the narrative of the love story of Thérèse
and Laurent. The Romantic hero, the lover, in this system represents the
artist, the one single individual whose genius encompasses all polarities.
The sense of Guattari's remark is that "becoming woman" is a way for men
to liberate themselves from hierarchical structures of power. This tactic
forces women, then, to double cross themselves in order to write—remarkable, indeed.[16] Because this fusion of the "I" and the "Not I" into one
individual is represented in romantic love as the creation of the romantic
couple, the "Not I" is represented as a woman, the object of desire. Much
like an alchemical process, the One becomes two, a second being born
from the imagination of the artist, which then reunites with the artist,
forming an androgynous One. The feminine half of a couple of romantic
lovers, is born, like Eve, of the male artist.

Proust describes this process in detail in *À la recherche du temps perdu*, a
novel whose major theme is the creative process:

> Quelquefois, comme Ève naquit d'une côte d'Adam, une femme naissait
> pendant mon sommeil d'une fausse position de ma cuisse. Formée du plaisir
> que j'étais sur le point de goûter, je m'imaginais que c'était elle qui me l'of-
> frait. Mon corps qui sentait dans le sien ma propre chaleur voulait s'y rejoin-

dre, je m'éveillais. Le reste des humains m'apparaissait comme bien lointain auprès de cette femme que j'avais quittée il y avait quelques moments à peine; ma joue était chaude encore de son baiser, mon corps courbaturé par le poids de sa taille. Si, comme il arrivait quelquefois, elle avait les traits d'une femme que j'avais connue dans la vie, j'allais me donner tout entier à ce but: la retrouver, comme ceux qui partent en voyage pour voir de leurs yeux une cité désirée et s'imaginent qu'on peut goûter dans une réalité le charme d'un songe. Peu à peu son souvenir s'évanouissait, j'avais oublié la fille de mon rêve. (4)

(Sometimes, too, just as Eve was created from a rib of Adam, so a woman would come into existence while I was sleeping, conceived from some strain in the position of my limbs. Formed by the appetite that I was on the point of gratifying, she it was, I imagined, who offered me that gratification. My body, conscious that its own warmth was permeating hers, would strive to become one with her, and I would awake. The rest of humanity seemed very remote in comparison with this woman whose company I had left but a moment ago: my cheek was still warm with her kiss, my body bent beneath the weight of hers. If, as would sometimes happen, she had the appearance of some woman whom I had known in waking hours, I would abandon myself altogether to the sole quest of her, like people who set out on a journey to see with their own eyes some city that they have always longed to visit, and imagine that they can taste the reality that has charmed their fancy. And then, gradually, the memory of her would dissolve and vanish, until I had forgotten the maiden of my dream.)

The tenacity of the problem Sand confronts in *Elle et lui* is seen, for example, in the way in which the novelist Nicolas Ségur formulates the dedication of his own fictional version of the Sand–Musset affair. The *dédicace* reads:

A ELLE qui a tant aimé et souffert
A LUI qui a si bien chanté ses souffrances d'amour.

*(To She, who so loved and so suffered
To He, who sang so well about what he suffered because of love).*

She suffers; he writes about it. This is how "she and he/*She and He,*" both the actual couple *and* Sand's novel are inscribed in literary culture.

In spite of the Romantic obsession with the feminine, the genius lover seeks a woman who does not parody femininity. Laurent despises women who dress in fancy ball gowns and act the role of coquette and thinks that he has found such a woman who is different from them in Thérèse.[17] For Laurent, Thérèse is not a female impersonator, she is more like a man. He tells her, "Vous devez avoir le coeur d'un homme, puisque vous en avez la force et le talent. Rendez-le-moi" (You must have a man's heart, since you have a man's strength and talent. Give it to me) (56). Thérèse responds with humor that, although she would like to be a man for him, she doesn't quite know how to go about it. In the tradition of the *asag,* their conversation is quickly transformed from one that might take place between male friends to one between lovers; when it does, jealousy and rage enter the picture: "Jusque là, ce charme d'amitié l'avait bercé et comme enivré; il devint tout à coup amer et glacé" (Hitherto the spell of friendship had lulled and, as it were intoxicated him; all of a sudden he became bitter, and cold as ice) (57). He begins his campaign to win her love. To one spate of passionate pleas for love Thérèse answers:

> Vous m'avez dit cent fois que vous me respectiez trop pour voir en moi une femme, par la raison que vous n'aimiez les femmes qu'avec beaucoup de grossièreté. Je me suis donc crue à l'abri de l'outrage de vos désirs. (63)
>
> *(You have told me a hundred times that you respected me too much to look upon me as a woman, because your love for women was altogether gross. So I believed that I was in no danger from the outrage of your desires.)*

Laurent pushes for a confession from Thérèse; if she is not moved by his words of love, then she must be in love with someone else.

In a scene contrived to insinuate to the reader the possibility that Thérèse's lover is another woman, Sand highlights the inevitability of sexual ambiguity given the terms of sexual difference as she has set them into play in her text. One night before Laurent and Thérèse become lovers, he lurks outside her enclosed garden while she receives a late night visitor—a woman. The rendezvous is described in a most ambiguous and mysterious way:

> Elle s'enferma avec cette personne mystérieuse, et Catherine leur servit un petit diner tout à fait succulent. Thérèse soignait et servait sa compagne, qui la regardait avec tant d'extase et d'ivresse, qu'elle ne pouvait pas manger. (45)
>
> *(She closed herself in with this mysterious person, and Catherine served them a delicious dinner. Thérèse took care of and served her companion, who looked at her with such ecstasy and tenderness, that she could not eat.)*

At this point in the narrative, the reader is more than ready to believe that this woman who has been described by Laurent as a "man disguised as a woman" is lesbian. Laurent cannot distinguish whether the second voice coming from the secluded garden is that of a man or a woman. He hears the woman he desires tell her companion in a voice filled with passion, "Je n'ai plus qu'un amour sur la terre et c'est vous" (I no longer have but one love on this earth—it is you) (49). As it turns out, the woman with whom Thérèse is dining is her mother. But the reader's readiness to accept the sexual ambiguity of the woman artist makes the point of Sand's suspenseful and ironic mini-drama: the woman artist is in the structural position of the masculine as an artist; as a lover, then, it follows that the object of her desire is a woman.

Unlike the reader, however, when Laurent hears the conversation he assumes that the ambiguous voice is masculine; his desire for a male rival informs his interpretation of the sexuality of the players in the scene. Sand writes, "Thérèse perdit d'abord son prestige aux yeux de Laurent, ce n'était plus qu'une femme pareille aux autres" (Thérèse lost her prestige in Laurent's eyes at first. She was no longer anything more than a woman like any other woman) (65). His desire becomes traditional; his relationship is no longer with Thérèse, but with the rival, "Seul, il le haïssait et le dénégrait en lui-même, attribuant tous les ridicules à ce phantôme, l'insultant et le provoquant dix fois par jour" (when he was alone, he hated him, decried him to himself, attributing all sorts of absurdities to that phantom, insulting him and challenging him ten times a day) (66). Sand and the reader are now complicit in their understanding of the nature of Laurent's desire. Despite her knowledge of the structure of desire and of the feminine role in that structure, Sand does not choose to save her heroine from becoming a woman like all the others. Laurent seduces Thérèse by using one of the most effective ploys of the feminine hero; he represents himself to her as a child, a helpless, devoted child. The femininity of the romantic hero, beginning with Tristan, and thematized by Rousseau, is grounded in identification with and desire for the mother. If we read the scene in which Thérèse dines with her mother in the light of this romantic cliché, the significance of its sexual ambiguity becomes clear. Because of the intricate pattern of sexual crossovers that occur in male writing, the structure of the double feminine can be read as heterosexual romance. This is not true if the writer, or the desiring subject is a woman. In that case, it is homosexual, since the crossover is to the feminine; for a woman, it is a move towards the same sex.[18]

There are moments in *Elle et lui* in which it seems that Thérèse believes Laurent's assessment of her as an artist. Before the novel ends, however, Sand's heroine refuses the relationship, which causes her to doubt her value as an artist—but not without a sense of loss as expressed in these final words to Laurent:

Adieu pour toujours! . . . Dieu condamne certains hommes de génie à errer dans la tempête et à créer dans la douleur. . . . Ta souffrance et ton doute, ce que tu appelles ton châtiment, c'est peut-être la condition de ta gloire. Apprends donc à le subir. Tu as aspiré de toutes tes forces à l'idéal du bonheur, et tu ne l'as saisi que dans tes rêves. Eh bien, tes rêves, mon enfant, c'est ta réalité, à toi, c'est ton talent, c'est ta vie; n'est-tu pas artiste?

Sois tranquille, va, Dieu te pardonnera de n'avoir pu aimer! . . . Les femmes de l'avenir, celles qui contempleront ton oeuvre de siècle en siècle, voilà tes soeurs et tes amantes. (180)

(Adieu forever! . . . God condemns certain men of genius to wander about in a tempest and to create in pain. . . . Your suffering and your doubt, which you call your punishment, may be the conditions of your glory. Learn, therefore, to submit to them. You aspired with all your might to ideal happiness, and grasped it only in your dreams. But your dreams, my child, are your reality, they are your talent, they are your life; are you not an artist?

Have no fear, God will forgive you for not being able to love! . . . The women of the future, they who will gaze at your work from century to century—they are your sisters and your lovers.)

Given the narrative of the love affair between Thérèse and Laurent, the events leading up to her final adieu, these words of absolution with which Thérèse relegates Laurent's capacity to love a woman to the world of representation, can only be read as ironic in spite of a temptation to read them as written by a passive, submissive, forgiving martyr. I do not believe that Sand could have written the words, "are you not an artist?" without also thinking, "and am *I* not an artist?".

In a reflective prefatory essay to a 1985 edition of Sand and Musset's *Lettres d'amour* (*Love Letters*), the novelist Françoise Sagan brings up the problem of the heterosexual couple when both partners are writers:

Elle et lui étaient supposés former un nouveau couple, le nouveau couple. . . . Mais ils étaient déjà, et malgré eux, et malgré tout ce que l'on pouvait en dire, ils étaient déjà, et encore, surtout, l'autre couple, le couple immuable, le couple le plus vieux et le plus classique au monde . . . .

Et qu'il l'appelait George, mon petit garçon, mon petit copain, et qu'il eût mal au coeur sur les bateaux pendant qu'elle s'en moquait en fumant des cigares, et qu'il s'assît et s'allongeât plus volontiers qu'elle, et qu'il eût des caprices et des nerfs de femme, tout cela n'empêchait pas que ce fût lui, lui, qui fût prédateur et que ce fût elle, elle, la victime. (10)

(She and he were supposed to form a new couple, the new couple. . . . But they were already, in spite of themselves, and in spite of everything one said about them, they were already that other couple—the immutable couple, the oldest and most classic couple in the world.

And even though he called her George, my little boy, my little buddy, and in spite of the fact that it was he who got sea sick on boats while she laughed at him and smoked cigars, and he who liked to recline stretched out, and he who had the whims and the nerves of a woman, none of this changed the fact that he, he was the predator and she, she was the victim.)

In this statement of the eternal problem of the woman artist in love, Sagan provides the major reasons why Sand gave up on writing the narrative of the romantic couple when both are artists to experiment with other narrative possibilities both in *Elle et lui* and elsewhere in her fiction. An example of such experimentation in *Elle et lui* refers directly to Rousseau's *ménage à trois* in *Julie*. In both *Julie* and *Elle et lui,* the romantic lovers live chastely with an older man; in Rousseau's novel they live with Julie's husband, Wolmar, and in Sand's with Thérèse's fiancé, Palmer. Both Wolmar and Palmer are described by their creators as noble, and both are depicted as detached from romantic passion. In Rousseau's conventional *ménage à trois,* the older man (Wolmar) is a patriarchal figure who represents traditional masculinity in contrast with the shared femininity of the childlike lovers. Saint-Preux describes his life with Julie and Wolmar at Clarens, Wolmar's estate as idyllic:

> Je sens plus de plaisir encore à me regarder comme l'enfant de la maison. . . . En fréquantant ces heureux époux, leur ascendant me gagne et me touche insensiblement, et mon coeur se met par degrès à l'unisson des leurs, comme la voix prend sans qu'on y songe le ton des gens avec qui l'on parle. (*OC,* II: 527)

> *(I take pleasure in seeing myself as the child of the family. . . . Spending time with these two happy spouses, their influence is starting to affect me imperceptibly and little by little my heart is beginning to beat in unison with theirs, as a voice takes on the tone of those with whom one is speaking)*

Sand's description of Laurent's happiness with Thérèse and Palmer in Italy resembles Saint-Preux's description of his childlike happiness at being with Julie and Wolmar on Wolmar's estate, "il (Laurent) ne quittait pas ses deux amis, se promenant avec eux en voiture . . . se faisant une joie d'enfant d'aller dîner dans la campagne en donnant le bras à Thérèse alternativement avec Palmer" (he [Laurent] never left his two friends, taking carriage rides with them, as joyful as a child when they went to have dinner in the country, alternately taking Thérèse's arm, and then Palmer's) (116). A mistranslation by George Burnham Ives reads: "Thérèse would take his (Laurent's) arm and Palmer's alternately" (125). The reversal of conventional mascu-

line and feminine roles by Sand who has Laurent taking Palmer and
Thérèse's arms alternately, is "rectified" by the translator who has Thérèse
playing the conventional feminine role.

Palmer's narrative function mimics Wolmar's in another way: both patriarchal figures test the romantic lovers. Wolmar leaves Saint-Preux and Julie
alone at the estate at Clarens to test their ability to control their passion,
creating a situation highly charged with desire and suffering. Palmer insists
that his fiancée, Thérèse, spend three days alone with Laurent. Sand's narrative differs from Rousseau's, however, in the heroine's response to the test,
to the suffering imposed on her by the two men, and to her position in triangular desire. Julie's role in Rousseau's version of the test resembles a
woman's role in a classic *asag*. In a letter filled with highly poetic and
Romantic feeling addressed to his friend Édouard, Saint-Preux describes
the intensity of his temptation during a romantic boat ride with Julie on
the lake at Clarens:

> Bien-tôt je commençai de rouler dans mon esprit des projets funestes, et
> dans un transport dont je frémis en y pensant, je fus violemment tenté de la
> précipiter avec moi dans les flots, et d'y finir dans ses bras ma vie et mes longs
> tormens. Cette tentation devint à la fin si forte que je fus obligé de quitter
> brusquement sa main pour passer à la pointe du bateau.
>
> Là mes vives agitations commencerent à prendre un autre cours; un sen-
> timent plus doux s'insinua peu à peu dans mon âme, l'attendrissement sur-
> monta le désespoir; je me mis à verser des torrens de larmes, et cet état
> comparé à celui dont je sortois n'étoit pas sans quelques plaisirs.
>
> . . . Voilà, mon ami, le détail du jour de ma vie où sans exception j'ai senti
> les émotions les plus vives. J'espère qu'elles seront la crise qui me rendra tout
> à fait à moi. (521)

> *(I soon began to turn fatal schemes around in my head, and in a state of rapture which
> I tremble to remember, I was fiercely tempted to hurl her into the water with me, and
> to end my life and my long torment there in her arms. That horrible temptation
> became so strong that I had to drop her hand abruptly and walk to the front of the
> boat.*
>
> *There my agitation took another course; a sweeter feeling flowed slowly into my
> soul, tenderness replaced despair. I began to cry torrents of tears and this state, com-
> pared to the one I had just been in, was not without pleasure.*
>
> *. . . There, my friend, is an account of the day on which I felt the strongest feel-
> ings of my life. I hope that they will be the crisis that will give me back to myself com-
> pletely.)*

Julie's function in Saint-Preux's account of the pleasure of intense suffering, which rendered him whole, is that of a blank page onto which he pro-

jects his experience. Once on the page, Julie is no longer necessary to Saint-Preux's rehabilitation. The irony of a parallel scene in which Julie actually drowns later in the novel is not lost on Sand. Saint-Preux is saved by writing, Julie first becomes language and then disappears into the watery abyss toward which Saint-Preux was drawn during the boat ride on the lake.

Sand's lovers undergo a similar test—also involving a boat trip—designed by Palmer, who insists that Thérèse accompany the ailing Laurent (who is by now her former lover) by row boat from Venice to Porto Venere, where he is to board a ship home to France. In contrast with Rousseau's scenario in which Saint-Preux wants to drag Julie into the water with him, in Sand's parodic version Thérèse saves Laurent from falling into the sea when he becomes "giddy" (132). In the end, Thérèse rejects both the romantic lover who tempts her to the abyss with his femininity, and the noble Palmer who cannot be for her a sublime love because of his Wolmar-like tendencies to rehabilitate her and treat her like a child. In words that echo those of the Princesse de Clèves to Nemours, Thérèse explains to Laurent her choice of celibacy over romantic love, "Nous ne nous retrouverons pas, Laurent, j'en ai la certitude. Chaque homme va vers son foyer d'attraction. Le repos m'appelle, et toi, tu seras toujours et partout attiré par la tempête" (170) (We shall not meet again, Laurent, I am sure. Each soul goes toward its center of attraction. Repose summons me, while you will always and everywhere be attracted by the tempest).

Laurent's disappointment takes the form of vengeance. He invites Thérèse to a masquerade ball in order to make it painfully clear to her that her femininity is a perpetual masquerade. As in *Consuelo,* Sand once again uses the metaphor of masquerade to analyze conflicting definitions of femininity. It is Laurent's intent to hurt Thérèse; Sand's intention in creating the scene is to highlight the fact that because Thérèse's sexuality is not conventional, there exists no possibility for her to enjoy the kind of sexual relationship enjoyed by other women. If he is the feminine poet, then her identity is that of a "man disguised as a woman," a mirror image of his artistic persona. If, on the other hand, he plays the part of libertine, she is cast as an ordinary woman—yet another construction of his imagination—but one he believes to be based on a natural division of the sexes. In her relationship with Laurent, Thérèse is always forced to play a role, yet when she sees Laurent at the ball, he wears no mask, nor do most of the men there. It is the women who are disguised, all in identical domino costumes. The voices of the other women mirror Thérèse's perception of herself when she is cast in the role of Laurent's mistress:

Elle se retourna et vit l'homme qu'elle avait tant aimé assis entre deux filles masquées, dont la voix et l'accent avait ce je ne sais quoi de mou et d'aigre tout ensemble qui révèle la fatigue des sens et l'amertume de l'esprit. (174)

(She turned and saw the man she had loved so well, seated between two masked damsels, whose voices and accent had that indefinable combination of limpness and sharpness which betrays exhaustion of the senses and bitterness of spirit.)

She characterizes them as "empty-headed creatures" whose vapidity causes Laurent to yawn. In a scene that recalls the *trobairitz,* Lombarda's "mirror without an image" (see chapter 2), Sand exploits the disguise motif to describe Thérèse's loss of self, "les habits et les dominos faisaient un font opaque, et la vitre devenait une glace noire où l'image de Thérèse se répétait sans qu'elle s'en aperçut" (the clothes and the dominos created an opaque background and the glass became a sort of black mirror, in which Thérèse's face was reflected unknown to her) (175). Laurent notices the immobile face in the mirror and comments to his women companions:

est-ce que vous ne trouvez pas ça effrayant, le masque? . . . une figure qu'on ne divine pas, que l'on ne connait pas, qui vous fixe avec cette prunelle ardente; je m'en vais d'ici, moi, j'en ai assez. (175)

(don't you find that ghastly, the mask? . . . a face that you can't guess, that you don't know, glaring at you with that ardent eye. I am getting out of here, I've had enough.)

Along with his invitation to the ball, Laurent had sent Thérèse a mask to wear. But Thérèse had rejected his mask, and brought another one, "made of Naples silk," which he does not recognize. Thérèse simultaneously accepts and rejects the identity that Laurent imagines for her. She wears the domino costume, like the other women, but chooses her own mask. Laurent flees once he realizes that he cannot control how Thérèse represents herself.

Sand has Thérèse skirt the abyss, but draw back: the call is heard, but the woman artist is not compelled to answer it; for Sand, creativity is a positive calling for a woman. It was, after all, her desire to write that had freed Sand from the prison of her marriage to Casimir Dudevant; writing, for Sand, is associated with pleasure, not with pain. The narrator of Sand's novel insists throughout that Thérèse must make a conscious effort to maintain the subjectivity that she has struggled to achieve; she must resist responding to either the lure of the abyss, or to the temptation of romantic love. This is how Sand describes the seduction of the abyss when the artist is a woman:

> Thérèse, disons-nous, trop côtoyé cet abîme pour n'en point partager quelquefois le vertige. Son propre talent comme son propre caractère avait failli s'engager à son insu dans cette voie désespérée. Elle avait eu cette exaltation de la souffrance qui fait voir en grand les misères de la vie, et qui flotte entre les limites du réel et de l'imaginaire. . . . (172)

> *(Thérèse, we say, had skirted that abyss too often not to have been made giddy by it more than once. Her own talent as well as her own character had well-nigh become involved, without her knowledge, in that desperate path. She had known that exaltation of suffering which shows one the miseries of life on a large scale, and which hovers on the boundaries between the real and the imaginary. . . .)*

The fact that Thérèse does not lose herself in the aspiration to the sublime, gives Laurent reason to believe that she is not an artist at all, but rather a rational—and hence conventionally masculine—woman whose intuition only resembles true art, a female impersonator, so to speak. For the male artist, the abyss is confused with the woman, with beauty, with love, and with art. For the female artist, to fall into the abyss would be to walk back through the looking glass into the prisonhouse of representation. Thérèse is in the classic double bind that characterizes *vagabondage* in the Romantic era. She is both attracted to and repulsed by the abyss associated with writing. Consequently, at times she sees herself as Laurent's destiny, reading his destructive desire to transform her into his muse as a sign of his artistic genius. Her desire to submit to the powerful attraction of a sublime passion undermines her belief in her own creative genius, which does not conform to the paradigm of the Romantic artist and for which there is no metanarrative.

Like the Princesse de Clèves before her, and Colette's vagabond Renée Néré after her, Thérèse suffers from a self divided into a woman in love and a woman determined to see the world through her own eyes. Like the princess, Thérèse chooses to renounce romantic passion. In *The Gay Science*[19] Nietzsche writes, "Supposing, however, that there should also be men to whom the desire for total devotion is not alien; well, then they simply are—not men" (319). The implication is that men who surrender to romantic passion are more like women than like men. For Sand, however, an actual woman who desires to be an artist must renounce both romantic love and the "aspiration to the sublime." Despite the implications of *vagabondage* and its attendant sexual exile, Sand's challenge to male femininity might be seen as an artistic victory for the woman writer, who exposes the travesty, and in so doing reappropriates the feminine position and the right to represent it.

CHAPTER 4

The Old Troubadour: George Sand

Liberté de pensée, liberté d'écrire et de parler, sainte conquête
de l'esprit humain!

*(Freedom of thought, freedom to write and to speak, sacred acquisition
of the human spirit!)*

—*George Sand,* Indiana

"Madame Dudevant, homme de lettres" (man of letters) is the
entry for George Sand in the Paris Almanach of 1837.[1] In the
process of becoming a writer, Sand had, in the language of
the Academy, become a man. This inversion of Sand's sex for the purpose
of classifying her as a professional writer stands in striking contradiction to
the prevailing Romantic notion of a writer's inevitable femininity, as well
as to postmodern descriptions of the writing subject as "becoming-
woman" (Deleuze and Guattari). Sand's "coming to writing" is by no
means a simple case of gender reversal.[2] Because "the feminine" is a figure
of the performance of subjectivity as self-difference in narratives of heterosexual desire since the era of the troubadours, a woman writing in the tradition, like her male counterparts, writes the feminine as self-difference.
That, in a word, is the nexus of the *troubadour effect* and *vagabondage*. Felix
Guattari defines the devilish nature of this structure in a remark about
Virginia Woolf (already cited in chapter 3) that "in order to become a
woman writer, she had to follow a certain trajectory of becoming as
woman, and for that she had to begin by being a man" (*Homosexualities* 62).
Guattari's sometime collaborator, philosopher Gilles Deleuze, has said that
"there is no becoming man, insofar as man presents himself as a dominant
form of expression that claims to impose itself on all matter" (*MP* 225).

How, then, does a woman writer figure self-difference? Pamela Caughie
writes with relation to the trajectory delineated by Deleuze, "the woman
writer stands in a very different relation to becoming—to writing—than
the man. Both must engage in a performance of femininity, only for the

123

woman writer that performance is not one of self-difference" (*Passing and Pedagogy* [1999] 167). Self-difference is, nonetheless essential to writing—to repeat a lesson learned from poststructuralist theory beginning with Barthes' "The Death of the Author." Barthes figures the performance of self-difference as a loss of identity, "beginning with the very identity of the body that writes" (142). Yet, as discussed in my Introduction, Barthes figures that body as a castrato, Zambinella, a male whose body and voice have been altered. The voice of the writer is a woman's voice, which emanates from a body whose male identity has been refigured as feminine for the purpose of exemplifying writing as self-difference. When Guattari says that one could probably find "even more remarkable things" in Sand than in Woolf's "becoming a man to become a woman," he has intuited a truth about Sand's writing that he does not pursue. Sand's heroines, Indiana, Lélia, Counsuelo, differ from Woolf's Orlando—a man who over the course of four centuries becomes a woman to write (see chapter 5)—in that the ways in which they cross over into subjectivity are more subtle. Sand's heroines are, however, no less subversive of the abysmal nature of the Romantic convention of sexual difference *qua* self-difference when the writer is a woman. Representations of Sand's life, in critical commentaries and in fiction, on the other hand, bear a closer resemblance to Orlando than to Sand's own heroines.

It is no surprise to anyone familiar with Sand lore that her femininity was often questioned, in spite of the prevailing convention of femininity as the *sine qua non* of a writer's self-difference. In a letter of 1835 to her friend Adolphe Guérot, Sand writes:

> Je n'ambitionne pas la dignité de l'homme. . . . Mais je prétends posséder aujourd'hui et à jamais la superbe et entière indépendance dont vous seuls croyez avoir le droit de jouir. . . . Prenez-moi donc pour un homme ou pour une femme, comme vous voudrez. Duteil dit que je ne suis l'un ni l'autre, mais que [je]suis un *être*. (*Corr.*, 2: 879–880)[3]

> *(I do not covet a man's position. . . . But I do claim to possess today and for always the superb and total independence which you believe that you alone have the right to enjoy. . . . Take me, then, for a man or for a woman, as you like. Duteil says that I am neither one nor the other, but that I am a* being.*)*

This statement did not keep Henry James from accusing Sand of appropriating life "exactly" as if she were a man, "and exactly is not too much to say," wrote James (in Barry [1977] xiii). It seems that Sand was constantly compelled to answer those who, like Guérot, represented her as a woman and as a writer in words that resemble a sort of gender mumbo jumbo.[4] Turgenev called the woman he thought of as a saint, "a brave man, and a good woman" (in Cate [1975] 731). Balzac, an ambivalent admirer, wrote in a letter to Madame Hanska, "she is masculine . . . she is an artist . . . she has the noble characteristics of a man, *ergo* she is not a woman" (*Corr.*, I: 584–585). Flaubert, for whom she was "cher maître," (dear master) uttered through tears at her funeral, "One had to know her as I knew her, to realize how much of the feminine there was in that great man" (in Cate 732). Elizabeth Barrett Browning waxed poetic about the beloved precursor whom she called "a large-brained woman" and "a large-hearted man," when she wrote, "True genius, but true woman! doest deny thy woman's nature with a manly scorn" (in Barry xiv). Juliette Adam is quoted as having said about Sand's failed love affairs, "Elle était amante et ne savait pas être maîtresse" (She was a lover and did not know how to be a mistress) (in Cate xxvii) and when the frail and dependent Frédéric Chopin who would later become her lover, first met her, he said, "This Sand! Is it really a woman?"[5]

Her contemporaries seemed to agree with Sosthènes de la Rochefoucauld that Sand was "a chameleon . . . everything can be found in that mind which is rational like a man's, and irrational like a woman's" (in Cate vii). More recently, in *Female Perversions,* Louise Kaplan provides a gloss on Flaubert's language, bringing the problem of describing the sexuality of a woman who writes to her ground-breaking study of female sexuality in contemporary America when she writes: "Sand, the epitome of the free woman to her own and later generations, never did acknowledge how much of the feminine there was in her masquerades as a man"—to wit, a woman writer becomes a feminine man (498). In a poem dedicated to George Sand in his collection called *Misgivings* (1979), Richard Howard likens Sand's assumption of the persona of a classical writer in a Nadar photo in which she is wearing a Racine-like wig, to "moral drag." For Howard, Sand's novels would not have warranted her being seen as a writer. Her life, on the other hand, and the choices she created for herself, merit her inclusion among "subversive poets." "Perhaps a genius though never a gentleman, you pose with a flamboyant frumpishness past the dull coquetries of sex, serenely heretical, efficient, real." According to the poem, it is only when she is past her prime as a writer and as a woman, that male impersonation—in this case posing as Racine—earns her the dubious distinction of being dubbed "real." Sand is worthy of praise only when she has moved beyond sexual desire into what the French call "the third age," a state of being that, in the poem, is a better lot than that of a "*grande amoureuse,*" which could never be more than a pretense for a woman who presumes to write. In essence, Howard expresses unmitigated disapproval of Sand's writing, and faint praise for the life she leads once she has moved beyond "the dull coquetries of her sex"—a harsh sentence pronounced on a woman for whom writing was her way of being in the world. Sand herself painfully understood how she was seen by her male contemporaries and which she sums up succinctly in *Elle et lui* when Laurent calls Thérèse, "un homme supérieur qui s'est déguisé en femme" (a superior man disguised as a woman) (41). The male poet's praise in both cases—Laurent's and Howard's—is for a woman's virility. Any sign of femininity in a woman writer is called a masquerade. Any sign of masculinity is "moral drag." Hollywood has made its share of cracks about Sand's sexuality as well. Take for example the following exchange in the 1946 film, *Humoresque,* about a beautiful young concert violinist (John Garfield), his "roommate" (Oscar Levant), and Joan Crawford playing Garfield's improbable love interest:

> Reporter: Is he your protégé
> Levant: My relationship with him is the same as the relationship between Chopin and George Sand.

In spite of making one laugh at the idea of Levant as George Sand, the joke, in the context of Crawford's role as Garfield's benefactor in the film, sends the message that both Sand and Crawford are female impersonators because they assume positions generally viewed as masculine.[6]

The curious inability on the part of men to call a woman who writes by the name of woman, and the resulting exclusion from sexual desire, are rendered with raw clarity by Colette in *Le pur et l'impur* (1941) in a scene astutely analyzed by Mary Lydon in her article, "Calling Yourself a Woman." In the scene, Colette suggests to a male friend, whom she calls Damien, that they go on a trip together," une paire de compagnons courtoisement égoïstes, commodes, amis des longs silences" (a pair of courteously egotistic companions, accommodating, comfortable with long friendly silences) (*Oeuvres,* III: 586). His reply, "Je n'aime voyager qu'avec des femmes" (I only care to travel with women) (*Oeuvres,* III: 586). Lydon describes Colette as possessing a certain "virility," "a psychic, mental, or perhaps even characterological trait that the Damiens of this world (alas, all too numerous) take to be antipathetic to, nay incompatible with, 'womanliness.'" Lydon's comments speak clearly to the problem of *vagabondage:*

> From the point of view of the woman who possesses it, on the other hand, this "suggestion of virility" need not and does not prevent her from "calling herself a woman," nor from aspiring to play the "woman's" part, on occa-

sion. The difficulty is that others (Colette would limit "others" here to men) may be misled, may allow this mysterious ingredient to mask or overpower what for want of a better word must be called "the woman" in one. Naturally, as soon as this happens one can no longer be "seen" as a possible female lead, though one may qualify admirably for the role of confidante, comrade-in-arms, or even, grotesquely, "old boy." (31)

Following up on the conversation that had clearly bothered her, given the amount of attention it receives, Colette recounts a conversation with her friend Marguerite Moreno who said, "Il n'y a vraiment pas de quoi. . . . Pourquoi ne te résignes-tu pas à penser que certaines femmes représentent, pour certains hommes, un danger d'homosexualité?" (There's no reason to be so upset. . . . Why don't you just accept the fact that for certain men some women represent the risk of homosexuality?) (*Oeuvres,* III: 587).[7] To which Colette replied, "Mais si tu dis vrai, qui nous tiendra pour femmes?" (But if what you say is true, then who will take us for women?) (*Oeuvres,* III: 587). In his poem, Howard depicts Nadar's image of Sand as beyond sexual desire and her youthful "coquetries." The correspondence Howard draws between Sand's right to be called a "poet" and a middle-aged woman's male impersonation, is an example of the double bind that exists for a woman who desires to write, and who possesses an equally strong desire to be "called a woman." Colette's disheartening realization that women's agency and her right to be "called a woman" are mutually exclusive is echoed by many twentieth-century women writers, too many for me to be able to mention even those on my personal list of favorites. Examples will undoubtedly flood into my reader's mind. I am moved by her recent death to single out Iris Murdoch, and her novel, *The Unicorn* (1963), a contemporary romance in the medieval style. Marian Taylor, an independent working woman who, when the novel begins, has just finished reading *La Princesse de Clèves,* is described as masculine in comparison with the romantic heroine, Hannah, the enchanting prisoner of her husband's "sexual feudalism," a woman with whom all the men in the novel are in love. Jamesie, one of the more masculine characters, makes the telling remark about Marian's difference from women like Hannah, "I've never known a woman like you. You're different. You're real. Like a man" (48).

A woman writer is kept in her place with what is to be construed, one must suppose, as flattery. Admission to the ranks of "one of the boys" keeps both her sexual energy and her agency in check—as in the ritual *asag* of *Fin'Amors,* a lady's access to the privileged relations of *compagnonnage.* She can never really be "one of the boys," of course, and will eventually and inevitably be exposed as an impersonator, legitimizing her exclusion from the symbolic order. Because of her sex, her authority is experience. The pleasure and freedom of experiment with its open-endedness is, according to the psychoanalytic model of oedipal desire, not available to her. In her book, *The In-Between of Writing: Experience and Experiment in Drabble, Duras and Arendt* (1993), Eleanor Honig Skoller makes a strong case for "women's desire for the symbolic order" against the background of a the-oretical environment in which experience is privileged as the ground of women's writing (11). Although concerned primarily with modernist and postmodernist women writers, Skoller's assessment of the problem of women's lack of access to the symbolic order applies to Sand as well:

> There has been a rather consistent effort by women to abdicate the register of the letter, by which the psyche and culture are constituted, to men who over the centuries have claimed it as their right. The letter is the province of men, and women stand at its gates, perpetual exiles, except for the occasional interloper who may get through only to be recognized as being like a man. (11)

Woman's desire for the symbolic order is essential to the experience of desire itself, which, in Skoller's words, "is what happens to the writer both before and during the writing" (27). Contrary to being a report of experi-ence as an unmediated occurrence, writing acts as a *philtre,* which creates desire in the writing subject. To relegate women's desire to the authority of experience, is to exclude women from what Skoller calls "literary experi-mentation," which, as Barthes has taught us in *Le plaisir du texte* (1973), is the key to "jouissance" (10). The variety of narrative forms representing a search for alternative ways to tell the story of desire in Sand's *oeuvre* gives testimony to her engagement with literary experimentation, often over-looked in women's writing because it is read as unmediated confession.[8]

Curtis Cate (1975) shines a light on the major reason for the production of sexually ambiguous aphorisms to describe Sand: her (hetero)sex life seemed to be in direct contradiction to her aspirations as a writer. In response to the accusation by the son of one of Sand's lovers, Stéphane Ajasson de Grandsagne, that Sand suffered from nymphomania, Cate writes, "George Sand's real trouble was nympholepsy—a frenzied pursuit of ecstatic rapture, a mystic yearning for the unattainably sublime, a desper-ate craving for the ineffably tender, for what James Joyce so beautifully termed 'the soft, sweet swoon of sin'" (239). In other words, Sand quested for the Absolute, for fusion with the Infinite, with the passion of a Roman-tic writer like any other. In the last chapter, I showed how desire for the Infinite in the Romantic era translates into male femininity. But, in the case of a woman who desires to write, expressions of ecstatic rapture and mystic yearning are viewed as the confessions of a nymphomaniac.

When, in a letter to Flaubert, Sand signed herself "le vieux troubadour (the old troubadour)," she undoubtedly had in mind a literary tradition with which she felt a strong affinity. Ironically, what attracts her to the kind of writing represented by troubadours is precisely what makes it so difficult for her to become a part of it. She faces the dilemma of a woman writing in a tradition in which femininity is the mark of a male writer's difference from other men and Woman represents the object of the mystic yearning associated with the Romantic quest, and its corollary, heterosexual desire. For Naomi Schor, "it is no accident that Sand repeatedly invokes the archetypal Western model of an ethical eros, the courtly love rituals sung by medieval troubadours" (Hollier, *NHFL* 772). In her book, *George Sand and Idealism* (1993), Schor expands on Sand's connection with the troubadours (61–62).[9] In a discussion of the tendency of idealism to turn against itself and lose its ethical force when it evolves towards allegory, she engages Julia Kristeva's description, in *Tales of Love* (1983), of how the troubadour poetics of *joi* lost its meaning when it evolved towards heterosexual romance (61). Kristeva writes about the two meanings (M1 and M2) of the courtly tradition, "One should, in short, always split the courtly message into an M1, made up of literal signification and having the Lady as referential object; and an M2, referring to joy alone and whose sign is the *song*" (Kristeva, *TL* 287–8; in Schor 61). Schor sees this move from ideal to allegory in which "the narrative level, at first only a pretext for the song, overtook the incantatory level" as analogous to the vicious circle of the collapse of idealism into "linear narrative and psychological realism" in the nineteenth century when realism became a major literary mode associated with masculinity and idealism was relegated to feminine writing (62). Sand remained an idealist, and consequently lost her place in the canon.

The trajectory suggested by Schor, with Kristeva, is of particular interest to me because I suggest the existence of a parallel trajectory. By recuperating in her later years (1866) the name of troubadour to describe herself as a writer, Sand takes us back to the ideal of the song as the direct inscription of *jouissance* (Kristeva's M2), a pleasure available in principle to both sexes, that is before *jouissance* becomes indistinguishable from its narrative pretext, heterosexual romance (Kristeva's M1)—a moment that occurs in the twelfth century, but which nevertheless parallels in structure Schor's trajectory, which she situates entirely within the nineteenth century. In early troubadour lyrics, the lady is identical to the unattainable *joi* of composition and should not be taken literally (see chapter 1). Once she is named, however, in romance narratives, the poetic ideal is lost to narrative realism and the writing position becomes unavailable to women—literally, but never of course figuratively. The writing analyzed in this chapter shows how Sand figured out how to move into the writing position by a double splitting of the subject. As discussed earlier in several contexts, writing depends on self-difference. In Lacanian theory, entry into language inevitably creates a division between "the subject of the enunciation and the subject of the *énoncé,* the 'I' who speaks and the 'I' who is represented in the discourse" (Belsey, *Critical Practice* 85). This split is complicated, I argue, when the subject is a woman, represented in the discourse of desire not as "I," but as "Not I," as "other," as "object"—the troubadours' "lady." Sand subverts the simple binary-split of "I" and "Not I" by figuring self-difference as an exchange of female identities, thereby disrupting the tradition of intersexual travesty and "blurring difference within difference" (Schor, "Female fetishism" [1986] 370). That's why the lady is a . . . troubadour.

In *Histoire de ma vie* (*Story of My Life*) (1848), Sand configures the course of her desire to participate fully in the *joi* of troubadour poetics, the *jouissance* of the imagination, in the language of a child's game called "crossing the river." In the autobiography, Sand transforms the memory of a childhood experience into a provocative metaphor for how women's writing challenges the simple binary split subject of traditional representations of self-difference. Further evidence of the importance of the game to Sand's recollection of her passage to writing is found in the way in which traces of the game's language appear throughout her fiction. The narrative of the game in *Histoire de ma vie* immediately precedes—suggestively, I think—an account of Sand's first attempts at writing, at age five (*OA,* I: 617). This juxtaposition situates the game in a context of memory and writing created by the writer's own design. In the scene, the five-year-old Aurore (Sand's name before adopting the *nom de plume* was Amantine-Lucile-Aurore Dupin) is playing with her half brother, Hippolyte, and her friend Ursule in her mother's room. The mother, Sophie, is totally absorbed in drawing, silent and oblivious to the children. The children's game also involves drawing; they draw a river in chalk on the tiles on the floor, a river that winds about the mother's room and—because of her position in the room—around the mother herself. In certain places, the imaginary river is so deep that the children can not cross it without getting wet. What was fun for the children has narrative interest for the autobiographer, who turns the game into a mini-drama of desire and the obstacle. The children are bent on overcoming the obstacle and crossing the river. It just so happens that situated on the other side, engaged in her own fantasy, is Aurore's mother, Sophie, the inaccessible feminine of George Sand's writing. Pre-

THE OLD TROUBADOUR: GEORGE SAND

dictably, the question of gender enters at this point in the narrative. Hippolyte, a boy, enjoys falling in, flapping about on the dry tiles, and lamenting his plight while the girls are immobilized by the fear of falling in. When Aurore arrives at the river's edge, she is engaged in a reverie described by Sand as separate from and yet as profound as the one her mother is in. The child is totally caught up in a hallucination, which Sand describes as follows:

> Pour mon compte, il ne me fallait pas cinq minutes pour m'y plonger de si bonne foi que je perdais la notion de la réalité et je croyais voir les arbres, les eaux, les rochers, une vaste campagne, et le ciel tantôt clair, tantôt chargé de nuages qui allaient crever et augmenter le danger de passer la rivière. (*OA*, I: 612)

> *(For my part, it was only a matter of five minutes before I had so completely and sincerely entered into it that I lost all sense of reality, and I believed that I saw trees, streams, rocks, a vast countryside, and a sky sometimes clear, sometimes filled with clouds that were about to burst making the river even more dangerous to cross.)*

Aurore loses herself in an imaginary scene, described by Sand as "tout un roman" (an entire novel), a well-constructed drama created from a primitive chalk trace (*OA*, I: 611). The danger imagined by the child caught up in creating a story suggests the real obstacles that stand in the way of the woman writer that the child Aurore will become. At the crucial moment of passage, the tactile sensation on Aurore's feet is one of fine grass and soft sand: "l'herbe était si fine, le *sable* doux" (the grass was so fine, the *sand* so soft) (*OA*, I: 612). The cross-channel pen name is already traced in the imaginary sand at the moment of crossing over. When Ursule warns Aurore that the water may reach her knees, Sand remembers herself as a child having said, "il ne s'agissait que de relever un peu nos jupes et d'ôter nos chaussures" (it was simply a matter of raising our skirts a bit and removing our shoes) (*OA*, I: 612). The shedding of the feminine dress, the cumbersome and perishable garb, will, in fact, occur years later in Paris. Sand explains the strategy of cross-dressing so closely associated with her in the popular imagination in a language which curiously resembles the language of the game, "Mais sur le pavé de Paris, j'étais comme un bateau sur la glace. Les fine chaussures craquaient en deux jours, . . . je ne savais pas relever ma robe" (On the paving stones of Paris, I was like a boat on ice. My delicate shoes fell apart in two days. I didn't know how to lift my dress) (*OA*, II: 117). Cross-dressing was in fact, Sand's mother's idea first—a revelation that recasts popular assumptions about Sand's male impersonation.

Sophie dressed "en garçon" when she was young and living in Paris with Sand's father, Maurice Dupin (*OA*, II: 117). Her daughter found the idea amusing and ingenious, and copied Sophie, inscribing her mother into her public, as well as her private, life.

The game ends when Hippolyte throws real water on the tiles to heighten the sensation. The girls' laughter rouses Sophie from her reverie and she in turn awakens her daughter from hers. Sand writes that her mother brusquely and angrily interrupts her hallucination at its most intense moment (au plus fort de mon hallucination [*OA*, I: 613]). The children's roles in this game are significant: Hippolyte, the boy, acts with confidence and abandon; Ursule exhibits fear of the unknown, fantasizing that shrimp will eat her feet; Aurore, in spite of being a girl, makes adjustments, and creates the possibility of crossing over into the magical "ludic" space. Sophie awakens her daughter from her hallucination at its peak, deferring *jouissance*.[10] Because of the interruption, the structure of the game is forever fixed for Aurore in incompletion and is played out repeatedly in Sand's writing, where it is consistently associated with the desire for the inaccessible feminine—represented in the game as the mother, Sophie—as self-difference. The river passage becomes what Sylvie Charron Witkin calls "un véritable roman d'aventures" (a true adventure novel), and is present throughout Sand's fiction as a metaphor for the passage to writing (146).[11] Sophie is associated with writing in an even more direct way later in the autobiography. When Aurore was seven years old, Sophie accepted an allowance from her mother-in-law, who wanted to be rid of her, and left Nohant for Paris, taking with her another daughter, Caroline, an illegitimate child born before she met Maurice Dupin, Sand's father. Sophie promised to send for Aurore, but never did. Heartbroken, the seven-year-old, who had lost her father when she was only five, spent the night before the rupture writing a long letter to her mother, a letter into which her heart "coulait à flots" (overflowed) (*OA*, I: 759). She placed the letter in a portrait of her paternal grandfather and begged her mother to leave one in its place for her before leaving. Her mother's response would have constituted a romantic fusion of their two beings in an exchange of letters. There was nothing, however, in writing from her mother in the morning, creating, it can be said, the daughter's desire—for writing.

The dangerous *traversée* of the child's game is replayed in Sand's first novel, *Indiana* (1831).[12] Like many of Sand's heroines, including Thérèse and Consuelo (chapter 3), Indiana is the figure of a woman searching for a position from which to write desire and to desire writing. Like many women writers before her, Sand tells two stories in *Indiana,* a romance and a story of writing. Sand revealed her intention in writing *Indiana* in the Preface to the 1842 edition in which she writes that the novel's purpose is to show "le rapport mal établi entre les sexes" (the poorly established relationship between the sexes) (2), words that remind us of Lacan's pithy representation of the nature and the problem of desire, "il n'y a pas de rapport sexuel" (there is no sexual relation). Sand blames society and social constructions of sexual difference for the unsuitable and intolerable situation that makes the expression "heterosexual love" an oxymoron. Sand's first novel resembles a *Bildungsroman* in that the heroine has many lessons to learn before moving beyond the two traditional stories of heterosexual relationships available to women writers, the marriage plot and the romance plot.

The first lesson, and an example of Sand's subversion of the simple binary split that marks self-difference in writing by men, involves an exchange of female identities. The relationship between Indiana and Noun, her maid, at first seems to be an example of a conventional use of literary doubles to represent the split image of Woman, the inaccessible, aristocratic lady and the sexually available servant. The doubling of Indiana and Noun is not a case of simple binarism, however, but a complex image of the double splitting of a woman writer's subjectivity. Noun's name, which in English means the name of a thing, a signifier, a substitute for the thing itself, is just one example in the novel of Sand's penchant for bilingual wordplay. Indiana, creole by birth, achieves social position through her marriage to the Frenchman, Delmare. Her servant Noun, also her *soeur de lait* (nursed at the same breast), is, on the other hand, a creole without social position. Indiana and Noun represent Sand's split heritage; her father was an aristocrat and her mother the descendant of bird sellers on the *quais* of the river Seine. The account, early in the novel, of Noun's suicide by drowning in the river on Indiana's property marks a nexus of autobiography and fiction. Noun's death in the river is the realization of the child Aurore's fear of getting wet. Indiana's survival, on the other hand, both as a heroine and the name of a novel, is the realization of the creative child's desire to cross over in spite of her fear that her skirt will be ruined. Noun's reasons for taking her life are related in the novel's first chapters during which we learn that she has been having an affair with Raymon, the novel's Lovelace, with whom Indiana also falls in love, and who will eventually drive the mistress, like the maid, to the river's edge.

In the novel's most explicitly erotic scene, played out between the characters Noun and Raymon, but with Indiana figured as the true object of Raymon's desire, he sees a double image of the two women reflected in a mirror:

Les deux panneaux de glace qui se renvoyaient l'un à l'autre l'image de
Noun jusqu'à l'infini semblaient se peupler de mille fantômes. Il épiait dans
la profondeur de cette double réverbération une forme plus déliée, et il lui
semblait saisir, dans la dernière ombre vaporeuse et confuse que Noun y
reflétait, la taille fine et souple de Madame Delmare. (82)

*(The two mirrored panels which reflected Noun's image from one to the other to
infinity, seemed inhabited by a thousand phantoms. In the depths of this double
reflection he recognized a more slender form, and in the last dim, blurred shadow of
Noun's reflection, he imagined he could grasp the slender, willowy form of Madame
Delmare.)*

This scene, which establishes that Indiana and Noun are doubles, mirror
images of the chimeric qualities of the Romantic heroine, is followed
immediately by Noun's suicide. Here, Sand exploits the convention of the
double for narrative experimentation in a scene, which, like several others,
alludes to the childhood game of "crossing the river." Sand describes
Indiana's actions, "elle se laissa tombée sur le gazon, encore blanchi par la
gelée du matin au bord de la petite rivière qui traversait le parc" (she let
herself fall down onto the grass, still white with morning frost, on the bank
of the little river that traversed the park) (98). Hypnotized by the rapidly
flowing water, she is drawn to the river's edge where she sees female clothing in the water. At first she recognizes the clothing but nothing else, and
the way in which the scene is narrated suggests that Indiana is seeing her
own reflection, self and other in a single image. But what she sees is Noun's
body floating in the river, not an uncomplicated mirror image à la Narcissus, but rather a grotesque parody of the myth of Ophelia—confirmed later
in the novel when Indiana's beloved dog, named Ophelia, dies in the same
manner (292). The myth of a writer's self-difference is cleverly glossed to
reveal an uneasy truth—a male writer's self-difference is often represented
by a dead woman. Ophelia and Narcissus combine in nineteenth-century
Romantic art; the image that Narcissus falls in love with becomes a separate
creature, a woman who exists outside of the poet in order to represent his
self-difference and to perish in his stead in the abyss of the sublime. Indiana
loses consciousness at the sight of Noun's body floating in the river; within
the same frame, Indiana is unconscious and Noun is dead. Indiana will,
however, eventually awaken to consciousness and to the recognition of the
dangerous appeal of the Ophelia role for women who desire heterosexual
romance. This subjectivity will allow Indiana to live to tell Noun's story to
the novel's narrator.[13]

Although *Indiana* is not read as frequently as Flaubert's *Madame Bovary*
today, Sand's novel, which tells the story of a bored bourgeois wife who has

a tragic adulterous affair with a Romantic hero and attempts suicide, is a significant precursor to Flaubert's Emma Bovary, a woman ruined by reading.
Sand's novel differs from Flaubert's in that Indiana, whose lover Raymon
accuses her of having read too many novels, survives (245). Like Madame de
Lafayette before her, Sand writes her heroine out of the traditional narrative
role as the object of desire, whereas Flaubert's heroine dies with a mirror in
her hand. The doubling of Noun and Indiana is central to Sand's subversion
of the romantic heroine, and Noun's death represents a powerful critique of
the Ophelia complex.

The novel's opening chapter establishes Indiana as a woman in search of
a voice. She already possesses what Naginski calls "a language of resistance," able to articulate her desire for liberation from her husband,
Delmare, whose language Naginski characterizes as "nothing more than a
pastiche of patriarchal power in marriage" (71; 64).[14] Delmare speaks in
clichés: "Qui est donc le maître ici, de vous ou de moi? Qui porte une jupe
et doit filer une quenouille. Pretendez-vous m'ôter la barbe du menton . . .
femmelette (Who is the master here, you or me? Who wears a skirt and
spins yarn. Do you think you can take my beard away from me, little lady);
and he also declares that, "les femmes sont faites pour obéir" (women are
made to obey) (233; 201). Indiana responds:

> Je sais que je suis l'esclave et vous le seigneur. La loi de ce pays vous a fait
> mon maître. Vous pouvez lier mon corps, garrotter mes mains, gouverner
> mes actions. Vous avez le droit du plus fort, et la société vous le confirme;
> mais sur ma volonté, Monsieur, vous ne pouvez rien. . . . Vous pouvez me
> commander, mais je n'obéirai jamais qu'à moi-même. (233–35)

> *(I know that I am the slave, and you are the lord. The law of this country has
> made you my master. You can tie up my body, shackle my hands, control my
> actions. You enjoy the right of the mighty, and society confirms it; but you cannot
> control my will, Sir. . . . You can command me, but I will never obey anyone but
> myself.)*

However quick-witted Indiana's responses to Delmare's patriarchal formulas might be, she is not yet able to distinguish between desire for agency and
desire to be desired. Her idea of freedom from the marriage plot is dictated
by the romance plot; she dreams of a liberator:

> Un jour viendra où tout sera changé dans ma vie, où je ferai du bien aux
> autres; un jour où l'on m'aimera, où je donnerai tout mon coeur à celui qui
> me donnera le sien; en attendant, souffrons. Taisons-nous, et gardons notre
> amour pour récompense à qui me délivrera. (64)

(The day will come when everything will change in my life, when I will do good for others; a day when I will be loved, when I will give my heart entirely to one who will give me his; in the meantime, we will suffer. Let us keep quiet, and save our love as the reward for he who will liberate me.)

Seduced by romantic clichés, Indiana sees Raymon as the liberator she seeks. Raymon is so skilled in the language of seduction that, as Sand writes with lovely irony, he even seduces himself:

En parlant ainsi Raymon s'exalta peu à peu, comme il avait coutume de faire en *plaidant* ses passions. La situation était puissante, romanesque; elle offrait des dangers. Raymon aimait le péril en véritable descendant d'une race de preux. (220)

(By speaking this way, Raymon became more and more excited, as he always did when he was pleading the cause of his passions. The situation was powerful, romantic—dangerous. Like a true descendent of the class of "preux," Raymon loved danger.)

Sand's ironic intent is contained in the word *preux*. The knight-lovers of troubadour poetry were called *preux,* a single word for an entire repertoire of chivalric qualities, a word that has disappeared from modern French usage—with the pertinent exception of Rousseau's hero, Saint-Preux (see chapter 3).

Flaubert's Emma Bovary falls in love with romantic clichéd language; she yearns to join "la légion lyrique de ces femmes adultères" (the lyrical legions of adulterous women) the heroines of the novels she had read (Flaubert 198). Twenty years earlier, Sand had written ironically that the heroine is not the only one seduced by a romantic hero's line. The man who uses romantic clichés to seduce impressionable women, arouses his own passion:

A force de réfléchir à son projet de séduction, il s'était passionné comme un auteur pour son sujet, comme un avocat pour sa cause, et l'on pourrait comparer l'émotion qu'il éprouva en voyant Indiana, à celle d'un acteur bien pénétré de son rôle, qui se trouve en présence du principal personnage du drame et ne distingue plus les impressions factices de la scène d'avec la réalité. (129)

(By thinking about his seduction plan, he had become passionate about it like an author for his subject or a lawyer for his case, and the emotion he felt when he saw Indiana might be compared to that of an actor engrossed in his role, who, when he finds himself confronted with the principal character in the play, can no longer distinguish between the illusions created on stage and reality.)

When she herself begins to write, Indiana begins to formulate a critique of the love narrative, a form that Raymon alternatively exploits or criticizes as it suits his purpose. Her "coming to writing" begins with a letter to Raymon in which she writes:

> C'est que j'étais folle; c'est que, selon votre expression cynique, j'avais appris la vie dans les romans à usage des femmes de chambre, dans ces riantes et puériles fictions où l'on intéresse le coeur au succès de folles entreprises et d'impossibles félicités. (250)

> *(It's that I was mad; according to your cynical expression I had learned about life from novels written for chambermaids, from those gay, childish works of fiction that inspire the heart to wish for the success of wild enterprises and impossible felicities.)*

Nancy K. Miller reads this letter as a challenge to the grounds of Raymon's literary judgment ("Arachnologies" [1986] 279). And it is not the only example of such a challenge. Noun writes a love letter to Raymon, which the reader does not read, and that Raymon does not finish reading because he is disgusted by the errors in grammar and spelling,

> Mais l'orthographe! Savez-vous bien ce qu'une syllabe de plus ou moins ôte ou donne d'énergie aux sentiments? Hélas, la pauvre fille à demi sauvage de l'île de Bourbon ignorait même qu'il y eût des règles à la langue. (49)

> *(But the spelling! Are you aware what a syllable more or less adds or detracts from the strength of feelings? Alas, the poor uncivilized girl from the Island of Bourbon did not even know that language had rules.)*

The narrator does not let Raymon's critique of Noun's writing slip by without comment, "c'était peut-être un chef-d'oeuvre de passion naïve et gracieuse" (it was perhaps a masterpiece of naive, delightful passion) (49).

Because what Raymon seeks is not an actual woman, but the representation of Woman in the clichéd tradition that is his standard, he is stupidly ruled by conventional structures of desire. He ceases to desire Indiana when she offers to leave her husband for him, thereby removing the desired obstacle, "Il aimait les obstacles, mais il reculait devant les ennuis" (He liked obstacles, but he withdrew in the face of annoyances) (195). Humiliated and rejected by Raymon, described as bored with "une intrigue épuisée" (a worn out plot), Indiana walks to the river's edge intending to kill herself (202). Once again, the scene is described in the language of the childhood game, "mais elle oublia de traverser le pont; et continua à longer la rivière absorbée dans une rêverie stupide. . . . elle s'était fait du suicide une sorte de volupté tentatrice" (but she forgot to cross the bridge; and continued to walk along the river absorbed in a stupid reverie. . . . suicide seemed to have a voluptuous appeal) (227). As in the game, cold water on her feet startles her and *jouissance*—in this case, death—is interrupted, not by the mother this time, but by Ralph. Although Ralph is present in the novel from the opening scene, his character's narrative function is enigmatic and underplayed until the two plots that prepare the reader to understand his role are played out: the bourgeois marriage plot and the romantic love plot. Once Delmare is dead, and Raymon is married, the reticent Ralph will move into position as the most important player in Sand's version of the story of desire . . . and of writing.

From the first page of the novel, Ralph's role exists outside traditional narrative structures. This is due primarily, it would seem, to the fact that unlike the traditional romance plot, the protagonist of *Indiana* is a woman, whose self-difference will eventually be represented by a man, not a woman. But, as I have shown, because of the *troubadour effect* in fictions of heterosexual desire, the gender shift is not a shift at all, but simply the second step of a woman writer's double move into the writing position. In *Indiana,* as in the tradition in general, the voice of *joi* is a feminine voice that emanates from a man's body.[15] Indiana does not merely "acquire a bridegroom rather than a bride" (Crecelius [1987] 60). The bridegroom, Ralph, is not a male version of the romantic heroine, the "Not I" of the romantic artist/lover. And although he lives with Indiana and Delmare in a pastiche of a Rousseauian *ménage à trois,* he is by no means a traditional romantic lover. Ralph does not possess the facility with the language of romance, which has been an integral part of the literary figure of the romantic lover since Tristan played the harp and sang a song of love and death in King Mark's court:

> Ralph avait si peu le talent de la persuasion, il était si candide, si mal-adroit. . . . Sa franchise était si raboteuse, sa logique si aride, ses principes si absolus! Il ne ménageait personne, il n'adoucissait aucune vérité. (157–58)

> *(He had so little talent for persuasion, he was so frank, so awkward. . . . his out-spokenness was so rough, his logic so dry, his principles so absolute. He manipulated no one, he did not soften the truth.)*

On the contrary, he is described as silent and brooding, unattractive really, a "crétin sans intelligence et sans voix" (cretin without intelligence and without a voice) (341). His lack of facility with the language of the literary establishment is later revealed as a virtue, the mark of his difference from

THE OLD TROUBADOUR: GEORGE SAND

Raymon (328). Ralph proves to be the true love poet, in search of truth and transcendence—an "old" troubadour—unlike Raymon who has transformed love's language into the discourse of seduction. Ralph does not even like novels—"il n'aime pas les romans" (128). He does not possess the language that ruins women like Indiana and Emma Bovary.[16] Because of this deficiency, however, he is not easily recognizable as a lover, rendering his relationship to Indiana unrepresentable within prevailing conventions of sexual difference in narratives of romantic love. Their relationship does conform, however, to Romantic poetics. The difference here is that the protagonist (and the writer) is a woman whose heroine's desire to represent self-difference is cast in precisely the same pattern of gender distribution as when the writer is a man. The gender trouble of the *troubadour effect* for a woman artist is revealed in *Indiana* as clearly as it was in *Elle et lui,* but differently.

Twice, Ralph saves Indiana from carrying the role of Ophelia in the romance plot to its traditional resolution. This does not mean, however, that *Indiana* is not a Romantic text, and as such preoccupied with the desire for the Infinite. Ralph's declaration of love for Indiana, which comes in Part IV of the novel, combines the discovery of a poetic voice with a *Liebestod,* a suicide pact between the two characters. In keeping with Romantic theory, Ralph's function in *Indiana,* as described by Naginski, is exemplary of a writer's transcendence:

> Originally lacking both skill or elegance in his manner of speaking, laconic and lackluster in his correspondence, he undergoes a linguistic metamorphosis that constitutes the crucial episode of the book. Significantly, Ralph's transformation into a poet-philosopher is as brusque and unexplained in the novel as Sand's own transmutation into a novelist, a parallel that helps shed light on his key role in the novel as the figure around whom so much of the plot crystallizes. (GS 67)

Ralph's transcendence conforms to another Romantic convention; it is effected through fusionary love for Indiana, symbolized by a suicide pact. Indiana agrees to the pact in the following words, "J'ai toujours été attirée vers le bord des eaux par une sympathie invincible, par le souvenir de ma pauvre Noun" (I have always been attracted to the water's edge by an invincible feeling, by the memory of my poor Noun) (323). The substitutions and the doubling between the autobiography and the first novel have come full circle with the mention of Noun at the water's edge. The game's language emerges in the conversation between Indiana and Ralph about the fatal trip. This time the fear of crossing over is gone, and Sand describes the trip in the following way, "jamais traversée ne fut si heureuse" (Never had a crossing been so happy) (323). The tone of the novel changes when Ralph and Indiana return together to the Island of Bourbon, where they lived as children, resolved to die together.

Sand rewrites the romantic plot yet again in the novel's conclusion. Because of a trick, equally theatrical as the one that brought Consuelo's husband, Albert, back to life as Liverani in a fictional cave in *Consuelo,* Ralph and Indiana do not die when they jump into the cave's analogue, Bourbon's Bernica Falls. The final chapter of *Indiana* ends when Ralph takes Indiana into his arms and they plunge together into the torrent. The fusionary *Liebestod* of Indiana and Ralph is, however, as much an illusion as the marriage of Consuelo and Albert performed according the rites of the "Invisibles." The conventional ending is followed by an appended conclusion in which the narrator tells how he met Indiana and Ralph on a deserted spot on the highest part of the Island of Bourbon. There, the couple, miraculously saved from death by the Romantic figure of a blonde, blue-eyed angel in a white robe with a golden belt, fills the narrator in on their lives since the failed suicide attempt. In short, like Consuelo and Liverani/Albert, Indiana and Ralph live together in a literary utopia, far from society and its laws, especially those concerning marriage. The Romantic cliché of fusionary love in paradise—the goal of the *Liebestod*—is intimately connected with the discovery of Ralph's voice. For Ralph, not Indiana, is the voice of *joi* at the end of the novel, "Son âme, longtemps roidie contre la douleur, s'amollit à la chaleur vivifiante de l'espérance. Le ciel descendit aussi dans ce coeur amer et froissé. Ses paroles prirent l'empreinte de ses sentiments" (His soul, which had been hardened against pain for such a long time, softened with the revitalizing warmth of hope. Heaven penetrated into his bitter and bruised heart. His words began to express his feelings) (324). Ralph's encounter with the Infinite brings the gift of language, the poet's greatest desire, the plenitude of subjectivity—*joi*. The moment of poetic revelation is cast in typical Romantic language as fusion with the feminine:

Une ardente sympathie religieuse l'initiait aux mêmes émotions; des larmes d'enthousiasme coulèrent de ses yeux sur les cheveux de Ralph. Alors la lune se trouva au-dessus de la cime du grand palmiste, et son rayon, pénétrant l'interstice des lianes, enveloppa Indiana d'un éclat pâle et humide qui la faisait ressembler, avec sa robe blanche et ses longs cheveux tressés sur ses épaules, à l'ombre de quelque vierge égarée dans le désert. (329)

(A profound religious affinity allowed her to experience the same emotions [as Ralph]; tears of compassion flowed from her eyes onto Ralph's hair. Then the moon

rose above the top of the tall palm tree, and its rays, shining through the interstices of the leaves, bathed Indiana in a light that made her in sheer white dress and long hair falling over her shoulders, look like the phantom of a virgin maid wandering about in the desert.)

The recurring image of a phantom marks a narrative event similar to those it has signaled before (i.e., the disappearance of one of Indiana's selves), sometimes represented as her double as in the case of Noun. When this last ghost disappears, it leaves behind a newly-discovered poetic voice, albeit Ralph's. Sand writes:

Le feu sacré qui dormait ignoré au fond de ses entrailles fit jaillir sa vive lumière. La première fois que cette conscience rigide se trouva délivrée de ses craintes et de ses liens, la parole vint d'elle-même au secours de la pensée, et l'homme médiocre qui n'avait dit dans toute sa vie que des choses communes, devint à sa dernière heure éloquent et persuasif comme jamais ne l'avait été Raymon. . . . Il est des instants d'exaltation et d'extase où nos pensées s'épurent, se subtilisent, s'éthèrent en quelque sorte. Ces rares instants nous élèvent si haut, nous emportent si loin de nous-mêmes, qu'en retombant sur la terre nous perdons la conscience et le souvenir de cette ivresse intellectuelle. . . . Qui peut nous raconter les rêves du poète avant qu'il se soit refroidi à nous les écrire? (328–29)

(The bright light of the sacred fire shot up after having lain dormant and unknown in the depths of his [Ralph's] being. The first time his strict conscience was freed from its fears and restrictions, words came spontaneously to the aid of his thoughts and, in his final hour, the ordinary man who, his whole life, had uttered only banalities became more eloquent and persuasive than Raymon had ever been. . . . There are moments of exaltation and ecstasy when our thoughts become, in a way, more pure, more subtle, more ethereal. These rare moments raise us up so high, carry us so far out of ourselves, that when we fall back to earth we lose the consciousness and the memory of that intellectual intoxication. . . . Who can relate the dreams of the poet before his emotion has cooled down so that he can write them?)

Words with which Sand describes her own intoxication with language in *Histoire de ma vie* resound in the description of Ralph's discovery of a voice. In the autobiography, she writes, "Je ne crois pas que rien puisse être comparé, dans la suite de notre vie intellectuelle, à ces premières jouissances de l'imagination" (I don't believe anything compares, in the rest of our intellectual life, with those first *jouissances* of the imagination) (*OA*, I: 618).

In Romantic narrative, the sex of the writing self is less important than the gender of the writing position. Because Romantic narrative depends so heavily on the heterosexual romance plot, however, that "something" that is "no thing,"—pace Shakespeare—becomes important. As noted earlier in reference to Shakespeare's sonnet XX, sexual difference is rendered unimportant in writing by men because the poet and the hero, through the power of representation, become women. Shakespeare's "master-mistress" represents the absence and the presence of sexual difference in a single term signifying the myth of androgynous fusion. In the sonnet, both the feminine and the masculine, however, are qualities found exclusively in males—in the poet and the beautiful boy. Actual women are "false women," female impersonators. The absence of the phallic "thing," in male writing, playfully veiled in Shakespeare's sonnet, signifies male self-difference; it is *literally* "nothing" in a woman. For this reason, in this tradition, female self-difference is quite literally unrepresentable.

In *Portrait of a Lady,* a novel whose language evokes *Indiana,* Henry James encodes Indiana's name in the name of his heroine, Isabelle Archer (I/Diana, the archer, goddess of the hunt) and Ralph Brown's name becomes Ralph Touchett (note the Franco/Anglo crossing-over of the two Ralph's surnames). Playing a similar role to Ralph Brown's in *Indiana,* Ralph Touchett is the character in *Portrait* who truly knows Isabelle. His words to his cousin, who has been caught up in both the romance plot and the marriage plot, sum up the dilemma central to Sand's fiction, "You wanted to look at life for yourself, but you were not allowed: you were punished for your wish. You were ground in the very mill of the conventional" (577).

This realization is at the heart of *Lélia* (1833), Sand's most abstractly theoretical critique of the Romantic myth of male self-difference *qua* sexual difference and the most explicit statement of *vagabondage* in Sand's major novels. The novel has been criticized as having no plot.[17] The novel's plot, I would argue, is the *vagabondage* plot: a woman's desire to write is an obstacle to heterosexual desire, and vice versa. Lélia, the heroine of the first novel signed with the full pseudonym, George Sand, is a poet. The first part of the novel is mostly a conventional exchange of letters between the romantic hero Sténio, and Lélia, the woman poet he desires. Sténio laments Lélia's coldness towards him, and in this sense, the novel begins in much the same way as *Elle et lui:* a romantic hero-artist laments the obstacles—created by the woman in question—to the fulfillment of his desire, which is to possess her. In both novels, the woman is also an artist—one might say that *Lélia,* a name which joins masculine (le) and feminine (la) signifiers in French, is the prototitle of *Elle et lui.*

The first time Lélia's physical appearance is described in detail in the novel, she is dressed in male attire for a masked ball, "elle avait le vêtement austère et pourtant recherché, la pâleur, la gravité, le regard profond d'un jeune poëte d'autrefois" (she had the austere and yet carefully chosen clothing, the palor, the seriousness, the deep gaze of a young poet from another age) (I: 100–1). The "old troubadour" insists on the description of Lélia's aura. The problem that plagues Lélia throughout the novel, the conflict between her masculine ambitions and her heterosexuality, is played out in the description of how the novel's protagonists, Sténio and Trenmor, see Lélia as they gaze at her in the same scene:

> Regardez Lélia . . . regardez . . . cette beauté physique qui suffirait pour constater une grande puissance, et que Dieu s'est plu à revêtir de toute la puissance intellectuelle de notre époque! . . . Peut-on imaginer quelque chose de plus complet que Lélia vêtue, posée et rêvant ainsi? C'est le marbre sans tache de Galatée, avec le regard chaste du Tasse, avec le sourire sombre d'Alighieri. C'est l'attitude aisée et chevaleresque des jeunes héros de Shakespeare: c'est Roméo, le poétique amoureux; c'est Hamlet, le pâle et ascétique visionnaire; c'est Juliette, Juliette demi-morte, cachant dans son sein le poison souvenir d'un amour brisé . . . Le jeune Raphaël devait tomber dans cette contemplation extatique, lorsque Dieu lui faisait apparaître une virginale idéalité de femme . . . Lélia réunit toutes ces idéalités, parce qu'elle réunit le génie de tous les poëtes, la grandeur de tous les héroïsmes. Vous pouvez donner tous ces noms à Lélia . . . (I: 102–03)

> (Look at Lélia . . . look at that physical beauty that would suffice to give her enormous power, and that God deigned to invest with all the intellectual power of our age! . . . Can one imagine anything more complete than Lélia dressed, standing and dreaming like that? It is Galatea's pure white marble, with Tasso's celestial gaze, with the solemn smile of Alighieri. It is the easy and chivalric attitude of Shakespeare's youthful heroes; it is Romeo, the amorous poet, it is Hamlet, the pale ascetic visionary; it is Juliet, a half-dead Juliet, hiding the poison of a broken love in her heart. . . . The young Raphael must have fallen into such a state of ecstatic contemplation when God revealed to him the virginal ideal image of woman. . . . Lélia unites all these ideals, because she unites the genius of all poets and the nobility of heroism.)

Lélia is both Romeo and Juliet, both Raphael and the women he painted; she is the artist and the artist's self-difference in a single ideal image. Because Lélia is a woman, she cannot represent the perfect fusion of "I" and "Not I" in the Romantic ideal of the artist; she cannot represent autonomous subjectivity. Rather, the portrait of Lélia is constructed by and under the gaze of Sténio and Trenmor, men who desire her. Their praise of her physical beauty and intellectual power is not unmitigated; she is flawed because of the very perfection that attracts them to her. In their eyes, she is unable to love; she cannot love because she does not love in a way that conforms to their received idea of Woman:

Lélia n'est pas un être complet. C'est un rêve tel que l'homme peut en créer, gracieux, sublime, mais où il manque quelque chose d'inconnu, quelque chose qui n'a pas de nom . . . l'amour Lélia ne l'a pas. Que'est-ce que donc que Lélia? Une ombre, un rêve, une idée tout au plus. Allez, là où il n'y a pas d'amour, il n'y a pas de femme. (I: 104–05)

(Lélia is not a complete being. She is a dream created by man, gracious, sublime, but where something unknown is missing, something which has no name. . . . Lélia does not have love. What is Lélia then? A shadow, a dream, an idea at best. Listen, where there is no love, there is no woman.)

Sténio and Trenmore repeat *Elle et lui*'s Laurent's complaint about Thérèse: he wants her to combine all of the qualities of beauty and intelligence which represent, as in a shadow or a dream, the artist's self-image, and at the same time be willing to deny her own artistic ambitions for the sake of love. The men in these novels do not hesitate, however, to criticize women who, unlike Lélia, play the role ordained for them by society's conventions; such women are unworthy of a man's love. The double bind of *Fin'Amors,* and the paradox of the *asag* are never more present than when the woman in question is herself an artist. The truth of the matter is that Lélia cannot love because she cannot find a man to satisfy both her artistic quest for the Infinite and her sexual passion. As signified by her double-gendered pseudonym, Lélia is in the position of both the male artist (le) and of feminine self-difference (la). It is the revelation that Lélia "could not love," taken literally, that created the scandal surrounding Sand's novel; Lélia's *vagabondage* was read as a confession on Sand's part of either frigidity or lesbianism.[18] Sand herself uses the word "vagabond" to describe Lélia's suffering:

Qu'est-ce que cette ame [sic] que vous m'avez donnée? Est-ce là ce qu'on appelle une ame [sic] de poëte? Plus mobile que la lumière et plus *vagabonde* que le vent, toujours avide, toujours inquiète, toujours haletante, toujours cherchant en dehors d'elle les alimens de sa durée et les épuisant tous avant de les avoir seulement goûtés! O vie, ô tourment! tout aspirer et ne rien saisir, tout comprendre et ne rien posséder! (emphasis added) (I: 225)

(What is this soul you have given me? Is this what they call the soul of a poet? More changeable than light and more vagabond *than the wind, always thirsty, always unsettled, always gasping for breath, always seeking outside of herself for lasting nourishment and always exhausting the source before having truly drunk from it! Oh life, oh torment, to aspire to everything and to achieve nothing, to understand everything and to possess nothing.)*

Sand states the sexual problem engendered by *vagabondage* abstractly but succinctly on the first page of Part III, often called "scandalous" by her critics, in which Lélia tells her sister, Pulchérie, that because of her desire for poetry she is "rendu impuissant par trop de puissance peut-être!" (rendered impotent [Sand uses masculine form of adjectives] by too much power perhaps!) (1). The discussion becomes explicitly erotic in a conversation between Lélia and Pulchérie that takes place at the river's edge, recalling the structurally analogous scenes in *Indiana* and *Histoire de ma vie*. As in the previously discussed river-crossing scenes, the scene tells once again, but in a different way, the story of how women's writing challenges the simple binary split subject of traditional representations of self-difference. The structure of the game replicates the desire for the inaccessible feminine as self-difference, and for access to the symbolic order; it replicates the search for a strategy to cross over into a position from which a woman can write self-difference. The split subject is represented in *Lélia* by the doubling of the biological sisters, Pulchérie and Lélia, reminiscent of the doubling of the adopted sisters, Noun and Indiana. The name, Pulchérie, beauty, establishes the subject's identification with the body in the form of a pleasure-loving courtesan. The name, Lélia, establishes the subject's identification with the double gender (le/la) of the poetic, androgynous mind in the form of a woman poet who suffers from the malady of the century's male poets, *le mal du siècle,* the disease named by Sand's lover, the poet Musset in *Confessions d'un enfant du siècle.*

After years of separation due to their different life styles, Pulchérie and Lélia meet again and, during the course of a conversation about their lives since their last meeting, they remember a summer day in their youth when they were drawn to the river's edge. Although it is Lélia who first recalls the moment, it becomes the occasion for Pulchérie to elaborate one of, if not *the,* richest expressions of the double feminine of desire in Romantic literature. Sand's text is more erotically explicit, for example, than Rousseau's treatment of the subject in the relationship between Claire and Julie. More important, Sand is clearly aware of the sapphic implications of the myth of sexual difference in romantic love, whereas Rousseau was as confused as his characters about the nature of their desire. As the scene begins, Lélia speaks:

Vous souvient-il de ce jour d'été, si lourd et si chaud, où nous nous arrêtâmes au bord du ruisseau . . . Nous nous entendîmes sur le gazon, et tout en regardant le ciel ardent sur nos têtes au travers des arbres, il nous vint un lourd sommeil, une profonde insousiance. Nous nous éveillâmes dans les bras l'une de l'autre sans nous être senti dormir. (I: 342–343)

(Are you reminded of that summer day, so heavy and hot, when we stopped by the edge of the stream. . . . We stretched out on the grass and while gazing at the blazing sky overhead through the trees, a heavy sleepiness and lethargy came over us. When we woke up in each other's arms, we were unaware of having slept.)

The *mise en scène* replicates the dreamy hallucinatory state associated with the river's edge in the autobiography. In this case, Pulchérie's dream is spotlighted, the side of the split-subject featured is not the budding novelist in search of the inaccessible feminine, but the sensual girl who identifies with the feminine; Sophie represents the feminine object in the "crossing the river" scene in *Histoire de ma vie*. Pulchérie reveals feelings to Lélia that she (Pulchérie) has repressed for years:

j'y ai pensé souvent avec une émotion pleine de charme, et peut-être de honte . . . je rêvai tout simplement d'un homme aux cheveux noirs qui se penchait vers moi pour effleurer mes lèvres des ses lèvres chaudes et vermeilles; et je m'éveillai oppressée, palpitante, heureuse plus que je ne m'étais imaginé devoir l'être jamais . . . Je vous regardais alors. O ma soeur, que vous étiez belle! Je ne vous avais jamais trouvée telle avant ce jour-là. Oh! vous étiez belle, Lélia! mais belle autrement que moi, et cela me troublait étrangement . . . il y avait je ne sais quoi de masculin et fort qui m'empêchait presque de vous reconnaître . . . Je recevais de la nature et de Dieu . . . ma première sensation de désir . . . Est-ce que vous ne vous souvenez pas de mon trouble et de mon rougeur? (I: 343–345)

(I think about it often with an emotion wrought with charm, and perhaps with shame. . . . I simply dreamt of a man with black hair who leaned over me to touch my lips with his own warm, flushed lips. I woke up overwhelmed, quivering, happier than I had ever imagined I could be . . . then I looked at you. Oh, my sister, you were so beautiful! I had never found you as beautiful as I did that day . . . Oh, you were beautiful, Lélia! but beautiful in a different way than me, and that troubled me strangely . . . there was something masculine and strong in the proud and cold expression on your sleeping face, which made you almost unrecognizable. . . . I received from Nature and from God . . . my first feeling of desire.)

Lélia is described as having black hair and large black eyes in the novel. The man with black hair who leans over Pulchérie to kiss her is Lélia in the guise of a male poet. Given the structure of the split subject, Pulchérie represents a woman's desire to be the object of the romantic poet's desire—the lady of troubadour poetry. Because the poet is a woman, Lélia, the desire to be the object of her sister's desire fills Pulchérie with shame; her desire—as figured in the conventional structure—is incestuous and lesbian. Pulchérie's desire is not literal, of course, that is to say, it is written as an ambiguous affirmation of lesbian desire.[19] As in previous replays of the river scene, the figure of a double appears in the water, but with a difference that can be seen in the following short exchange between the sisters:

> Vous me fîtes pencher sur l'eau, et vous me dîtes—Regarde-toi, ma soeur: ne te trouves-tu pas belle?—Je vous répondis que je l'étais moins que vous.— Oh! tu l'es bien davantage, reprîtes-vous. Tu ressembles à un homme. (I: 342–349)

> *(You made me bend over and look at myself in the water. "Don't you find yourself beautiful?" you said. I answered that I was not as beautiful as you. "You are more beautiful," you said. "You look like a man.")*

Pulchérie's shame, and her need to heterosexualize her desire for Lélia is a prelude to Lélia's own confession to her sister that she envies her ability to feel sexual passion, something that Lélia has never known. Pulchérie was initiated into a life of (hetero)sexual passion on that hot summer day when she fell in love with her sister, imagining that her sister was a man who desired her. What Lélia herself sees when she looks in the water, however, is a woman who is not desirable—to a man. The only position available to her is that of the vagabond, "toujours avide, toujours inquiète, toujours haletante, toujours cherchant en dehors d'elle les alimens de sa durée et les épuisant tous avant de les avoir seulement goûtés!" (always thirsty, always unsettled, always gasping for breath, always seeking outside of herself for lasting nourishment and always exhausting the source before having truly drunk from it!) (I: 225).[20]

Lélia describes her *vagabondage* to Pulchérie; her sexual problems are directly related to her desire to write:

> La poésie m'avait créé d'autres facultés, immenses, magnifiques, et que rien sur la terre ne devait assouvir. La réalité a trouvé mon âme trop vaste pour y être contenue un instant . . . je ne pouvais être en amour l'égale de per- sonne. La froideur de mes sens me plaçait au-dessous des plus abjectes femmes, l'exaltation de mes pensées m'élevait au-dessus des hommes les plus passionés . . . Mon âme orageuse se plaisait à ce ballottement funeste qui l'u- sait sans fruit et sans retour . . . Il lui fallait des obstacles . . . de grands travaux à poursuivre . . . C'était une carrière, une gloire; homme, j'eusse aimé les combats . . . peut-être l'ambition de régner par l'intelligence, de dominer les autres hommes par des paroles puissantes. Femme, je n'avais qu'une destinée noble sur la terre, c'était d'aimer. (II: 11–18)

(Poetry created other powers in me, immense, magnificent, which nothing on earth could satisfy. My soul was too vast to be contained by reality for an instant. . . . In love I was unable to be the equal of anyone. Because of the coldness of my senses I was beneath the most abject of women, the loftiness of my thoughts raised me above the most passionate men. . . . My stormy soul took pleasure in being tossed about in this deadly way which wore it out with neither fruit, nor return. . . . It [my soul] needed obstacles . . . great works to pursue . . . a career, glory. . . . Had I been a man, I would have enjoyed combat . . . perhaps the desire to rule by my intelligence, to dominate other men with my powerful words. . . . As a woman, I had but one noble destiny on earth, to love.)

Clearly, Lélia cannot represent herself as a man, but because she wants to write, she cannot represent herself as a woman, either. Self-difference is foreclosed to her.

Similar to the hero of the romance plot of *Elle et lui,* the principal male character in *Lélia* is the heroine's rival. Like Lélia, Sténio is a poet; like Laurent, Sténio cannot satisfy the woman he loves because of what Sand calls in *Indiana,* the ill-defined relationship between the sexes. In the 1839 revision of *Lélia,* Sand describes the problem with the relationship between the sexes in what reads as if it were in explicitly feminist terms:

Quel lien autre que celui de la force pourra exister désormais entre celui qui a le droit d'exiger et celle qui n'a pas le droit de refuser? . . . Il n'y a donc pas de véritable association dans l'amour des sexes; car la femme y joue le rôle de l'enfant, et l'heure de l'émancipation ne sonne jamais pour elle. (I: 170–71)

(What relationship, other than that of power, can henceforth exist between he who has the right to exact and she who has no right to refuse? . . . There is no true association in the love between the sexes, because the woman's role is that of the child and the hour of emancipation never rings for her.)

The sexual problem created by the impossibility of mutual love between the sexes in turn creates the appearance of frigidity in women who desire such mutuality. Sténio is depicted as oscillating between male femininity in his guise as a Romantic poet, and brutal, aggressive, selfish virility in his role of heterosexual lover. Like Thérèse in *Elle et lui,* Lélia does not blame Sténio for his inability to love a woman, but blames the social construction of sexual difference, which comes into direct conflict with the ideals of mutual love expressed in literature. Sténio's femininity is established early in the novel, and is a constant theme until his death by suicide, when the character Magnus mistakes the cadaver of the pale, golden-haired young poet for a woman. Lélia prefers a chaste relationship with a feminine romantic hero to what seems to her to be the only alternative, a sexual relationship with an insensitive, selfish lover (II: 28).

Descriptions of sleepy voluptuousness and balmy breezes involving Lélia and Sténio recall Pulchérie's description of the afternoon she and Lélia spent together. In that scene, Lélia, in the role of man-poet, remains asleep, allowing Pulchérie's *jouissance*. In another scene, following it, the sleepy Lélia puts her arm around Sténio, assuming the same position she had in Pulchérie's hallucination, and Sténio awakens (II: 28). Lélia's *jouissance* is interrupted because she has assumed the masculine position with Sténio, a man who is feminine when he writes, and masculine when he is in bed with a woman. Being awakened from a creative dream is a theme that runs through the metaphoric river scenes. In the first scene, Lélia leans over Pulchérie, her double, in a dream that brings pleasure to Pulchérie, for whom the figure of the poet Lélia is interchangeable with that of a romantic male hero. When, in the second scene, Lélia leans over the feminine Sténio, he wakes up and reverts to masculinity, a transformation that destroys her pleasure. This double bind reminds us of Claire's dream of an ideal relationship in *La nouvelle Héloïse,* same-sex friendship imbued with heterosexual fantasy (chapter 3).

In Pulchérie's dream, desire is triangular, there are two women and a man, Lélia's double. Later in the novel, the dream is realized when Sténio mistakes Pulchérie for Lélia and they have sex—echoes of Noun and Raymon's tryst in *Indiana.* Read in conjunction with Pulchérie's dream, the second triangle establishes both Pulchérie and Sténio as Lélia's doubles. Pulchérie stands in for Lélia which allows Sténio to consummate his passion for Lélia; by becoming Lélia, Pulchérie enjoys fusion with the man-woman of her dreams. Lélia remains, by choice, in a state of *vagabondage.*

The erotic double-crossing in *Lélia* is intimately bound up with the impossibility for a woman to both write and enjoy a sexual relationship with a man for whom she represents self-difference. Pulchérie sums up Lélia's problem when she tells her that in order to enjoy sex with Sténio, Lélia should cross-dress ("vous travestir") (II: 97). What Pulchérie suggests is tantamount to female impersonation. The only way for Lélia to enjoy "un plaisir réel" (real pleasure) with a man is to impersonate a woman (II: 97). Sand's depiction of the woman poet's situation, then, is that, as a writer, she is in the position of a man for whom self-difference is male femininity. Sténio expresses his fantasy of Lélia in the following words, "Vous savez bien, Lélia, que je ne voudrais pas une femme seulement. Mais vous, qui êtes Dieu et âme, ne pouvez-vous être femme un seul jour dans mes bras?" (You know, Lélia, that I do not want just a woman. But you, who are God and soul, can't you be a woman in my arms for just one day?) (II: 115).

Pulchérie, a courtesan and Lélia's double, makes her living by doing just such performances of the feminine. She invites Lélia into her world, dressed to resemble Pulchérie, herself. The cross-dressing is so convincing that Sténio, who has a conversation with Lélia disguised as Pulchérie, later mistakes the "real" Pulchérie for Lélia. When they have sex, he is convinced that Lélia has finally behaved like a woman in love. Is it any wonder that *Lélia*'s critics find the sexuality of the novel impossible to comprehend? On the one hand, Lélia represents the vagabond, a woman who chooses writing over the price of sexual pleasure, telling a confused Sténio, "Vous avez confondu le plaisir avec le bonheur" (You have confused pleasure with happiness) (II: 147).[21] On the other hand, disguised as Pulchérie, she enjoys uninhibited sexual pleasure.

If the truth be told about reactions to *Lélia,* Pulchérie's sexual promiscuity is easy to understand, it is Lélia's desire for celibacy that is truly scandalous to the reader who desires the romance plot. It is the scandal of the vagabond to find *joi* in writing and not in being another poet's muse.[22] To further complicate matters, the poet, according to Sand, does not really want his muse to become an actual woman. As Sténio says, "il ne faut pas posséder ce qu'on admire, parce qu'on le souillerait et qu'on n'aurait plus rien à désirer" (one must not possess what one admires, because that would be to sully it, and one would have nothing left to desire) (II: 197). To be without desire is to be without a muse. He sums up his feelings for Lélia in terms that echo the *troubadour effect,* "Je sais aujourd'hui Lélia toute entière, comme si je l'avais possédée; je sais ce qui la faisait si belle, si pure, si divine: c'était moi" (Today I know Lélia completely, as if I had possessed her; I know what made her so beautiful, so pure, so divine: it was me) (II: 293). Sand's poet-lover understands why he is incapable of loving a woman, "femme! tu n'es que mensonge! homme! tu n'es que vanité!" (Woman, you are but a lie, man, you are only vanity) (II: 296). I do not read *Lélia* as a failed experiment in revising the romance plot, but as a prototype, the first fully drawn narrative of the *vagabondage plot*.

Lélia (1833) concludes with a *Liebestod*—or, more accurately, a deconstruction of the classic love-death. The scene is a recreation of the river-crossing, and the *mise en abîme* of sexual cross-overs that make the reader's ride a very bumpy one. In this version, Sténio's suicide doubles Noun's performance of the Ophelia plot. The following is a description of the suicide scene, as discovered by Magnus, a mad priest in love with both Lélia and Sténio:

Magnus retourna au bord du lac . . . A mesure que la lumière augmentait, il crut distinguer à ses pieds des caractères tracés sur le sable. Il se baissa, et lu:

"Magnus, tu diras à Trenmore que j'ai tenu ma parole. Il me retrouvera ici . . ." Après cette inscription, la trace d'un pied, un léger éboulement de sable. . . . Sur un tapis de cresson d'un vert tendre et velouté, dormait pâle et paisible le jeune homme aux yeux bleus. Son regard était attaché au ciel, dont il reflétait encore l'azur dans son cristal immobile, comme l'eau dont la source est tarie, mais dont le bassin est encore plein et limpide. Les pieds de Sténio étaient enterrés dans le sable de la rive . . . (II: 321)

(Magnus returned to the bank of the lake. . . . As the light grew brighter, he thought he could make out letters traced in the sand. He bent down, and read, "Magnus, tell Trenmore that I kept my word. He will find me here . . . ." After the inscription, the trace of a foot, a little hill of sand, then nothing but the steep incline where the dust of the sloped earth held no more prints, and the lake with its water-lilies and a few dark weeds in the white fumes. . . . On a carpet of watercress, green and tender, pale and peaceful slept the young man with blue eyes. His gaze was fixed on the sky, whose azure was reflected in its motionless crystal, like water whose source is impure, but whose basin is still full and clear. Sténio's feet were buried in the sand on the shore.)

In *Indiana,* there are several mentions of Noun's footprints in the sand at the river's edge, prints that recall the frightened feet of the child, Aurore, venturing into the imaginary river in her mother's room. In a major step toward making the connections between the Ophelia plot and the femininity of the male poet, Sand writes the death of Sténio in the language of the Ophelia plot:

Sa tête reposait parmi les fleurs au froid calice qu'un faible vent courbait sur elle. Les longs insectes qui voltigent sur les roseaux étaient venus par centaines se poser sur lui. Les uns s'abreuvaient d'un reste de parfum imprégné à ses cheveux mouillés; d'autres agitaient leurs robes de gaze bleue sur son visage, comme pour en admirer curieusement la beauté, ou pour l'effleurer du vent frais de leurs ailes. C'était un si beau spectacle que cette nature tendre et coquette autour d'un cadavre. (II: 321)

(His head rested among flowers whose cold calyxes the wind bent down over it. Long insects who fly among the weeds had come by the hundreds to hover round him. Some drank the dregs of the perfume with which his wet hair was permeated; others fluttered their blue gauze dresses around his face, as if to curiously admire its beauty, or to gently touch it with the cool breeze of their wings. What a beautiful spectacle it was, tender and coquettish nature attending a corpse.)

There can be no doubt as to Sand's intention to fix the male poet's identity as feminine. When Magnus sees Sténio's body he cries out, "O femme! o beauté!" (Oh woman! oh beauty!) (II: 351). Like Indiana's reaction at seeing Noun's corpse floating in the river at Delmare's estate at Langy, Magnus faints when he discovers Sténio floating in the steaming lake. As if to reinforce the crossovers occurring in the scene, the narrator describes Magnus's reaction, "il perdait courage comme une femme" (He lost courage, like a woman) (II: 323). Sténio is clearly figured as woman in the suicide scene. But what of Lélia? With Sténio's death, Lélia returns to the scene, "une femme errante et seule dans la nuit" (a woman wandering and alone in the night), condemned to wander alone, like a wind off the water, for all eternity, Lélia is love's vagabond (II: 353).

In what I read as an ironic turn at the novel's conclusion, Lélia gazes on Sténio's dead body and says the words that male poets have addressed to the women of their poems since the dawn of heterosexual romance:

Te voilà, comme tu étais alors, frêle adolescent, encore sans vigueur et sans désirs, étranger aux ivresses et aux souffrances de la vie physique. Fiancé de quelque vierge aux ailes d'or, tu n'avais pas encore jeté ton anneau dans les flots orageux de nos passions . . . Tu as bien fait de mourir, Sténio, ta grande âme étouffait dans ce corps délicat et frêle, dans ce monde sans soleil. Nous n'étions pas dignes de toi: tu nous as refusé ton amour, tu nous as retiré tes désirs et tes caresses. Retourne à Dieu, ange fourvoyé dans nos voies impures. Protège-nous, pardonne-nous de ne t'avoir rien donné de ce que tu demandais. C'est que nous étions des hommes et que tu valais mieux que nous. (II: 367)

(There you are, as you once were, frail adolescent, still without vigor and without desires, a stranger to intoxication and to the suffering of the physical life. Fiancé of a golden-winged angel, you had not yet thrown your ring into the stormy sea of our passions. . . . You did well to die, Sténio, your great soul was stifled in that frail and delicate body, in a world without sun. We were not worthy of you: you refused us your love, you took your desires and your caresses away from us. Return to God, angel led astray on our impure paths. Protect us, pardon us for not having given you what you asked for. It is that we were men, and you were better than we are.)

A woman who dares to represent a man as the object of desire the way Lélia represents Sténio as the inaccessible feminine, doomed to die in order to maintain the poet's desire for the Infinite, will be punished. Magnus sees Lélia as a devil, whom he mistook for a woman, and strangles her (II: 379). Sténio and Lélia are buried like Tristan and Iseut in twin tombs; Sand's lovers, however, are buried on opposite banks of the water. In *Lélia,* Sand, in effect, desacralizes the tombs which have haunted romantic love narratives since the twelfth century, appropriating them as a symbol of *vagabondage:*

Les deux flammes mystérieuses se tinrent quelque temps sur le milieu du lac, comme si *elles* eussent eu de la peine à se séparer. Puis *elles* furent chassées toutes deux en sens contraire, comme si *elles* allaient rejoindre chacune la tombe qu'*elle* habitait. (emphasis added) (II: 382)

(Two mysterious flames stayed for a time in the middle of the lake, as if it were diffi-cult for them to separate. Then they were chased in opposite directions, as if each were going to return to the tomb it inhabited.)

In a typical linguistic trick, Sand evokes the double feminine of roman-tic lovers by substituting *"elles"* (feminine they) for *"flammes"* (flame, femi-nine noun in French). In French, but not in the English translation, the passage reads as if it were two women who are seeking fusion, but are chased back to separate tombs. Read as an allegory for a woman seeking to reconcile heterosexual desire and the desire to write, *Lélia* is a bitter cri-tique of a writing process in which a male writer's transcendence depends on the appropriation of a dead woman's identity. The ending of the 1839 version of *Lélia* was changed significantly by Sand to place even more emphasis on Lélia's desire for writing. The change, as I see it, was a direct response to critics who read *Lélia* as a confession of Sand's sexual frigidity. In the version of 1839, Lélia is not murdered; her death scene is trans-formed from one that might occur in a novel more in the mimetic tradi-tion—*Indiana,* for example—to a metaphoric alternative, which better conveys the literary experimentation that characterizes *Lélia*'s form. Before her death, which comes because she is worn out by "l'élan poétique" (poetic fervor), Lélia speaks of her desire:

Depuis dix mille ans j'ai crié dans l'infini: Vérité, vérité! Depuis mille ans, l'infini me répond: Désir, désir! O Sibylle désolée, ô muette pythie, brise donc ta tête aux rochers de ton antre, et mêle ton sang fumant de rage à l'é-ume de la mer car tu crois avoir possédé le Verbe tout-puissant et depuis dix mille ans tu le cherches en vain. (II: 159)

(For ten thousand years I have cried out into the infinite: Truth, truth! For a thou-sand years, the infinite has answered me, Desire, desire! Oh, grieving Sibyl! oh mute Phythis, smash your head against the rocks of your cave, and mingle your blood smol-dering with rage with the foam of the sea, for you think you once possessed the all-powerful Word, and for ten thousand years you have been seeking it in vain.)

The conclusion of the new *Lélia* moves the novel away from the romance plot, which figures the object of poetic desire as a woman (of either sex), and re-figures the object of the poet's desire as writing. The

153

new ending also moves beyond the conclusion of *Indiana* in which Ralph's character is a figure for the poetic voice. In the 1839 version of *Lélia,* a woman poet lives beyond the *Liebestod,* to enjoy, for a brief moment, *jouissance* of an unambiguously female poetic voice—unambiguous in the sense that sexual difference is irrelevant to a woman who must renounce sexual desire in order to enjoy the plenitude of poetic desire.

CHAPTER 5

The Vagabond: A Modern Heroine

And she plunged her pen neck deep in the ink. To her enormous surprise, there was no explosion. She drew the nib out. It
was wet, but not dripping. She wrote. The words were a little
long in coming, but come they did.

—*Virginia Woolf*, Orlando

$\mathcal{R}$ ousseau's autobiography, *The Confessions* (1782–89), is generally
considered to herald the *official* advent into the literary canon of
the sexually ambiguous romantic hero. I underscore "official"
because I am challenging the heterosexuality of the romantic hero in the
literary canon as far back as troubadour lyric poetry and medieval romance.
The heterosexuality of artist-heroes of autobiographical texts by male writers after Rousseau, such as Goethe's *The Sufferings of Young Werther* (1774),
Novalis's *Heinrich von Ofterdingen* (1800), Chateaubriand's *René* (1802),
Constant's *Adolphe* (1816), Byron's *Manfred* (1817), Shelley's *Epipsychidion*
(1821), and Flaubert's ironic portrait of the Romantic artist, *L'Éducation
sentimentale* (*Sentimental Education*) (1869), is explicitly dubious. The
women they yearn for are unavailable, dead, or so unbelievable as to be parodies of femininity fashioned to expose the romantic hero's love of women
either as a great sin, because it involves incestuous desire—or a great joke.[1]
One of the more blatant examples of the ridiculous role women play is
found in Flaubert's *L'Éducation sentimentale* in which Frédéric, the artist-
hero, is overwhelmed with desire for Marie Arnoux—angelic, virtuous, and
married. His desire intensifies when she offers a song as a *divertissement* for
her guests after a dinner party attended by the enamored would-be romantic lover. The passage that describes the effect of Marie's song on Frédéric
begins with what I see as a parody of the voice of pleasure:

> Frédéric ne comprit rien aux paroles italiennes. Cela commençait sur un
> rhythme grave, tel qu'un chant d'église, puis, s'animant crescendo, multipliait
> les éclats sonores, s'apaisait tout à coup; et la mélodie revenait amoureuse-

155

ment, avec une oscillation large et paresseuse. Elle se tenait debout, près du clavier, les bras tombant, le regard perdu. Quelquefois, pour lire la musique, elle clignait ses paupières en avançant le front, un instant. Sa voix de contralto prenait dans les cordes basses une intonation lugubre qui glaçait, et alors sa belle tête, aux grands sourcils, s'inclinait sur son épaule; sa poitrine se gonflait, ses bras s'écartaient, son cou d'où s'échappaient des roulades se renversait mollement comme sous des baisers aériens; elle lança trois notes aiguës, redescendit, en jeta une plus haute encore, et, après un silence, termina par un point d'orgue. (*OC*, II: 26)

(Frédéric did not understand a single one of the Italian words. The song began with a solemn measure, like plain chant; next, growing faster and livelier, it broke into repeated bursts of sound; then it suddenly subsided, and the melody returned tenderly, with a lazy, sweeping lilt.

She stood next to the piano, with her arms by her sides and a faraway look in her eyes. Occasionally she bent her head forward to read the music, blinking her eyes for a moment. In the low notes her contralto voice took on a mournful intonation which had a chilling effect on the listener, and then she leant her lovely head with its great eyebrows towards her shoulder; suddenly she raised it again, with flames in her eyes; her bosom swelled, her arms stretched out, her neck bent slightly as she warbled, as if under ethereal kisses; she sang three piercing notes, came down the scale again, threw out one higher still, and after a moment's silence, finished with a sustained cadence.)

Flaubert's description of Marie Arnoux's musical expression borders on the ludicrous; its excess resonates with Wayne Koestenbaum's description of the vicarious bliss of heterosexual fusion, which, in his version of the voice of pleasure, emanates from the "queen's throat." The scene is an example of what I have called the supplementarity of the voice of pleasure (see Introduction). It is also a pertinent example of an important linguistic phenomenon, inseparable from poetic language, which Julia Kristeva names the *semiotic.*

In "Maternité selon Giovanni Bellini" (Maternity according to Giovanni Bellini from *Polylogue*), Julia Kristeva explains the process and the problem of sublimation in art:

Au carrefour du signe et du rythme, de la représentation et de la lumière, du symbolique et du sémiotique, l'artiste parle à la place où elle n'est pas où elle ne sait pas. Il marque ce qui, en elle, est corps jouissant. . . . Car, par la symbiose de sens et de non-sens, de représentation et de jeu de différences, l'artiste dépose dans le langage et à travers son identification avec la mère . . . , sa jouissance spécifique.

Toutefois, l'homme de l'art occidental explicite mieux que quiconque cette dette de l'artiste au corps maternel et/ou cette arrivée à l'existence symbolique de la maternité—c'est-à-dire la jouissance trans-libidinale, la relève de l'érotisme par le langage de l'art. (*Polylogue* [1977] 414)

*(At the intersection of sign and rhythm, of representation and light, of the symbolic and the semiotic, the artist speaks from a place where she (the woman) is not, where she does not know. He delineates what, in her, is a body experiencing bliss (*un corps jouissant*). . . . Because, through a symbiosis of meaning and nonmeaning, of representation and play of differences, the artist falls into language, and through identification with the mother . . . into his own specific jouissance.*

    Craftsmen of Western art reveal better than anyone else the artist's debt to the maternal body and/or motherhood's entry into symbolic existence—that is, translibidinal jouissance, *eroticism taken over by the language of art.)*

Kristeva's description of desire in art as "éclatant dans le langage, l'embrassant de fond en comble de façon si *singulière* qu'elle défie les *généralisations*" (exploding into language, embracing it from top to bottom in such a *singular* fashion that it defies *generalization*) corresponds very well to Madame Arnoux's song (*Polylogue* 163). Madame Arnoux is the voice of Frédéric's pleasure, his *joi*. She is the *dame* of troubadour lyrics, her voice produces, gives materiality to his desire. Her song represents what Philippe Willemart, writing about Proust's character Swann, calls "la jouissance sans objet" (*jouissance* without an object) (1993). Willemart's reference is to the effect on Swann of the little musical phrase which he associates with Odette in *Swann's Way*, the first volume of Proust's *À la recherche du temps perdu*. His desire mediated by the musical phrase, Swann experiences the plenitude of sexual bliss in Odette's absence. Her presence, on the other hand, is an obstacle to *jouissance* (Willemart, 34).

Kristeva emphasizes throughout her writings that women's access to writing depends on the dissolution of the sexual determination of language. For Kristeva writing is "poetic language," or the *semiotic*, which is different from standard discourse, which she calls the *symbolic* (*La révolution du langage poétique* [1974] 79). Poetic language does not deal rationally with those objects or concepts which words in ordinary discourse seem to encase, but works, consciously or not, with the sounds and rhythms of words.[2]

In my reading of *L'Éducation sentimentale*, two of the structures at the heart of romantic love narratives create desire in Flaubert's hero: *compagnonnage*, ideal male friendship, and the courtly model of mimetic desire, desire shared by a lord and his vassal which is made flesh in the illusive figure of the lady. In *L'Éducation sentimentale*, Flaubert places the theme of Frédéric's enduring love for his male friend, Deslauriers, in contrapuntal relationship to the young artist's illusory and preposterous heterosexual loves. Frédéric is the feminine half of the couple formed by the two friends, "apercevant Deslauriers, Frédéric se mit à trembler comme une femme adultère sous le regard de son époux" (seeing Deslauriers, Frédéric began to tremble like a guilty wife under her husband's gaze) (*OC*, II: 24). Frédéric's heterosexual relationships in the novel, like those in Rousseau's autobiography and fiction, are rendered ambiguous by his femininity. The other structure essential to heterosexual romance since *Fin'Amors* is the courtly model of mimetic desire. The earliest and best known example of this model is the mutual desire of King Mark and Tristan, made to appear heterosexual by the presence of Iseut. Flaubert's *L'Éducation sentimentale* suggests, in less than subtle ways, that Frédéric is more in love with Jacques Arnoux, Marie's husband, than with Marie herself. Frédéric's mimetic desire for Arnoux extends beyond Arnoux's wife to his mistress, Rosanette, one of the most parodic figures of femininity in modern literature. Flaubert further elaborates on the romantic hero's sexual ambiguity by describing Frédéric not only as the feminine half of the novel's enduring couple, Frédédric and Deslauriers, an unmistakable instance of *compagnonnage,* but on several occasions Frédéric is unequivocally the feminine object of Jacques Arnoux's attentions as well, recalling Mark's fascination with Tristan's youth and beauty in the classic text of triangular desire. Frédéric has a sexual fantasy involving Arnoux, Arnoux's mistress Rosanette (also called the Marshal) and himself, which brings the association between the artist's femininity and his masochistic impulses into focus in Flaubert's ironic post-romantic portrait of the obscure objects of an artist's desire:

> . . . il lui semblait qu'il était attelé près d'Arnoux, au timon d'un fiacre, et que la Maréchale, à califourchon sur lui, l'évantrait avec ses éperons d'or. (*OC*, II: 54)

> *(he thought of himself harnessed side by side with Arnoux in the shafts of a cab, and the Marshal, sitting astride him, was tearing his belly open with her golden spurs.)*[3]

In spite of these pertinent examples, it is not until the twentieth century that male homosexual desire explicitly supercedes—in canonical texts—the conventional plots of desire narratives, i.e. triangular desire and the obstacle. The spurious heterosexual heroine as the object of male mimetic desire is supplanted by forbidden homosexual objects or by writing itself in representations of the femininity *qua* masochism of the male writer who suffers for art. Sometimes the two passions—homosexual desire and writing—are represented as counterparts, as in André Gide and Thomas Mann, for example. In two of the most celebrated European works of the early twentieth century, Gide's *L'Immoraliste* (*The Immoralist*) (1902) and Mann's *Der Tod in Venedig* (*Death in Venice*) (1912), the object of the transgressive desire to write is represented as a beautiful boy. Literary representations of the beautiful object of writing continue to be figured as "feminine," however, because of their status as object of "masculine" desire in the signifying system that organizes Western thought. Furthermore, in spite of the frequent substitution of a beautiful boy for the object of desire in novels of this period, the desire to write is still unequivocally commingled and therefore confused with sexual desire. The nexus of writing and eroticism as a structuring principle is by no means limited to twentieth century works; it appeared as the troubadour notion of *joi*. The 1998 film *Love and Death on Long Island* (Richard Kwietniowski), which revisits Mann's *Death in Venice,* makes the relationship between writing and desire for the "beautiful boy" visually explicit. In the film, a sixty-something distinguished British writer (John Hurt) named Gilles D'eath falls in love with an American screen and television teenage idol (Jason Priestly). This inappropriate desire takes D'eath to the 1990s *fin de siècle* site of decadence, America, to pursue the object of his desire. The movie ends with the pages of an interminable fax (a twentieth-century *fin de siècle* version of the romantic cliché, the farewell letter) from the writer to the boy. What remains to be seen after D'eath is writing.

To collapse the eroticism of fictional characters and the eroticism of writing into a single libidinal drive does not, however, change the fact of women's exclusion from subjectivity, and from the pleasure associated with the act of writing.[4] Consider the passage from *Orlando* quoted in this chapter's epigraph in which Virginia Woolf writes ironically about the identification of the act of writing with male sexuality, and writing, or the written, with the "feminine" body—be it a woman, a beautiful boy, or a blank page. The problem of *vagabondage* cannot be accommodated by the terminology that currently exists to define sexism in literature; it goes beyond the problem of "reading"—specifically the plethora of sexist images of woman in fictional depictions of heterosexual desire—to a problem of "writing."[5] While the problem of woman's role as an imagined or absent object of male desire is a serious one, the more challenging problem is that of agency, and the gender of the writing subject. If, in narratives of desire, a writer is "masculine" and writes the "feminine" as self-difference, heterosexual women whose models for writing belong to the tradition I have been describing, are virtually excluded from the erotic pleasure intimately associated in this tradition with writing. (Callahan, "Vagabondage" 201).

When the pleasure of writing, and not its product, becomes a self-conscious literary theme, *vagabondage,* implicit in women's writing since the *trobairitz,* emerges as a dominant recurring plot in narratives by women. Colette establishes the vagabond, a woman compelled to choose between sexual pleasure and writing, as a modern heroine in *La vagabonde* (*The Vagabond*) (1911). An autobiographical novel, *La vagabonde* was written during the period immediately following Colette's divorce from her first husband Willy, who had signed her early novels with his own name. For this reason, although her novels were bestsellers, Colette herself had no income from them. After the divorce that left her destitute, she earned her living as a pantomime performer in the music halls that were popular in France in the early decades of the twentieth century. The experience spawned rich material for future works, including *La vagabonde,* the first novel signed with the now legendary single name "Colette," the ostensibly feminine signature which was in fact the surname of her father, Jules Colette. In this novel, about which biographer Judith Thurman writes, "This is literature, and adheres to a standard of spiritual truthfulness that was new for Colette," Colette raises the question of whether or not a relationship that does not conform to the heterosexual romance or marriage plot can properly be called *love* (197).[6] Suggestively, this issue comes up in the only passage in *La vagabonde* that touches on lesbianism.[7] In one of the many passages that prepares the heroine, Renée Néré, to renounce her fiancé, Max, she reflects on his inability to understand female homosexuality:

> À quoi bon lui expliquer? . . . Deux femmes enlacées ne seront jamais pour lui qu'un groupe polisson, et non l'image mélancolique et touchante de deux faiblesses, peut-être réfugiées aux bras l'une de 'autre pour y dormir, y pleurer, fuir l'homme souvent méchant, et goûter, mieux que tout plaisir, l'amer bonheur de se sentir pareilles, intimes, oubliées . . . À quoi bon écrire, et plaider, et discuter? . . . Mon voluptueux ami ne comprend que l'amour . . . . (*Oeuvres,* I: 1207)

> (*What would be the good of explaining to him? Two women enlaced will never be for him anything but a depraved couple, he will never see in them the melancholy and touching image of two weak creatures who have perhaps sought shelter in each other's arms, there to sleep and weep, safe from man who is often so cruel, and there to taste, better than any pleasure, the bitter happiness of feeling themselves akin, frail and forgotten. What would be the good of writing, and pleading, and discussing? My voluptuous friend can only understand love.*)

Knowing the role played by women together in Colette's other writings, we understand that the words, "can only understand *love,*" are not meant to be taken at face value—Colette does not mean that two women cannot love each other. Elaine Marks writes of "the preponderant role played by women, alone and together . . . as mothers and daughters, as sisters, as friends" in Colette's writings, and brings out the important role played by Colette as a "foremother" in "creating a language capable of speaking the unspoken in Western literature—female sexuality with woman as namer" ("Lesbian Intertextuality" 362; 363). Marks also makes the point, however, that lesbian relationships are as unsatisfactory in Colette's world as heterosexual relationships. She writes, "Women who love women come together in Colette's world because they are fleeing from a painful experience with a man and are looking for a *retraite sentimentale* [emotional refuge]. Lesbianism is a *pis aller* [last resort]" (369). She concludes that what remains in Colette's writing is "the single woman writing alone about woman's sexuality," an earmark of what I call the *vagabondage* plot (369). The implication of the phrase "can only understand *love,*" coming when it does in the novel at a moment when Renée is beginning to question the meaning of Max's "love" for her, is that his definition of the word is absolutely and unequivocally formed by the conventions of heterosexual romance. Although the passage contains a moving description of two women in each other's arms, the point here is not whether women can love each other, but whether any "writing, pleading or discussion" can convince the world, represented by Max, to call any relationship that does not conform to narrative conventions of heterosexual romance, love. Renée's impasse is a double bind: She is torn between the conventional happiness she feels when in love with a man and the self-loathing she feels when she plays the role of the woman in love. And the love she feels for women can be named only within a tradition of heterosexual romance that denies it.

In *Le deuxième sexe* (*The Second Sex*) (1949), Simone de Beauvoir paints a fully developed portrait of what Colette means by the condition of being a "woman in love" in a chapter of the same name (*l'amoureuse*).[8] Both Colette and de Beauvoir focus on the *amoureuse*'s desire for a master who will assimilate her existence into his own ("elle sera intégrée à son existence à lui" (she will be integrated into his existence) (De Beauvoir, *Le deuxième sexe,* II: 557). De Beauvoir writes that this is viewed by women not as masochism, but as the dream of "l'union extatique" (ecstatic fusion), which I argue is the single most important—and dangerous—legacy of *Fin'Amors* (*Le deuxième sexe,* II: 557). De Beauvoir takes philosophical distance and writes about "*l'amoureuse*" as an object of a discourse on the social construction of femininity. Colette, on the other hand, explores the split subjectivity of the woman writer when she recognizes "*l'amoureuse*" as one of the personae produced when her heroine writes.

In the first part of the novel, Renée, a recent divorcée, supports herself by performing in a music hall. Her ex-husband is an artist whose constant cruelty, rather than alienating her, only reinforced her masochistic bondage to him. Renée's situation is similar to that of Sand's Thérèse-Jacques (*Elle et lui*) in that in both novels, the woman is both an artist herself and an embodiment of her lover's representation of a woman in love (see chapter 3). Renée recalls how her husband, Taillandy, represented her:

> Taillandy a fait mon portrait aussi, autrefois. On ne sait plus que c'est moi, cette petite bacchante au nez lumineux, qui porte sur le milieu du visage sa tache de soleil comme un masque de nacre, et je me souviens encore de ma surprise, à me découvrir si blonde. (*Oeuvres*, I: 1082)

> *(Once upon a time Taillandy did my portrait too. No one now remembers that I was the model for his picture of the little bacchante with the shiny nose, where a splash of sunlight falling on her face, makes it look like a mask of mother-of-pearl. I still remember my surprise at finding myself so blonde.)*

All of Taillandy's "women" were blonde, all constructed to resemble his ideal romantic heroine. As he says, "Je ne veux pour modèles que mes maîtresses, et pour maîtresses que mes modèles!" (I want no models but my mistresses, and no mistresses but my models!), inviting comparison with director Roger Vadim's tendency to transform all the actresses in his films into the same woman—e.g. Brigitte Bardot (*And God Created Woman* [1956]) or Jane Fonda (*Barbarella* [1968])—and to either marry them, or make them his mistresses (*Oeuvres*, I: 1082). During the time that Renée was married to Taillandy, she found his portraits irresistible, in spite of the humiliation of his constant infidelities with these so-called model-mistresses.

Oddly enough, Renée was able to write while under Taillandy's spell. Her control of language erased the humiliation of suffering for love. She describes "la volupté d'écrire" (the voluptuous pleasure of writing) as "la lutte patiente contre la phrase qui s'assouplit, s'assoit en rond comme une bête apprivoisée" (the patient struggling with a phrase, until it becomes supple and sits down, curled up like a tamed animal) (*Oeuvres*, I: 1084). For Renée, sexual pleasure is so connected to writing that the one activity produces desire for the other; the way language submits to her ("like a tamed animal") reminds her so much of her own submission to Taillandy that writing arouses her sexual desire to play the role of the written (the "woman in love"), not of the writer. One of the most puzzling aspects of Renée is that although writing gives her the strength to eventually leave Taillandy, she denies herself the pleasure of writing after their divorce. This is one of the "slippery knots" of *vagabondage,* the double bind of a woman writer whose erotic pleasure has been nurtured by the convention of heterosexual romance.[9] Even though Renée is in control when she writes, her sexual fantasies of submission to a master do not disappear. This is why when the novel opens, Renée has vowed never to fall in love again. In spite of her determination, the second part of the novel constitutes a heterosexual romance narrative. A wealthy suitor named Max desires Renée. The first time she allows him to kiss her passionately, she describes herself as conforming to earlier descriptions of how she controls a phrase when she writes:

> mon regard de chienne soumise, un peu penaude, un peu battue, très choyée, et qui accepte tout, la laisse, le collier, la place aux pieds de son maître . . . . (*Oeuvres*, I: 1160)

> (*my look of a submissive bitch, slightly shamefaced, slightly beaten, very petted, and who will accept everything, the leash, the collar, the place at her master's feet*).

Renée has internalized Taillandy's portraits of her, and they mediate her desire for a master. She is caught between two identities, that of a writer able to control a phrase until it is a submissive animal, and that of a woman in love; the two identities are described by Colette as structural doubles—the name Renée Néré is fact a palindrome, a figure of self-reference, of writing. In *La vagabonde,* the move to writing does not assure uncomplicated subjectivity for a woman in love with romantic literature. The threads of *vagabondage* are tightly woven, and almost impossible to separate in this novel which names and, in my view, definitively describes the complexity of the problem.

> "Écrire! pouvoir écrire! cela signifie la longue rêverie devant la feuille blanche, le griffonage inconscient, les jeux de la plume qui tourne en rond autour d'une tache d'encre, qui mordille le mot imparfait, le griffe, le hérisse de fléchettes, l'orne d'antennes, de pattes, jusqu'à ce qu'il perde sa figure lisible de mot, mué en insecte fantastique, envolé de papillon-fée . . .
>
> Écrire. . . . C'est le regard accroché, hypnotisé par le reflet de la fenêtre dans l'encrier d'argent, la fièvre divine qui monte aux joues, au front, tandis qu'une bienheureuse mort glace sur le papier la main qui écrit. Cela veut dire aussi l'oubli de l'heure, la paresse aux creux du divan, la débauche d'invention d'où l'on sort courbatu, abêti mais déjà récompensé, et porteur de trésors qu'on décharge lentement sur la feuille vierge, dans le petit cirque de lumière qui s'abrite sous la lampe . . .
>
> Écrire! verser avec rage toute la sincérité de soi sur le papier tentateur . . .
> Écrire! . . . J'éprouve bien, de loin en loin, le besoin, vif comme la soif en

été, de noter, de peindre . . . Je prends encore la plume, pour commencer le jeu périlleux et décevant, pour saisir et fixer, sous la pointe double et ployante, le chatoyant, le fugace, le passionnant adjectif. . . . Ce n'est qu'une courte crise, la démangeaison d'une cicatrice. . . . (*Oeuvres*, I: 1074)

(To write! To be able to write! It means spending long hours dreaming before a white page, scribbling unconsciously, letting your pen play round a blot of ink and nibble at a half-formed word, scratching it, making it bristle with darts and adorning it with antennae and paws until it loses all resemblance to a legible word and turns into a fantastic insect or a fluttering creature half butterfly, half fairy. To write is to sit and stare, hypnotised, at the reflection of the window in the silver ink-stand, to feel the divine fever mounting to one's cheeks and forehead while the hand that writes grows blissfully numb upon the page. It also means idle hours curled up in the hollow of the divan, and then the orgy of inspiration from which one emerges stupefied and aching all over, but already recompensed and laden with treasures that one unloads slowly on to the virgin page in the little round pool of light under the lamp. To write is to pour one's innermost self passionately upon the tempting page. . . . From time to time I feel a need, sharp as thirst in summer, to note and describe. And then I take up my pen again and attempt the perilous and elusive task of seizing and pinning down, under its flexible double pointed nib, the many-hued, fugitive, thrilling adjective. . . . The attack does not last long; it is but the itching of an old scar.)

This passage doubles in turn the novel's most explicitly erotic scene between Max and Renée:

Car les lèvres qui me baisent . . . sont bien les mêmes qu'hier . . . Soudain, elles changent, et je ne reconnais plus le baiser, qui s'anime, insiste, s'écrase et se reprend, se fait mouvant, rythmé, puis s'arrête comme pour attendre une réponse qui ne vient pas . . . Je remue imperceptiblement la tête, à cause des moustaches qui frôlent mes narines, avec un parfum de vanille et de tabac miellé. . . . Oh! . . . tout à coup, malgré moi, ma bouche s'est laissée ouvrir, s'est ouverte, aussi irrésistiblement qu'une prune mûre se fend au soleil. . . . De mes lèvres, jusqu'à mes flancs, jusqu'à mes genoux, voici qui renaît et se propage cette douleur exigeante, ce gonflement de blessure qui veut se rouvrir et s'épancher—la volupté oubliée . . .

Je laisse l'homme qui m'a réveillée boire au fruit qu'il presse. Mes mains, raidies tout à l'heure, s'abandonnent chaudes et molles dans sa main, et mon corps renversé cherche à épouser son corps. Pliée sur le bras qui me tient, je creuse son épaule un peu plus, je me serre contre lui, attentive à ne pas disjoindre nos lèvres, attentive à prolonger confortablement notre baiser. (*Oeuvres*, I: 1159–60)

(For the lips that kiss me are just the same as yesterday. . . . But all of a sudden they change, and now I no longer recognize the kiss, which quickens, insists, falters, then

begins again with a rhythmical movement, and finally stops as if waiting for a response which does not come.

I move my head imperceptibly, because of his moustache which brushes against my nostrils with a scent of vanilla and honeyed tobacco. . . . Oh! . . . suddenly my mouth in spite of itself, lets itself be opened, opens of itself as irresistibly as a ripe plum splits in the sun. And once again there is born that exacting pain that spreads from my lips, all down my flanks as far as my knees, that swelling as of a wound that wants to open once more and overflow—the voluptuous pleasure that I had forgotten.

I let the man who has awakened me drink the fruit he is pressing. My hands, stiff a moment ago, lie warm and soft in his, and my body, as I lie back, strives to mould itself to his. Drawn close by the arm which holds me, I burrow deeper into his shoulder and press myself against him, taking care not to separate our lips and to prolong our kiss comfortably.)

The identification of erotic pleasure with the symbolic "wound" often associated with writing creates a double bind for Renée:[10]

Tout est contre moi. Le premier obstacle où je bute, c'est ce corps de femme allongé qui me barre la route, un voluptueux corps aux yeux fermés, volontairement aveugle, étiré, prêt à périr plutôt que de quitter le lieu de sa joie. . . . C'est moi, cette femme-là, cette brute entêtée au plaisir. "Tu n'as pas de pire ennemi que toi-même." (*Oeuvres*, I: 1217–18)

(Everything is against me. The first obstacle I run into is the female body lying there, which bars my way, a voluptuous body with closed eyes, deliberately blind, stretched out and ready to perish rather than leave the place where its joy lies. That woman there, that brute bent on pleasure is myself. "You are your own worst enemy.")

In the novel's third section, Renée literally writes herself out of her decision to marry Max, and chooses instead the role of, what I call "pleasure's vagabond" (Callahan, "Vagabondage" 202). What begins as a story of exile from both romance and writing ends with the discovery that writing is not inevitably tied to sexual submission. Renée comes to see possibilities for writing that transform the nature of its pleasure. This breakthrough occurs while Renée, engaged to Max, is on one last road trip with her music hall troupe before their marriage. Max makes the mistake of writing a letter to Renée, which reveals the conventional nature of his perception of their relationship: "Vous aurez à vous toute la terre, jusqu'à ne plus aimer qu'un petit coin à nous, où vous ne serez plus Renée Néré, mais Madame Ma Femme! (the whole world will be yours, until you come to love nothing but a little corner of our own where you will no longer be Renée Néré but My Lady Wife) (*Oeuvres*, I: 1209).[11]

Colette identifies this letter as the only "real love letter" Renée has received from Max, suggesting once again that love is only "real" love when expressed according to certain fixed formulas; this one being that a woman has no identity besides that of the man she loves. Consequently, women's subjectivity depends on renouncing love, that is, renouncing *received* ideas of "love" and happiness. Renée has to explain this notion to Max, who does not understand why she has chosen not to marry him, when he knows that he makes her happy. She answers, "Il n'y a pas que le bonheur qui donne du prix à la vie" (Happiness is not the only thing that gives life its value) (*Oeuvres*, I: 1232). *Vagabondage* is neither happiness nor unhappiness, it is freedom *from* happiness as it is defined by romantic love narratives. As Renée puts it:

> Je m'échappe, mais je ne suis pas quitte encore de toi, je le sais. Vagabonde, et libre, je souhaiterai parfois l'ombre de tes murs. . . . Combien de fois vais-je retourner à toi, cher appui où je me repose et me blesse. Combien de temps vais-je appeler ce que tu pouvais me donner, une longue volupté, suspendue, attisée, renouvelée . . . la chute ailée, l'évanouissement où les forces renaissent de leur mort même . . . le boudonnement musical du sang affolé . . . l'odeur de santal brûlé et d'herbe foulée . . . Ah! tu seras longtemps une des soifs de ma route! (*Oeuvres*, I: 1232)

> *(I escape from myself, but I am still not free of you, I know it. Vagabond and free, I will sometimes long for the shade of your walls. . . . How many times shall I return to you, dear prop on which I rest and wound myself. How many times shall I cry for what you were able to give me: a long drawn-out voluptuousness, suspended, fanned, renewed, the winged fall, the swooning in which one's strength is renewed by its own death. . . . Ah, how long shall I not thirst for you upon my road!)*

The move from feminine to today's notion of feminist in *La vagabonde* is in no way a moment of jubilation for Renée. It does, after all, involve forsaking happiness, described as basically limited in a woman's case to sexual happiness:

> un appétit dévorant de tout ce qui est bon, luxueux, facile, égoïste, un besoin de me laisser rouler sur la pente la plus moelleuse, de renfermer le bras et les lèvres sur un bonheur tardif, tangible, ordinaire et délicieux . . . . (*Oeuvres*, I: 1196)

> *(a devouring appetite for all that is pleasant, luxurious, easy and selfish, a need to let myself slide down the softest slope, and embrace with arms and lips a belated happiness that is tangible and ordinary and delicious.)*

In the novel's epiphany, which I have discussed in my introduction, Renée comes to the stark, absolute realization that the only thing that matters is "de posséder par les yeux les merveilles de la terre!" (to possess the world through [my own] eyes) (*Oeuvres,* I: 1221). Although the scene is written in such a way that it moves us to rejoice with Renée in her freedom to reinvent her definition of happiness, it does not change the unsatisfactory resolution of the *vagabondage* plot—solitude and sexual isolation.

Virginia Woolf's modernist classic *Orlando* (1928) is an ingenious, ironic rendering of the *vagabondage* plot with a wickedly fantastic, unbelievable, and skeptical to a fault—happy ending. Woolf's novel tells the story of a thirty-six year-old woman who begins the process of "coming to writing" as a sixteen-year-old aristocratic male poet—with shapely legs—in the Elizabethan Age. When, in 1928, Orlando develops a distinctive voice as a writer, she has been a woman since the reign of the "Merry Monarch," Charles II (1660–1685). Woolf wrote in her diary that she wanted *Orlando* to be "half laughing, half serious: with great splashes of exaggeration" (*A Writer's Diary* 117–18). The result is a humorous but nonetheless serious account of the social and literary history that a woman confronts when her most compelling desire is to write. Both Proust's *À la recherche du temps perdu* and Woolf's *Orlando* tell the story of how the novel we hold in our hands came into being. Like Proust's narrator Marcel, Orlando is a frustrated writer when the novel begins. Both novels end when their protagonists are finally able to write—with a difference; in the process of becoming a writer, Orlando becomes a woman.

Orlando begins with the words "HE—for there could be no doubt of his sex," which, as Pamela Caughie notes, "arouse our doubt" because "the stress on what is obvious makes it seem unnatural" (Woolf 13; Caughie, *Virginia Woolf and Postmodernism* [1992] 78).[12] By drawing our attention to a pronoun, Woolf points to the fact that the writing subject is culturally predetermined as masculine; with one and the same stroke of the pen she places that masculinity in question.[13] The novel does not question Orlando's masculinity per se, but rather the erotic confusion produced when the performance of gender in the writing veils, like a garment, the body of the writer: "the women . . . perched on his knee, flung their arms around his neck and, guessing that something out of the common lay hid beneath his duffle cloak, were quite as eager to come at the truth of the matter as Orlando himself" (29). Writing and sexual identity is the dominant theme of *Orlando* from the beginning of the novel. Orlando is, above all else, a writer, "Never had any boy begged apples as Orlando begged paper; nor sweet meats as he begged ink" (76). As a writer, he must learn to distinguish between representation and reality:

He was describing, as all young poets are for ever describing, nature, and in order to match the shade of green precisely he looked (and here he showed more audacity than most) at the thing itself, which happened to be a laurel bush growing beneath the window. After that, of course, he could write no more. Green in nature is one thing, green in literature another. Nature and letters seem to have a natural antipathy; bring them together and they tear each other to pieces. (17)

Catherine Belsey calls the desire to represent nature realistically "expressive realism," which she describes as "the theory that literature reflects the *reality* of experience as it is perceived by one (especially gifted) individual, who *expresses* it in a discourse that enables other individuals to recognize it as true" (*Critical Practice* 7). The limitations of language impede Orlando's writing, and the following is a description of his frustration:

He sighed profoundly, and flung himself—there was a passion in his movements which deserves the word—on the earth at the foot of the oak tree. He loved, beneath all this summer transiency, to feel the earth's spine beneath him; for such he took the hard root of the oak tree to be; or, for image followed image, it was the back of a great horse he was riding; or the deck of a tumbling ship—it was anything indeed, so long as it was hard, for he felt the need of something which he could attach his floating heart to. . . . To the oak tree he tied it and as he lay there, gradually the flutter in and about him stilled itself . . . as if all the fertility and amorous activity of a summer's evening were woven web-like around his body. (19)

The images that come to Orlando are not mirrors of nature; the freedom to create images depends on the recognition that language, as Saussure demonstrated, is not mimetic, but a system of differences. Woolf evokes this aspect of language by contrasting Orlando's fluttering to the oak's stability, his softness to the oak's hardness. Moreover, Woolf chooses images bound to make the reader think straight away of sexual difference, which is at the root of the problem with literary representations of desire.

Discussing a scene in Woolf's novel *Between the Acts,* which is strikingly similar to this one in *Orlando*—both involve rolling about in the grass—Eleanor Honig Skoller makes the point about representation when she writes:

In *Between the Acts,* she [Woolf] depicts the end of those whalebone bindings that encase the woman's body, when she had Mrs. Manresa say: "'And what do I do? Can I say it aloud? . . . I take off my stays . . . and roll in the grass.' She laughed wholeheartedly. She had given up dealing with her figure and thus gained freedom."

Just as Woolf celebrated the demise of the corset, letting the body go, so she attempted to dissolve the mimetic stays holding language fast to the real world. She had already written in her diary during the composition of *The Waves*, "there must be a great freedom from 'reality.'" (Skoller 1)

Both this passage and the passage quoted above from *Orlando* define the freedom to write, characterized by Skoller as letting go of the "mimetic stays holding language fast to the real world." Woolf challenges the representational model of the relationship between representation and experience. At the same time, her novel underscores the enduring fact that a culture's signifying system naturalizes social constructions. As Belsey puts it, "language insists on a difference, which readily comes to seem fundamental, *natural*" (49). She gives the example of sexual difference, illustrating the point with Lacan's well-known, and self-explanatory image of twin doors with "Ladies" written on one, "Gentlemen" on the other (49).

Orlando's efforts to think about language in a new way, as signifying difference, not mimetic, begin in this crucial scene. Woolf shows how sexual difference translates fluently as self-difference; the oak tree is hard and stands erect, Orlando is soft and fertile. If Orlando's socially constructed gender as an Elizabethan man is masculine, the gender of the poet who loosens the stays of mimesis is marked as feminine. Woolf centers our attention on the social fact of the naturalized polar distinction between masculine and feminine early in the novel. For example, in the early part of the novel, Woolf relates how attractive Orlando is to the woman who lends her name to the era, Queen Elizabeth I, who, Woolf writes, "flashed her yellow hawk's eyes upon him as if she would pierce his soul. The young man withstood her gaze, blushing only a damask rose as became him" (24). Elizabeth saw him as a poet, "she read him like a page" (25). In his role as Elizabeth's page, in both senses of the word, Orlando is in a role associated with femininity. On the other hand, in his life as a young man filled with sexual desires, however, he is in another, doing "what nature bade him," that is, bedding as many young lasses as he can (28). Because of the femininity he exhibits in his role as poet, Orlando appeals to the queen, who sees him as a "damask rose." He is also a man who plucks girls like flowers, "Girls were roses, and their seasons were short as the flowers'. Plucked they must be before nightfall . . . ." (27). In the first pages of her novel, then, Woolf charts in quick succession a series of related but conflicting images of her main character's sexual identity, a complex network of gender crossovers. By doing so, she draws our attention to the mistaken identification of representation and nature, expressed in such a way as to prepare the reader to recognize the exceptional relationship a writer has not only to gender, but also to sex. As regards social realities, a writer's gender is constructed from without; and so, as a young man of his time, Orlando feels compelled to pluck girls like flowers.

The third and most confusing term of the structure here is that the poet's self-representation as a fertile body inhabited by amorous longings and desiring to fuse with the strong, phallic oak tree, also takes the form of descriptions of young girls. With words that foreshadow Orlando's audacious act of writing as a woman in the 1920s, described in my epigraph to this chapter, Woolf brings up a further complication. The representation of the poet's self-difference as the feminine does not mean that the position occupied by what is conventionally perceived as "the writer" is not masculine. The male writer has it both ways. Woolf describes how Orlando, identifies the act of writing with masculine sexuality at the same time that he identifies woman with writing and with a poet's self-difference:

> He plunged his quill so deep into the inkhorn that the ink spirted over the table, which act, explain it how one may (and no explanation perhaps is possible—Memory is inexplicable), at once substituted for the face of the Princess a face of a very different sort. But whose was it, he asked himself? . . . "A poet, I dare say." (79–80)

We have come full circle back to the false identification of representation and nature. The gender of a writer's social persona, then, is constructed according to society's definition of sexual difference while the writer constructs the gender of the writing subject as self-difference.

Woolf turns the tables on men writing the feminine as self-difference by having Orlando, now a Duke, and British ambassador to Constantinople, fall into a deep sleep lasting seven days and emerge from his trance as a woman (137). The serious purport of Woolf's joke is that, in spite of having undergone a sex-change, Orlando remains essentially unchanged:

> Orlando had become a woman—there's no denying it. But in every other respect, Orlando remained precisely as he had been. The change of sex, though it altered their future, did nothing whatever to alter their identity. Their faces remained, as their portraits prove, practically the same. His memory—but in future we must, for convention's sake, say "her" for "his," and "she" for "he"—her memory then, went back through all the events of her past life without encountering any obstacle. (138)

One could argue, Woolf suggests in this passage, either that Orlando is still a man, or possibly that she had always been a woman (139). The subtleties of Woolf's language in the sex-change scene, I would argue, point to the fact that all writers for whom writing is identified with erotic pleasure, are figured in the feminine. As Roland Barthes writes in *Grain of the Voice,* "Being in love is a unisex situation in that exactly the same tonality can be found in a man who loves a woman or a man, and a woman who loves a man or a woman" (293).[14] The question then becomes, what does it mean for a poet to be a "woman"? Woolf's humor brings the writer's body into play. Orlando's fantastic sex-change allows him to inhabit a woman's body and to experience a woman's *jouissance.* When Orlando sails from Turkey to England, he sheds the gender-blurring Turkish trousers for a "lady's" skirts and delights in the pleasure of his own skin for the first time. Woolf describes Orlando's delight, "Never have I seen my own skin (here she laid her hand on her knee) look to such advantage as now" (154). Ironically evoking romantic love narratives, Woolf names the ship on which Orlando first dresses like a "lady," the *Enamored Lady* (153). The woman in love is a persona representing *joi,* the ecstasy achieved by projecting the self outside of the self in the form of a woman (155). Even more ironic is Orlando's reaction to himself as a woman. Orlando, who as a young man had "insisted that women must be obedient, chaste, scented, and exquisitely appareled," now realizes that women attain these graces "by the most tedious discipline." "Heavens!" she (Orlando) thought, "what fools they make of us—what fools we are!" (158). The women men create for themselves—make fools of the men. The move from the representation of male self-difference to the illusion of the real presence of women occurs almost without notice.

Typical of Woolf's style is the subtle use of pronoun shifts to make her point that there is no real man or real woman called Orlando whose body and sexual feelings change with her wardrobe. The changes in Orlando's body provoke similar changes in others, as in the case of the Archduchess Harriet, a woman when she is in love with Orlando, the man, but swiftly transformed into a man when confronted with Orlando's sex-change (179). Upon reflection the reader realizes that Orlando's attraction to his first love, Sasha, was due to the uncertainty of her sex (37). Anticipating Judith Butler's provocative theory that sex, like gender, is a cultural construction, a performance, Woolf describes Sasha in terms of unstable sexual identity, "her sex changed far more frequently than those who have worn only one set of clothing can conceive" (Butler 333; Woolf 221). Woolf's rendering of sex as a cultural performance is enriched by the way in which she makes the connection between sex-change and sexual desire which, in *Orlando,* results in heterosexuality and homosexuality being uncertain and shifting categories. It seems that whether Orlando is a man or a woman is a matter of indifference to those who are attracted to the poet. Playful indifference to the sex of a romantic lover is conventional. Take for example Cherubino, the eternally popular character in Mozart's (*The Marriage of Figaro*) (1786), whose beautiful and pleasurable singing voice and talent as a writer of romantic verse make him equally desirable as either a boy or a girl. The gender of an individual whose sexual identity is unstable is marked, however, as feminine—much is made of Cherubino's female travesties when forced to hide among women domestics to escape the wrath of his lord, Count Almaviva. Ambiguous sexuality is marked as feminine in a patriarchal culture in which to represent masculinity as ambiguous would be to dismantle the signifying system. In the troubadour tradition, the romantic couple is composed of two lovers, both of whom are feminine. This is the sense of one of the major revelations of Woolf's novel:

> As all Orlando's loves had been women, now, through the culpable laggardry of the human frame to adapt itself to convention, though she herself was a woman, it was still a woman she loved; and if the consciousness of being of the same sex had any effect at all, it was to quicken and deepen those feelings which she had had as a man. (161)

Lest her reader, looking for a simple explanation for the sexual confusion of the work, see *Orlando* as a lesbian novel, and Orlando's sex-change as a narrative gimmick, revealing the novel as a thinly disguised account of her relationship with Vita Sackville-West, Woolf has Orlando fall passionately in love with, and marry, a man.[15] The love story that ends the novel would seem to be either heterosexual, involving a woman (Orlando in the 1920s) and a man (Marmaduke Bonthrop Shelmerdine) or, if it is homosexual it involves two men, Orlando and Shelmerdine. Knopp writes, "*Orlando* is obviously not about the sapphic love of Vita and Virginia even in a disguised way. The hero/heroine loves men and women over the course of four hundred years, but no one of these is the subject" (1988) (28). It seems clear that there *is* a subject, however—the subject is writing. Woolf's exploration of a poet's coming to writing leads to both male femininity and to the double feminine of the eroticism of the romantic couple. The object of desire for the writer, whether a man or a woman, is the feminine as self-difference.

When Orlando realizes she loves Shelmerdine, the issue becomes how to classify their relationship. Is it homosexual, or heterosexual? If it is homosexual, are Shel and Orlando both men?, or both women? "An awful suspicion rushed into both their minds simultaneously. 'You're a woman, Shel! . . . You're a man, Orlando!' " (252). Ah! we might be moved to say to ourselves, so it is heterosexual after all, just not in the way we thought.

Shel sees Orlando's "original" sex. But what does Orlando see? Orlando is a poet. He sees Shel, the object of his desire, as the "she"—She(l/elle)—of all poetry. Woolf uses the words, "awful suspicion" to describe the realization that a woman, Orlando, has assumed the masculine role of writer, relegating her lover to a conventionally feminine role. In spite of the positive effects of the move (both sexes can play the roles of subject and object of desire, subject and object of writing), the idea of a feminine man remains "awful" because of the social fact of sexual difference. The social and historical conditions for the exclusion of women from writing, analyzed so brilliantly by Woolf in *A Room of One's Own* (1929), can be neither dismissed nor transcended with a series of gender-blurring jokes. Once married, Orlando doubts the legitimacy of having it both ways. She reflects on what she seems to have gotten away with, and wonders, "if one still wished, more than anything in the whole world, to write poetry, was it marriage? She had her doubts" (264). At several points in the novel, Orlando prides herself on having gotten through customs "by the skin of her teeth" with "contraband," meaning that she has "passed" as a woman in spite of her desire to write (265).[16] The question of whether or not femininity is incompatible with a woman's desire to write persists in Woolf's novel. Woolf's determination, in *Orlando* and elsewhere, "to expose the categories by which identity is determined and legalized" (Caughie, *VWP* [1991] 81) lead me to conclude that Orlando's question is rhetorical, meant to remind the reader that the temptation to identify with the role of a "woman in love" threatens her desire to write—and vice versa. Woolf's writer's doubts do not last long, however. Straightaway, Woolf writes Orlando out of her dilemma with humor and vigor:

> But she would put it to the test. She looked at the ring. She looked at the ink pot. Did she dare? No, she did not. But she must. No, she could not. What should she do then? Faint, if possible. But she had never felt better in her life.
> "Hang it all!" she cried, with a touch of her old spirit. "Here goes!"
> And she plunged her pen neck deep in the ink. (264)

The rest of the passage, quoted above in my epigraph, is a hymn to *joi*. The double pleasure of sex with Shel and the *joi* of writing do not exist simultaneously in *Orlando,* for once Orlando's pen is plunged deep in ink, Shel virtually disappears from her life to sail around Cape Horn (264). In the final pages of the novel, the vagabond husband is described in poetic terms, as a phantom spirit—the sexual exchange is consummate, he has become writing:

"Marmaduke Bonthrop Shelmerdine!" she cried, standing by the oak tree.
The beautiful glittering name fell out of the sky like a steel blue feather.
She watched it fall, turning and twisting like a slow falling arrow that cleaves
the deep air beautifully. He was coming, as he always came, in moments of
dead calm; when the wave rippled and the spotted leaves fell slowly over her
foot in the autumn woods; when the leopard was still; the moon was on the
waters, and nothing moved between sky and sea. It was then that he came.
All was still now. It was near midnight. The moon rose slowly over the
weald. Its light raised a phantom castle upon earth. There stood the great
house with all its windows robed in silver. Of wall or substance there was
none. All was phantom. (328)

While it is true that the modernist reference that Shel's metamorphosis
brings to mind is the new invention, the metallic bird, the airplane, it is also
significant that Woolf describes Orlando's vision of Shel as a "steel blue
feather." The choice of "steel" to describe what Orlando sees when she
follows Shel's trajectory brings his identification with writing to the attention of a reader accustomed to Woolf's language play: stele, stylo, style.[17]
The color blue has evoked a writer's desire for creative space since the
Romantic era, when that color symbolized the search for the Infinite in
writing and painting. The final words of the novel, "And the twelfth stroke
of midnight sounded; the twelfth stroke of midnight, Thursday, the eleventh
of October, Nineteen Hundred and Twenty-eight," announce the completion of *Orlando*. The novel is a love affair with writing, any resemblance to
a romantic love narrative is purely coincidental, and highly amusing. Both
Orlando and Shel are vagabonds. Although Orlando is a successful writer at
the novel's completion, and ostensibly a happily married woman, coming
to writing has taken four centuries and a sex-change, which renders the
heterosexuality of the marriage of Orlando and Shel indeterminate.

Orlando was published the same year as Colette's autobiographical
novel, *La naissance du jour* (1928). In this work, Colette severs the ties that
bind happiness to convention, and develops an explicitly experimental narrative. The words with which Colette congratulates one of her reviewers,
André Billy, on having "sniffed out" the truth of the novel, "vous avez flairé
que dans ce roman le roman m'existait pas" (you sniffed out the fact that
the novel doesn't exist in this novel) affirm that for her, the novel, in the
conventional sense of the genre, is dead (*Oeuvres*, III: 1389). From now on,
her writing will not depend on conventional novelistic plots. With the
words "for the first time since I turned sixteen, I will have to live—or even
die—without my life or my death depending on a love" in *La naissance du
jour*, Colette completes the story begun in *La vagabonde* (*Oeuvres*, III: 349).
The two novels exist in the same relationship to each other as do Sand's

Lélia and *Indiana* (see chapter 4). Like *La vagabonde,* in form and plot *Indiana* is a novel in keeping with the conventions of its time. *Lélia,* however, like *La naissance du jour,* is an experimental critique of the representation of sexual difference in Romantic myths of the artist, and Sand's most theoretical exploration of *vagabondage. Lélia* shows how women's writing challenges the simple binary split subject of traditional representations of self-difference. The encounter between Pulchérie and Lélia by the river stands as one of the most richly suggestive expressions of the double feminine of desire in literature and reveals Sand's awareness of the sapphic implications, especially for women writers, of the myth of sexual difference in Romantic love narratives.

Colette's *La naissance du jour,* also involves a critique of the myth of sexual difference in traditional representations of romantic love and reveals the double feminine of the structure of desire. In Colette's novel, the two women who represent the split subject of the writer are not sisters, but mother and daughter. Mari McCarty's description of the split subjectivity necessary to writing emphasizes the difference between Colette's mother and the fictional character, Sido:[18]

> Writing became her way to create a written self, a "Colette" who wrote herself into existence. In this enterprise, Sido is her guide, her "model." We cannot take Sido to mean Colette's flesh and blood mother, but rather Colette's *idea* and *reconstruction* of her mother in the text. . . . Colette finds her identity with Sido in the mirror, which reveals an older Colette "little by little taking on her likeness." Reminded of Sido by her own reflection, Colette creates a second self to serve as confidante and observer of her own actions. (in Strand [1995] 144–45)

The strong identification between the writer and the mother succeeds in doing several things at once: it brings the mother into existence, and at the same time, remembering the mother brings the daughter into existence—again—as a writer; more important, it brings the mother back to life in a narrative that forcefully resists the conventional collapse of the difference between the mother and language. The mother exists in the text as herself, and as the daughter's self-difference. Neither woman loses her identity as an individual, and the relationship produces writing.[19]

As in Sand's *Lélia,* the relationship between the two women in *La naissance du jour* exists in counterpoint to a heterosexual passion. In Colette's novel, the narrator, a novelist whose name is "Colette," sends her young suitor, Vial, away after spending what the French call "une nuit blanche," a night without sleep (evoking its linguistic analogue, un mariage blanc [a

marriage without sex]—thus, a night without sex), during which instead of
the passionate sex he desires, she explains in passionate language the reasons
for her decision to give him up:

> Faire peau neuve, reconstruire, renaître, ça n'a jamais été au-dessus de mes
> forces. Mais aujourd'hui il ne s'agit plus de faire peau neuve, il s'agit de
> commencer quelque chose que je n'ai jamais fait. Comprends donc, Vial,
> c'est la première fois, depuis que j'ai passé ma seizième année, qu'il va falloir
> vivre—ou même mourir—sans que ma vie ou ma mort dépendent d'un
> amour. (*Oeuvres*, III: 317)

> *(Begin again, rebuild, be born again, that has never been beyond my capacities. But
> today, it is no longer a question of beginning again, it is a question of starting some-
> thing that I have never done. Understand then, Vial, this is the first time since I was
> sixteen years old that I am going to have to live—or even die—without my life or my
> death depending on love.)*

Her passion that night was spent on conceiving a new beginning, a new
subjectivity, free from the romance plot. Significantly, I think, Colette links
her narrator linguistically to Renée Néré when she describes her behavior
with Vial that night as follows, "Je vagabonde cette nuit autour de Vial, à la
manière du cheval que l'obstacle importune, et qui fait le gentil, avec mille
folâtries de cheval, devant la barrière" (I spend that night "vagabonding"
around Vial, like a horse aggravated by an obstacle, pretending to be nice,
frolicking in front of the barrier like a frisky horse) (*Oeuvres,* III: 317). Her
desire for Vial represents an obstacle to the more compelling desire to jump
the fence like a wild horse in search of vagabond pleasure. She resists Vial,
and this time the renunciation of romance is absolute. As Vial flees by the
window, his form gradually disappears, creating the illusion of a metamorphosis into "halliers, embruns, météores, livre sans bornes ouvert, grappe,
navire, oasis . . ."(thicket, fog, meteors, [a] boundless open book, [a] bunch
of grapes, [a] ship, [an] oasis) (*Oeuvres*, III: 371). Like the fleeting images of
Shel in *Orlando,* Vial is transformed from a figure of the lover into a figure
for writing—a "boundless open book."

The story of the narrator's renunciation of heterosexual romance (the
"*Princesse de Clèves*" plot) is interwoven with the story of a mother's love
for her daughter, and the daughter's recognition of the mother's subjectivity. Colette structures the text in such a way that the maternal writing is
inscribed on the pages created by Vial's disappearing form as scenes from
the narrator's life during the time covered in the narrative—the twenty-
four hours of French classical tragedy—are interspersed with excerpts of
letters from Sido. The femininity of the split subject is structural in West-

ern narrative. Woolf's Shel becomes a woman, the "She" of poetry, before becoming Orlando's writing. Vial disappears, leaving an open book on whose pages the narrator of *La naissance du jour* writes Sido as self-difference. Unlike the oedipal paradigm, however, for Colette the split subject necessary for writing does not depend on the mother's disappearance, but on her reappearance. It is the case with Colette, as with other women writers discussed in this book, that although the mother is suppressed for a time, generally corresponding to the daughter's period of male-identification, she is resurrected in later texts—in "coming to writing" texts. This is the ultimate meaning of the novel's title *La naissance du jour*, which in French includes the word for "birth" (naissance); the mother—for many women writers—gives birth to the writer. Unfortunately, the English translation, *Break of Day*, does not convey this meaning. It is Sido who teaches her daughter how to give up everything, save what is essential for the supreme happiness of self-realization. Colette needs only a few words to convey the beauty of that lesson, which she calls "le chic suprême du savoir-décliner . . ."(the supreme elegance of knowing how to diminish) (*Oeuvres,* III: 371)—it is also possible that Colette intended a pun, since the verb "decliner" also refers to a grammatical process, thus the mother's lesson extends beyond love to writing (166).

The Sido of *La naissance du jour* teaches Colette how to renounce passion for the promise of a more "contemplative self"—a lesson learned in a more austere fashion by the Princesse de Clèves from her mother, three centuries earlier (Ward-Jouve [1987] 148). The major difference between the narrator of *La naissance du jour* and her predecessor, the Princesse de Clèves, is that Colette clearly names the desire to write as the motive for the heroine's quest for freedom from heterosexual romance. When she reproduces the last letter Sido wrote to her before her death, Colette's commentary on the letter emphasizes Sido's intimate connection to writing:

La dernière lettre, ma mère en l'écrivant voulut sans doute m'assurer qu'elle avait déjà quitté l'obligation d'employer notre langage. Deux feuillets crayonnés ne portent plus que des signes qui semblent joyeux, des flèches partant d'un mot esquissé, de petits rayons, deux "oui, oui" et un "elle a dansé" très net. Elle a écrit aussi, plus bas, "mon amour"—elle m'appelait ainsi quand nos séparations se faisaient longues et qu'elle s'ennuyait de moi. Mais j'ai scrupule cette fois de réclamer pour moi seule un mot si brûlant. Il tient sa place parmi des traits, des entrelacs d'hirondelle, des volutes végétales, parmi les messages d'une main qui tentait de me transmettre un alphabet nouveau, ou le croquis d'un site entrevu à l'aurore sous des rais qui n'attendraient jamais le morne zénith. De sorte que cette lettre, au lieu de la contempler comme un confus délire, j'y lis un de ces passages hantés où par jeu l'on cacha un visage dans les feuilles, un bras entre deux branches, un torse sous des noeuds de rochers. (*Oeuvres*, III: 371)

(No doubt my mother wrote that last letter to assure me that she no longer felt any obligation to use our language. Two penciled sheets have on them nothing more than apparently joyful signs, arrows emerging from an embryo word, little rays, 'yes, yes' together, and a single 'she danced', very clear. Lower down she had written, 'my love,' her name for me when our separations had lasted a long time and she was longing to see me again. But this time I feel a scruple in claiming for myself so burning a word. It has a place among strokes, swallow-like inter-weavings, plant-like convolutions—all messages from a hand that was trying to transmit to me a new alphabet or the sketch of some ground-plan envisaged at dawn under rays that would never attain the sad zenith. So that instead of a confused hallucination, I see in that letter one of those haunted landscapes where, to puzzle you, a face lies hidden among the leaves, an arm in the fork of a tree, a body under a cluster of rock.)

In this passage, the daughter translates the mother's cryptic message as the possibility of a "new alphabet." The meaning of the mother's letter is interpreted by the daughter from signs and figures hidden beneath leaves and rocks. By describing her mother's writing as a "sketch of a plan" that would never see the light of day—a version of the title of the daughter's book—Colette describes far more than Sido's cryptic message; she describes the repression of women's writing. The daughter's task is to claim for herself the "burning word," symbol of the mother's desire, and to transform a single word into a book.

There exists an uncanny similarity between the language used to describe Sido's final letter to her daughter in *La naissance du jour* and the passage on writing cited earlier from *La vagabonde,* in which Colette describes writing as

la plume qui tourne en rond autour d'une tache d'encre . . . jusqu'à ce qu'il perde sa figure lisible de mot, mué en insecte fantastique, envolé de papillon-fée. (*Oeuvres*, I: 1074)

(letting your pen play round a blot of ink . . . until it loses all resemblance to a legible word and turns into a fantastic insect or a fluttering creature half-butterfly, half-fairy)

The desire to write is in the hand transforming ink blots into figures; the desire exists in both the mother and the daughter. The daughter, by writing, gives legible form to that desire, in doing so explodes the myth that women want only to be written as the body, the object of desire—that they do not desire to write. In Colette's model of the maternal presence in language, the daughter's writing does not replace the mother as it does in the oedipal model. Her presence, on the contrary, is essential not only to the process of language acquisition, but even more important to the knowledge that pleasure has many forms, and speaks many languages. In the following passage from *No Voice is Ever Wholly Lost* (1995), psychoanalyst Louise J. Kaplan illuminates the connection between loss and creativity and in so doing offers a scenario of restoration and recovery from the perverse behavior that was the subject of her widely known earlier study, *Female Perversions: The Temptations of Emma Bovary*:

> [B]ecause the reciprocal dialogue between infant and parent establishes certain everlasting connections between each individual life and some larger human community, self-mortification and destruction are not our only responses to loss of dialogue. Our cultural attainments, the sentences we utter or sign, our poems, dances, monuments, paintings, symphonies, songs, are all a way of refinding and restoring lost dialogues. (240)

In Colette's case, the voice of the mother's desire accompanies the daughter in her "coming into writing."

It was in 1964, with *Une mort très douce* (*A Very Easy Death*) that de Beauvoir, in my opinion, comes into "writing" as I have defined it elsewhere in this chapter, and comes out, so to speak, as a woman. This breakthrough book is about her mother Françoise de Beauvoir's illness and death. The revelations of *Une mort très douce* come as a surprise to readers familiar with her previous writings; this, the slimmest volume written by de Beauvoir, stands as her fullest expression of desire and subjectivity. Jean Paul Sartre, de Beauvoir's sometimes lover, primarily her best friend, once wrote that "Un livre de femme, c'est un livre qui refuse de prendre à son compte ce que font les hommes. Beaucoup d'hommes n'ont jamais écrit que des livres féminins" (a woman's book is a book which refuses to take into account what men do. Many men have never written anything but feminine books) (*Situations* (1964), IX: 18–18).[20] Sartre's words resonate with the problem of the *troubadour effect,* that *real* writers—as opposed to authors—write feminine books . . . and they're men. The textual flaw here is in the move from the word femme (woman) to féminin (feminine); the illusion of the *troubadour effect,* whereby "woman" becomes "male self-difference" with a stroke of the pen: the books are not women's books, but "feminine" books—there's a difference.

Une mort très douce is a woman's book, written by a woman for a woman. It is a love letter from a daughter to a mother whom she does not learn to love until she writes a book about her death. Moreover, in this book, de

Beauvoir defines woman's desire more clearly even than in *Le deuxième sexe* in which she writes about women in general. In *Une mort très douce*, writing about and identifying with her mother gives de Beauvoir the freedom to write about herself as a woman. She is a good example of one of the more difficult aspects of *vagabondage*: women feel compelled to exile themselves from their own sex in order to write—they see themselves as men, in the male-identified role of writer. When they realize, as Jane Gallop has shown, that brains and drive do not give a woman a man's status, that in fact they're women and will be seen and treated as such in whatever "academy" they dare to enter, the discovery can be demoralizing.[21]

In 1972, de Beauvoir wrote, "writing has remained the great affair of my life." This declaration explains her distinctive way of being in the world far more than notions about her difference from "ordinary women." Desire is the key to subjectivity, and in her case, the desire to write was stronger than the desire to be a "woman in love." By the time she made this statement, she had written *Une mort très douce*, a process through which she seems to have gained a deeper understanding of how difficult it is for a woman to achieve autonomy when—as in her mother's case—her strongest desire is to be both loved and in love.

Une mort très douce marks a progression from separation from the mother to an acceptance of an affinity with her. Acceptance in this text, as in Colette's writings about Sido, is expressed initially as the daughter's identification with the mother's body. It does not stop there, however, but is transformed, through writing, to the restoration of the mother as a person whose identity is not confined to her body. In this way, the daughter restores her own identity as a woman, an identity also not confined to her body. In all the women discussed in this and previous chapters, the mother is initially suppressed. Not until later in their lives did these women writers return to the mother as a well-spring of their own agencies. The mother's presence in the daughter's most mature and often most experimental writing, is made eminently clear by Woolf, de Beauvoir, Colette, and, as we shall see, by Marguerite Duras as well. It took a long time for de Beauvoir, who as a young philosopher and writer was so male-identified that she had contempt for women like her mother, to accept herself as a woman. In *Une mort très douce*, the turning point takes place during a conversation with Sartre:

> Je parlai à Sartre de la bouche de ma mère . . . et ma propre bouche, m'a-t-il dit, ne m'obéissait plus: j'avais posé celle de maman sur mon visage et j'en imitais malgré moi les mimiques. Toute sa personne, toute son existence s'y matérialisaient et la compassion me déchirait. (43–44)

(I talked to Sartre about my mother's mouth . . . and he told me that my own mouth was not obeying me anymore; I had put Maman's mouth on my own face and in spite of myself, I copied its movements. Her whole person, her whole being, was concentrated there, and compassion wrung my heart.)

Once identification—expressed here as compassion—is established, representations of mother and daughter begin to merge. The text moves in a marked way from a third person narrative of the mother's illness to the first person as de Beauvoir writes herself as the object of her own gaze, "Je traverse le jardin. J'entre dans le hall" (I go through the garden, I go into the hall) (66–67). De Beauvoir's representation of the daughter's awareness of the mother's part in the construction of the daughter's identity as a woman reaches the height of its intensity at the moment of the mother's death, "dans chaque cellule de mon corps, je m'unissais à son refus, à sa révolte" (in every cell of my body, I identified with her resistance [to dying], with her revolt) (150). In a final—and unexpected—move, she writes of a dream in which her mother "se confondait avec Sartre, et nous étions heureuses ensemble" (blended with Sartre, and we were happy together) (147). De Beauvoir is able, through writing, to realize the double feminine (the adjective *heureuses* is feminine plural in French) of the fantasy of fusion which is the central myth of heterosexual romance. The strategy of blending the mother with the male object of desire is an illuminating example of how a woman writer manages to express her self-difference as a couple who is heterosexual but comprised of two feminine figures. The complexity of the image produced in de Beauvoir's dream about her mother's face blending with Sartre's is reminiscent of the effect produced in Sand's *Lélia* when Pulchérie recognizes her sister Lélia's face as that of the man in her dream.

De Beauvoir brings her mother to life in *Une mort très douce*—by naming her, by telling her story from birth to marriage to widowhood to the grave. By one and the same process, she brings to life the full complexity of being a woman writer. It would have been less messy to continue as male-identified, and to forget the female body. What I have discovered, however, in the process of understanding the woman writer of heterosexual desire is that "coming into writing" for a woman does not permit such a lapse of memory. The reappearance of the mother after an initial repression is a recurring structure when women write about desire. Examples of this structure are by no means limited to the writers I have chosen to discuss, or to works in French and English. To give just one example, in *El Cuarto de Atrás (The Back Room)* (1978), written in post-Franco Spain, Carmen Martín Gaite compares women's desire for subjectivity to an entire society's struggle to break from a tradition of repression. In this novel, too, the daughter's renunciation of romance is linked to the mother's desire for language.

In her autobiography, *L'Amant* (*The Lover*) (1984) Marguerite Duras specifies the connection between forgetting the mother's physical body, and restoring the mother to life in writing. Duras reveals in *L'Amant* that before writing this book, she had long since forgotten the woman she calls "the" mother. She writes, "C'est fini, je ne me souviens plus. C'est pourquoi j'en écris si facile d'elle maintenant, si long, si étiré, elle est devenue écriture courante" (It's over. I no longer remember. That's why I write about her so easily now, so long, so entirely. She has become flowing writing) (38). There is a step, however, in both de Beauvoir's and Duras's texts between forgetting the mother and restoring her in representation; that step is the daughter's resistance. The writing daughter's ambivalence towards the passivity associated with the mother's body in the daughter's social consciousness is never completely resolved. In *L'Amant,* the mother's presence rises to the surface of the text and remains close to the surface, and unresolved in each book thereafter. For example, in *La mer écrite* (*The Written Sea*), published following Duras's death in 1996, the mother is evoked homophonically (in French the words for sea [*la mer*] and for mother [*la mère*] are homonyms) in the book's title in which it becomes almost the only written language that remains in a book whose format is a series of photographs with short written captions. I do not want to romanticize either *Une mort très douce,* or *L'Amant;* to do so would be to create yet another myth of fusion. Both the writing and the mother continue to exist for the daughter; the mother does not become writing in the Romantic sense of ideal fusion of "I" and "Not I" into a writing subject and the written. That the feeling towards the mother remains ambivalent is inevitable—and that's what makes *vagabondage* so labyrinthine.

For Duras, like de Beauvoir, the desire to write is what distinguishes her from her mother: "Ce qui était suffisant pour elle ne l'est plus pour la petite." (What was enough for her is not enough for the girl) (11). About the curbs on female desire, Duras writes:

> Ce manquement des femmes à elles-mêmes par elles-mêmes opéré m'apparaissait toujours comme une erreur. Il n'y avait pas à attirer le désir. Il était dans celle qui le provoquait ou il n'existait pas. Il était déjà là dès le premier regard ou bien il n'avait jamais existé. Il était l'intelligence immédiate du rapport de sexualité ou bien il n'était rien. Cela, de même, je l'ai su avant l'*experiment*. (28)

> *(This lack of women to themselves, by themselves has always seemed to me to be a mistake. It wasn't necessary to attract desire. Either it was in the woman who aroused*

it or it did not exist. Either it was there from the first look or it didn't exist. Either it was the instant comprehension of a sexual relationship or it was nothing. That, likewise, I knew it before the experiment.*)*

In a process corresponding to the one that I have shown in Colette and de Beauvoir, Duras evokes the double, continuing presence of both mother and daughter in a narrative of female desire which she calls "the experiment," choosing to use the English word in French to underscore the difference between experience and experiment (Skoller 27). The French word for experiment is *expérience*. Duras's choice of English is a determined effort to convey her conviction that autobiography is not a written account of unmediated "experience"; the life constructed in autobiography is not "experienced" until it is written (*L'Amant* 14).

The experiment is written as a narrative, the story of the first and defining sexual liaison of a fifteen-year-old narrator who is Duras herself, but at a time when she had a face that is no longer recognizable as hers. The forgotten body, then, is not only the mother's but also her own when it was ripe for sexual pleasure. Writing of her relationship to herself at the age of her narrator, she says:

> Je pense souvent à cette image, que je suis seule à voir encore et dont je n'ai jamais parlé. Elle est toujours là dans le même silence, émerveillante. C'est entre toutes celle qui me plaît de moi-même, celle où je me reconnais, où je m'enchante. *(9)*

> *(I often think of that image which only I can still see and about which I have never spoken. It is always there, in the same silence, amazing. It is the only one of all the images of myself which pleases me, the only one in which I recognize myself, which enchants me.)*

The narrator's body, like the mother's body in the texts we have been discussing is a representation, both when it is repressed, and when it is resurrected. The mother represents the daughter's self-difference, herself as a woman who doesn't write and as such has an important role to play in the *vagabondage* plot. What was enough for the mother is not enough for the daughter. "La mère n'a pas connu la jouissance" (the mother had never known *jouissance*), Duras writes (50). At fifteen years old, the daughter had "le visage de la jouissance" (the face of *jouissance*); the space existed in her for desire (15). The romance plot does not kill desire in the daughter, who frees herself from its conventional language by refusing to allow the lover to say the words that would position him as agent and her as the object of his desire; she forbids him to say "I love you."

It is the mother who puts her on the ferry "to cross the river," to return to school in Saigon from the mother's home in Sadec. The mother, like Sophie in Sand's *Histoire de ma vie,* is central to the girl's desire "to cross over," while she herself lacks agency. When the narrator of *L'Amant* meets her Chinese lover on the ferry, she is wearing the mother's clothes, including a man's hat with a flat brim. Duras writes, "l'ambiguïté déterminante de l'image, elle est dans ce chapeau" (the ambiguity that defines the image is in that hat) (19). The ambiguity is created by the combined image of the masculinity of the hat and the femininity of the almost transparent dress of real silk and gold lamé high heels. Duras writes that at first she could not remember where she got the hat, thinking that perhaps she had borrowed it from the mother of her friend Hélène. When she finds an old family photograph, she sees her mother, in the center, among Duras and her two brothers—wearing the hat and looking uncomfortable. The photograph is important because it recalls a moment in the narrator's life when the mother was at the center of the image, before the daughter forgot her—which is necessary to the writing process.

Duras explains that her writing before *L'Amant* was not really writing, "Je n'ai jamais écrit, croyant le faire, je n'ai jamais aimé, croyant aimer, je n'ai jamais rien fait qu'attendre devant la porte fermée" (I had never written, believing that I was doing so. I had never loved, believing that I loved. I had done nothing but wait before a closed door)(35). She was just another writer in love with the inaccessible, repressed mother. In this book, the mother's reappearance identifies her explicitly as the daughter's object of desire. The mother does not remain repressed, replaced by either writing, or by the illusory heroine of heterosexual romance. The process of substitution works in reverse. In a move similar to the one made by de Beauvoir in the scene in which her mother's face blends with Sartre's, Duras transforms "the lover" progressively into "the mother" in the book's erotic scenes. The transformation begins with the description of his body the first time they have sex, "il est imberbe, sans virilité autre que celle du sexe" (he's hairless, nothing masculine about him but his sex) (49). After the first time, she tells him that her mother will die, and that her death is connected to what has happened with the lover. It is when she says these words that she notices that she desires him ("je m'aperçois que je le désire") (51). He asks her what she's thinking about and she tells him, "je pense à ma mère" (I'm thinking about my mother) (56). As the writing progresses, the transformation of the lover into the mother becomes more explicit:

> Ainsi j'étais devenue son enfant. C'était avec son enfant qu'il faisait l'amour chaque soir. Et parfois il prend peur, tout à coup il s'inquiète de sa santé

comme s'il decouvrait qu'elle était mortelle et que l'idée le traversait qu'il pouvait la perdre. . . . Et ce dégoût aussi qu'elle a quelquefois de la vie, quand ça la prend, qu'elle pense à sa mère et que subitement elle crie et pleure de colère à l'idée de ne pas pouvoir changer les choses, faire la mère heureuse avant qu'elle meure, tuer ceux qui ont fait ce mal. Le visage contre le sien il prend ses pleurs, il l'écrase contre lui, fous du désir de ses larmes, de sa colère. Il la prend comme il prendrait son enfant. (122–23)

(I had become his child. It was with his own child he made love every evening. And sometimes he takes fright, suddenly he's worried about her health, as if he suddenly realized she was mortal and it suddenly struck him he might lose her. . . . And the loathing of life that sometimes seizes her, when she thinks of her mother and suddenly cries out and weeps with rage at the thought of not being able to change things, not being able to make her happy before she dies. . . . His face against hers he receives her tears, crushes her to him, mad with desire for her tears, for her anger. He takes her as he would his own child.)

The masculinity of the gendered lover of the book's title (*L'Amant* is markedly masculine in French) is erased by his transformation into the mother in the text itself.

Jeffrey Skoller's film, *The Malady of Death* (1994), inspired by Duras's text of the same name, refocuses the familiar male gaze on the self, its actual object, and not on a woman. In Duras's text, the woman's body is not feminine in and of itself, but by comparison with the male body. It is described as "cette forme imberbe, sans accidents musculaires ni force" (that hairless unmuscular body without strength) (Duras, *La maladie de la mort* [*The Malady of Death*] [1982] 8). To describe a woman's body in such a way directs attention not to the female body, but to the male body, which *it is not*. In his film, Skoller exploits the possibilities opened up by Duras's ambiguities by removing the image of the woman altogether; the text is given to a woman's disembodied voice (in a voiceover) and to different male bodies, which represent the sexual encounter on screen. The female body is never seen, but is heard and described, while the male body is seen from a multitude of angles, vulnerable, feminine, masculine, translucent, old, young, black, white—several men play the protagonist, their individual identities made unclear by the angle, distance and motion of the camera. This technique foregrounds the male protagonist's reason for hiring the woman, his desire to explore his own body, to know how he himself experiences pleasure and is justified by the opening passage of Duras's text:

Vous ne devriez pas la connaître, l'avoir trouvée partout à la fois, dans un hôtel, dans une rue, dans un train, dans un bar, dans un livre, dans un film, en vous-même, en vous, en toi, au hasard de ton sexe dressé dans la nuit qui appelle où se mettre, où se débarasser des pleurs qui le remplissent. (7)

(You wouldn't have known her, you'd have seen her everywhere at once, in a hotel, in a street, in a train, in a bar, in a book, in a film, in yourself, in you (vous), in you (toi), when your sex grew erect in the night, seeking somewhere to put itself, somewhere to shed its load of tears.)

Skoller's artistic choices stem from his belief that conventional cinematic techniques used to represent sexual pleasure fail when they ignore the primary source of pleasure, which is its production or creation in the desiring subject (Skoller, notes on *The Malady of Death*). Whether that subject be writer or filmmaker, reader or viewer, the experience of pleasure is inseparable from its performance.

The ultimate pleasure in *L'Amant* occurs when the narrator imagines a voyeuristic erotic scene when she would deliver her classmate, Hélène Lagonelle, to the Man from Cholen, her Chinese lover. She imagines him making love to Hélène until both women cry out with pleasure. The definitive climax would be simultaneous orgasm with Hélène Lagonelle through the mediation of "the lover." In this scene of split subjectivity, Duras frees herself to write an erotic scene, which she controls without destroying the language of desire. She gains access to subjectivity by writing the scene of pleasure. At the same time, she identifies with the woman in the contrived scene. Hélène Lagonelle's name is constructed on a series of linguistic signs that refer to the feminine, the article "*la*," the pronoun "*elle*," and its homophonic twin, the letter "l" (the character is often referred to as H.L.). There is no moment when the image of woman's difference is assimilated by male desire in a figure for the romantic ideal of androgynous fusion. The narrator submits to pleasure, she does not submit to a man. In fact, she forbids the "lover" to say the words "I love you" until the final paragraph of the novel when she is already well established as a writer. The passage suggests that although years have passed since the fifteen-year-old girl left Saigon for France to become a writer, she has not replaced the Man from Cholen as the generic "lover." She tells the story over and over in novels, plays and films, until she finally calls her own autobiography *L'Amant*—in the masculine—establishing representation as the vagabond's *joi*:

Des années après la guerre, après les mariages, les enfants, les divorces, les livres, il était venu à Paris avec sa femme. Il lui avait téléphoné. C'est moi. Elle l'avait reconnu dès la voix. Il avait dit: je voulais seulement entendre votre voix. . . . Il savait qu'elle avait commencé à écrire des livres, il l'avait su par la mère qu'il avait revue à Saigon. . . . Et puis il le lui avait dit. Il lui avait dit que c'était comme avant, qu'il l'aimait encore, qu'il ne pourrait jamais cesser de l'aimer, qu'il aimerait jusqu'à sa mort. (141–42)

(Years after the war, after marriages, children, divorces, books, he came to Paris with his wife. He phoned her. It's me. She recognized him at once from the voice. He said, I just wanted to hear your voice. . . . He knew she'd begun writing books, he'd heard about it through her mother whom he'd met again in Saigon. . . . And then he told her. Told her that it was as before, that he still loved her, he could never stop loving her, that he'd love her until death.)

The last word of the book is death. The book held in the reader's hand constitutes what remains of the love story, without the book, there is no lover.[22]

In the final passage of *Jazz* (1992), Toni Morrison's narrative voice exhorts the reader to free herself from conventional plots and remake the novel. The means to do this are in the reader's hands because Morrison's narrator refers to the very book that the reader holds. The reader is free to reread the novel she has just finished reading, picking up other voices, other themes, reading the same material differently. Morrison sends the reader back through the novel in search of clues to the narrator's identity. Responding to Morrison's invitation, I discovered the novel's *vagabondage* plot, involving Violet, Joe's wife, Dorcas, his mistress, and Wild, a Lilith figure with whom he is obsessed, believing that she is his "real" mother who abandoned him at birth. Like the women writers discussed in this and in previous chapters, Morrison writes two stories in *Jazz,* one a typical story of romantic love involving Joe Trace's tragic affair with Dorcas, and the other a story of writing and women's agency involving Violet, Wild, Dorcas, and the ambiguous narrator.

The romance plot of *Jazz* conforms to the belief embedded in Western narrative since the twelfth century, that romantic love is the key to self-realization. Joe Trace and Violet are a married couple who have come from the South to New York years before 1926, the time of the tragic events that begin the novel's action.[23] Joe has murdered his teenage lover Dorcas, and Violet has come to the funeral home with a knife, and tried to disfigure the corpse—to kill a dead woman, so to speak—before being thrown to the church floor by mourners. The rest of the story is a journey back in time and place—typically, for Morrison, to the South—to discover the personal and social reasons for the tragedy. In keeping with a conventional romance plot, Joe falls in love not with Dorcas, but with his own difference. He characterizes himself as having been a "new negro" all his life constantly seeking an identity, remaking himself again and again, seven times in all (129).[24] Joe's search for the self began when he named himself Joe Trace; his parents had disappeared "without a trace" and he was the "trace" they disappeared without (122). The name "trace" can also be said to signify the search for identity through language. When he meets Dorcas, Joe is still searching, but this time it is different, "But all I lived through, all I seen, and not one of those changes prepared me for her" (129). In Joe's latest transformation which provokes the novel's action, he sees romantic love as the key to self-realization. For Joe, Dorcas represents the missing half of an original self, belonging to a lost paradise:

> I told you again that you were the reason Adam ate the apple and its core. That when he left Eden, he left a rich man. Not only did he have Eve, but he had the taste of the first apple in the world in his mouth for the rest of his life. The very first to know what it was like. . . . You looked at me then like you knew me, and I thought it really was Eden. . . . (133)

Joe does not see Dorcas, he sees himself in Dorcas's eyes. Like Balzac's Paquita, "the girl with the golden eyes" (*La Fille aux yeux d'or*), Dorcas's eyes are a mirror in which Joe believes his "true" identity to be reflected. Like Paquita's lover, Henri de Marsay, Joe murders the woman in whose eyes he sees his own desire reflected. In both cases, once the woman has served her purpose, she dies. Like the key and meter of composed music, the traditional plot structure is preserved: A man seeks self-realization in romantic love. He projects his desire onto a woman conceived in his imagination as a figure of the "first" and "only" woman; "I" and "Not I" fuse, and the woman disappears—tragically. In an interview for *Inrockuptible,*[25] a French magazine featuring articles on contemporary music and other forms of popular culture, Toni Morrison describes *Jazz* as a literary version of jazz improvisation; "There is no musician in the book, the literary structure itself fills that role. . . . That is my contribution, jazz is so important because it is composed by the musician herself and does not depend on another's composition. In the case of *Jazz,* the book writes itself" (53). The book is both the musician and the music, a formal organization that defies the imposition of ready-made structural positions such as the writer and the written, the surveyor and the surveyed, the subject and the object of writing. When, on the last page of the novel, we discover that the mysterious narrator is the very book we are reading, we recognize in Morrison's "modernist whimsy and wickedness" a strategy designed to thwart our desire to know the sex of the narrator (Leonard [1993] 39).

The improvised plot of *Jazz* isolates and reconfigures the essential components of the romance plot, without essentially changing its structure or diminishing its appeal. In Morrison's novel, the narrator does not control the composition, but allows the other characters to speak in their own voices. Gates compares this structure to Duke Ellington's jazz compositions "constructed, or scored, for his individual musicians and their peculiar timbres, their particular *sounds*" (Gates [1993] 54). As in the musical form Morrison appropriates for the novel's title, *Jazz* generates new combinations of sounds and voices without abandoning the structural frame of the underlying composition. Specifically, it brings into play the stories of the individual women behind the feminine types (the mother [Wild], the madwoman [Violet], the *femme fatale* [Dorcas]) that function in traditional romance narratives as male self-difference. The women return in Morrison's novel, not as Joe's self-difference, but as solo voices.

Like the musical form, *Jazz* does not end when it ends; it finishes first with an unexpected yet conventional resolution before moving on to a lyrical yet disruptive coda. In the first ending, Joe and Violet's married love endures his infidelity with Dorcas. Morrison describes Joe and Violet's reconciliation as follows:

> They are under the covers because they don't have to look at themselves anymore; there is no stud's eye, no chippie glance to undo them. They are inward toward the other, bound and joined by carnival dolls and the steamers that sailed from ports they never saw. (228)

Having survived violent desire, and thanks in great part to their age, Joe and Violet settle into a comfortable love, in a space filled, however, with romantic images of lost paradises. The narrator, sure that one of them would have killed the other, expresses surprise at this resolution, "I missed it altogether" (220). Bringing to light one of the paradoxes of the history of romantic love, the narrator characterizes Joe and Violet's "public love" as a retreat into each other. The oxymoronic notion of *undercover public love* reminds us that the fusionary love of the heterosexual couple was once an anti-social concept; read today as "true" love, the narrative of violence has gone public. In an improvised coda, the narrator suggests that there is another narrative of desire that has remained anti-social: "I envy them their public love. I myself have only known it in secret, shared it in secret and longed, aw longed to show it—to be able to say out loud what they have no need to say at all" (229). Public expression of the narrator's love (of writing) is forbidden, while Joe and Violet's story of desire, violence and the restoration of order can be published—as a novel. Because male writers since the troubadours have been allowed full and public expression of *joi* through metaphors such as the passion of a spurious heterosexual couple, it seems that Morrison's narrator-writer is a woman. The words spoken by the narrator in the book's final passage tend to confirm this conclusion. They show how writing is figured as the feminine, specifically a woman's body. Morrison's words also show how a woman writer who expresses *joi* in the traditional way risks sounding like a "woman in love":

> That I have loved only you, surrendered my whole self reckless to you and nobody else. That I want you to love me back and show it to me. That I love the way you hold me, how close you let me be to you. I like your fingers on and on, lifting, turning. I have watched your face for a long time now, and missed your eyes when you went away from me. (229)

When a male writer expresses the pleasure of writing thus, he transcends the limits of the "I" and fuses with writing as self-difference. This is not the case for a woman writer whose identity is intimately associated with the body equated in the passage with writing. Morrison deploys the metaphor of jazz to disturb the set form that assumes a fixed correlation between writing and a woman's body. An important character in the novel's *vagabondage* plot is Wild, a "crazy woman," a vagabond spirit, who may or may not be Joe's mother (178). Drucilla Cornell situates the allegory of Wild "at the heart of the novel" and sees "an association between the woman writer and this figure" ("Wild Woman and All That Jazz" [1995] 313–314). She writes, "In Morrison's allegory, we are forced to confront the operation of the psychical fantasy of Woman on the woman writer herself" (314). With the creation of Wild, Morrison joins the ranks of women who write about the necessity of dealing with a mother's agency as a person whose identity is not contained in images of the maternal. If Joe is to be free, he has to give up the eternal search for an imagined "real" mother; it is the search for the maternal that disrupts order in the novel, not Dorcas's seductive ways. Joe tells Dorcas as much when he tells her about his past: "Don't ever think I fell for you, or fell over you. I didn't fall in love, I rose in it. I saw you and made up my mind. My mind. And I made up my mind to follow you too. That's something I know how to do from way back" (135). Dorcas represents not only Joe's self-difference, the "first woman," lost with paradise; she is also a substitute for Wild. Morrison connects the two women with a repertoire of shared symbolic details, such as Dorcas's green shoes and the hoof marks on her cheeks, which by evoking Wild's green dress and the tracks to her cave-like dwelling, make the substitution apparent. Joe knows that Dorcas is a substitute:

> Take my little hoof marks away? Leave me with no tracks at all? In this world the best thing, the only thing is to find the trail and stick to it. I tracked my mother in Virginia and it led me right to her, and I tracked Dorcas from borough to borough. I didn't even have to work at it. (130)[26]

Dorcas refuses to reveal the name of her murderer before she dies. She does speak, however, and her last words reveal a truth far more important to the novel's integrity than the material fact of who shot her. Her final words, "Listen. I don't know who is that woman singing but I know the words by heart," link Dorcas even more closely textually to Wild than do the symbolic dress and the hoof marks; she hears Wild's song which replaces the lover's name, bringing Wild's importance into focus in the crucial scene of the novel's action. In Morrison's novel, the presence of Wild's song in the scene of Dorcas's death functions in two ways; it is a critique of the conventional wisdom that says that a sexually promiscuous woman deserves to die, and it brings the wild woman's voice into play as disrupting the patriarchal order, which demands Dorcas's confession. Wild's song represents the voice of women who refuse to conform to narrative convention. The narrator describes Wild's nonconformity in relation to Joe's desire for self-realization, "his house was full of motherlessness—and the chief unmothering was Wild's" (167). Wild is a Lilith figure, "local people used the story of her to caution children and pregnant girls," and as such she refuses, as Dorcas does in the end, to play the role of Eve in man's story (167). Since he was a teenager, Joe has wanted to find Wild and transform her into a conventional maternal figure:

> She wouldn't even have to say the word "mother." Nothing like that. All she had to do was give him a sign, her hand thrust through the leaves, the white flowers, would be enough to say that she knew him to be the one, the son she had fourteen years ago, and ran away from, but not too far. (37)

With words recalling *Jazz*'s epigraph, to the effect that Wild wouldn't have to use language, just give him a sign, Morrison sums up the maternal role in narrative. Wild's resistance to conforming to the maternal role in the son's search for identity both intrigues and upsets Joe:

> Wild was always on his mind, and he wasn't going to leave for Palestine without trying to find her one more time. . . . Above and to his left hibiscus

thick, savage and old. . . . The scrap of song came from a woman's throat, and Joe thrashed and beat his way up the incline and through the hedge, a tangle of muscadine vines, Virginia creeper and hibiscus rusty with age . . . he saw tracks enough to know she was there. He called out, "Anybody there?" The song stopped, and a snap like the breaking of twigs took its place. "Hey! You in there!" Nothing stirred and he could not persuade himself that the fragrance that floated over him was not a mixture of honey and shit. He left then, disgusted, and not a little afraid. (176–77)

Joe is attracted by the idea of the maternal, but disgusted by female presence. Like the musical form it is modeled on, Morrison's technique in *Jazz* is to pick up each chapter with a response to a note sounded at the end of the preceding one. For example, at the end of one chapter Joe enters a cave where Wild is thought to live; there he finds objects associated throughout the novel with both Wild and Dorcas, but Wild herself is nowhere to be found. "But where is *she?*" are the words which end Joe's search for Wild—and the chapter (184). Answering the question, the following chapter begins with the words, "There she is," this time, however, the pronoun *she* refers to Dorcas (187). Finding her at a party, dancing without him, "satisfied, content. . . . Happier than she has ever been anytime," Joe shoots her dead (188). The mother's song (Dorcas's final words, "I know that song by heart") must be silenced, sacrificed to the son's quest for self-realization. Dorcas's memory of Wild's song is a moment in Morrison's novel which is analogous to Colette's recollection of Sido's last letter, De Beauvoir's reaction to the sound of her mother's name at the funeral service, and Duras's restoration of the missing image of her mother—wearing the hat—to the center of the photograph.

The story of writing does not end with Wild/Dorcas's death. The narrator at the end of the book takes up Wild's song:

Who would see her, a playful woman who lived in a rock? Who could, without fright? Of her looking eyes looking back? I wouldn't mind. Why should I? She has seen me and is not afraid of me. She hugs me. Understands me. Has given me her hand. I am touched by her. Released in secret. Now I know. (221)

Wild is mother to the book. In a discussion of Sand's *François le champi,* Ann Berger writes:

She does not conceive of the return to the mother as a regression to the state of nature, a recrossing of the threshold of language acquisition. Rather she thinks of it as a passage beyond divisions (nature/culture, body/language)created precisely by placing the mother outside the sociocultural order.

Contrary to what a Lacanian or Kristevan analysis would have us believe, . . . it is the mother who guarantees access to the symbolic order . . . ("Let's Go to the Fountain" 8–9)

Mothering is redefined in *Jazz*. Wild, though mother to the book, is "unmother." Although Violet has no children, she is a mother in another way; she gives birth to Dorcas by telling her story the way Peter raises the biblical Dorcas from the grave (Acts 9: 36–42).

The novel's action begins with Violet killing a dead woman. She kills Dorcas in order to resurrect both Dorcas and herself; the repetition of the violence against women in narratives of desire reveals Violet's "wild" side. "Violent they called her now;" Violent is Violet's other self, "she sat in the drugstore sucking malt through a straw wondering who on earth that other Violet was that walked about the City in her skin; peeped out through her eyes and saw other things" (75; 89). Violet's self-realization depends not on the repression of her "wild" side, but on its release:

> But if *that* Violet was strong and had hips, why was she proud of trying to kill a dead girl, and she was proud. Whenever she thought about *that* Violet, and what *that* Violet saw through her own eyes, she knew there was no shame there, no disgust . . . . *that* Violet is not somebody walking round town, up and down the streets, wearing my skin and using my eyes shit no *that* Violet is me! (98)

Like Violet, Morrison's Sula is also a dangerous woman because she had, Morrison writes, "a gift for metaphor" and an "idle imagination"; she was "an artist with no art form" (*Sula* 121). By inventing Dorcas's story, Violet finds a creative outlet. She transforms herself from the kind of "dangerous woman" like Sula, into a creative woman who releases "the woman who scared everybody." The narrator's secret is out. She is a woman.

In an example of the double feminine of narratives of desire, Violet cannot fall in love with herself until she first falls in love with Dorcas (15). Violet's love for Dorcas is different from Joe's, however. While both seek to know themselves through Dorcas, Violet also comes to know her as a separate person, "based on careful investigation"—for Joe, Dorcas is nothing more than the representation of his own desire (28). Morrison manipulates language to tell a story of language and the construction of "woman"—the desire to feel like a woman is a desire to conform to a social construction. Morrison's syntax conveys the message that girls are taught by representations of "woman" to desire their own death; they seek their murderers. Girls like Dorcas are willing to sacrifice themselves to lovers like Joe "because he made them feel like women—which, she thought, was what Dorcas was looking for. Murderer" (76). When Violet resurrects Dorcas, she brings a part of herself back to life; in keeping with the *vagabondage* plot, she expresses the restoration of her wild side as a tribute to her own mother: "Now I want to be the woman my mother didn't stay around long enough to see. *That* one. The one she would have liked and the one I used to like before" (208).

CHAPTER 6

The Voice of Pleasure:
The Troubadour Continuum

I, René Gallimard, you see, I have known and been loved
by . . . the Perfect Woman.

—*David Henry Hwang*, M. Butterfly

Nobody's Perfect.

—*Joe E. Brown in* Some Like it Hot

The primary focus of contemporary debates challenging the hete-
rocentrism of Western culture has been the modern period. By
naming and defining the *troubadour effect,* and demonstrating its
tenacity in Western narratives of desire since twelfth-century Occitania,
this study shows that there is nothing new about the heterophobia and
misogyny of landmarks of modern and postmodern popular culture, which
convey the message that the perfect woman is a man. Since its introduction
into culture in the erotic lyrics of the troubadours, romantic love has not
been heterosexual. Nor is it homosexual. The woman in narratives of
desire is an illusion, a representation of a male artist's desire to transcend
conventional masculinity and express his difference from other men. The
perfect woman of Western romance is a man, and the sexual arrangements
in narratives of desire in Western culture are most aptly described as heterosexuality without women.[1]

In *Black Sails,* published in German in 1979 and in English translation
in 1999, Austrian novelist Erich Wolfgang Skwara retells the Tristan story.
His modern character, Tristan, a failed writer, and his constant companion,
called simply "the director," live in exile in Paris. They send for a former
lover of Tristan's, an actress by profession, to join them in Paris. Although
the plot of Skwara's narrative is intentionally obscure, it seems that the two
men's intention is for Tristan and the woman called simply "the actress" to

give a performance of heterosexual desire under the gaze of the patriarchal "director"; the actress will play the role of "the girlfriend" (17). The actress is confused. Since this is not a play, but "real life," why is the director always with the spurious heterosexual couple? "If she had not had the memory of passionate nights spent with Tristan in Munich, she would have suspected that the two men in front of her were misogynists, in love with each other" (24). She would have been mistaken. For although Tristan does not desire her as a woman, his desire conforms to the model for desire in heterosexual romance. Skwara's hero, who has been around for "a thousand years in fact," is a poet in love with neither the director, nor the actress, whose murder allows Tristan to dream of her and to eventually write their story. (153, 168). Tristan is in love with writing and because of this Skwara's modern hero is yet another example of the *troubadour effect*. He writes to the actress:

> To begin to write and expire somewhere just as our union initially befell us and began somewhere. To be with you in the writing, actress, to live and sleep with you and, in the writing, to achieve a necessary mutual fulfillment. For I've always known we were meant for each other. (103–4)

Although the actress is meant to read Tristan's letter as a love letter, expressing desire with her as its object, Skwara's Tristan, like the medieval lover, does not desire a woman, he desires to represent self-difference:

> Beloved, today I'm suffering an agony of longing for you. . . . I look down at my linen trousers and think of your precious face that I likewise have a right to kiss, since my head is filled with the loveliest thoughts about you. Trade me your outer for my inner self. . . . Someone must survive you after all. I love you, my actress. For me no other woman exists. (164–5)

Skwara's actress, like women readers for centuries, is "flattered" and "intoxicated" by the language of heterosexual desire (106). And so it continues. The thousand-year-old Tristan continues to seduce.

The danger to the subjectivity and the right to desire—not to mention the threat to their lives—of women who mistake male femininity for heterosexual romance is easier to discern in the romances and novels I have discussed than it is in less classic, but equally, and perhaps even more dangerous examples of the troubadour continuum in modern and postmodern popular culture. In the following pages I show how one might read some of these cultural events from the historical and cultural perspectives established in the preceding chapters. The examples offered are selective and random, and are drawn mainly from film and television. They are by no means exhaustive, but are meant to suggest the existence of a continuum which can be traced in any genre—popular art, performance art, advertising, popular music, etc.—representing heterosexual desire.

Billy Wilder's *Some Like It Hot* (1959), for example, penetrates a *mise-en-abîme* of cross-dressing and *homovestism* (Louise J. Kaplan's term) to pose an important question: who are the female impersonators in this film—Jack Lemmon and Tony Curtis, male actors who cross-dress to play Daphne and Josephine? or Marilyn Monroe who plays Sugar Cane as a caricature of Monroe's own screen persona? The title of Wilder's film, *Some Like It Hot*, summons up its analogue, *As You Like It,* Shakespeare's classic comedy of layered sexual masquerade—a boy actor plays Rosalind who plays Ganymede who plays Rosalind in a mock wedding ceremony with Orlando. In Wilder's film, out-of-work musicians Jack Lemmon and Tony Curtis cross-dress to join an all female band, according to the classic comic formula, their cross-dressing, like Rosalind's, is based on exigency. The comic effect that makes this film a classic, and not just a superb performance of drag by actors Lemmon and Curtis, is generated by the juxtaposition of their performance of femininity with Monroe's.[2] At a given moment in the film, the female impersonators are shown to be the "real ladies," when they tell the other "girls" to "watch their language."

The *troubadour effect*—the tacit motif of romantic love narratives in Western culture, to the effect that it takes a man to be a "real woman"—is evident in a scene when the camera lingers on Curtis's glamorously made-up face as he gazes with desire at Marilyn Monroe. In this, the film's only serious love scene, Curtis is in drag. While he looks longingly at Monroe, light and shadow play on his face, transforming him from a comic impersonator into a woman in love. When he moves toward the unsuspecting Monroe and kisses her, the lesbianism of the kiss shocks those in the audience who are convinced by the uncanny camera work that Curtis is a real woman. At the moment of fusion, when the (heterosexual) couple is formed, it is—as we have seen consistently in the romantic tradition— constitutively feminine.

To cite another example of a similar phenomenon, in *Tootsie* (Sydney Pollack, 1982), Michael Dorsey (Dustin Hoffman) sees his female self, Dorothy Michaels (also played by Hoffman), as a "representation of his better self hidden within" (Belle-Metereau [1985] 202). By the time Dorothy and Julie Nichols (Jessica Lange) move toward each other, drawn together by mutual desire to share an erotic kiss, the viewer is convinced by Hoffman's remarkable impersonation of a woman, that the relationship is lesbian, not heterosexual. Our sense of the relationship is confirmed by the dialogue between Julie and Michael in the film's final scene, which takes place after Julie discovers the truth, that Dorothy is a man. Julie admits that she "misses Dorothy," and Michael responds, "you don't have to. She's right here." In keeping with the troubadour tradition, the heterosexual Michael has been feminized by his transformation into Dorothy—Dorothy is to Michael what Claire is to Saint-Preux in Rousseau's *Julie ou la nouvelle Héloïse* (see chapter 3), making Julie's name a delightful example of cultural serendipity. (Or is it?)

The general acceptance and even approval of the absence of women's heterosexual desire from representations of desire in Western culture is attested to by the popularity of *Tootsie,* a more disturbing film in my view than *Some Like It Hot.* Viewers, like Julie, miss Dorothy at the film's conclusion, convinced that a female impersonator is a better partner for the loving and loveable Julie than an actual man—or woman. Given that the actor who plays Dorothy is Dustin Hoffman, it goes without saying that she is not a pretty woman. In spite of the sometimes comic effect of Dorothy's sexual encounters with men, however, the film's message is that she is sexually attractive in spite of her singular physical unattractiveness because she knows how to express a woman's desire better than an actual woman does, including Julie. One of Dorothy's major roles in the film is to tell Julie what to desire. Julie ends up desiring Dorothy, a false woman who disappears at the film's conclusion; the only desire remaining at the film's conclusion is Michael's.

Michael's feminization accomplishes two goals: the ideal fusion of "I" and "Not I" essential to the artist and its representation as the fusionary love of a woman and a feminized man. Once Michael has attained these goals, his femininity is retained only in his private eroticism with Julie. Similar to the structure of Chrétien de Troyes' *Érec et Énide* (see chapter 1), in public, Michael is once again a man, with all of the privileges of masculinity, now enhanced by the validation of his artistic genius.[3] Michael's self-realization is played against the background of the perfectly malleable figure of Julie, whose capacity to love either a man or a woman is governed by Michael's *gender du jour.* Julie is culture's dupe, forced to suffer needless self-doubt about her sexuality in order to demonstrate the absolute power of the *troubadour effect.*

Michael and the viewer, on the other hand, know the *so-called truth,* that their relationship is *really* heterosexual. The same play on the truth or lie of heterosexual romance is found in *Victor/Victoria* (Blake Edwards 1982) in which the character played by James Garner has inside knowledge that his relationship with the female impersonator played by Julie Andrews is *really* heterosexual. In Edwards' remake of Reinhold Schunzel's 1933 *Viktor und Viktoria,* Andrews plays an impoverished singer who is out of work—the prevailing pretext for comic transvestism in these films. She becomes a successful stage performer in Paris when she agrees to impersonate a man impersonating a woman. Garner's character is a wealthy American whose name, King Marchand, represents his undisputed claim to conventional masculinity. King is unnerved when he finds out that the woman (Andrews) to whom he finds himself attracted is supposed to be a female impersonator. To validate his conviction that a man like himself could never fall in love with another man, he manages to spy on her in the bathtub. As Bell-Metereau points out so trenchantly, however, it is no accident that director Blake Edwards has Garner "hiding in a closet" when he confirms his heterosexuality (227).

In *Some Like It Hot,* when Curtis plays the ostensibly heterosexual love scenes with Monroe, he sheds his female garb for the equally parodic costume of a wealthy playboy à la Cary Grant. Curtis's character does not play the heterosexual scenes as himself, a womanizing trombone player, but as a male impersonator. The choice of Grant, the paradigmatic romantic lover in American cinema, is by no means random. Grant's brief moment of transvestism in the 1938 film, *Bringing up Baby* (Howard Hawks) is often cited as a "wink" at gay Hollywood where Grant's own sexual ambiguity was well known (Garber 396). By showing that masculinity is as much a masquerade as femininity, Wilder calls the heterosexuality of all of the love scenes, including those *played as heterosexual,* into question. This is not to say, however, that the scenes should be read as homosexual. The questions I raise about the heterosexuality of romantic lovers in Western narrative challenge the grounds for reading homosexuality as its "other."

Many films involving female impersonation, comedies and serious dramas alike, have appeared since 1959 and the success of *Some Like It Hot.* The phenomenon has been given serious attention by critics, for example Rebecca Bell-Metereau (*Hollywood Androgyny* 1985) and Marjorie Garber (*Vested Interests* 1992), whom I have cited in these pages. Garber's book shows how the transvestite figure functions to disrupt received notions of fixed and stable sexual identity; she exhorts her reader not to "look through it [the transvestite figure] on a way to a story about men and women" (17). My focus differs from Garber's in that my point is that when a female impersonator enters into a relationship with another character in a narrative, the image that results *is* the story of men and women in Western representation.

At the end of *Some Like It Hot,* Curtis returns to a typical "male" persona, supposedly at this point his character's "real" self and he and the archetypal "female" sex object, Monroe, constitute a heterosexual couple—as do Michael and Julie, King Marchand and Victoria, Rosalind and

Orlando at the conclusion of Shakespeare's *As You Like It*. In none of these well-known romantic comedies, however, has "falling in love" been performed as heterosexuality. The reappearance of the heterosexual couple satisfies the public need for the *philtre*, an illusion that has formed our desire for its representation since the twelfth century. Sugar Cane, the character played by Marilyn Monroe, like the *dame* of troubadour lyrics has no original female self to return to: she is arrested in the role of female impersonator in the spurious heterosexual couple of the narrative's resolution.[4] Curtis's character, like the troubadour lover, is enhanced by his performance of the feminine without losing the privileges of masculinity. Wilder does not leave the viewer with a heterosexual image, however. In the film's oft-cited coda, Jack Lemmon, whose female persona, Daphne, has been wooed throughout the film by Osmond, played by Joe E. Brown, tells his would-be heterosexual beau that he is really a man. Osmond's response, "Nobody's perfect," stands as one of the classic comic lines in film history. The line's currency, and the film's status as one of the greatest comic films in the history of the genre, attests to an unstated consensus that an inadmissible truth about our culture's misogyny and heterophobia has been revealed in an acceptable way.

Comedy is not the only genre in which the truth about heterosexual narrative is revealed by a transvestite messenger. *The Kiss of the Spider Woman* (Hector Babenco 1985), *M. Butterfly* (H.D. Hwang, 1988; film version by David Cronenberg 1993), and *The Crying Game* (Neil Jordan 1992) are serious dramas exemplifying the *As You Like It/Some Like It Hot* phenomenon. In both the film *The Kiss of the Spider Woman,* starring William Hurt, Raul Julia, and Sonia Braga, and the novel by Manuel Puig (1976), the implication is that actual women lack the moral fabric to play the role of romantic heroine. *M. Butterfly* and *The Crying Game* carry the message that the perfect woman is a man.

The heterosexual couple in *The Kiss of the Spider Woman* is represented by two men who are cellmates in an Argentine prison: Molina, a homosexual transvestite window dresser and Valentin, a heterosexual revolutionary. Molina, played in the film by William Hurt, entertains his companion, Valentin, by telling the plots of his favorite movies. In the telling, Molina takes on the feminine qualities of the heroines of the elaborately reenacted narratives. The transformation of Molina into a woman is underscored in the film by the interpolation of clips of a tragic love story of desire, betrayal, and death, starring Sonia Braga, the Spider Woman of the title. Valentin, played by Raul Julia, is disgusted at first by Molina's female impersonations. Eventually however, after Molina has betrayed him and he has been weakened by his torturers, he falls under the spell of the narrative *philtre* prepared by Molina who nurses him, and the two men have sex. When he is released from prison, the once cowardly Molina risks his life to take a message to Valentin's revolutionary comrades. In the course of the narrative, Molina metamorphosizes from a comic female impersonator into a *real* woman who, through love, musters the courage to die for her lover. The transformation takes the form, significantly, of Molina mimicking the maternal to the point of becoming his own mother in scenes depicting his care of the very ill Valentin.[5] The substitution is pervasive; Molina also replaces the women in the film clips with a superior male version. Like the *dame* of *Fin'Amors,* the Spider Woman lacks the necessary courage for true love. Molina fulfills her feminine destiny in her place.

The hero of *The Crying Game*, Fergus (Stephen Rae), is also a revolutionary. He is responsible for guarding Jody (Forest Whitaker), a young British soldier held captive by members of the IRA. Jody and Fergus spend hours talking, during which time Jody shows Fergus a picture of Dil, the perfect woman (Jaye Davidson), and asks Fergus to take care of Dil after his inevitable execution. Jody is not executed by Fergus, but is killed trying to escape. Predictably, Fergus, whose desire for Dil has been mediated by the gentle prisoner, finds her and falls in love with Jody's perfect woman. Dil's status as the voice of pleasure is confirmed the first time Fergus sees her performing the film's title song, "The Crying Game." As the two prepare to make love for the first time, the viewer and Fergus learn at the same time that Dil, who represents the perfect woman and the voice of pleasure, is a man. The revelation scene is a shocker: as Dil undresses, the camera zooms in on her penis. Fergus vomits, and his retching might be seen as mirroring the reaction of viewers also taken in by actor Jaye Davidson's performance of femininity. The female impersonator is the only sympathetic woman in the film; evil is personified in Fergus's former IRA comrade and lover, Jude, played by Miranda Richardson. The names Jody and Jude resemble each other in the same way that Jude resembles the biblical name of Jesus's nemesis, Judas. Before Dil pumps Jude full of bullets in the film's violent climax, Fergus asks Dil to take off her makeup and cut her long hair. When they make love for what Fergus believes will be the last time, given that his former IRA associates are closing in on him, it is as two men. The film does not leave the viewer with an image of homosexual lovers, however. In a coda, a familiar technique for representing tacit cultural truths in artistic landmarks, Fergus is in prison for Jude's murder and Dil, for whom he has taken the blame, visits him. Dil is once again in drag, and to the uninformed eye, the film closes on the image of the perfect woman in love with a stereotypically virile man jailed for revolutionary acts. Viewers come to understand from *The Kiss of the Spider Woman* and *The Crying Game* that falling in love is the ultimate revolutionary act. As the camera moves away from the newly reconfigured heterosexual couple, Percy Sledge's rendition of the song "When a Man Loves a Woman" is heard, involving both film and popular music in the creation of the illusion. The writer and director of *The Crying Game,* Neil Jordan, said about the film, "Its a love story beyond sex." Not so. Dil's appeal as a character is that she is a man who is also the perfect woman.

René Gallimard, the protagonist of D.H. Hwang's 1988 play, *M. Butterfly* is an unwitting traitor, unaware that he has committed a revolutionary act by falling in love with a Chinese spy, Song Liling with whom he has a passionate affair for twenty years before discovering that the woman he loves is a female impersonator.[6] His reaction to the discovery of Song's biological sex echoes the message of *The Crying Game:* once you have known a woman created by a man, actual women are undesirable. Gallimard is devastated when he learns the truth, but remains in love with Song:

> I'm a man who loved a woman created by a man. Everything else—simply falls short. . . . I've finally learned to tell fantasy from reality. And, knowing the difference, I choose fantasy. (III: 3)

His desire for the representation of the perfect woman blinds him from the truth for a long time. In words that convey the message of *Tootsie* in a more serious drama, Song explains how she conned him, "only a man knows how a woman is supposed to act" (II: 7).

The conclusion of *M. Butterfly* brings us back to the *troubadour effect.* Gallimard is in love not only with a representation of femininity, but with the voice of pleasure as embodied in Cio Cio San, the heroine of Puccini's opera *Madame Butterfly.* In prison for having passed information to Song, Gallimard brings the representation of the feminine back to its original site, his own body. He picks up a kimono and speaks:

> I've played out the events of my life night after night, always searching for a new ending to my story one where I leave this cell and return forever to my Butterfly's arms.
>
> Tonight, I realize my search is over. That I've looked all along in the wrong place. And now, to you, I will prove that my love was not in vain . . . by returning to the world of fantasy where I first met her.
>
> There is a vision of the Orient that I have. Of slender women in chong sams and kimonos who die for the love of unworthy foreign devils. Who are born and raised to be the perfect women. Who take whatever punishment we give them, and bounce back, strengthened by love, unconditionally. It is a vision that has become my life. (III: 3)

He makes up his face to resemble an oriental woman, dons the kimono, is handed a knife, and says:

> Love warped my judgment, blinded my eyes, rearranged the very lines on my face . . . until I could look in the mirror and see nothing but . . . a woman.
>   The love of a Butterfly can withstand many things—but how can it face the one sin that implies all others? The devastating knowledge that underneath it all, the object of her love was nothing more, nothing less than . . . a man. It is 19__. And I have found her at last. In a prison on the outskirts of Paris. My name is René Gallimard—also known as Madame Butterfly. (III: 3)

As the music of the "Love Duet" from Puccini's opera blasts over the loudspeakers, Song appears, dressed as a man. He stares at the dead Gallimard and says two words: "Butterfly? Butterfly?" which are also the final words of Puccini's opera, uttered in desperation by Butterfly's seducer, Lieutenant Pinkerton. Hwang explains the ending of his play in an afterword: "the Frenchman fantasizes that he is Pinkerton and his lover is Butterfly. By the end of the piece, he realizes that it is he who has been Butterfly, in that the Frenchman has been duped by love; the Chinese spy, who exploited that love, is therefore the real Pinkerton" (96). Song's name represents her function in Gallimard's story; she is the voice of pleasure, the song a masculine diplomat dares not sing in public, his private fantasy of self-difference. Gallimard has it both ways; for a major part of the narrative, he has played the role of Tristan, a man in love with the perfect woman, and in the end he is Iseut, a woman who dies for love of a man. None of which is strange considering that the first operatic "divas" were castrati. As Susan Leonardi and Rebecca Pope conclude in *The Diva's Mouth* (1996), this does not mean that there were no women opera singers during the eighteenth century, but that the public preferred the castrati to actual women (38).

There are examples of the troubadour continuum, which, like the canonical literary examples I have analyzed in this study, do not involve explicit female impersonation. A scene from the film, *Philadelphia* (1993), for example, is a good illustration of how the *troubadour effect* persists in contemporary culture in a work that deals primarily with homosexual eroticism. In one scene, a gay man in the final stages of AIDS (Tom Hanks) expresses the joy of love in the face of death to his straight lawyer (Denzel Washington), by acting out the drama and emotion of a recording of the diva Maria Callas singing "La mamma morta," an aria from Giordano's opera *Andrea Chénier* (1896). The lawyer's homophobia dissolves—for at least this privileged moment in the film—as he listens to Callas's rendition of the aria, which ends with the words "sono amore" (I am love), while watching Hanks' character's uninhibited participation in the pleasure that her voice allows him to experience. Washington's character participates—in spite of himself—in the gay man's experience, and for a moment the voice of pleasure renders the social categories of homosexuality and heterosexuality invisible and irrelevant.

"Sono amore," I am love, I sound (sonare) love. The "I" who is love and sounds love is experienced as a representation of a desiring subject who is male. In other words, there is no female presence on the screen. The voice, however, that transports these two men is a woman's. The "I" in *sono amore,* is rhetorical, an effect of language. This being the case, it would seem to follow, then, that such an experience transcends sex. That this is not so, however, can be seen in the life of the woman Maria Callas, which, from a postmodern perspective, might be said to mirror her status as the voice of pleasure. Callas was a woman who presumed to desire in life as well as in art; a woman whose capacity for desire moved beyond representation, beyond lending a female voice to male desire. It seemed that Callas was destined to be punished for her desire, and like the fictional examples of *vagabondage* discussed in previous chapters, the punishment was disappearance: the mandated weight loss; exile from the Metropolitan Opera by Rudolph Bing; and displacement from the Island of Scorpios by the lean, beautiful boy ideal of femininity, Jackie Kennedy Onassis. In the end, after Onassis's death, Callas took on the appearance of a specter in, for example, the often reproduced image of her peeking out from behind a transparent curtain in her Paris apartment where she was soon to die like Iseut—the disappearance of a body whose heart has died with her lover, or more to the point, with her lover's desire. When a woman desires too much, she is either a disembodied voice, or a social outcast. When a man desires too much, he is an artist and a woman. Such are the peregrinations of the *troubadour effect.*

Nicholas Ray's 1954 western, *Johnny Guitar,* illustrates how the cowboy of the American epic is a hero in the tradition of the knights of medieval epics. In his book on cultural history, called *John Wayne's America* (1997), Gary Wills says that Wayne's success as an epic masculine type is, in part, due to a certain feminization. According to Wills' sources, Wayne modeled his unique way of standing and walking on Roman statuary, specifically the statues of David by Donatello and Michelangelo. The models for Wayne's virility described by Wills as "beyond masculinity" were, then, two world classics of feminine male beauty (12–27). *Johnny Guitar,* a cult classic in France, is described by François Truffaut as "a Western that is dream-like, magical, unreal to a degree delirious" (107–8). Zeroing in on a quality akin to Truffaut's choice of "delirious," Leo Charney (1990) argues that the film "brings forth *excess* in an attempt to contain it," seeing the women characters in the film as fulfilling this role (31, emphasis added). Charney argues that the film subordinates "the female plot to the reaffirmed masculinity of Johnny Guitar" (31). Musical references, such as the names of the film's male rivals Johnny Guitar (Sterling Hayden) and The Dancing Kid (Scott Brady), convey and contain feminine excess. Like *M. Butterfly,* the music played at the conclusion of *Johnny Guitar* suggests sexual illusion: in Peggy Lee's sultry rendition of the title song, the words "there never was a man like my Johnny" are in the tradition of double entendre illustrated earlier, with reference to the language play ("the one thing to my purpose nothing") of Shakespeare's Sonnet XX (chapter 2).

Johnny Guitar (Sterling Hayden) is a gunfighter who has renounced a gun in favor of a guitar. His masculinity, however, is undisputed; without a gun, he is still the "best shot in the west." The gunfighter that Johnny Logan (Johnny Guitar's real name) used to be is never represented on screen; masculinity is unrepresentable except as self-difference, figured in the film by Johnny's love interest, Vienna (Joan Crawford). As the film begins, Johnny returns after a long absence, during which he has undergone a change from gunslinger to vagabond singer. His arrival coincides with attacks on Vienna by a group bent on driving her out of town on the pretext that she is involved with members of a criminal gang. The group is led by Vienna's rival, Emma Small (Mercedes McCambridge), whose hatred stems not from the trumped up charges against Vienna, but from jealousy; Emma sees Vienna as her rival for the affections of The Dancing Kid. Vienna's first appearance emphasizes her masculine qualities. The camera angle gives the impression of height and power as Vienna descends a staircase into the saloon she owns, dressed in black shirt and pants, a heavy silver and leather belt, and sporting a stance and a strut in the manner of John Wayne.[7] One of her male saloon employees confirms the visual image, commenting, "Never seen a woman who was more a man. She thinks like one, acts like one, and sometimes makes me feel like I'm not." Another man adds, "for the first time I'm workin' for a woman, and likin' it." The romantic heroine of *Johnny Guitar* is masculine enough for the hero to love her with the same intensity reserved for other men—in the tradition of *compagnonnage,* and still feminine enough to represent his self-difference.

Johnny rides into town like a typical western hero, but with a difference; instead of a gun, he carries a guitar. The guitar connects him to the troubadour tradition and designates him as the film's romantic hero. Johnny's arrival inspires a costume change in Vienna. The powerful woman who makes her employees doubt their own masculinity puts on femininity for

WRITING THE VOICE OF PLEASURE

her reunion with the feminized man who has given up his gun for a troubadour's guitar; the feminized romantic hero meets the illusory feminine
woman. Alternately wearing a sexy red nightgown and a virginal white
dress whose voluminous skirt emphasizes a small waist, actress Crawford's
sharply contoured features are highlighted by harsh make up and short
upward brushed hair, placing the femininity of the costume in relief.
Johnny seduces a reluctant Vienna by having her repeat in her voice words
he provides: "I have waited for you." "I would have died if you hadn't
come back." "I love only you." Vienna is the female voice Johnny needs to
express the excess of his desire; she is the troubadour's lady, the voice of
pleasure. A man's feelings spoken by a woman whose femininity is performative, characterize the film's only love scene.[8]

When Vienna and Johnny are forced to run for their lives to escape
Emma's gunfighters, she removes the long white dress and enacts an elaborate parody of cross-dressing. Vienna and Johnny duck into a dark, roman-
tically lit cave under her saloon, where she finds the masculine attire she
took off to play the role of Johnny's woman. She retreats into an obscured
part of the cave from which the viewer—and Johnny—see clothes flying,
spoofing those film scenes in which a stage-door "Johnny" watches feminine clothes appear over a screen that veils a woman performer changing
costumes behind it. One is reminded as well as George Sand's use of a cave
as the *mise en scène* for equally parodic episodes of "putting on" and "taking
off" traditional sex roles in *Consuelo* (see chapter 3). When Vienna reappears, she is dressed as she was in her first appearance, more manly than any
man. These clothes, however, will be shed in turn when Vienna and Johnny
swim across a river to find a place to hide and their clothes get wet. In a
more complex scene of cross-dressing, Johnny borrows clothes from his
rival for Vienna's love, the Dancing Kid, with whom they have found
refuge from Emma's pursuit. Johnny and the Dancing Kid are predictably
the same size; Vienna is smaller and must put on the clothes of a very young
boyish cowboy, Turkey, who has been hanged by Emma's avenging posse.
Turkey, the boy, the victim, and scapegoat, was never considered to be as
much of a man as the others, but his death brings him respect in the end.
And now the masculinity of Vienna, a woman in boy's clothes will also be
tested in an *asag* reminiscent of medieval romance. Vienna must betray all of
her pacifist principles and face off against Emma; she is wounded and is
spared having to kill Emma who is killed by, and kills the Dancing Kid,
eliminating the obstacles to Johnny and Vienna's desire. When Johnny and
Vienna walk off into the sunset in the last scene, Johnny is much taller than
Vienna, who appeared so tall in the film's first shot of her. Order is
restored; sexual difference is reestablished. Ray has made sure, however, that

the astute viewer will be aware of its restoration as myth, as illusion, and as pure representation.

Representation is the also the underlying theme of Kevin Smith's *Chasing Amy* (1997), a romantic comedy whose popularity attests to the appeal of the themes and structures of the troubadour continuum to contemporary twenty-something filmgoers. The film's irony turns on the occupation of its main characters, they write—comic books. Heterosexual romance serves the romantic hero, Holden (Ben Affleck), in a perfectly traditional way; by falling in love with Alyssa (Joey Lauren Adams) Holden becomes a better writer, producing a new comic book, called "Chasing Amy," which represents—for him—the kind of personal writing he has been striving for. Once Alyssa becomes writing for Holden, she has served her purpose. Holden's romance with Alyssa is summed up by a metaphor—Chasing Amy—conceived in the film by Silent Bob, a character played by the film's writer and director, Kevin Smith. Silent Bob, as his name indicates, does not speak except to create the metaphor that gives Holden's new strip, and Smith's own film, its title. Holden's story is transformed into representation by Silent Bob's metaphor. Some things never change; writing in *Chasing Amy* is represented as heterosexual romance. Holden's metaphor is borrowed from Smith, who borrows it from the tradition that produced "Chasing Amy" or "Chasing *Ami*."

Holden's creative endeavor is different from existing comic book plots in which men perform heroic feats together in a variety of versions of *compagnonnage*.[9] Its main plot is, in principle, heterosexual desire. In my view, Smith's plot suggests that today's comic book resembles the poetry of twelfth-century Provence in which heterosexual love is an experimental plot. For this reason, *Chasing Amy* is an apt example of the troubadour continuum in the culture of fin de siècle America. A romance narrative in the tradition of *Fin'Amors,* the relationship at the center of the film's narrative focus is the *compagnonnage* of Holden and his best friend and collaborator Banky (Jason Lee), not Holden's relationship with Alyssa. The heroine of the film's heterosexual romance plot is a lesbian. Alyssa's lesbianism is, however, a red herring. Alyssa's sexual preference is not the obstacle to heterosexual romance; the obstacle is Holden's friendship with Banky. The obstacle to the heterosexual plot disappears when Alyssa gives up her lesbian lifestyle for Holden. *Chasing Amy* contains the inevitable romantic scene depicting fusionary heterosexual love between a woman who has proven that she is worthy to be loved by becoming a man's *compagnon* and a man who is different from other men in that he is capable of loving a woman with the same intensity as he loves his male *compagnon*.

Alyssa, like Sand's Thérèse Jacques, and other heroines before her in the romantic tradition, falls in love with the romantic hero in spite of herself. When she rushes into Holden's arms for the inevitable fusionary kiss, Alyssa is a parody of the romantic heroine. The viewer is divided, disappointed that Alyssa gives up her unique identity to participate in Holden's dream of self-realization, but at the same time taking pleasure in the familiar kiss which symbolizes androgynous fusion. Typical of the *Fin'Amors* tradition, in spite of their fusion, and her sacrifice, Holden is not convinced that she is worthy of his love because he finds out that besides her lesbian affairs, Alyssa has also had kinky heterosexual sex. Since his own sexual experience has always been orthodox, he feels inadequate. Interestingly, her mature lesbianism does not bother him as much as her adolescent heterosexual encounters, confirming the conventional wisdom that sex between women doesn't count. When Alyssa counters Holden's attacks on her sexual morality with the words, "I'm an experimental girl," Smith's film touches on the conflict between women's agency and heterosexual love which I have associated throughout this book with *vagabondage*.

In *The Notebooks of Malte Laurids Brigge* (1910), Rainer Maria Rilke depicts the departure from tradition by imaginative women as the troubadour's worst fear:

> But a woman loved, who yields is still far from being a woman who loves. . . . How he thought then of the troubadours who feared nothing more than being answered. (212)

A woman free to return a man's desire intrudes on the solitary pleasure of the joy of desiring, which Rilke insightfully associates with the troubadours:

> For he had loved and loved again in his solitude; each time with waste of his whole nature and with unspeakable fear for the liberty of the other. Slowly he learned to penetrate the beloved object with the rays of his feeling, instead of consuming it in them. And he was spoiled by the fascination of recognizing through the ever more transparent form of his beloved, the expanse it opened to his desire infinitely to possess. (212)

Rilke's rendering of the writer's relationship to women confirms the continued presence in the Western poetic tradition since the troubadours of the collapse of difference between a poet's *joi* and an (imaginary) woman. Alyssa is the troubadour's—and Holden's—worst fear, an experimental girl, more artistic than Holden, she sings as well as writes. In that both are artists, and that her sexuality is unorthodox, the relationship between

Holden and Alyssa has much in common with that of Thérèse Jacques and Laurent in Sand's *Elle et lui* (chapter 4). While listening to Alyssa sing in a lesbian bar, The Meow Mix Club, Holden enjoys an encounter with the voice of pleasure. Thinking Alyssa's song is for him, he enjoys a few moments of uninhibited joy, snapping his fingers and swaying rather awkwardly to the music. Even though it turns out that Alyssa's song is meant for a woman, it acts as a *philtre,* mediating Holden's desire to go beyond the boundaries that have, until now, defined his sexuality (using a hackneyed cliché, Smith blames Holden's repressed sexuality on his Catholic school education in New Jersey). Holden has fallen in love with his own capacity to love a sexually experimental girl. The ideal relationship continues, however, to be his friendship with Banky, which is threatened by Alyssa in the same way that Érec's relationship with Énide threatens the coherence and stability of the masculine world of the Knights of the Round Table in Chrétien de Troyes's story discussed in chapter 1.

A classic example from the comic book canon, "Archie," is the prototype for the characters Holden and Banky. Archie and Jughead are constantly threatened by the inappropriate and irrelevant presence of the comic's female types, the blond Betty and the brunette Veronica. When *Chasing Amy*'s only overtly homosexual male character, Hooper, suggests that Banky and Holden are mirror images of Archie and Jughead, Holden concludes that Banky harbors latent homosexual desire for him. His desire to please Banky and to prove to Alyssa that he is as "experimental" as she is leads him to suggest a *ménage à trois.* Banky agrees to the experiment, but Alyssa says that her experimental days are over: "You turned out to be all I was looking for." She walks out on the two friends, saying to Banky as she leaves, "he's yours again." She is wrong, however, to mistake what has transpired for proof of either Banky or Holden's homosexuality. The heterosexual romance is over, but so is the equally spurious homosexual plot.

One year later, the three characters meet again at the Comicon convention. Although Holden shares some wistful gazes (contrived to move the viewer) with both Banky and Alyssa, he has what he yearned for. He has discovered a personal writing style. The film ends when Holden walks out the door, leaving two people who compromised their own sexual identities so that he could write. Alyssa has a new lesbian lover, and Banky is alone working on the old strip.

The Crying Game and *Chasing Amy* simultaneously create and reveal the inherent absurdity of the heterosexual romantic couple. Contemporary popular culture derives this and other structures of desire from the same classical models it seeks to subvert. *Seinfeld,* characterized by cultural anthropologist Eric Gans as unmatched as a cultural marker for the 1990s, is brilliant in its practiced avoidance of representing desire as heterosexual.[10] In spite of outspoken references by Kramer and others to the show's "gay" subtext, viewers are not offended by this message as in the case of *Ellen,* a sitcom similar to *Seinfeld* in format as well as in the fact that both Seinfeld and De Generes began their careers as stand-up comics. The decision to remove the *philtre* from the prevalent and highly successful format of non-threatening friendships with sexual undercurrents was the end of *Ellen.* When De Generes decided to have her character come out as a lesbian, De Generes's own sexual preference off-screen, the *Truman Show*-like result made network executives and viewers alike squeamish. The popularity of shows like *Three's Company, Bosom Buddies, Magnum P.I., Friends,* to mention only a few, attests to our desire for the *philtre.* The season after the character Ellen came out, the show carried a warning that its contents could be dangerous to children. No such warning has ever accompanied *Seinfeld* and shows like it, in spite of their implications of homoeroticism.

The problem is not only the issue of homosexuality, but of lesbianism. Male homosexuality has a history of heroic representation, not so female homosexuality. This difference stems from cultural expectations about woman's agency. Women are traditionally represented either as lacking agency, or, if they acquire it, it is to serve the narrative structure that demands that a woman have agency only to surrender it to fusionary love. The latter narrative device is the one Sand, Colette, and other women writing in the vagabond tradition have foregrounded in their novels. A woman who dares assume a non-negotiable subject position, closing off the option that she might one day "melt into romantic longing and the desire for union" in the tradition of women in love, can no longer play the role required of women (Gornick [1997] 3).

The *philtre,* lost when writer De Generes conflated representation and reality, prolongs deferral of closure. Deferral, as Gans points out, is the very essence of *Seinfeld.*[11] During its final year, the series became more and more explicit about the absence of heterosexuality. The notion that the lack of heterosexual love might mean the presence of homoeroticism is introduced, but as a comic *effect* that serves as a *philtre.* Unreliable messengers proclaim the show's "gayness"; Kramer, the postmodern voice of the absurd, and Newman, whose name reads like a warning label—god help us all if this guy is the "new man." The *philtre* permits moments such as the last scene in the "Reverse Peephole" episode (January 15, 1998) when the series' star, Jerry, is seen on the street wearing a fur coat that has been the major prop in the episode's thematic gag about "dandies" and "fancy boys" who wear "man furs." He is carrying a European men's "carry-all" which Elaine has convinced him to buy for its practicality since he doesn't like the look of an overstuffed wallet in his pocket. When the "carry-all" is stolen, a policeman refuses to pursue the thief until Jerry admits that it is really a "purse." The last time we see Jerry, he is crying out to anyone who will listen, "It's not a purse, it's European!" The construction of the American notion of masculinity is the central theme of this episode. As usual, masculinity is constructed in relationship to male self-difference or femininity. Comic effects are produced when Jerry is forced by circumstances to experience a woman's vulnerability.

A recent commentary on the show's history poses a question as to why Elaine, the only actual woman among the main characters, "spends so much time acting like one of the boys," when she is really a "riot grrl with a certain *Camelot*-like grace" (Wild [1998] 66). Elaine's gender role-playing is not as puzzling in the context of the literary tradition that produced Camelot. Elaine is at once the boys' *compagnon,* and the voice of their pleasure. Unlike Ellen, Elaine's sexual desire does not make her unavailable to play this latter role. Wild goes on to say:

> Jerry Seinfeld had said that the decision was made to add a major female character because the show initially "lacked estrogen." But, in the hands of Louis-Dreyfus, Elaine Benes quickly became more than just a demographic, estrogen-laced throwaway. She was the excitable girl of our dreams—a woman with the grace to make a simple exclamatory phrase like "get out!" ring out like poetry. (Wild 33)

Elaine's sexual desire is excessive, but because it is also ridiculous, she can still be the "girl of our dreams." The ongoing narrative of her sex life allows the male friends to share sexual experiences with each other and with Elaine, as *representation.* Her final and most consistent lover in the series, Puddy, is abysmally stupid, but good in bed. Puddy wears a fur coat for real, unlike Jerry who puts it on like drag. The inappropriateness and castrating nature of Elaine's sexual desire is placed in relief by Puddy's inappropriateness and effeminacy. This comic representation of the poor use to which Elaine puts her agency makes the viewer wonder if she wouldn't be better off with Jerry, with whom she is supposed to have had a romantic relationship before the show began. The absence of any representation of their sexual relationship on the show is important to the key comic strategy of deferral. Jerry's best friend, George, suggests from time to time that because Jerry has slept with one of his girlfriends, he should sleep with Elaine. This suggestion has nothing to do with Elaine, nor does it make any sense as an exchange—the symmetry is off. It has to do with George's mimetic desire. Elaine's agency exists only when the man in question is stupid and effeminate. In her relationship with the show's more credible men, George and Jerry, on the other hand, she is an object of exchange in George's fantasy about living Jerry's sex life.

Kramer participates in the troubadour continuum as well. He spends an entire episode riding around on a test run with a car salesman. When the two are running out of gas, they transform a perfectly safe situation into a dangerous adventure by reenacting the final scene of *Thelma and Louise* (Ridley Scott 1991). When they floor the gas pedal and hold hands, they mimic the same actions performed by those film heroines. Thelma and Louise's grand gesture included a kiss, making it a parody of the *Liebestod* of the paradigmatic romance, *Tristan and Iseut*. Their *compagnonnage* is a pastiche of classic buddy movies such as *Butch Cassidy and the Sundance Kid* (George Roy Hill 1969). Could it possibly be an accident that Sundance's name is so reminiscent of The Dancing Kid in *Johnny Guitar,* or that his sidekick's name is Butch? The episode of Kramer's test ride has rich implications for viewers knowledgeable about American popular culture. The *Tristan* legacy provides a historical perspective on the cultural representations framing the comic episode.

The most blatant example of how the show consistently points to what it is possible to get away with if the taboos against conflating reality and representation are understood—don't ask, don't tell—is the January 29, 1998 episode, "The Cartoon," in which Jerry's best friend George dates Jerry's double. Although both George and Jerry vehemently deny the resemblance, everyone else, especially Kramer—often the voice of truth in the world according to *Seinfeld*—agrees that Janet looks just like Jerry. Kramer and Elaine perpetuate the "homosexual panic" created by the implications of the resemblance. When Kramer comes right out with it and says to George, "You're gay!" the hilarity of the moment, like the last line of *Some Like It Hot,* makes the truth of the structure of desire admissible.[12] Hilarity is not the effect produced by the entire episode, however. When George and Jerry are alone discussing this, they become paranoid at the possibility of their homosexuality and desperately seek out Kramer to deflect attention from what could be a serious threat to their friendship. When George desperately tries to discover other reasons for his attraction to Janet, the Jerry look-alike, he asks her what the first thing he said to her was. Janet responds: "You told me I was the prettiest girl at the party." Since Janet really does look like Jerry Seinfeld, she is not very pretty. George knows this, and so must pursue his inquiry. She says that the next thing he did was to ask her for gum. "So," he thinks, "its not about looks, its about gum!" Gum, not her resemblance to Jerry, is what is holding this (heterosexual) relationship together. The scene pushes the envelope, turning into comedy of the absurd when gum gets stuck in Janet's hair forcing her to cut it so short that she looks even more like Jerry. When she emerges from the shower, having just washed her newly-cut hair, dressed in Jerry's signature blue oxford button-down shirt, George runs away from the relationship, and from his fear that the madman Kramer might be right about his desire for his best friend.[13] George's desire is not homosexual, he does not desire another man. He desires a man who is a more perfect woman than any woman he has ever met . . . or ever will.

Jerry is Mom.[14] All of the series' episodes are shot around Jerry's kitchen, stocked with comfort food. Interestingly, all of the male characters' mothers have played central roles in particular episodes throughout the series' run. It hardly seems coincidental that Elaine's mother has, to my knowledge, never been mentioned. By way of contrast with Jerry's role as mother to the family of friends, the men's actual mothers fall far short of the maternal ideal.

The Janet episode is not the first time that Jerry's resemblance to a woman has been the subject of a show. In Spring 1996, the season ended with a teaser about fusionary love; Jerry tells George that he is in love. By the first episode of the next season Jerry's heterosexual romance is already a thing of the past, he says that he had to break it off because he realized that the woman he was in love with was just a female version of himself—she too was a comic, and what was even more disconcerting, she looked just like him. Jerry never has another brush with "the real thing;" impossible, since, like René Gallimard, he had known and been loved by the perfect woman.

In the end, the structure of the relationships between and among the four main characters—Jerry, George, Elaine, and Kramer—cannot be reduced to repressed homosexual desire, or any one of the variants of sexual desire treated during the series' nine year run. *Seinfeld*'s appeal, and its status as an example of the troubadour continuum, is that it allows millions of viewers, whose ideas of sexual relationships are formed by the Western narrative of heterosexual romance, to laugh openly at the absurd idea that a man might love a woman with the same intensity that he loves his male friend.

David Wild proposes that at some time in the future, one will look back at *Seinfeld* and write a book about the show called "Homoeroticism on the West Side: George and Jerry, a love story for our times?" I am suggesting that to read this love story as new or contemporary is to have missed the point of Western love narratives since the twelfth century. Another problem with Wild's fictitious book title lies with the term "homoerotic." Jerry's appeal is not masculinity. He is yet another version of the perfect woman of Western representation.

$\mathcal{N}otes$

INTRODUCTION

1. The expression "minimizing none of its charm" is from Nancy Mitford's translation of *La Princesse de Clèves* (36).
2. See especially Denis de Rougemont and René Nelli, whose books, respectively, *Love in the Western World* (1939) and *L'Érotique des troubadours* (1963) are foundational to the study of medieval philosophies of love. Although I take issue with many of their conclusions, especially concerning the presence of women in romantic love narratives, this study owes much to their scholarship, especially in regard to the relationship between the troubadours and Catharism.
3. In an interview with Frédéric Beigbeder published in *Le Figaro littéraire* (March 9, 2000), Sollers responded to the question "wouldn't you rather be having lunch right now with a woman rather than with me," with the following remark: "A man is a woman like the others" (Un homme est une femme comme les autres) (8). It can be said that this comment confirms the spurious meaning of "heterosexuality" for a man who writes novels whose subject is desire.
4. See Carol Siegel's work on modern forms of homophobia and their connection to cultural aesthetics, particularly a paper on Lawrence's *Lost Girl,* read at the 1995 MLA, and another article in *Genders* (1995), "Compulsory Heterophobia: The Aesthetics of Seriousness and The Production of Homophobia." In the paper on *Lost Girl,* Siegel makes the point that heterophobia is essential to the construction of homophobia in contemporary feminist theory, which "retains (from psychoanalytic theory) homosexuality as a repository for historically forbidden desires" (3).
5. My discussions of how literature provides models for social behavior are framed by the theories of mimetic and triangular desire developed by René Girard in *Mensonge romantique et vérité romanesque (Deceit, Desire and the Novel)*(1960). Two of Girard's theoretical tenets are important to my own work: first, his argument that the desire that governs romantic passion is triangular in that its structure inevitably involves two men who desire the same object; second, his belief that

models of desire in literature create desire in the reader. To expand on Girard's first premise, it is not a woman that men desire, but each other's desire and each other's subjectivity. Girard does not pursue the issue of the illusory nature of the woman in Western representations of desire, nor the implications of this phenomenon for women's access to heterosexual desire.

6. In "Compulsory Heterosexuality" (1980) Adrienne Rich calls on feminists to "take the step of questioning heterosexuality as a 'preference' or 'choice' for women" (51). "The rewards will be great," she writes, "a freeing-up of thinking, the exploring of new paths, the shattering of another great silence, new clarity in personal relations" (51). At one point in the development of a political position, Rich proposed that heterosexually identified women make the distinction—for purposes of speculation—between "lesbian existence," by which she means "consciously desired genital sexual experience with another woman," and the "lesbian continuum." Rich later reneged on her invitation to heterosexually-defined women to place themselves on the lesbian continuum, defined by Rich as "a range—through each woman's life and throughout history—of woman-identified experience." Her reason: because it offers to "women who have not yet begun to examine the privileges and solopsisms of heterosexuality . . . a safe way to describe their felt connections with women, without having to share in the risks and threats of lesbian existence" (51, 73). By closing ranks to exclude heterosexually-identified women from the range of woman-identified experience, I fear that Rich replicates their exclusion from subjectivity and desire in the so-called heterosexual narrative tradition which she condemns.

7. The work of Eve Kosofsky Sedgwick in *Between Men* (1985) and *Epistemology of the Closet* (1990) moves Girard's theories into the politics of sexual identity by stressing the homosexuality of the triangular structure. I, too, challenge the heterosexuality of desire in Western representation, but argue that desire in romantic love narratives is not homosexual either. It is rather an expression of *joi,* a complex poetic rendering of the erotic pleasure of writing developed by the troubadours in twelfth-century Provence.

8. Courtly love is a term coined by Gaston Paris to embrace the various philosophies of heterosexual love in the Middle Ages. Courtly love is a composite of sex roles, codes and rituals derived from *Fin'Amors,* a specific twelfth-century philosophy of ideal love invented by the troubadours of Occitania. The rituals of *Fin'Amors,* which include the *asag* or love test, and the exchange of hearts involving the androgynous fusion of the lovers, are inextricable from the structure of desire in romantic love narratives. For a complete history and analysis of the poetics of *Fin'Amors,* popularly known as courtly love since Paris's coinage in 1883, see especially Nelli, *L'Érotique des troubadours* (1963). My bibliography also contains an extensive list of related works.

9. Nelli describes the homosexualization of heterosexuality in troubadour poetry throughout *L'Érotique des troubadours.* See especially the extensive treatment of the ritual of "the exchange of hearts", and the conclusion (209–220, 338). For

the best example of Nelli's application of *Fin'Amors* to contemporary eroticism, see "Tirésias ou les métamorphoses de la passion" (1980).

Because his writings have not been translated into English, Nelli's work is not often cited by anglophone scholars and critics. It is also important to address a misconception. While it may be true that French medieval scholars have diverging opinions about Nelli's personal devotion to Cathar practices and for that reason some characterize him as a bit of an eccentric, there is no disagreement about either the integrity or the thoroughness of his research on the troubadours, nor about its value to scholarship in that area.

10. The term "the feminine" belongs rather to philosophy and art of the 1890's than to the era of the troubadours. I use it here in spite of this, because I believe that the notion of the (eternal) feminine ordinarily associated with Goethe, Nietzsche, Schopenhauer and writers after them to refer to male creativity, is as old as the twelfth-century philosophy of *Fin'Amors*.

11. In *Sexual Politics* (1969), Kate Millett sums up feminist objections to the commonly held idea that courtly love brought about an improvement in women's status, "One must acknowledge that the chivalrous stance is a game the master group plays in elevating its subject to pedestal level. Historians of courtly love stress the fact that the raptures of the poets had no effect upon the legal or economic standing of women and very little upon their social status. As the sociologist Hugo Beigel has observed, both the courtly and romantic versions of love are 'grants' which the male concedes out of his total powers. Both have had the effect of obscuring the patriarchal character of Western culture . . . " (37).

12. See Harold Nicholson's *Good Behavior* (1955) for a discussion of how class systems are constructed by changing male behavior, especially his treatment of chivalry.

13. Le *joi* in troubadour poetry is a masculine noun designating the pleasure of composing. It is often also used metonymically to designate the pleasure of loving a lady with *Fin'Amors*. Throughout this book, I use the Provençal word, *joi* to designate the particular pleasure of writing which can be confused with the pleasure of loving a woman. I do this to avoid confusion with the modern French feminine noun, *joie,* the equivalent of the English word "joy." In the text of the chapter on the troubadours of Occitania, I will discuss the problems with the term, including its relationship to the equally problematic word, *jouissance* (sexual bliss). Jean-Charles Huchet discusses how linguistic problems associated with confusion about the meaning of *joi* complicate our understanding of troubadour sexuality in *L'Amour discourtois* (1987) (203–211).

14. One explanation for this linguistic phenomenon (*dame/don*) is the influence of Hispano-Arabic poetry of the period which would have been spread by the troubadours who visited Spain, including the first troubadour, Guillaume IX. Many of the Arabic influences are frankly homosexual in content, a phenomenon that supposedly "disappears" in the western European tradition. This

theory originates with A.R. Nykl, *Hispano-Arabic poetry and Its Relations with the Old Provençal Troubadours*(1946).

15. Baudelaire writes, "La femme est *naturelle, c'est-à-dire abominable*" (Woman is natural, that is to say, abominable). This contemptuous statement is written in the context of the poet's admiration for the decadent figure of the Dandy—the feminine man.

16. In *Gynesis: Configurations of Women and Modernity* (1985), Alice Jardine situates the trope of "the feminine" as the "space of alterity to be explored" in language within the discourse of modernity (25). She defines *gynesis* as "the putting into discourse of 'woman' as that *process* diagnosed in France as intrinsic to the condition of modernity; indeed, the valorization of the feminine, woman, and her obligatory, that is, historical connotations, as somehow intrinsic to new and necessary modes of thinking, writing, speaking. The object produced by this process is neither a person nor a thing, but a horizon, that toward which the process is tending: a *gynema*" (25). Jardine cites Barthes, Derrida, Deleuze and Guattari as male theorists who seek to escape the history of the subject under patriarchy by imagining a subject which "feminizes" itself. Jardine's superb study shows clearly how the problem of "woman-as-writing" creates a double bind for "women's relationship to the alterity of modernity" (117). My study traces the problem of woman as the effect of men writing self-difference at least as far back as the emergence of the troubadour lyric in the twelfth century. Jardine raises the question of women theorists' relationship to language and subjectivity, while I raise the question of women's relationship to writing heterosexual desire.

    In *Sexual Personae* (1990), Camille Paglia credits homosexual men with having made the greatest contribution to Western literature and art by inventing "femininity," as a "systematic reconceptualizing of the brute facts of female nature." For Paglia "femininity" is a male persona. I would argue, however, that male homosexuality is not the structure of desire in western art, but rather the desire of a feminized male for his own self-difference figured not as another man, but as a woman.

17. Donald Furber and I did an extensive study of the ambiguity of the sexual relations in the myth of Tristan and Iseut in *Erotic Love in Literature: From Medieval Legend to Romantic Illusion* (1982). With the help of the many theoretical works on sexual difference that have since appeared, I have developed the theory of the *troubadour effect* and the consequences of male femininity on women's agency, both as writers and as desiring subjects.

    The study that established the Tristan myth as the one great European myth of romantic love is Denis de Rougemont's classic *Love in the Western World*.

18. See chapter 3 for a discussion of Sand and Rousseau.

19. For a full explanation of the meaning of "trobar" see William Paden's introduction to *The Voice of the Trobairitz* (1992).

20. In keeping with the fashion, George Sand signed her letters to Flaubert, "le vieux troubadour."

21. In "The Spiritual Canticle," John of the Cross writes:

> Allí me dio su pecho
> allí me enseñó sciencia muy sabrosa
> y yo le di de hecho
> a mí sin dexar cosa:
> allí le prometí de ser su esposa.

> *(He held me to his chest and taught me a sweet science. Instantly I yielded all I had—keeping nothing—and promised then to be his bride.)*

My colleague Susan Cavallo reminded me of these verses of the "Spiritual Canticle."

For a thorough discussion of *joi,* and the inevitable feminization of mystic poets, see Marie-Christine Hamon's article, "Le sexe des mystiques" in *Ornicar?, 20/21,* 1980, p. 159–80.

By way of comparison with the ways in which women mystics represent self-difference, I recommend Marie-Florine Bruneau's book on Marie de l'Incarnation (1599–1672) and Madame Guyon (1648–1717). Bruneau makes the point that their writing produces a negative mysticism, a place where "nothing is left of the self." Bruneau writes:

> postmodern male critics' neglect, not only of female autobiographers, but also of gender, might be due to the fact that they have not gone far enough in the deconstruction of the self. They still hold masculinity as a fixed, stable, and essential identity, one they will not relinquish despite the wreckage of identity they themselves have instigated. (219)

Bruneau's commentary corroborates the point that I make throughout this study that because the position of Woman is available to male writer's seeking to express the difference of the self from the self, or to question the subject and its identities, they do not go further than moving into a position which they designate as feminine.

22. For a discussion of the end of the heroic age in French literature see Furber & Callahan, *Erotic Love in Literature* (84–116).

23. In the first chapter of *Popular Culture: An Introduction,* Carla Freccero asks, "Why study popular culture . . . ?" (2). One of the many convincing reasons given—and which corresponds to my reason for including a chapter on popular culture in this book—is the following:

> This project is also about changing our position as "mere" consumers of mass culture and making us into critics, meaning that we approach our culture critically and we analyze it, not only in order to denounce it, but in order to understand the ways it works on us, the ways we are implicated in it. It is about understanding how our culture represents us and how we are represented in it (17).

24. Janice Mouton appropriates the term *flâneuse*, usually used in its masculine
form (*flâneur*), to describe the heroine of Agnès Varda's *Cléo de cinq à sept* (Cleo
from 5 to 7) (1961). Mouton portrays the way in which Cléo lays claim to subjectivity in words which recall Colette's vagabond's decision to possess the
marvels of the earth through her own eyes, forgetting the feminine role she had
hitherto been playing:

> When she enters the street, her expression tells us she refuses to engage
> in the masquerade of feminine spectacle and is taking on a new role of
> participant-observer in the city.
>
> Cleo embarks on a journey—by foot, in the city streets—during the
> course of which she takes on an identity so rare for women in Western
> culture that its feminine form, "flâneuse," is rarely mentioned.

It is interesting to note that Varda is perhaps best known for a 1985 film,
Sans toit ni loi, retitled *The Vagabond* for distribution in the USA.

25. The body of critical and theoretical writing to which I refer appeared mainly
between 1985 and 1991, following the publication in 1979 of the ground-
breaking volume edited by Elaine Marks and George Stambolian, *Homosexualities in French Literature* and includes: Alice Jardine's *Gynesis* (1985) and the
volume of essays she edited with Paul Smith, *Men in Feminism* (1987), Eve
Kosovky Sedgwick's *Between Men* (1985), *The Poetics of Gender,* edited by
Nancy K. Miller (1986), Mary Ann Doane's *The Desire to Desire* (1987), Teresa
de Lauretis's *Technologies of Gender* (1987), Dorothy Kelly's *Fictional Genders*
(1989), Joan de Jean's *Fictions of Sappho* (1989), Judith Butler's *Gender Trouble*
(1990), Camille Paglia's *Sexual Personae* (1990), Louise J. Kaplan's *Female Perversions* (1991), Marjorie Garber's *Vested Interests* (1991), *Displacements,* edited by
Miller and DeJean (1991), and Madeleine Kahn's *Narrative Transvestism* (1991),
to mention only those that have been especially important to the (re)conceptu-
alization of my thesis. These works are in addition to the classic *textes de base*
that problematize the issue of the sex of the writer, including Luce Irigaray's *Ce
sexe qui n'en est pas un* (*This Sex Which is not One*) (1977), Roland Barthes' "La
mort de l'auteur" (The Death of the Author) (1968), *S/Z* (1970), and *Fragments
d'un discours amoureux* (*Fragments of a Lover's Discourse* (1977), Gilles Deleuze
and Félix Guattari's *Anti-Oedipe* (1972), and Jacques Derrida's *Epérons* (*Spurs*)
(1978).

26. All translation of citations from "The Death of the Author" are from *The Rustle
of Language* (1986, orig. 1984), translation by Richard Howard. The French text
can be found in the *Oeuvres complètes* (1993–94, volume 2, pp. 491–495). The
English "neuter" is rendered as "neutre" in the French version of the essay.

27. For an extensive discussion of my interpretation of eroticism in Balzac's *Comédie
Humaine,* see Furber & Callahan, *Erotic Love in Literature,* pp. 157–185.

CHAPTER 1

1. For further reading on male friendship in Antiquity, see Dover, *Greek Popular Morality* (1975), and Boswell, *Christianity, Social Tolerance and Homosexuality* (1980). For a discussion of the difficulties of distinguishing between classical male friendship and romance in twelfth-century literature, see Dronke, *Medieval Latin and the Rise of European Love Lyric* (1968).

2. Because the term *joi* does not translate into the English joy, I will use the French term in future references to this complex notion. In *Les troubadours* (1971), Henri Irénée Marrou describes its complexity and the problem of translating the masculine Provençal word *joi* into the modern French word *joie,* which is feminine. The sense of the meaning of *joi* in troubadour poetry is developed throughout this chapter.

3. The rites and rituals include the exchange of blood, which becomes the exchange of hearts in *Fin'Amors,* and sleeping with a sword between *compagnons* on the battlefield which becomes the *asag* in *Fin'Amors.* The conventions of *compagnonnage* appear elsewhere at around the same time, for example, in the Galician *cantigas de amigo.*

4. Languedoc included the geographic regions of Limousin, Poitou, Basse-Auvergne, and Aquitaine. The first courts to be poetry centers in the first half of the twelfth century were Poitiers, Ventadour, Turenne et Clermont. After 1150 at the latest, the taste for troubadour poetry spread to Le Haut et le Bas Languedoc and the counts of Toulouse were among its most ardent supporters. The area known today as Provence furnished a relatively small number of poets; it wasn't until the time of Raimon-Béranger (1209–45) that the court of Aix became a literary center (Jeanroy, *Les chansons de Guillaume IX* [1913] passim).

5. Anthologies of troubadour poetry are often confusing in this regard. The present study, however, is not a study of troubadour poetry per se, but of a writing effect present in the poetry. For a general overview of the history of the troubadours see Henri-Irénée Marrou's, *Les troubadours* (1971), a concise pedagogical text which appears in the History division of Seuil's series *Points.*

   René Nelli's *L'Érotique des troubadours* is an exhaustive study of troubadour eroticism that also includes an overview of the history of troubadour poetry.

   Several good sources in English for the history of the troubadours are Davenson, Egan, Goldin, Lindray, and Topsfield.

6. Both Marrou and Nelli include thorough discussions of the converging influences on the literary renaissance of the twelfth century, including Arab love poetry of the tenth century in which the woman was addressed in the masculine form.

7. According to Alfred Jeanroy, without the troubadours, Dante and Petrarch would have been very different poets (15). Two centuries after the destruction of Occitania, Dante chose one of the earliest troubadours, Arnaut Daniel, as the exemplar of the poets who have sung of love, and in the *Purgatorio* dedicated

verses in Provençal to Arnaut. This is the only instance of a language other than Italian in the *Divine Comedy*.

8. In a book on modern poetry published in 1998, Martine Broda makes the connection between the absence of an object of desire in early twentieth-century lyric poetry and the "équivalence entre 'chanter' et 'aimer'" (equivalence between 'to sing' and 'to love') in troubadour lyrics. She defines troubadour *joi* as the "ecstasy of unending desire." Broda's book, *L'Amour du nom: Essai sur le lyrisme et la lyrique amoureuse* (*Love of the name: essay on lyricism and the love lyric*, is discussed in a review of three books on poetry in *Le Monde du livre* of 20 March, 1998. The reviewer emphasizes the continued presence in poetry since the troubadours of a specific aspect of desire: "l'objet n'est rien, mais le désir est tout" (the object is nothing, the desire is everything).

9. In *L'Amour discourtois,* Huchet provides a rich array of examples of the joy of desiring without another object than the language of desire itself in poetry by Guillaume IX (La Dame et le "dreyt nien" [the Lady and pure nothingness]), Jaufré Rudel (Le chant de l'absence [the song of absence]), Cercamon (la langue divisée [divided language]), and Bernard de Ventadorn (Le "joy").

10. In Provençal, *gensor* meant "beau" or "joli" (handsome or pretty). Topsfield's translation of *gensor* as lady is in keeping with the metonymic process whereby qualities of refinement sought by the male poet came to signify the presence of a "lady." The metonymy is borne out in the rest of the poem.

11. In her review of Dominique Rabate's volume of essays, *Figures du sujet lyrique,* Susan F. Crampton writes that Michel Collot's article "Le Sujet lyrique hors de soi" (The lyric subject outside itself) presents an innovative perspective. "Collot taps examples from Rimbaud and Ponge to illustrate the notion that lyric poetry is purely immanent. Collot holds that a more positive and a more transitive mode of expression is produced once the modern lyric subject is displaced, embracing the alterity of separation" (*The French Review,* Vol. 73, No. 4, March 2000, 738). My work on the troubadours shows that from the first lyric poets in the twelfth century, the lyric subject exists outside itself in the figure of the lady.

12. In *Marcabru et le fonti sacre* (1948) Guido Errante reads this transition as the moment when ideal male friendship *degenerates* into courtly love (186).

13. It is this displacement, which he sees as an example of sublimation in art, that is the focus of Jacques Lacan's interest in troubadour poetry.
    The ways in which sexual difference translates into oppositional roles such as those enacted by lovers in sado-masochistic relationships has been fully elaborated in Mario Praz's *Romantic Agony* (1933).

14. All references to Marcabru's poetry are to the De Jeanne edition of his works.

15. In a recent (1998) book, *La poésie et son autre* (*Poetry and its other*), John E. Jackson's thesis is that the object of desire in modern lyric poetry since Rimbaud is the language which allows the poet to represent the self as other. My thesis is that male self-difference constituted in language is the object of desire in lyric poetry since the twelfth century.

16. Nelli gives the following history of the use of the word "lady" (domna) in "L'Amour courtois" (115–116):

> Mais l'originalité propre des troubadours a peut-être été de reconnaître, par la façon même dont ils la nommaient, la légère masculinisation de la Dame. Ils l'appellaient Monseigneur. . . . Appeler 'seigneur' sa dame, c'était , sans nul doute, pour le troubadour, lui conférer la valeur, lui attribuer un rôle actif, masculin.
>
> *(But the true originality of the troubadours was perhaps to recognize, by the very name which they gave them, the moderate masculinization of the woman. They called her Monseigneur. . . . To call his lady 'seigneur' (sir) was undoubtedly for the troubadour to bestow value on her, to attribute to her an active role, masculine.)*

17. As explained in the Introduction, prior to *Love in the Western World,* the most influential source for the culture of Occitania, was Napoléon Peyrat's *Histoire des Albigeois* (1870), the first sustained study of the rise and subsequent annihilation of Catharism in southern France, which according to Krystel Maurin (1995), specialist on the presence of Cathar themes in modern literature, represented the end of a fascination on the part of several generations of Romantic writers with medieval Occitania. The fascination had begun, however, in 1803 with Fabre d'Olivet's *Le Troubadour* which brought the word "troubadour" into fashion and with it the "troubadour style" in painting and architecture. We can assume that George Sand who signed her letters to Flaubert, "le vieux troubadour," was one of the Romantics caught up in the fashion (See chapter 4). For a recent look at the "troubadour style" in Romantic art see the pages written by Josephine Le Foll, in the catalogue of an exhibit held at the Musée des Beaux Arts in Nantes, France in 1995–96 on French Romantic painting from 1815 to 1850 *Les années romantiques: La peinture en France de 1815–1850* (1995).

18. Of the New Testament, John's gospel was especially important to the doctrine of the Two Principles because of one particular line, "et sine ipso factum est nihil quod factum est" (John 1: 4), which the Cathars translated differently from the Catholics. The Catholics translated the line as "and nothing which was made was made without him." The Cathar translation reads "and without him, nothing (nothingness) was created." The Cathars translated nihil as "nothingness." Cathar metaphysics is founded on a dualist interpretation of the Scriptures. For Cathars, there exist two separate creations, a true creation by God, and a second creation, which is an illusion. The second creation exists in this "base world," and so all of visible creation is false. The material world emanates from an evil principle (Brenon, *Le vrai visage* [1995] 62). In Cathar theology, in the end, the veil of illusion will be lifted and the material world will disappear into its original "nothingness" (nihil). Love will prevail and everyone will be redeemed.

19. The ambiguity surrounding the Cathar practice of sexual abstinence is pointed out by John Boswell, whose *Christianity, Social Tolerance and Homosexuality*

(1980) made a distinguished contribution to the study of the connections between religious and sexual mores from the early Christian era until the fourteenth century. He says of this change of mentalities that although dualists opposed all sexual pleasures, homosexual acts were considered less serious than heterosexual ones because they did not result in reproduction of the *despised* human body (129).

20. Gaston Paris coined the term courtly love in 1883 (see Introduction). To be accurate, the philosophy of love invented by the troubadours was called *Fin'Amors,* pure love, and was a rare and privileged sentiment whose rites and rituals were elaborate and strict. As *Fin'Amors* became popular in the courts of Occitania, it became less sincere, and often resembled a game which it was by the time André Chapelain wrote his treatise on love in the thirteenth century. The general term courtly love can be applied to these later versions, but should not be used to describe *Fin'Amors*. René Nelli distinguishes between *Fin'Amors* and later corruptions in *L'Erotique des troubadours.* I will define *Fin'Amors,* and the codes and rituals which contribute to the creation of the *troubadour effect,* later in this chapter.

21. Anne Brenon, the curator of the CRNEC, Centre René Nelli des Etudes Cathares, a paleontologist whose *Le vrai visage du Catharisme (The True Face of Catharism)* (1995) is an important revisionist study, undertakes the task of revising Rougemont's work with a certain nostalgia, calling it "the celebrated *Love in the Western World* of our youth" (198). In a conversation, Brenon spoke to me of Rougemont's influence on her as a student. This is a striking example of how the same erroneous accounts which scholars must revise attracted them to the area of research in the first place.

22. The idea that troubadour eroticism haunts today's sexual relations is mentioned by a writer concerned with popular culture, Naomi Wolf, who in *The Beauty Myth* (1991) writes that "the catalogue of features, developed by the troubadours, first paralyzed the beloved woman into beauty's silence" (59).

23. The *Book of the Two Principles* was discovered in Florence and published by Father Dondaine in 1939. There is a recent critical edition with notes and translation by Christine Thouzellier, published in Paris by CERT in 1973.

The best known example of using Inquisition records to investigate Cathar history is Le Roy Ladurie's *Montaillou.*

At the René Nelli Center for Cathar Studies (CNREC), a team of scholars and archivists, headed by director Anne Brenon, author of *Le vrai visage du Catharisme (The True Face of Catharism)* (1995), works to revise and advance the history of Occitania. In addition to setting the record straight on the doctrines and daily life of medieval Cathars, disentangled from "mythological Catharisms" (Brenon 9), the current generation of scholars is also concerned with correcting the misrepresentation of the nature of the relationship between the Cathars and the troubadours. While it is true that the conflation of social reality and representation is a problem, it is also true that to disengage the two can itself distort that reality which we call culture. Historians working at the

CRNEC are only too aware of this dilemma. The most reliable sources available at this time are books and articles by Brenon, Duvernoy, Maurin, Roquebert, Thouzellier, and Wakefield. The most extensive study is Roquebert's multi-volume work.

24. The source of this anecdote about Bélibaste is Anne Brenon (conversation, November, 1995). For more on Bélibaste, see Duvernoy.

25. This period is referred to as "The Renaissance of the Twelfth Century." See Charles Homer Haskins. *The Renaissance of the Twelfth Century* (1927). Boswell refers to Gothic architecture, biblical scholarship, the study of medicine, law and classical literature, architecture, science, economics, and agriculture as part of the "cultural efflorescence" (265).

26. Boswell points out that there was a widespread belief at the time that the Albigensians practiced sodomy in order to avoid procreation. He sees this practice as relevant to his thesis that until the crusades in the thirteenth century, homosexual practices were tolerated in Europe. Boswell's book confirms the general sense in scholarship that it is impossible to speak of conventional heterosexuality when dealing with Occitania.

27. Although there has been no formal Cathar movement since the middle ages, Nelli calls himself a "cathar d'aujourd'hui" (a Cathar of today), the title of one of his autobiographical writings. It is difficult to classify Nelli's writings, since their subject range is great and includes: history, for example *Le musée du Catharisme* (1964), *Le phénomène cathare* (1964), *Dictionnaire des hérésies méridionales* (1967), *La vie quotidienne des Cathares du Languedoc au XIIIe siècle* (1969), *Les Cathares* (1972), *Histoire du Languedoc* (1974), *Écrivains anticonformistes du Moyen-Age occitan* (1977); literary history and criticism, including his two most important books on the history and significance of *Fin'Amors*, *L'Érotique des troubadours* (1963) and *Un art d'aimer occitanien du XIIIe siècle: Le roman de Flamenca* (1966); a study of the surrealist poet Joë Bousquet (1975); history of spirituality, *Spiritualité de l'hérésie: le Catharisme* (1953); psychoanalytic theory, "Tirésias ou les métamorphoses de la passion" (1980); the history of eroticism, *L'Amour et les mythes du coeur* (1952), *Érotique et civilisations* (1972); and his own bilingual poetry in French and Provençal, *Arma de Vertat:Poemas de Renat Nelli* (1952); and an essay on "L'Amour courtois" in *Sexualité humaine* (*Human Sexuality*) in 1970 which merges his scholarship with his vision of the finality of intersexual eroticism.

28. The structure of *Fin'Amors* differs from the structure of desire as described by René Girard (*Deceit, Desire and the Novel*)for whom two men desire each other's desire, represented by a woman. Eve Sedgwick (*Between Men*) has studied the homosociality of this structure. An analysis of *Fin'Amors* tells us that there are not three players in the ritual exchange of hearts, but that the woman plays two parts: she is both the male friend and the object of desire.

29. Former Chicago Bulls player Dennis Rodman's words at the championship rally in Chicago's Grant Park (June 16, 1998) provide a contemporary, albeit caricatural example, of the intimate connection between *compagnonnage* and

misogyny/heterophobia. Rodman said, "I've always said I'd never get married. Never have a wife. If I had to marry anybody, it'd be these twelve guys" (*Chicago Tribune,* June 17, 1998). Known for his off-court transvestism, particularly for appearances in an elaborate wedding gown and veil, Rodman's sexual persona represents in a single outrageous, but socially acceptable (and cheered) image, how the heroic tradition subverts heterosexuality. Ironically, on stage at the rally were the "Lovcabulls," the team's sexy female cheerleaders, complete with pom-poms—the compulsory (for the illusion of heterosexuality), excessive, and ridiculous female presence.

30. The use of the term "sodomite" can also be read to refer to sexual practices which prevent pregnancy. However, the fact that so many commentaries besides Rougemont's question the conventional heterosexuality of troubadour eroticism using a variety of terms would seem to indicate that there is a general sense among those who have looked long and hard at this poetry that the sexuality cannot be unequivocally defined as heterosexual.

31. See C.S. Lewis's *Allegory of Love* (1891), T.S. Eliot's *The Wasteland* (1922), Julia Kristeva's *Histoires d'amour* (1983), and George Duby's *Mâle Moyen Âge* (1988).

32. For the history of the myth of Tristan and Iseut, from the Celtic oral tradition, the twelfth-century fragmented versions of the troubadours Béroul and Thomas which Joseph Bédier united in a continuous narrative in 1900, to nineteenth and twentieth-century versions, adaptations, and evocations, see the 1995 Pléiade volume of *Tristan et Yseut.*

33. I use the term troubadour to refer to both troubadours and trouvères. There were women troubadours, called *trobairitz,* to whom I return in chapter 2.

   According to the *Oxford Companion to French Literature* (1987), the *"langue d'oc"* was spoken south of the line running roughly from the mouth of the Gironde eastward to the Alps. The *"langue d'oui",* which prevailed and became the French language, was spoken north of this line. Present day Provençal retains, more than French, the character of Latin in respect of its vowel sounds, also to a greater degree its inflections; it is softer and more harmonious than the northern language (393).

34. There is an explicit reference to *Fin'Amors* in the fragment attributed to Béroul. After Tristan and Iseut are discovered in the forest by King Mark, the lovers decide to part forever. Iseut gives Tristan a jasper ring with a promise to go to him if ever he should send the ring back to her as a sign that he needs her. Iseut says that she makes the promise for *"fine amor"* (75, line 2723).

35. Césareo Bandera discusses the relationship between the philtre and representation in "Literature and Desire: Poetic Frenzy and the Love Potion."

36. Another symbol of androgynous fusion in the Tristan story as we know it today is the honeysuckle, a plant that dies when the vine and flower are separated. This symbol, which Bédier integrated into his narrative version, comes from a *lai* by Marie de France. A discussion of Marie de France follows in a later section of the book devoted to women writers and the problem of *vagabondage.* For an excellent essay which situates Marie de France in the historical moment

around the date 1180, see Joan Ferrante's contribution to Hollier's *New History of French Literature* (1989) (51–55).

37. My argument here goes counter to Kevin Kopelson's proposition that the romantic ideal of fusion is essentially heterosexual, based on the "complementarity of sexual difference" (*Love's Litany* [1994] 4). Kopelson and I share, however, a point of departure. As he puts it so well, "even if conceptions of love are now passé and fragmentary, they are not necessarily inconsequential. They are active, if residual, cultural elements that have played and continue to play a crucial and underexamined role in the construction of sexuality" (2). Kopelson argues that since both love and *homo*sexuality are literary effects, literature is an appropriate place to investigate the construction of *homo*sexuality. I argue as strongly that *hetero*sexuality is a literary construction—and an illusion—dating from the earliest representations of romantic love. My major difference from Kopelson is that he sees love in literature as an appropriate place to explore the construction of homosexuality, while I argue that although the heterosexuality of the literary representations of love is an illusion, it is not homosexual either.

38. For further analysis of related elements in *Tristan and Iseut* see Furber & Callahan, *Erotic Love in Literature*.

39. According to legend, Arthur was a sixth-century British chieftain who died in the Battle of Camlan in 537 in Cornwall. In the *Morte d'Arthur*, written in 1470, Malory makes Arthur a legendary hero by pulling together all of the fragments of the myth that grew up around him, and Mallory added Excalibur—the sword that symbolized the right to the throne of England. The fragments are as follows: in 1148 Geoffrey of Monmouth in the *Historia regum Britannicae* wrote of a Celtic legend about Arthur and provided a national hero to Britain. The story moved to France: Wace is the first to mention the Round Table in 1155, Robert de Boron added the Grail and Merlin. Mallory collected all the stories.

40. All of the romances of the period include scenes involving threats of violence to the heroine's body which border on pornography.

41. The imprisonment of Fenice may represent an historical reference to the fact that Eleanor of Aquitaine was imprisoned by her husband in 1174 because of her part in political conspiracies (Ferrante, *New History of French Literature* 51).

42. The masculine form, *mi dons,* is used for example in the famous canso of Bernart de Ventadorn, "Can vei la lauzeta mover." See Angelica Rieger's "Was Bieiris de Romans Lesbian" in *The Voice of the Trobairitz* (Paden [1992] 74).

CHAPTER 2

1. The epigraph is from Fowles' preface to *The Lais of Marie de France,* Hanning and Ferrante. Fowles pays tribute to Marie in *The Ebony Tower* (1974), a collection of tales based in part on Marie's *lai, Eliduc.*

2. According to Diana Faust, the exordium, a declaration of the obligation to use one's God-given talents, is common among writers of the period (17).

3. Two books that give the history of the correlation between France's so-called femininity, and its anti-feminism, are Edward Berenson's *The Trial of Madame Caillaux* (1992), which shows how "feminine" privilege has an adverse effect on justice in the fascinating story of the wife of a powerful French cabinet minister who murdered the editor of *Le Figaro* for publishing articles damaging to her husband's career, and the historian Mona Ozouf's *Les mots des femmes* (1995), which responds to this paradoxical correlation with a survey of the work of France's best known women writers.

4. See Berenson for a discussion of the loss of women's rights at the time of the French Revolution (105–106).

5. See chapter 1 on Occitania for an extensive discussion of the evolution of the notion of *joi*.

6. My discussion of the theme of silence in medieval romances is informed by R. Howard Bloch's chapter 5, "The Old French Lay and Modes of Male Indiscretion" in his 1991 study, *Medieval Misogyny and the Invention of Western Romantic Love*. His analysis of the *lais* of Marie de France is especially important for the emphasis on the enclosure of a code of poetic expression within a love story.

7. Marie's lai is thought to date from 1165, prior to the written versions of Thomas (1170–73) and Béroul (ca.1180). In the 1995 Pléaide edition of all of the versions of the Tristan legend, Mireille Demaules concludes that although Marie herself says that the source of *Chèvrefeuille* is a *lai* by which she means an oral version, a song either sung by Irish harpists or performed by Breton *jongleurs*, textual evidence exists to indicate that Marie had also seen a written version, probably one which has since been lost (1288).

8. Sand has satirized certain male writers' envy of her abundant productivity in *Elle et lui* (*She and He*) (see chapter 3).

9. Camille Paglia argues in *Sexual Personae* that the male homosexual is one of the great forgers of Western identity, and that "major peaks of Western culture have been accompanied by a high incidence of male homosexuality" (22). Even if that were true, it would not account for femininity as a writing effect, although it might help explain the connection between homophobia, misogyny, and heterophobia. At the 1993 meeting of the Midwest Modern Language Association, in a paper on the "gays in the military" debate, Russ Christensen described the relationship between homophobia and heterophobia as follows, "Our usual word 'homophobia' denotes a condition which is in fact better named 'heterophobia.' What has passed for a 'fear of same-sex affection in males is really a fear of 'difference,' a male fear of 'the feminine' which we shall assume to be a part of most male persons. What culture is fond of calling male 'homophobia' is really a species of misogyny. The term 'unit cohesion' touted by our Senators these days—really means *heterophobia*. The Marine Corps was full of such 'heterophobes.'"

NOTES

10. A trobairitz is a woman who composes: the term combines the root of "trobar" to compose with the Provençal suffix *airitz,* expressing a feminine agent in contrast to the masculine *ador* (from the Latin -or and -ix as in imperator, imperatrix). According to William Paden, editor of *The Voice of the Trobairitz* (1992), the most extensive collection of critical essays on the *trobairitz* to date, there is only one use of the term in medieval Occitan, in the romance, *Flamenca,* "The heroine of the romance becomes involved with the knight who will become her lover; at one point, when her maid thinks of the perfect response, she congratulates her as a *bona trobairis,* a good trobairitz" (13).

The names of the *trobairitz* are: Alais, Alamanda, Almucs de Castelnou, Azalais d'Altier, Azalais de Porcairagues, Beatritz de Romans, Carenza, Castelloza, Clara d'Anduza, Countess of Die, Garsenda (Countess of Proensa), Gaudairenca, Gormonda de Monpeslier, Guillelma de Rosers, H. (Domna), Isabella, Iselda, Iseut de Capio, Lombarda, Maria de Ventadorn, Tibors.

There are only two complete extant editions of the poems of the *trobairitz.* The first is Oskar Schultz-Gora, *Die provenzalischen Dichterinnen* (1888). The other is Jules Véran, *Les poétesses provençales du moyen âge* (1946), which draws almost entirely from Schultz-Gora. Information on the lives of the *trobairitz* comes mainly from the *vidas,* brief biographies that precede the poems in manuscripts. The earliest collections of poems with *vidas* provided French translations, and a few other French and Spanish versions appear in anthologies. Meg Bogin's *The Women Troubadours* (1976) is the first full-length study of the *trobairitz* and includes the first edition of their works in English translation. Bogin provides an historical background and a cursory introduction to the form and themes of the poetry; the chief value of Bogin's book lies in the translations of the poems and in her provocative—if sketchy—discussion of the ambiguous role of women in *Fin'Amors.*

11. See Callahan, "Les Trobairitz," (1991) for biographical information on the women troubadours.

12. Marianne Shapiro's rigorous feminist reading of trobairitz poetry in a 1978 article in *Signs,* focuses on strategies for finding a voice in courtly love poetry revealed in *trobairitz* lyrics.

13. Lacan describes the split subject as necessary to the entry into language which inevitably creates a division between the "I" who speaks and the "I" who is represented in the discourse. Similarly, the subject who writes is divided from the subject who is represented in the discourse, which in the case of the troubadour effect is replaced by a woman (see Belsey, Critical Practice [1984], chapter 4 passim).

14. See chapter 1 for a discussion of the troubadour desire to suffer.

15. In *Bonds of Love* (1980), Jessica Benjamin describes the problem of the double bind for women who seek agency in the following way, "The conflict between the identificatory love that enhances agency and the object love that encourages passivity is played over and over in women's efforts to reconcile autonomous activity and heterosexual love" (115).

16. The title itself, *L'Heptaméron,* was not Marguerite de Navarre's choice. After her death the collection passed through many hands before being published by

Claude Gruget in 1559 with this title. Marguerite had called the collection simply *Nouvelles* (Tales). It was not until 1853 that the unabridged version of *L'Heptaméron* was finally compiled.

17. See Callahan & Furber (*Erotic Love in Literature*) for a discussion of the ways in which Marguerite shows the impossibility of knowing the real motivation behind sexual behavior given the existence of three conflicting philosophies of love (courtly love, erotic naturalism and neo-platonism) in the Renaissance (55–58).

   Marcel Tetel refers to the conscious design of *L'Heptaméron* and to the ingenious techniques that mirror and communicate the major themes: the duplicity in human behavior and the relativism of truth.

18. Eve Kosofsky Sedgwick explores the homosocial and homosexual implications of triangular desire in her innovative study of the role of women in the transactions between men, *Between Men: English Literature and Male Homosocial Desire* (1985). My reading of Marguerite de Navarre shows her awareness—in the sixteenth century—of the problem Sedgwick has defined for contemporary feminist, queer, and gender studies: namely, that the bond between male rivals in an erotic triangle is stronger than the bond between either of them and the beloved (woman) who is their mutual object of desire (21).

19. Jacques Lacan, writes, "C'est qu'il me semble naturel de reconnaître en Marguerite Duras cette charité sévère et militante qui anime les histoires de Marguerite d'Angoulême . . . ." (It seems to me natural to recognize in Marguerite Duras that severe and militant charity which inspires Marguerite d'Angoulême's tales) ("Hommage fait à Marguerite Duras du ravissement de Lol V. Stein" [1975] 98).

20. Christopher Isherwood compares the appeal of beautiful boys to that of women: "Why do I prefer boys? Because of their shape and their voices and their smell and the way they move. And boys can be romantic. I can put them into my myth and fall in love with them. Girls can be absolutely beautiful but *never romantic*" (emphasis added) (in Vidal, "Review of Christopher Isherwood's *Lions and Shadows*" 1976).

21. See Furber & Callahan for an extensive discussion of Neoplatonism, Shakespeare's *Venus and Adonis,* and the spread of Neoplatonism from Italy to France and England.

22. Critics Camille Paglia and Eve Kosovsky Sedgwick have identified themselves with gay men.

23. I use the term the age of chivalry to encompass the medieval period which gave rise to the knight/warrior/lover as hero, and the dissipation of this ideal with the decadence of the courtly tradition in the second half of the seventeenth century, which culminated in the libertinage of eighteenth-century fiction.

24. The theme of gallantry is introduced by Madame de La Fayette on the first page of the novel, "La magnificence et la galanterie n'ont jamais paru en France avec tant d'éclat que dans les dernières années du règne de Henri second"

(Magnificence and gallantry have never appeared in France with such pomp as in the first years of the reign of Henry II) (69).

25. Erich Fromm makes this point about erotic love very clearly in *The Art of Loving* (1956), his widely read book on the variety of ways in which love is defined in western culture. He defines erotic love as "the craving for complete fusion, for union with one other person. It is by its very nature exclusive and not universal; it is also perhaps the most deceptive form of love there is" (48). In *Erotic Love in Literature* Donald Furber and I discuss the sexual ambiguity inevitably created by the ideal of androgynous fusion.

26. A few well known examples of the variety of forms the *philtre* assumes in literature include: love at first sight (e.g. the moment in Madame de Lafayette's *Princesse de Clèves* where the lovers, the Princess and the Duc de Nemours, instantly recognize each other when they dance, although they have never met), optical illusion (e.g. the scene in Balzac's *La fille aux yeux d'or* [*The Girl with the Golden Eyes*] in which Paquita's bedroom is visually transformed, including shape and color, at the moment when Henri falls in love for the first time in his life), intense exchange of glances (e.g. the remarkable ocular duel fought by Valmont and Madame de Tourvel in Laclos' *Les Liaisons dangereuses,* in the famous "She is conquered" letter (CXXV). The metaphors for the *philtre*'s power are consistently visual.

27. In *Repertoire I* (1960), Michel Butor puts forth the idea that the pavilion scene is a rare example of female fetishism in literature (74–78).

28. In contemporary literature, novelist and art historian Anita Brookner has explored the phenomenon of "women ruined by literature" in *Providence* (1982). The heroine, Kitty Maule is a British professor of French literature who confuses her own relationship with one in a novel she is teaching.

29. In keeping with the interpretation that the princess's withdrawal at the end of the novel is to a place associated with her participation in the representation of desire, Naomi Schor sees the convent as well as home as "a new and inviolable space of erotic reverie." ("The Portrait of a Gentleman" 118)

CHAPTER 3

1. Montesquieu, "Mes pensées," *Oeuvres complètes,* 1: 1234.

2. References to the woman-like nature of Don Juan types continue to show up. In an article in the New York Times (October 1, 1997) Dinitia Smith reports a telephone conversation with psychoanalyst Lydia Flem about Casanova, the renowned eighteenth-century Don Juan, in which Flem says, "I think he is a man who can understand women. Because, in a certain way, a part of him is like a woman."

3. Allan Bloom describes Rousseau's purpose in a chapter on Rousseau in *Love and Friendship* (1993): "He introduced them all to the romantic taste—ideal and sincere—to take the place of their *gallantry,* which he treated as a school of

vanity. . . . Edmund Burke spotted it at its birth and recognized it as the sexual revolution accompanying the political revolution, the private life suitable to modern public life" (39). In keeping with the theme of his study, the loss of Eros in contemporary society, due in major part to feminism, and the liberation of women's desire, Bloom praises Rousseau's idealization of femininity, a sign of sublimation in art, as a high point in the representation of love in literature.

4. The creation of a "*preux*" of the golden age of chivalry is structurally analogous to Rousseau's creation of a mythic "golden age" of man's "goodness" in the two Discourses, *Sur les sciences et les arts* (*On the Sciences and the Arts*) (1750) and *Sur l'origine et les fondements de l'inégalité parmi les hommes* (*On the Origin and the Foundations of Inequality among Men*) (1755).

5. The choice of "*chérubin*" is not without irony, given that the most celebrated trouser role of all time is Mozart's Cherubino of *The Marriage of Figaro.* Mozart's trouser roles, now sung by mezzo sopranos, were originally sung by castrati.

6. In "William Faulkner as a Lesbian Author," Frann Michael writes (about Faulkner): "the erotic relationship is carried out, if not between two females, then still between two feminines. Writing is a lesbian act" (145). Michael jokes about calling Faulkner a lesbian author. But establishes a theoretical basis for the notion. The same might be said of Rousseau.

7. Annie Leclerc is best known in the United States as having collaborated, with the internationally known French feminist theorist, Hélène Cixous, on *La venue à l'ecriture* (*Coming to Writing*) (1977).

8. In "Reading Women: Rousseau's Case," William Ray describes Julie's role in the novel as "not just providing an example for the culturally less-sophisticated to emulate, but also by provoking a fantasy of possession and then deflecting it into a project of self-possession through cognitive containment and self-expression." Similar to Lacan's reading of the role of *Fin'Amors* in the history of desire in the West, Ray calls the relationship between Julie and Saint-Preux an example of "masculine sublimation" (440). See chapter 1 for a brief discussion of Lacan's theory of sublimation and art.

9. In spite of the fact that it was Madame de Warens who "initiated" Rousseau into sex, the experience—as recounted in the *Confessions* was far from satisfactory for either partner, and was not repeated because, according to Rousseau, he loved this woman whom he called "Maman" too much to possess her (*OA* 197).

10. See Joel Schwartz *The Sexual Politics of Jean-Jacques Rousseau* (1984) for a discussion of the role of imagination in creating men's desire for women and Rousseau's view of the feminine plot of romantic love.

11. The term "*romanesque*" is not easy to translate. One of the best explanations of its difference from the term "*romantique*" is found in René Girard's *Mensonge romantique, vérité romanesque,* translated as *Deceit and Desire in the Novel* although a more literal translation would be, "Romantic lie, novelistic truth." On the one hand, Rousseau is evoking a novelistic (romanesque) tradition in this

instance; and on the other, an architectural tradition associated with the Middle Ages, the temporal origin of the myth of romantic love.

12. For example: in "Quelques reflections sur Jean-Jacques Rousseau," (Some reflections on Jean-Jacques Rousseau) written for the *Revue des deux mondes* in 1841; in "Les Charmettes," an account of an 1861 visit to the country retreat that Rousseau shared with Madame de Warens; and in Sand's preface to an 1847 Charpentier edition of Rousseau's *Confessions.*

   We are reminded of the connection between the two writers in recent scholarship as well. In "L'Image de Voltaire et de Rousseau chez George Sand," Béatrice Didier shows "la présence d'un écrivain chez un autre écrivain" (the presence of one writer in the work of another writer) (1979) (263).

   In an article comparing Sand's and Rousseau's autobiographies, Gita May attributes Sand's "quasi-mystical" devotion to Rousseau's writing to the pleasure of having found a "soul-sister" (une âme-soeur) (42).

13. Johnson's statement is particularly troublesome in the context of feminist literary criticism of the last 20 years in which, as Elaine Marks writes, "experience has become the Divine Providence of a secular religion, the sole guarantee of authenticity in speech and writing" ("Feminism's Wake," 102). For a thoughtful discussion of the authority of experience, and the exclusion of women from the symbolic order in the feminist literary enterprise, see Eleanor Honig Skoller's *The In-Between of Writing: Experience and Experiment in Drabble, Duras and Arendt* (1993).

14. See Lucy Maccallum-Schwartz ("Sensibilité et Sensualité") (1983) for a more fully developed discussion of Liverani's unique place among Sand's male characters.

15. Writing about Wordsworth, Susan J. Wolfson remarks, "The crossover into feminine gender turns out to be not just the peculiar aberration of men like the superstitious speaker of 'The Thorn'; it is an integral part of Wordsworth's own way with words in the poetics of 'feeling'" (1994) (29).

16. For the creation of the formulation *"devenir-femme,"* (becoming woman) see Gilles Deleuze and Felix Guattari, *L'anti-Oedipe* (1972) and the chapter by that name (devenir-femme) in *Mille plateaux* (1980). In *The Technologies of Gender* (1987), Teresa de Lauretis takes issue with Guattari and Deleuze, along with Derrida, Foucault, and Lyotard, for using woman as a metaphor for male subjectivity. She writes, "only by denying sexual difference (and gender) as components of subjectivity in real women, and hence by denying the history of women's political oppression and resistance, as well as the epistemological contribution of feminism to the redefinition of subjectivity and sociality, can the philosophers see in 'women' the privileged repository of 'the future of mankind'" (24).

17. In *Female Perversions: The Temptations of Emma Bovary* (1991), Louise Kaplan calls women dressing in the clothes of their own sex —like female impersonators, a female sexual perversion which she names *homovestism* (251).

18. This crossover reminds us of the psychoanalytic model of female oedipal desire in which a woman must change her love object from the mother to a man.

NOTES

19. See Translator's Introduction of *The Gay Science* for the connection between Nietzsche's title *Die fröliche Wissenschaft: la gaya scienza* and *gai saber*, the Provençal term for the art of poetry (5).

CHAPTER 4

1. Cited by Georges Lubin (*Corr.*, 3:853).
2. The term "coming to writing" is borrowed from the title of a 1976 essay by Hélène Cixous published in *Entre l'écriture* (1986). As Mary Lydon explains in *Skirting the Issue* (1995), "la venue à l'écriture" (coming to writing) differs from Cixous's more familiar concept of "l'écriture féminine" (feminine writing) in that "coming to writing" describes "a process, rather than a prescription" (Lydon 23).
3. Isabelle Naginski signals this citation in the first chapter on Gynography and Androgyny of her book, *George Sand: Writing for her Life* (1991), the most thorough study of Sand as a writer to date.
4. For a more extensive list of the language used to describe Sand as a woman whose gender is blurred because of her desire to write, see Donna Dickerson, *George Sand: A Brave Man—the Most Womanly Woman* (1988) and Renée Winegarten, *The Double Life of George Sand: Woman and Writer* (1978).
5. Curtis Cate says that this remark by Chopin was "reported" (xxv).
6. Thanks to my friend and astute reader, Tom Cox, for this and other nuggets from the wealth of cultural knowledge, erudition, and just plain savvy which he has brought to our conversations about this book.
7. Marguerite Moreno's words recall Baudelaire's comment to the effect that "men who love intelligent women are pederasts," cited by Bernard Henri-Lévy, one of France's new generation of so-called "intellectuals," in *Les hommes et les femmes* (1993), a conversation between Henri-Lévy and feminist writer Françoise Giroud (153).
8. Jane Nicholson reports in the Fall, 1996 *George Sand Studies* that in the December, 1996 issue of *Smithsonian,* Robert Wernick opines, "She never had the gift for creating unforgettable characters like her contemporaries Balzac and Dickens—at least in her novels, for in real life she did create one character that seems sure to live on indefinitely. That character is, of course, George Sand" (132).
9. Schor opposes Idealism and Realism as aesthetic categories, and argues that Sand's disappearance from the canon cannot be ascribed in any simple terms to her gender, but because she is associated with a devalorized representational mode, Idealism. The reasons advanced by Schor for Sand's espousal of a poetics of Idealism when male writers of the period had embraced Realism provide yet another angle from which to consider the issues surrounding gender and the writing subject.
10. The difficulty of finding a suitable English equivalent to the French *jouissance* have been discussed—among others—by Stephen Heath, in "Translator's Notes" (Barthes, *Image-Music-Text* [1977] 9).

11. In an article in which she further develops the trope of the river in Sand's fiction, especially *François le champi, André, les maîtres sonneurs* et *La Petite fadette,* Sylvie Charron Witkin credits me as her source for the notion of crossing the river as a metaphor for the passage to writing in Sand's fiction ("Rivières et fontaines dans les romans champêtres" [1992] 145).

12. Sand had written novels in collaboration with Jules Sandeau prior to writing *Indiana. Indiana* is the first novel she wrote alone.

13. Although I will not pursue this line of argument here since it would take me too far from the focus of this book, I cannot let the problem of Noun's cultural difference from Indiana go without comment. Noun's status as the "other woman," the maid, the woman of color, whose presence in the novel figures Indiana's self-difference is an issue that demands attention, not only in Sand's novel, but in general. One aspect of such a discussion is that if woman figures the male writer, it follows that women writers wanting to represent self-difference look for alternative figures of difference, since "man" is unavailable.

14. I read Naginski's chapter on the importance of language in defining various characters' difference from each other in *Indiana* while revising a paper I gave at the MLA in 1985 on "Crossing the River, Sand's crossing over into writing in *Histoire de ma vie* and *Indiana*" for inclusion here. I am indebted to her work for helping me to refine my discussion of *Indiana.*

15. Kathryn Crecelius writes in *Family Romances* that one finds in *Indiana* "reversals occasioned by the gender of the protagonist" (60). I do not read the gender inversions as simple reversals, however, but as twice-reversed, like the river. For the romantic hero(ine), Indiana, moreover, the reversals are no less complex than the ones I laid out briefly in the opening pages of this chapter for her creator, George Sand.

16. Crecelius remarks that "Sand gives Indiana a chance that is denied to Emma Bovary, that for happiness outside of the novelistic world she had created for herself and men like Raymon had fostered" (70).

17. Naginski makes the point that Sand wrote *Lélia* twenty-five years before Flaubert wrote a "novel about nothing." Sand was, according to Naginski, "setting forth the existence of a new type of fiction, whose main quality would be nothingness." For a discussion of criticisms of Sand's experimentation in *Lélia,* see *GS,* 105–107.

18. *Lélia* is the most extreme example of Sand's fiction being read as confessional. The explicit discussion of Lélia's sexual problems created a scandal at the time of its publication. Sand was confused with her heroine as recently as 1952 when André Maurois called his biography of Sand, *Lélia.* Maurois' biography includes what is in my view a truly scandalous reading of Lélia's sexuality as evidence of Sand's sexual frigidity.

19. In *Fictions of Sappho,* Joan de Jean asks a pertinent question, "Is woman's writing sapphic even if woman herself isn't?" (17).

20. Naginski characterizes Lélia as the "epitome of the solitary woman" (126). According the Naginski, the solitary woman was shocking for the period.

21. Lélia's words foreshadow a similar passage in Colette's *La vagabonde*. When Renée Néré breaks off from her fiancé Max in order to become a writer, he counters her argument by saying, "but I make you happy," to which Renée responds, "Yes, but happiness is not the only thing that gives life its value." See chapter 5 for my discussion of *La Vagabonde*.

22. Women writers such as George Sand, were considered a social evil by the influential nineteenth-century historian, Jules Michelet (1798–1874) (*La femme* [1981] 69–70). Roland Barthes's characterization of Michelet's sexuality as "lesbianism" provides an opportunity for me to make the point that *the troubadour effect* is not limited to poets and romantic—thus, effeminate—male writers. Michelet is not only read as a traditional male, but as a defender of traditional sex roles. *Vagabondage,* then, results not only from male writers' conscious desire to be women, but from a tradition which fosters "male lesbianism" in the most unlikely male writers (Barthes, *Michelet* [1987] Orig. French 1954] 153).

CHAPTER 5

1. In the film *In and Out,* Kevin Kline's character discovers that he is gay just as he is about to marry a woman whose femininity is rendered ridiculous by Joan Cusack's comic portrayal.

2. The correspondence between Kristeva's poststructuralist description of sublimation in art, and *joi,* the goal of troubadour poetics is not coincidental. Kristeva's first published work (*Le texte du roman* [*The Text of the Novel*])(1970) deals with the birth of the novel in the late medieval period, and *Histoires d'amour* (*Tales of Love*) (1983), which shows how the Western discourse of love is related to the psychoanalytic process of transference, goes back to twelfth-century troubadour poetics for early examples of the narcissism intrinsic to representations of romantic love.

3. Examples of the masochistic male desire implicit in the courtly model abound in popular culture. In Quentin Tarantino's film *Pulp Fiction* (1994), John Travolta, an American example of an iconic beautiful boy ever since he was the object of the gaze of both men and women in *Saturday Night Fever* (1977), plays a role in which he is a caricature of his own cult image. Travolta's relationship with the film's heroine, played by Uma Thurman, duplicates Tristan's relationship to Iseut. Thurman plays the wife of a mob boss. The boss, known to be violently jealous, orders Travolta's character to take his wife out dancing while he is out of town. The rest follows the narrative structure in a predictable way, including a *philtre* scene in a restaurant when Travolta and Thurman share a fatal drink and dance together. Travolta, the actor, whose youthful *Saturday Night Fever* beauty has faded, reminds the viewers of what he represents in American culture by doing some of the dance steps from the earlier film. After the dance, the newly formed "romantic" couple is destined for trouble.

The beautiful boys of film are inevitably cast as Tristan figures involved in triangular desire with more powerful, conventionally masculine types. The relationship between the characters played by Warren Beatty (hairdresser) and Jack Warden (rich business mogul) in *Shampoo* (1975) is another example.

4. This was the point of my article "Vagabondage."

5. One of the main concerns of early feminist criticism was "images of women in literature." Jane Gallop discusses this phase of feminist criticism in *Around 1981* (1992).

6. In *Secrets of the Flesh: A Life of Colette* (1999), Judith Thurman reports Paul D'Hollander's remark that *Claudine in Paris* was the only novel about love that Colette ever wrote. Thurman interprets, "By which he means the only novel in which she treats romantic love uncritically" (122). This, says Thurman, is the reason Willy liked it so much.

7. Colette writes more extensively of lesbian love in several other works, notably *Claudine à l'école* (1900), *Les vrilles de la vigne* (1908), *Le pur et l'impur* (1932).

8. In another chapter of *The Second Sex*, "La femme indépendante" (The Independent Woman), De Beauvoir cites the example of Colette's vagabond, Renée Néré, as an example of a woman whose choice of a career as a writer forces her into "une solitude desséchante" (a withering solitude) (*Le deuxième sexe* II, 615). For de Beauvoir this fate is the result of women writers not going far enough in establishing their independence once they have clearly seen through the romance plot. She writes, "mais c'est à partir de là que tout commence: la femme épuise son courage à dissiper des mirages et elle s'arrête effrayée au seuil de la réalité" (but this is where it all begins: the woman [writer] exhausts her courage dissipating illusions and she stops terrified at the threshold of reality) (*Le deuxième sexe* II, 635).

9. Judith Thurman quotes a critic writing for *Comoedia* about the narrator of Colette's 1908 novel, *Tendrils of the Vine*: "an emancipated woman writer, artist, and rebel . . . savagely and resolutely alone" but "unconsciously still fixated on her childhood." Thurman comments, "And this (*Tendrils*) is her allegory for the loss of self and the dawn of vigilance, for the discovery of her voice and her gifts, and for the conflict between autonomy and the yearning for submission that will inform her work for the next forty years" (181).

10. Baudelaire's use of the symbolic wound as a metaphor for his "femininity" occurs, for example, in the poem "Moesta et Errabunda" (*Les fleurs du mal*) and in his short prose poem, "Confitéor de l'artiste."

11. The same kind of statement by the fiancé is the turning point in *Pinky* (Elia Kazan 1949) in which the protagonist gives up marriage for a "career." The difference is that the heroine of Pinky is a black woman whose career is training "colored girls" to be nurses. Here the sexist issue is inflected by the racial in that the protagonist's self-assertion is in the service of racialist desires to see colored women in their proper place. Writing is not an option for Pinky.

12. J.J. Wilson remarks that in the first sentence of *Orlando*, Woolf says just what she does not want us to think; Judy Little writes that the sentence "immediately and

comically" dismantles the male subject with "interruptive qualifications;" "the first sentence is what every sentence in the book is about and what every sentence continues to produce and unproduce in rhetorical play" (1981) (179; 183).

13. For an analysis of Woolf's discussion in *A Room of One's Own* (1929) of the gendering of the position of the writing subject as masculine see Pamela Caughie and Anne Callahan, "The Rhetoric of Virginia Woolf's Feminism" (220–21).

14. Given Barthes general tendency to equate being in love with being "feminized" (*Fragments d'un discours amoureux*) (*Fragments of a Lover's Discourse*), this statement confirms my conclusion regarding the voice of the writer in *Orlando*.

15. The reasons for *Orlando* being read as simply autobiographical are valid ones. The photos of Orlando published with the novel are of Vita and Vita's son, Nigel Nicolson, who calls *Orlando* "the longest and most charming love letter in literature" (1973) (202). Woolf herself, however, has written much about the problem of representation and reality, and warns against confusing fiction with the historical reality which informs it (the citation about the representation of "green" quoted earlier in this chapter, for example). In a paper given at a meeting of the M/MLA (1996), Nancy Cervetti made a strong argument against reducing *Orlando* to an "escapade" or a "love letter."

16. The notion that Orlando, a man who has become a woman, has gotten away with "passing," not because of her sex, but because of the subject position she inhabits as a writer is a joke in keeping with Woolf's persistent effort to dismantle categories of identity, making labels, such as masculine and feminine, and even male and female, impossible to situate on individual bodies. Caughie's most recent book, *Passing and Pedagogy,* redefines conventional notions of "passing" as assuming a fraudulent identity to the recognition that any assumption of a subject position is "passing," and that to recognize this dynamics is not only *not* fraudulent, but ethical and responsible.

17. My research assistant, Gina Zupsich, brought the wordplay suggested by the "steel" feather to my attention.

18. Claude Pichois remarks that although Sidonie Landoy Colette played an important role in her daughter's life, Sido is a "personnage" (fictional character) (*OC,* II: lii-liii).

19. Curiously, as Judith Thurman makes the point, Colette shook herself free—often brutally—of "the maternal yoke" (Colette's words) when it came to her relationship with her own daughter (251).

20. Sartre was probably thinking of Flaubert, the subject of Sartre's lengthiest study of a single writer, *L'Idiot de la famille* (*The Family Idiot*) (1971) when he made this statement. His study brings up Flaubert's sexual ambiguity throughout.

21. Gallop discusses the problem of being a woman in the academy in a chapter entitled "The Female Body" in *Thinking through the Body* (1988). In *A Room of One's Own,* Woolf describes her reaction to not being allowed to enter the library at the male university where she is an invited lecturer.

NOTES

22. Sanford Ames gave the title *Remains to be Seen* to the volume he edited on Duras, emphasizing the durasien theme that there is no experience, including love, until it is written. What remains (what the remains are) is the story.
23. For an explanation of the importance of the year 1926, see Gates (53).
24. "New Negro" was a common expression among black intellectuals in the 1920s. In his essay, "The New Negro" (1925), in the collection by the same title, Alain Locke distinguishes the New Negro as an agent of his own representation from the old Negro of minstrelsy.
25. The interview appeared in the July 1993 issue of *Inrockuptible* (53). "Inrockuptible" is untranslatable; it is a word coined by the creators of the widely-read publication that plays on the words "rock" and "incorruptible." In format, style and readership, the magazine resembles the American publication, *Interview* founded by Andy Warhol.
26. The importance Morrison gives to the hoof marks is confirmed in the name Dorcas, the Greek version of the Aramaic name Tabitha, meaning gazelle.

CHAPTER 6

1. That sexual difference remains central to the standard plot of romantic love in contemporary literature, which now must include film, is discussed by Lucy Fischer in a chapter of *Shot/Countershot* entitled "Kiss Me Deadly: Heterosexual Romance" (1989).
2. The parodic nature of Marilyn Monroe's femininity is attested to by the title of Dean MacCannell's article in *Diacritics* (1984), "Marilyn Monroe was not a Man" (114).
3. Teresa De Lauretis has suggested another arena in which it takes a man to be a woman by commenting that in a scene in which Dorothy rebels against the sexism of her boss, feminism becomes palatable to a general filmgoing public because it comes from a man masquerading as a woman, and not from an actual woman (*Alice Doesn't* [1984] 57).
4. Film culture tells us that while there are acceptable alternatives to stereotypical heterosexual gender roles for men, the same is not true for women like Sugar Cane. In buddy films, and other paradigms of male bonding, in which masculine and feminine roles alike are played by men, such as *The Odd Couple* (1968), *Three Men and a Cradle* (1985), and the German film, *Men* (1985), women are eliminated altogether from domestic scenes which are "normal" in every other sense. Their message is that men can become women and go on very nicely without them. Masculinity is not privileged behavior for a woman, however.
5. I discuss the problem of the maternal and representation in chapter 5.
6. *M. Butterfly* is a fictionalized version of a true espionage case reported in 1986 involving a French diplomat, Bernard Bouriscot, who was unaware that his lover for twenty years was a spy and a man.

7. The use of John Wayne as a model for male impersonators of both sexes is standard movie fare. This is "hysterically" illustrated in the French play and film, *La cage aux folles,* when the male actor who is the feminine partner in a homosexual couple has to imitate a man for a social occasion and comes up with John Wayne as a model. The comic effect is produced when a female impersonator, obviously a consummate actor, is incapable of impersonating a man. His representation is a caricature which does not resemble a man but a female impersonator impersonating a man.

8. Jennifer Peterson sees Vienna as an example of "performative femininity" (1996) (11).

9. The homoerotic implications of comic book *compagnons* such as Batman and Robin have become a topic of discussion in contemporary criticism associated with "Queer Studies."

10. Gans's commentaries on *Seinfeld* can be found at the "anthropoetics" web site for which he writes a weekly column called "Chronicles of Love and Resentment." <http://www.humnet.ucla.edu/humnet/anthropoetics/views/vw131.htm>

11. One of the reasons Gans's claim that *Seinfeld* has had a real cultural impact is that it defers "sentimentality," which, for Gans, is the central preoccupation of culture.

12. In "Cloud Cover: (Re)Dressing Desire and Comfortable Subversions in Caryl Churchill's *Cloud Nine,*" (1998) James M. Harding makes the point that "comfortable subversions," such as the one in *Some Like It Hot,* exist not only in works produced for a heterosexual audience, but also in those whose intended audience is homosexual such as Churchill's play, which came out of a workshop on sexual politics. He writes:

> Churchill's play does not deconstruct heterosexual presumptions but, rather, enforces a repressive mode of expression, a passing under duress. *Cloud Nine* makes acceptance of gay male and lesbian desire easy because it represents these forms of desire in terms that reinforce heterosexuality (260).

13. Thanks are due to two of my students, Gina Zupsich and Patricia Clemente, for the time they spent viewing Seinfeld tapes and discussing the themes and structures of the series with me. We had a lot of fun in the process, for which I am also grateful.

14. Janet—Jerry's double with whom George falls in love—is played by Tracy Nelson, the daughter of actor and rock musician Ricky Nelson, who starred with his parents, Ozzie and Harriet Nelson and his brother David in the prototype of early sitcoms centered on the nuclear family. *Seinfeld* exploits the structural paradigm of shows like "The Nelsons," and "Father Knows Best" for the purpose of creating an alternative family, held together not by family ties, but by shared neuroses. Casting Tracy Nelson as Jerry's double creates a certain uncanny symmetry because Jerry's role in *Seinfeld* doubles Harriet Nelson's.

Works Cited

Ames, Sanford S. "A Severe and Militant Charity." *L'Ésprit Créateur* XXVIII, no. 2 (Summer 1988): 89–96.

Anderson, Bonnie S. and Judith P. Zinsser. *A History of Their Own: Women in Europe from Prehistory to the Present.* Vol.1. New York: Harper & Row, 1988.

Arthurian Romance: Seven Essays. Ed. D.D.Owen. Edinburgh: The Scottish Academic Press, 1970.

Balzac, Honoré de. *La fille aux yeux d'or.* Paris: Livre de poche, 1983.

———. *Illusions perdues.* Paris: Livre de poche, 1962. *Lost Illusions.* Trans. Herbert J. Hunt. Middlesex: Penguin Books, 1971.

———. *Lettres à Madame Hanska.* 4 vols. Paris: Bibliophiles de l'Originale, 1967.

Bandera, Césareo, "Literature and Desire: Poetic Frenzy and the Love Potion." *Mosaic* VIII (1975): 33–52.

Barbour, Richard. "'When I Acted Young Antinous': Boy Actors and the Erotics of Jonsonian Theater." *PMLA* 110, no. 5 (October 1995): 1006–1023.

Barry, J. *Infamous Woman: The Life of George Sand .* New York: Doubleday, 1977.

Barthes, Roland. "The Death of the Author." *The Rustle of Language.* Trans. Richard Howard. New York: Hill and Wang, 1986. 49–55.

———. *Le degré zéro de l'écriture.* Paris: Seuil, 1953.

———. *Fragments d'un discours amoureux.* Paris: Seuil, 1977.

———. *Image, Music, Text.* Trans. Stephen Heath. New York: Hill & Wang, 1977.

———. *A Lover's Discourse.* Trans. Richard Howard. New York: Hill & Wang, 1978.

———. *Michelet.* Trans. Richard Howard. New York: Hill & Wang, 1987. Orig. French, 1954.

———. *Oeuvres complètes.* 2 vols. Paris: Seuil, 1993–94.

———. *Le plaisir du texte.* Paris: Seuil, 1973.

———. *The Rustle of Language.* Trans. Richard Howard. New York: Hill & Wang, 1986.

———. *S/Z.* Paris: Seuil, 1970. *S/Z* Trans. Richard Miller. New York: Hill & Wang, 1974.

Baudelaire, Charles. *Oeuvres complètes.* Paris: Éditions Robert Laffont, S.A., 1980.

Beauvoir, Simone de. *Le deuxième sexe.* 2 vols. Paris: Gallimard, 1949. *The Second Sex.* Trans. H. M. Parshley. New York: Vintage, 1953.

————. *Une mort très douce.* Paris: Gallimard (Folio), 1964.

Bec, Pierre. *Les saluts d'amour du troubadour Arnaud de Mareuil.* Toulouse: Privat, 1961.

————. *Anthologie des troubadours.* Paris: 10/18, 1979.

Bédier, Joseph. *The Romance of Tristan and Iseut.* New York: Pantheon, 1965.

Bédier, Joseph. *Le Roman de Tristan et Iseut.* Alfortville: H. Piazza, 1946. Orig. 1900.

Bell, Roseann P., Bettye J. Parker, & Beverly Guy-Sheftall. *Sturdy Black Bridges: Visions of Black Women in Literature.* New York: Anchor/Doubleday, 1979.

Bell, Quentin. *Virginia Woolf: A Biography.* New York and London: Harcourt Brace Jovanovich, 1972.

Bell-Metereau, Rebecca. *Hollywood Androgyny.* New York: Columbia University Press, 1985.

Belperron, P. *La joie d'amour.* Paris: Plon, 1948.

Belsey, Catherine. *Critical Practice.* London: Methuen, 1980.

————. *Desire: Love Stories in Western Culture.* London: Blackwell, 1994.

Benjamin, Jessica. *The Bonds of Love.* New York: Pantheon Books, 1988.

Bennington, Geoffrey, and Jacques Derrida. *Jacques Derrida.* Paris: Seuil, 1991.

Berenson, Edward. *The Trial of Madame Caillaux.* Berkeley: University of California Press, 1992.

Berger, Anne. "L'Apprentissage selon George Sand." *Littérature* (October, 1987): 73–83.

Berger, John. *Ways of Seeing.* London: British Broadcasting Corporation and Penguin Books, 1972.

Berry, A. *Bernart de Ventadour.* Paris: Rougerie, 1958.

Bloch, R. Howard. *Medieval Misogyny and the Invention of Western Romantic Love.* Chicago & London: University of Chicago Press, 1991.

————. and Frances Ferguson. *Misogyny, Misandry and Misanthropy.* Berkeley, Los Angeles, London: University of California Press, 1989.

————. "Tristan, the Myth of the State and the Language of the Self." *Yale French Studies* L, no. 1 (1974): 61–81.

Bloom, Allan. *Love and Friendship.* New York, London: Simon & Schuster, 1993.

Bloom, Harold. *The Anxiety of Influence: A Theory of Poetry.* London & New York: Oxford University Press, 1974.

Boccaccio, Giovanni. *Decameron.* Firenze: Felice Le Monnier, 1965.

Bogin, Meg. *The Women Troubadours.* New York: Paddington Press, 1976. French edition, *Les femmes troubadours.* Trans. Jeanne Faure-Cousin (1978).

Bousquet, Joë. *La tisane de sarments.* Paris: Denoël, 1936.

Bossis, Mireille. "L'Homme-dieu ou l'idole brisé dans les romans de George Sand." *George Sand: Colloque de Cerisy.* Ed. Simone Vierne. Paris: SEDES, 1983. 179–87.

————. "Les Relations de parenté dans les romans de George Sand." *Cahiers de l'Association Internationale des Études Françaises* 28 (1976): 297–314.

Boswell, John. *Christianity, Social Tolerance and Homosexuality: Gay People in Western*

Europe from the Christian Era to the Fourteenth Century. Chicago: University of Chicago Press, 1980.

Brenon, Anne. *Les Femmes cathares.* Paris: Perrin, 1992.

———. *Le vrai visage du Catharisme.* Toulouse: Labatières, 1991.

Broda, Martine. *L'Amour du nom: Éssai sur le lyrisme et la lyrique amoureuse.* Paris: José Corti, 1998.

Brookner, Anita. *Providence.* London: Grafton Books, 1982.

Bruneau, Marie-Florine. *Women Mystics Confront the Modern World.* Albany: State University of New York Press, 1998.

Butler, Judith. *Gender Trouble: Feminism and the Subversion of Identity.* New York and London: Routledge, 1990.

Butor, Michel. *Repertoire I.* Paris: Éditions de Minuit, 1960.

Byron, George Gordon Byron, Baron. *Works.* New York: Octagon, 1966.

Callahan, Anne. "Élle e(s)t Lui: L'Énvers et L'Éndroit de l'Autre Romantique." *George Sand: Collected Essays.* Ed. Janis Glasgow. Troy, N.Y.: Whitston Publishing Co., 1985. 239–250.

———. "Mediation of Desire in *La Princesse de Clèves.*" *Approaches to Teaching La Princesse de Clèves.* Eds. Faith E. Beasley and Katherine Ann Jensen. New York: Modern Language Association, 1998. 165–174.

———. "La Nouvelle Elle et Lui: Sand Reads Rousseau." *Rousseau et la Critique/Rousseau and Criticism,* Eds. Lorraine Clark and Guy Lafrance. Pensée libre No. 5. Ottawa: North American Association for the Study of Jean-Jacques Rousseau, 1995. 171–180.

———. "The Trobairitz." *French Women Writers.* Eds. Eva Martin Sartori and Dorothy Wynne Zimmerman. New York, Westport Ct, London: Greenwood Press, 1991. 495–503.

———. "Vagabondage: Marguerite Duras." *Remains to be Seen: Essays on Marguerite Duras.* Ed. Sanford S. Ames. New York: Peter Lang, 1988. 197–205.

Camproux, Charles. *Histoire de la littérature occitane.* Paris: Payot, 1953.

———. *Le joy d'amour des troubadours.* Montpellier: Causse et Castelnau, 1965.

Capellanus, Andreas. *The Art of Courtly Love.* Trans. John J. Parry. New York: Columbia University Press, 1990.

Castiglione, Baldassare de. *Book of The Courtier.* New York: Penguin, 1976.

Cate, Curtis. *George Sand, A Biography.* Boston: Houghton Mifflin, 1975.

Caughie, Pamela. *Passing and Pedagogy.* Urbana and Chicago: University of Illinois Press, 1999.

———. *Virginia Woolf and Postmodernism: Literature in Quest and Question of Itself.* Urbana and Chicago, University of Illinois Press, 1991.

———. "Virginia Woolf's Double Discourse." *Discontented Discourses: Feminism/Textual Intervention/Psychoanalysis.* Ed. Marleen S. Barr and Richard Feldstein. Urbana and Chicago: University of Illinois Press, 1989. 41–53.

Caughie, Pamela with Anne Callahan. "The Rhetoric of Virginia Woolf's Feminism." *Virginia Woolf's Miscellanies: Proceedings of the First Annual Conference on*

Virginia Woolf. Eds. Mark Hussey and Vara Neverow-Turk. New York: Pace University Press, 1992. 215–223.

Cervetti, Nancy. "The Breeches, Petticoats, and Pleasures of *Orlando,*" paper presented at the annual meeting of the M/MLA, Nov.,1996.

Charney, Leo. "Historical Excess: *Johnny Guitar's* Containment." *Cinema Journal* 29 (Summer 1990): 23–34.

Charron Witkin, Sylvie. "Rivières et fontaines dans les romans champêtres." *George Sand Today.* Ed. David A. Powell. Lanham, New York and London: University Press of America, 1992. 145–153.

Chrétien de Troyes. *Arthurian Romances.* New York: Penguin, 1991.

———. *Érec et Énide.* Paris: Champion, 1977.

———. *Romans de la Table Ronde: Le cycle aventureux.* Paris: Gallimard, 1970.

Christensen, Russ. "Gays in the Military." MMLA conference paper, 1993.

Cixous, Hélène. *Entre l'écriture.* Paris: des femmes, 1986.

———. and Catherine Clément. *La jeune née.* Paris: 10/18, 1975.

Colette. *Lettres à Marguerite Moreno.* Paris: des femmes, 1985.

———. *Lettres de la Vagabonde.* Paris: Flammarion, 1961.

———. *La Naissance du jour.* Intro. Claude Pichois. Paris: Flammarion, 1984.

———. *Oeuvres.* 3 vols. Paris: Gallimard, Bibliothèque de la Pléiade, 1984–91.

Conley, Tom. "A Malady of More." *Remains to be Seen.* Ed. Sanford S. Ames. New York: Peter Lang, 1988. 137–151.

Constant, Benjamin. *Adolphe.* Paris: Flammarion, 1989.

Cornell, Drucilla. "The Doubly-Prized World: Myth, Allegory, and the Feminine." *Cornell Law Review* 75, 3 (March 1990): 644–98.

———. "The Wild Woman and all that Jazz." *Feminism Beside Itself.* Eds. Diane Elcon and Robym Wiegman. New York: Routledge, 1995. 313–321.

Crampton, Susan F. "Review of *Figures du sujet lyrique.*" *The French Review,* Vol.73, no. 4, March 2000, 738.

Cranston, Maurice. *The Solitary Self: Jean-Jacques Rousseau in Exile and Adversity.* 2 vols. Chicago: University of Chicago Press, 1997.

Crecelius, Kathryn. *Family Romances: The Early Novels of George Sand.* Bloomington: Indiana University, l987.

Crosland, Margaret. *Colette: The Difficulty of Loving.* London: Peter Owen, 1973.

Curtius, Ernest Robert. *European Literature and the Latin Middle Ages.* New York: Pantheon, 1953.

Daly, Pierrette. *The Feminization of the Novel.* Gainesville: University of Florida Press, 1991.

Dante Alighieri. *The Divine Comedy.* 3 vols. Trans. Allen Mandelbaum. New York: Bantam, 1980–84.

De Jean, Joan. *Fictions of Sappho 1546–1937.* Chicago and London: The University of Chicago Press, 1989.

———. "Lafayette's Ellipses: The Privileges of Anonymity." *PMLA.* Vol. 99. no. 5 (October 1984): 884–902.

———. "Salons, 'Preciosity,' and Women's Influence." *A New History of French Literature.* Ed. Denis Hollier. Cambridge, Mass.: Harvard University Press, 1989. 297–303.

———. and Nancy K. Miller, eds. *Displacements: Women, Tradition, Literatures in French.* Baltimore: Johns Hopkins University Press, 1991.

———. *The Politics of Tradition: Placing Women in French Literature. Yale French Studies,* Number 75, 1988.

DeJeanne, J.M.L. *Poésies complètes du troubadour Marcabru.* Toulouse: Privat, 1909.

de Lauretis, Teresa. *Alice Doesn't: Feminism Semiotics, Cinema.* Bloomington: Indiana University Press, 1984.

———. *The Practice of Love: Lesbian Sexuality and Perverse Desire.* Bloomington & Indianapolis: University of Indiana Press, 1994.

———. *Technologies of Gender: Essays on Theory, Film and Fiction.* Bloomington & Indianapolis: University of Indiana Press, 1987.

Deleuze, Gilles and Felix Guattari. *L'anti-Oedipe.* Paris: Éditions de Minuit, 1972.

———. *Mille plateaux.* Paris: Éditions de Minuit, 1980.

DeMan, Paul. *Allegories of Reading.* New Haven: Yale University, 1979.

De Rougemont. Denis. *Love in The Western World.* New York: Schocken, 1990. Orig. French *L'Amour et l'Occident* (1939).

Derrida, Jacques. *De la grammatologie.* Paris: Éditions de Minuit, 1967. Trans. Gayatri Chakravorty Spivak. *Of Grammatology.* Baltimore: Johns Hopkins University Press, 1974.

———. *The Post Card: From Socrates to Freud and Beyond.* Trans. Alan Bass. Orig. French *La Carta Postale* (1980). Chicago and London: The University of Chicago Press, 1987.

———. "The Purveyor of Truth." *Yale French Studies* 52 (1975): 31–114.

———. *L'Écriture et la différence.* Paris: Seuil, 1967.

———. *Spurs: Nietzsche's Style.* Trans. Barbara Harlow, Chicago: University of Chicago Press, 1979. Orig. French *Éperons.* Paris: Seuil, 1978.

Dickenson, Donna. *George Sand: A Brave Man—the Most Womanly Woman.* Oxford: Berg, 1988.

Didier, Béatrice. "Le corps féminin dans *Lélia.*" *Revue d'Histoire littéraire de la France* (1976): 634–43.

———. *L'Écriture-femme* Paris: PUF, 1981.

———. "L'Image de Voltaire et de Rousseau chez George Sand." *Revue d'Histoire Littéraire de la France* (mars-juin 1979): 251–64.

———. Introduction to George Sand, *Lélia* Vol. I. Meylan: Éditions de l'Aurore, 1987. 5–50.

———. Preface to *Indiana* Paris: Gallimard (Folio), 1984. 5–17.

Doane, Mary Ann. *The Desire to Desire: Women's Film of the 1940's.* Bloomington: Indiana University Press, 1987.

———. *Femmes Fatales: Feminism, Film Theory, Psychoanalysis.* New York: Routledge, 1991. 44–75.

Dover, Kenneth. *Greek Popular Morality*. Oxford: Oxford University Press, 1975.

Dronke, Peter. *Medieval Latin and the Rise of European Love-Lyric*. Oxford: Clarendon Press, 1968.

———. "The Provençal Trobairitz: Castelloza." *Medieval Women Writers*. Ed. Katharina M. Wilson. Athens: University of Georgia Press, 1984. 131–52.

Duby, Georges. *Dames du XIIe siècle. I. Héloïse, Aliénor, Iseut et quelques autres*. Paris: Gallimard, 1995.

———. *Dames du XIIe siècle. III. Ève et les prêtres*. Paris: Gallimard, 1996.

———. and Michelle Perrot, eds. *A History of Women in the West*. 5 vols. Cambridge, Mass. Harvard University Press, 1992–94.

———. "Les 'jeunes' dans la société aristocratique du Nord-Ouest au XIIe siècle." *Hommes et structures au Moyen Âge*. Paris: La Haye, 1973.

———. *The Knight the Lady and the Priest: The Making of Modern Marriage in Medieval France*, Trans. Barbara Bray. London: Penguin, 1985. Orig. French *Le chevalier, la femme et le prêtre*. Paris: Hachette, 1981.

———. *Mâle Moyen Âge: De l'amour et autres essais*. Paris: Flammarion/Champs, 1988.

Duras, Marguerite. *L'Amant*. Paris: Éditions de Minuit, 1984. Trans. Barbara Bray. New York: Harper & Row, 1986.

———. *Écrire*. Paris: Gallimard, 1993.

———. *India Song*. Paris: Gallimard, 1973.

———. *La maladie de la mort*. Paris: Les Éditions de Minuit, 1982.

———. *La mer écrite*. Turin: Marval, 1996.

Duvernoy, Jean. *Dissidents du Pays d'Oc*. Toulouse: Privat, 1994.

Duvernoy, Jean, M. Roquebert, P. Labal, P. Martel. *Les cathares en occitanie*. Paris: Fayard, 1982.

Eisinger, Erica Mendelson, and Mari Ward McCarthy, eds. *Colette, the Woman, the Writer*. University Park: Pennsylvania State University Press, 1981.

Eisner, Sigmund. *The Tristan Legend: A Study in Sources*. Evanston: Northwestern University Press, 1969.

Eliot, T.S. (Thomas Stearns). *The Waste Land, and Other Poems*. San Diego: Harcourt, Brace, Jovanovich, 1988.

Errante, Guido. *Marcabru e le fonti sacre dell'antica lirica romanza*. Florence: Sansoni, 1948.

Fallon, Eileen. *Words of Love: A Complete Guide to Romance Fiction*. New York: Garland Publishing, 1984.

Farnell, Ida. *The Lives of the Troubadours: Translated from the Medieval Provencal, with Introductory Matter and Notes, and with Specimens of Their Poetry Rendered into English*. London, 1986.

Farewell, Marilyn R. "Heterosexual Plots and Lesbian Subtexts: Toward a Theory of Lesbian Narrative Space." *Lesbian Texts and context: Radical Revisions*. Eds. Karla Jay and Joanne Glasgow. New York: New York University Press, 1990. 91–103.

Faust, Diana M. "Women Narrators in the *Lais* of Marie de France." *Women in French Literature* Ed. Michel Guggenheim. Stanford French and Italian Series. Saratoga, California: Animi Libri, 1988. 17–29.

Feminine Sexuality. Eds. Juliet Mitchell and Jacqueline Rose. New York: W.W. Norton, 1982.

Ferrante, Joan. "Marie de France." *A New History of French Literature.* Ed. Denis Hollier. Cambridge, Mass.: Harvard University Press, 1989. 50–56.

———. "Notes Toward the Study of a Female Rhetoric in the Trobairitz." *The Voice of the Trobairitz.* Ed. William Paden. Philadelphia: University of Pennsylvania Press, 1992. 63–72.

———. and George D. Economou. *The Pursuit of Perfection: Courtly Love in Medieval Literature.* Fort Washington, New York: Kennikat Press, 1971.

———. *Woman as Image in Medieval Literature from the Twelfth Century to Dante.* New York: Columbia University Press, 1975.

Fichte, Johann Gottlieb. *Science of Knowledge.* Trans. Peter Heath and John Lachs. New York: Appleton-Century-Crofts, 1970. 2 vols. Orig. German *Wissenschaftslehre* (1794).

Fischer, Lucy. *Shot/Countershot: Film Tradition & Women's Cinema.* Princeton: Princeton University Press, 1989.

Fitzgerald, Penelope. *The Blue Flower.* Boston, New York: Houghton Mifflin Company, 1995.

Flaubert, Gustave and George Sand. *Correspondance Flaubert-Sand.* Paris: Flammarion, 198l.

Flaubert, Gustave. *Madame Bovary.* Paris: Gallimard (Folio), 1972.

———. *Oeuvres complètes.* 2 vols. Paris: Seuil (l'Intégrale), 1964.

———. *Sentimental Education.* Trans. Robert Baldick. Middlesex: Penguin Books, 1964.

Foucault, Michel. *The History of Sexuality.* 3 vols. Trans. Robert Hurley. New York: Vintage, 1988.

———. "What Is an Author?" *Textual Strategies: Perspectives in Post-Structuralist Criticism.* Ed. Josué V. Harari. Ithaca: Cornell University Press, 1979. 141–160.

Freccero, Carla. "Margaret of Navarre." *A New History of French Literature.* Ed. Denis Hollier. Cambridge, Mass.: Harvard University Press, 1989. 145–148.

———. *Popular Culture: An Introduction.* New York and London: New York University Press, 1999.

Fromm, Erich. *The Art of Loving.* New York: Harper & Row, 1989. Orig. 1956.

Furber, Donald and Anne Callahan. *Erotic Love in Literature: From Medieval Legend to Romantic Illusion.* Troy, N.Y.: Whitston Publishing Co., 1982.

Gaite, Carmen Martín. *The Back Room.* (1978) Trans. Helen R. Lane. New York: Columbia University Press, 1983. Orig. Spanish *El cuarto de atrás* (1978).

Gallop, Jane. *Around 1981: Academic Feminist Literary Theory.* New York: Routledge, 1992.

———. *Thinking Through the Body.* New York: Columbia University Press, 1988.

Gans, Eric. *Madame Bovary: The End of Romance.* Boston: Twayne, 1989.

Garber, Marjorie. *Vested Interests: Cross-dressing and Cultural Anxiety.* New York: Harper Perennial, 1993.

Gates, Henry Louis, Jr. *"Jazz."* *Toni Morrison: Critical Perspectives Past and Present.* Eds. Henry Louis Gates, Jr. and K.A. Appiah. New York: Amistad, 1993. 52–58.

George Sand: Collected Essays. Ed. Janis Glasgow. Troy, N.Y.: Whitston, l985.

Gerson, Noel B. *George Sand: A Biography of the First Modern Liberated Woman.* London: New English Library/Mentor, 1975.

Gide, André. *L'Immoraliste.* Paris: Mercure de France, 1902.

Gilbert, Sandra M. and Susan Gubar, *The Madwoman in the Attic: The Woman Writer and the Nineteenth Century Literary Imagination.* New Haven: Yale University Press, 1979.

Girard, René. *Deceit, Desire, and the Novel.* Trans. Yvonne Freccero. Baltimore & London: The Johns Hopkins Press, 1965. Orig. French *Mensonge romantique, et vérité romanesque.* Paris: Grasset, 1961.

Giraudon, Liliane, and Jacques Roubaud, Eds. *Les Trobairitz: Les Femmes dans la lyrique occitane. Action poétique* 75 (1978).

Giroud, Françoise and Bernard-Henri Lévy. *Les hommes et les femmes.* Paris: Oliver Orban, 1993.

Goethe, Johann Wolfgang von. *The Sufferings of Young Werther and Elective Affinities.* New York: Continuum, 1990.

Goldin, Frederick. *Lyrics of the Troubadours and Trouvères.* New York: Doubleday Anchor Books, 1963.

———. *The Mirror of Narcissus in the Courtly Love Lyric.* Ithaca: Cornell University Press, 1967.

Gornick, Vivian. *The End of the Novel of Love.* New York: Beacon Press, 1997.

Guattari, Félix. "Liberation of Desire." *Homosexualities and French Literature.* Eds. Elaine Marks and George Stombolian. Ithaca: Cornell University Press, 1979. 56–69.

Hamon, Marie-Christine. "Le sexe des mystiques." *Ornicar?* 20/21. 1980: 159–80.

Harari, Josué V, ed. *Textual Strategies: Perspectives in Post-Structuralist Criticism.* Ithaca: Cornell University Press, 1979.

Harding, James M. "Cloud Cover: (Re)Dressing Desire and Comfortable Sub-versions in Caryl Churchill's *Cloud Nine.*" *PMLA* 113. 2 (March 1998): 258–272.

Haskins, Charles Homer. *The Renaissance of the Twelfth Century.* New York: Meridian Books, 1968. Orig. 1927.

Hass, Robin. "*Archetypus, Imaginatio,* and *Inventio:* the Poet as *Artifex* and the Creation of a Feminized Language, Subject and Text." *Proceedings of the Medieval Association of the Midwest* IV (1997): 16–39.

Hoepffner, E. *Les poésies de Bernart Marti.* Paris: Champion, 1929.

Hollier, Denis, ed. *A New History of French Literature.* Cambridge, Mass and London: Harvard University Press, 1989.

Hovey, Tamara. *A Mind of Her Own: A Life of the Writer George Sand.* New York and London: Harper and Row, 1977.

Howard, Richard. *Misgivings: Poems.* New York: Atheneum, 1979.

Huchet, Jean-Charles. *L'Amour Discourtois" La Fin'Amors chez les premiers trouba-dours.* Toulouse: Privat, 1987.

Huchet, Jean-Charles. "Nom de femme et écriture féminine au moyen age." *Poétique* 12 (1981): 407–430.

Huffer, Lynne. *Another Colette: The Question of Engendered Writing.* Ann Arbor: University of Michigan Press, 1992.

Huizinga, J. *The Waning of the Middle Ages.* London: St. Martins, 1924.

Hwang, David Henry. *M. Butterfly.* New York: New American Library, 1986.

Irigaray, Luce. *Ce sexe qui n'en est pas un.* Paris: Éditions de Minuit, 1977.

Jacobs, Alphonse. Preface to George Sand and Gustave Flaubert, *Correspondance Flaubert-Sand.* Paris: Flammarion, 1981. 7–24.

Jacobson, Howard. *Ovid's Heroides.* Princeton, New Jersey: Princeton University Press, 1974.

James, Henry. "George Sand (1899)." *Notes on Novelists.* New York: Charles Scribner's Sons, 1914.

———. *Portrait of a Lady.* New York: Modern Library, 1983.

Jardine, Alice A. *Gynesis: Configurations of Woman and Modernity.* Ithaca and London: Cornell University Press, 1985.

———. and Paul Smith, Eds. *Men in Feminism.* New York and London: Methuen, 1987.

Jean de Meun. *Le roman de la rose.* Ed. Félix Lecoy. 3 vols. Paris: Champion, 1966.

Jeanroy, Alfred. *Les chansons de Guillaume IX, duc d'Aquitaine* (Les Classiques français du moyen-âge). Paris: Champion, 1913.

———. *Les chansons de Jaufré Rudel.* Paris: Champion, 1924.

Johnson, Barbara. "Gender and Poetry: Charles Baudelaire and Marceline Desbordes-Valmore." *Displacements: Women, Tradition, Literatures in French.* Eds. Joan DeJean and Nancy K. Miller. Baltimore: The Johns Hopkins University Press, 1991. 163–181.

———. "The Lady in the Lake." *A New History of French Literature.* Ed. Denis Hollier. Cambridge, Mass.: Harvard University Press, 1989. 627–32.

John of the Cross, Saint. *The Poems of Saint John of the Cross.* Bilingual. Trans. Willis Barnstone. Bloomington and London: Indiana University Press, 1968.

Kahn, Madeleine. *Narrative Transvestism: Rhetoric and Gender in the Eighteenth-Century Novel.* Ithaca, N.Y.: Cornell University Press, 1991.

Kaplan, Louise J. *Female Perversions: The Temptations of Emma Bovary.* New York: Doubleday, 1991.

———. *No Voice is Ever Wholly Lost.* New York: Touchstone (Simon & Schuster), 1995.

Kelly, Dorothy. *Fictional Genders: Role and Representation in Nineteenth-Century French Narrative.* Lincoln and London: University of Nebraska Press, 1989.

Kelly, Joan. "Early Feminist Theory and the *Querelle des femmes, 1400–1789.*" *Signs* 8 (1982): 4–28.

Knopp, Sharon. "'If I Saw You Would You Kiss Me?': Sapphism and the Subversiveness of Virginia Woolf's *Orlando*. *PMLA* 103 (1988): 24–34.

Kopelson, Kevin. *Love's Litany: The Writing of Modern Homoerotics.* Stanford: Stanford University Press, 1994.

Koestenbaum, Wayne. *The Queen's Throat: Opera, Homosexuality and the Mystery of Desire.* New York: Poseidon Press, 1995.

Kristeva, Julia. *Desire in Language.* New York: Columbia University, l980.

———. *Polylogue.* Paris: Seuil, 1977.

———. *La révolution du langage poétique.* Paris: Seuil, 1974.

———. *Sens et non-sens de la révolte.* Paris: Fayard, 1996.

———. *Tales of Love.* Trans. Leon S. Roudiez. New York: Columbia University Press, 1987. Orig. *Histoires d'amour.* Paris: Denoël, 1983.

———. *Le texte du roman: Approches semiologiques d'une structure discursive transformationelle.* The Hague: Mouton, 1970.

———. "Woman Can Never Be Defined." *New French Feminisms.* Eds. Elaine Marks and Isabelle de Courtivron. New York: Schocken, 1984.

Labé, Louise. *Oeuvres complètes.* Préface, François Rigolot. Paris: Flammarion, 1986.

Lacan, Jacques. *Écrits.* Paris: Seuil, 1966.

———. "Hommage à Marguerite Duras du ravissement de Lol V. Stein." *Marguerite Duras.* Ed. François Barat and Joël Farges. Paris: Éditions Albatros, 1975.

———. "L'Amour courtois en anamorphose." in *Seminaire VII: L'éthique de la psychanalyse.* Ed. Jacques-Alain Miller. Paris: Éditions du Seuil, 1964. 167–84.

———. *Le séminaire, livre XX: Éncore.* Paris: Éditions du Seuil, 1975.

Laclos, Pierre Chaderlos de. *Oeuvres complètes.* Paris: Gallimard, Bibliothèque de la Pléiade, 1951.

Lafayette, Madame de. *The Princess of Clèves.* Trans. Nancy Mitford. New York & Middlesex: Penguin Books, 1978.

———. *The Princess of Clèves.* Trans. Terence Cave. Oxford and New York: Oxford University Press, 1992. French edition *La Princesse de Clèves.* Paris: GF-Flammarion, 1980.

Lambert, Malcolm. *Medieval Heresy: Popular Movements from the Gregorian Reform to the Reformation.* Oxford: Blackwell, 1992.

Leclerc, Annie. *Origines.* Paris: Bernard Grasset, 1988.

LeFoll, Joséphine. "Le style troubadour." *Beaux Arts Magazine: Les années romantiques: la peinture française de 1815–1850.* Paris: RMN, 1995: 34–42.

Le Roy Ladurie, Emmanuel. *Montaillou.* Trans. Barbara Bray. New York: George Braziller, Inc.,1978. Orig. French *Montaillou, village occitan de 1294 à 1324.* Paris: Gallimard, 1975.

Leonard, John. "Jazz." *Toni Morrison: Critical Perspectives Past and Present.* Eds. Henry Louis Gates, Jr. and K.A. Appiah. New York: Amistad, 1993, 36–48.

Leonardi, Susan J. and Rebecca A. Pope. *The Diva's Mouth: Body, Voice and Prima Donna Politics.* New Brunswick, New Jersey: Rutgers University Press, 1996.

WORKS CITED

Lesser, Wendy. *His Other Half: Men Looking at Women Through Art.* Cambridge and London: Harvard University Press, 1991.

Levine, Laura. "Men in Women's Clothing: Anti-Theatricality and Effeminization from 1579–1642." *Criticism* 28 (1986): 126–136.

Lewis, C.S. *The Allegory of Love: A Study in Medieval Tradition.* Oxford: Oxford University Press, 1965.

Lichtenstein, Jacqueline. "Making up Representations: The Risks of Femininity." *Representations* 20 (Fall 1987): 77–87.

Locke, Alain. ed. *The New Negro.* New York: Atheneum, 1992. Orig. 1925.

Loomis, Roger Sherman. *The Development of Arthurian Romance.* London: Hutchinson University Library, 1963.

Lorris, Guillaume de et Jean de Meun. *Le roman de la rose.* Paris: Flammarion, 1974.

Love, Jean. "*Orlando* and Its Genesis: Venturing and Experimenting in Art, Love, and Sex." in *Virginia Woolf: Revaluation and Continuity.* Ed. Ralph Freedman. Berkeley: University of California Press, 1980.

Lubin, Georges. Introduction to George Sand. *Oeuvres autobiographiques.* Vol. I. Paris: Gallimard Bibliothèque de la Pléiade, 1970, pp. xiii–xxviii.

———. *Nohant.* Paris: Caisse Nationale des Monuments Historiques et des Sites, 1976.

Lukacher, Maryline. "La communauté à venir: La fiction Sandienne entre 1832 et 1845." *Romanic Review.* Vol. 82 4 (November 1990): 409–424.

———. "Consuelo ou la défaite politique de la femme." *George Sand Studies.* Volume XII. 1 & 2 (Spring 1993): 26–35.

Lydon, Mary. *Skirting the Issue: Essays in Literary Theory.* Madison: University of Wisconsin Press, 1995.

Lyons, John. "The Emergence of the Novel." *A New History of French Literature.* Ed. Denis Hollier. Cambridge, Mass.: Harvard University Press, 1989. 350–354.

Maccallum-Schwartz, Lucy. "Sensibilité et sensualité: rapports sexuels dans les premiers roman de George Sand (1831–1843)." *Colloque de Cerisy.* Ed. Simone Vierne. Paris: Sedes, 1983.

MacCannell, Dean. "Marilyn Monroe Was Not a Man." *Diacritics* (Summer 1987): 114–127.

Malory's *Le Morte d'Arthur: King Arthur and the Legends of the Round Table.* Intro. Robert Graves. New York: Mentor, 1962.

Mann, Thomas. *Death in Venice.* New York: The Modern Library, 1970. Original German, 1912.

Marie de France. *Les lais de Marie de France.* Trans. Pierre Jonin. Paris: Librairie Honoré Champion, 1977.

———. *The lais of Marie de France.* Trans. Robert Hanning & Joan Ferrante. Forward by John Fowles. New York: Dutton, 1978.

Marin, Louis. *De la représentation.* Paris: Gallimard, 1994.

Marks, Elaine. *Colette.* New Brunswick, N.J.: Rutgers University Press, 1960.

———. "Feminism's Wake." *Boundary* 2.12.2 (Winter 1984): 99–110.

————. "Lesbian Intertextuality." *Homosexualities and French Literature.* Eds. Elaine Marks and George Stombolian. Ithaca: Cornell University Press, 1979. 353–377.

————. and Isabelle de Courtivron, Eds. *New French Feminisms.* New York: Schoken Books, 1981.

Marrou, Henri-Irénée. *Les troubadours.* Paris: Seuil, 1971.

Maurin, Krystel. *Les Ésclarmonde: La femme et la féminité dans l'imaginaire.* Toulouse: Privat, 1995.

Massardier-Kenney, Françoise. "*Indiana:* Lieux et personnages féminins." *Nineteenth-Century French Studies.* Vol. 19 1 (Fall 1990): 65–71.

Maurois, André. *Lelia: The Life of George Sand.* London: Jonathan Cape, 1953.

May, Gita. "Des *Confessions* à l'*Histoire de ma vie* Deux auteurs à la recherche de leur moi." *Présence de George Sand.* No. 8., May, 1980, p. 40–47.

McClary, Susan. *Feminine Endings: Music Gender, and Sexuality.* Minnesota & Oxford: University of Minnesota Press, 1991.

McKenna, Andrew. *Violence and Difference: Girard, Derrida and Deconstruction.* Urbana and Chicago: University of Illinois Press, 1992.

Michael, Frann. "William Faulkner as Lesbian Author." in *Men Writing the Feminine.* Ed. Thaïs Morgan. Albany: State University of New York Press, 1994. 139–157.

Michelet, J. *La femme* Paris: Flammarion, 1981.

Miller, Nancy K. "Arachnologies: The Woman, The Text, and the Critic. *The Poetics of Gender.* Ed. Nancy K. Miller. New York: Columbia University Press, 1986. 270–296.

————. ed. *The Poetics of Gender* New York: Columbia University Press, 1986.

————. *Subject to Change: Reading Feminist Writing.* New York: Columbia University Press, 1988.

————. "Woman of Letters: The Return of Writing in Colette's *The Vagabond.*" *Subject to Change: Reading Feminist Writing.* New York: Columbia University Press, 1988.

————. "Women's Autobiography in France: For a Dialectics of Identification," *Women and Language in Literature and Society.* New York: Praeger, 1980.

Millett, Kate. *Sexual Politics.* Urbana & Chicago: University of Illinois Press, 1969.

Miravel, Raimon de. *Du jeu subtil à l'amour fou.* Trans. René Nelli. La Grasse: Éditions Verdier, 1979.

Mitchell, Juliet. *Psycho-analysis and Feminism.* New York: Vintage, 1975.

Modleski, Tania. *Feminism Without Women.* New York: Routledge, 1991.

————. *Loving with a Vengeance: Mass-Produced Fantasies about Women.* New York: Methuen, 1982.

Moers, Ellen. *Literary Women: The Great Writers.* New York: Doubleday, 1976.

————. "Fraternal George Sand." *The American Scholar* 48 (Spring 1979): 221–26.

Moi, Toril. "Desire in Language: Andreas Capellanus and the Controversy of Courtly Love." in *Medieval Literature: Criticism, Ideology, and History.* Ed. David Aers. New York: Saint Martin's Press, 1986. 11–33.

————. *Sexual/Textual Politics.* New York: Methuen, l985.

Molière, Jean-Baptiste Poquelin. *Oeuvres complètes.* Paris: Garnier, 1962.

Molina, Tirso de. *El burlador de Sevilla.* New York: Dell Publishing Co., 1965.

Molnar, Geza von. *Romantic Vision, Ethical Context: Novalis and Artistic Autonomy.* Minneapolis: University of Minnesota Press, 1987.

————. *Novalis' 'Fichte Studies': The Foundations of His Aesthetics.* The Hague & Paris: Mouton, 1970.

Montesquieu, Charles de Secondat, baron de. *Oeuvres complètes.* Ed. Roger Caillois. 2 vols. Paris: Gallimard, 1949 and 1951.

Morgan, Thais E., ed. *Men Writing the Feminine: Literature, Theory, and the Questions of Genders.* Albany: SUNY Press, 1994.

Morrison, Toni. *Jazz.* New York: Knopf, 1992.

Mouton, Janice. "From Feminine Masquerade to Flâneuse." *Cinema Journal* 40, no. 2, Winter 2001: 3-16.

Murdoch, Iris. *The Unicorn.* London: Penguin Books, 1966. Orig. Viking Press, 1963.

Musset, Alfred. *Oeuvres complètes.* Paris: Seuil (L'Intégrale), 1963.

Musset, Alfred de and George Sand. *Correspondance.* Paris: Hermann, l983.

Naginski, Isabelle Hoog. *George Sand: Writing for Her Life.* New Brunswick and London: Rutgers University Press, 1991.

Navarre, Marguerite de. *L'Heptaméron.* Paris: Garnier Frères, 1967.

Nelli, René. "L'Amour courtois." *Sexualité humaine.* Paris: Aubier-Montaigne, 1970. 97–130.

————. *L'Amour et les mythes du coeur.* Paris: Hachette, 1952.

————. "L'Amour provençal." *Revue de Synthèse.* Centre International de Synthèse. Vol. LXIV (juillet-décembre 1948): 31–38.

————. *Arma de Vertat: Poemas de Renat Nelli.* Toulouse: Messatges, 1952.

————. *Un art d'aimer occitanien du XIIIe siècle: le roman de Flamenca.* Toulouse: Institut d'études occitanes, 1966.

————. *Les Cathares.* Paris: Grasset, 1972.

————. "La continence Cathare." *Études carmélitaines.* (1952): 139–151.

————. *De l'amour provençal.* Toulouse: Éditions I.E.O., 1951.

————. *Dictionnaire des hérésies méridionales.* Toulouse: Privat, 1967.

————. *Écrivains anticonformistes du Moyen-Age occitan.* 2 vols. Paris: Phébus, 1977.

————. *L'Érotique des troubadours.* 2 vols. Toulouse: Privat, 1963.

————. *Érotique et civilisations.* Paris: Weber, 1972.

————. *Histoire du Languedoc.* Paris: Hachette, 1974.

————. *Joë Bousquet: sa vie, son oeuvre.* Paris, Albin Michel, 1975.

————. *Le Musée du Catharisme.* Toulouse: Privat, 1964.

————. *Le phénomène Cathare.* Collection Perspectives Philosophiques, Morales et Iconographiques. Paris: PUF, 1964.

————. *Le Roman de Flamenca: un art d'aimer occitanien du XIIIe siècle.* Carcassonne: Institut d'Études Occitanes, 1989.

————. *Spiritualité de l'hérésie: le Catharisme.* Paris: PUF, 1953.

————. *Le Tiers-amour.* Paris: Denoel, 1938.

————. "Tirésias ou les métamorphoses de la passion." *Nouvelle Revue de Psychanalyse.* 21 (1980): 133–142.

————. and René Lavaud. *Les Troubadours.* Paris: Desclée de Brouwer, 1960.

————. *La Vie quotidienne des cathares du Languedoc au XIIIe siècle.* Paris: Hachette, 1969.

Newhouser, Frederick. *Fichte's Theory of Subjectivity.* Cambridge: Cambridge University Press, 1990.

Newton, Esther. *Mother Camp: Female Impersonators in America.* Chicago: University of Chicago Press, 1972.

Nichols, Stephen G. "The Old Provençal Lyric." *A New History of French Literature.* Ed. Denis Hollier. Cambridge, Mass.: Harvard University Press, 1989. 30–36.

Nicholson, Jane. "Guest Editor's Column." *George Sand Studies.* Vol. XV, nos. 1 & 2 (Fall, 1996): 1–3.

Nicholson, Linda J. Ed. *Feminism/Postmodernism.* New York: Routledge, 1990.

Nicolson, Harold. *Good Behavior.* Boston: Beacon Press, 1955.

Nicolson, Nigel. *Portrait of a Marriage.* New York: Athenaeum, 1973.

Niel, Fernand. *Albigeois et Cathares.* Collection "Que sais-je?". Paris: PUF, 1955.

Nietzsche, Friedrich. *The Gay Science.* Trans. Walter Kaufman. New York: Vintage Books, 1974.

Noble, Peter S. *Love and Marriage in Chrétien de Troyes.* Cardiff: University of Wales Press, 1982.

Nochlin, Linda. "Why Have There Been No Great Women Artists?" *Art and Sexual Politics.* Ed. Thomas B. Hess and Elizabeth C. Baker, N. Y.: Collier Books, 1973. 1–43.

————. *Women, Art, and Power and Other Essays.* New York: Harper and Row, 1988.

Novalis. (Georg Friedrich Philipp von Hardenberg) *Henry von Ofterdingen.* Trans. Palmer Hilty. New York: Ungar Press, 1974.

Nykl, Alois Richard. *Hispano-arabic poetry and its relations with the Old Provençal Troubadours.* Baltimore: J.H. Furst, 1946.

O'Brien, Dennis. "George Sand and Feminism." In *George Sand Papers: Conference Proceedings 1976.* Eds. Natalie Datlof, Edwin L. Dunbaugh, Frank S. Lambasa, Gabrielle Saver, William S. Shiver, Alex Szogyi, and Joseph G. Astman. New York: AMS Press, 1980. 76–91.

O'Brien, Justin. "Albertine the Ambiguous: Notes on Proust's Transposition of Sexes." *PMLA* 64 (1949): 933–52.

Olivet, Fabre d'. *Le troubadour, poésies occitaniques du XIIIe siècle.* Traduites et publiées par Fabre-D'Olivet. Seconde partie. Paris: Henrichs, Librairie de Dupont, 1803.

Olsen, Tillie. *Silences.* New York: Delacorte Press, 1978.

Ovid. *Heroides and Amores.* Loeb Classical Library, 1914.

————. *Metamorphoses.* Trans. Mary M. Innes. New York and Middlesex: Penguin Books, 1955.

Ozouf, Mona. *Les mots des femmes: Éssai sur la singularité française.* Paris: Fayard, 1995.

Paden, William D, Ed. *The Voice of the Trobairitz: Perspectives on the Women Troubadours.* Philadelphia: University of Pennsylvania Press, 1992.

Paglia, Camille. *Sexual Personae: Art and Decadence from Nefertiti to Emily Dickinson.* London & New Haven: Yale University Press, 1990.

Painter, Sidney. *French Chivalry.* Ithaca: Cornell University Press, 1961.

Paris, Gaston. "Études sur les romans de la Table Ronde." *Romania* XII, 1883.

Parsons, John C. *Eleanor of Castile.* New York: St. Martin's Press, 1995.

Peterson, Jennifer. "The Competing Tunes of *Johnny Guitar:* Liberalism, Sexuality, Masquerade." *Cinema Journal* 35, 3 (Spring 1996): 3–18.

Peyrat, Napoléon. *Histoire des Albigois.* 3 vols. Paris, 1870–72.

Pirotte, Huguette. *George Sand.* Paris: Ducolot, l980.

Praz, Mario. *The Romantic Agony.* London, New York: Oxford University Press, 1970. Orig. 1933.

Press, Alan R. Ed., Trans. *Anthology of Troubadour Lyric Poetry.* Austin: University of Texas Press, 1971.

Proust, Marcel. *A la recherche du temps perdu.* 8 vols. Paris: Gallimard (Folio), 1987–1990.

Puig, Manuel. *Kiss of the Spider Woman.* Trans. Thomas Colchie. New York: Alfred A. Knopf, 1979.

Rabine, Leslie. "George Sand and the Myth of Femininity." *Women and Literature* 4 (1976): 2–17.

———. *Reading the Romantic Heroine: Text, History, Ideology.* Ann Arbor: University of Michigan Press, 1985.

Radway, Janice. *Reading the Romance: Women, Patriarchy, and Popular Literature.* Chapel Hill: University of North Carolina Press, 1984.

Ray, William. "Reading Women: Cultural Authority, Gender, and the Novel. The Case of Rousseau." *Eighteenth-Century Studies.* 27:3 (1994): 421–448.

———. *Remains to be Seen: Essays on Marguerite Duras.* Ed. Sanford S. Ames. New York: Peter Lang, 1988.

Rich, Adrienne. "Compulsory Heteroxexuality and Lesbian Existence, *Signs* 5 no. 4 (Summer 1980). Rpt. in *Blood, bread and poetry: Selected Prose 1979–85.* New York: W.W. Norton & Co., 1986. 23–75.

Richardson, Alan. "Romanticism and the Colonization of the Feminine." in *Romanticism and Feminism.* Ed. Anne Mellor. Bloomington: Indidna University Press, 1988. 13–25.

Richardson, Lula McDowell. *The Forerunners of Feminism in French Literature of the Renaissance from Christine de Pisan to Marie de Gournay.* Baltimore: Johns Hopkins Press; Paris: PUF, 1929.

Richardson, Samuel. *Clarissa, or, The History of a Young Lady.* 8 vols. Stratford-Upon-Avon: Shakespeare Head Press (published by Basil Blackwell), 1930.

Rigolot, François. "Préface." *Louise Labé: Oeuvres complètes.* Paris: Flammarion, 1986.

———. "Louise Labé." in *French Women Writers.* Eds. Eva Martin Sartori and Dorothy Wynne Zimmerman. New York, Westport Ct, London: Greenwood Press, 1991. 262–272.

Rilke, Rainer Marie. *The Notebooks of Malte Laurids Brigge*. Trans. M.D. Herter Norton. New York: W.W. Norton & Co., 1964.

Rivière, Joan. "Womanliness as Masquerade." in *Formations of Fantasy*. Ed. Victor Burgin, James Donald and Cora Kaplan. London: Methuen, 1986.

Rogers, Nancy. "Psychosexual identity and the erotic imagination in the early novels of George Sand." *Studies in the Literary Imagination*. XII 2 (Fall 1979): 19–36.

Roiphe, Katie. *The Morning After: Sex, Fear, and Feminism on Campus*. Boston: Little, Brown, 1993.

Le roman de Flamenca in *Les Troubadours*. Trans. Nelli and Lavaud. Paris: Desclée de Brouer, 1960. 621–1063.

Roquebert, Michel. *L'Épopée Cathare*. 4 vols. Toulouse: Privat, 1970–1989.

Rorty, Richard. *Contingency, Irony and Solidarity*. Cambridge; New York: Cambridge University Press, 1989.

Rose, Jacqueline. "Femininity and Its Discontents." *Sexuality in the Field of Vision* London: Verso, 1987. 90–94.

Rousseau, Jean-Jacques. *Les confessions*. Préface de George Sand. Paris: Charpentier, 1847.

———. *Correspondance complète de Jean-Jacques Rousseau*. 51 vols. Ed. R.A. Leigh. Geneva, Banbury, and Oxford: Oxford University Press, 1965–95.

———. *Oeuvres complètes*. 2 vols. Paris: Gallimard, Bibliothèque de la Pléiade, 1959–64.

Russo, Vito. *The Celluloid Closet: Homosexuality in the Movies*. New York: Harper and Row, 1987.

Sagan, Françoise. "Préface." *Sand & Musset: Lettres d'amour*. Paris: Hermann, 1985.

Sainte-Beuve, Charles Augustin. *Les grands écrivains français: Dix-Neuvième siècle, les romanciers*. Paris: Garniers Frères, 1927.

Sand, George. *Consuelo. La Comtesse de Rudolstadt*. Eds. Simone Vierne and René Bourgois. 3 vols. Meylan: Éditions de l'Aurore, 1983.

———. *Correspondance*. Ed. Georges Lubin. 25 vols. Paris: Garnier, 1964–1990.

———. *Consuelo. La Comtesse de Rudolstadt*. 3 vols. Meylan: Éditions de l'Aurore, 1983.

———. *François le champi*. Ed. André Fermigier. Paris: Gallimard (Folio), 1976.

———. *Letters to Marcie*. Trans. Betsy Wing. Chicago: Academy Press, 1988.

———. *La petite Fadette*. Paris: Garnier-Flammarion, 1967.

———. "Les Charmettes." *Revue des deux mondes*. XXVI. (1841): 703–716.

———. *Nouvelles*. Ed. Eve Sourian. Paris: des femmes, 1986.

———. *Élle et lui*. Meylan: Les Éditions de l'Aurore, 1986. English translation. *She and He* George Burnham Ives, Chicago: Academy Press, 1978.

———. *Indiana*. Paris: Éditions d'aujourd'hui, 1976. Based on text of original 1842 edition.

———. *Indiana*. Ed. Béatrice Didier. Paris: Gallimard (Folio), 1984.

———. *Lélia*. (1833 edition) Ed. Pierre Reboul. Paris: Garnier, 1960.

———. *Lélia*. (1839 edition) Ed. Béatrice Didier. 2 vols. Meylan: Éditions de l'Aurore, 1987.

————. *Oeuvres autobiographiques.* Ed. Georges Lubin. 2 vols. Paris: Bibliothèque de la Pléiade, 1970–71.

————. *Oeuvres de George Sand.* Paris: Calmann Lévy, l894.

————. *Oeuvres de George Sand.* Paris: Michel Lévy Frères, 1873.

————. "Pourquoi les femmes à l'Académie française?" Nohant, 20 mai, 1863 in *Questions d'art et de littérature.* Eds. Henriette Bessis and Janis Glasgow. Paris: des femmes, 1991. First published in 1878.

————. "Quelques Reflections sur J.-J. Rousseau." *Mélanges.* Paris: Perrotin, 1843.

————. *Story of My Life.* A Group Translation of *Histoire de ma vie.* Ed. Thelma Jurgrau. Albany: State University of New York Press, 1991.

————. *Valentine.* Ed. Aline Alquier. Meylan: Éditions de L'Aurore, 1988.

Sankovitch, Tilde. "Lombarda's Reluctant Mirror: Speculum of Another Poet." *The Voice of the Trobairitz.* Ed. William Paden. Philadelphia: University of Pennsylvania Press, 1992. 183–193.

Sarde, Michelle. *Colette: Free and Fettered.* New York: Morrow, 1980. Orig. French *Colette libre et entravée.* Paris: Stock, 1978.

————. *Regards sur les françaises.* Paris: Stock, 1983.

Sartre, Jean Paul. "Flaubert." in *Flaubert: A Collection of Critical Essays.* Ed. Raymond Giraud. Englewood Cliffs N.J.: Prentice-Hall, 1964.

————. *L'Idiot de la famille.* Paris: Gallimard, 1971.

————. *Situations.* Paris: Gallimard, 1964.

Saslow, James M. *Ganymede in the Renaissance.* New Haven: Yale University Press, 1987.

Saussure, Ferdinand de. *Course in General Linguistics.* Trans. Wade Baskin. London: Fontana, 1974.

Schor, Naomi. "Female Fetishism: The Case of George Sand." In *The Female Body in Western Culture.* Ed. Susan Rubin Suleiman. Cambridge, Harvard University Press, 1986, 363–72.

————. *George Sand and Idealism.* New York: Columbia University Press, 1993.

————. "The Portrait of a Gentleman: Representing Men in (French) Women's Writing." *Representations* 20 (1987): 113–33. In *Misogyny, Misandry, and Misanthropy.* Eds. R. Howard Block and Frances Ferguson. Berkeley: University of California Press, 1989.

Schultz-Gora, Oskar. *Die provenzalischen Dichterinnen.* Lepizig: Fock, 1888.

Schwab, Gabriele. *The Mirror and the Killer Queen: Otherness in Literary Language.* Bloomington, Indiana University Press, 1996.

Schwartz, Joel. *The Sexual Politics of Jean-Jacques Rousseau.* Chicago: University of Chicago Press, 1984.

Schwartz, Lloyd. "Elizabeth Bishop." *The New Yorker Magazine,* September 13, 1991.

Sciolino, Martina. "Objects of the Postmodern 'Masters': Subject-in-Simulation/Woman-in-Effect." *Men Writing the Feminine.* Ed. Thaïs Morgan. Albany: State University of New York Press, 1994. 157–172.

Sedgwick, Eve Kosofsky. *Between Men: English Literature and Male Homosexual Desire.* New York: Columbia University Press, 1985.

————. *Epistemology of the Closet.* Berkeley, Los Angeles: University of California Press, 1990.

Ségur, Nicolas. *Elle et lui à Venise.* Paris: Albin Michel, 1928.

Shakespeare, William. *William Shakespeare, The Complete Works.* Oxford: Clarendon Press, 1956.

Shapiro, Marianne. "The Provençal Trobairitz and the Limits of Courtly Love." *Signs* 3 (1978): 560–71.

Shelley, Percy Bysshe. *The Complete Poetic Works.* Oxford: Clarendon Press, 1972.

Sichtermann, Barbara. *Femininity: The Politics of the Personal.* Minneapolis: The University of Minnesota Press, 1986.

Siegel, Carol. "Compulsory Heterophobia: The Aesthetics of Seriousness and the Production of Homophobia." *Genders* 21 (1995): 319–338.

Sivert, Eileen. "*Lélia* and Feminism: French Texts/American Contexts." *Yale French Studies* 62 (1981): 45–66.

Skoller, Eleanor Honig. *The In-Between of Writing: Experience and Experiment in Drabble, Duras and Arendt.* Ann Arbor: University of Michigan Press, 1993.

Skoller, Jeffrey. *Notes on The Malady of Death.* Chicago, 1994.

Skwara, Erich Wolfgang. *Black Sails.* Trans. Derk Wynand. Riverside, California: Ariadne Press, 1999. Orig. German, 1979.

Sollers, Philippe. *Passion fixe.* Paris: Gallimard, 2000.

Stambolian, George and Elaine Marks, Eds. *Homosexualities and French Literature: Contexts/Critical Texts.* Ithaca and London: Cornell University Press, 1979.

Stoppard, Tom. *The Invention of Love.* New York: Grove Press, 1997.

Strand, Dana. *Colette: A Study of the Short Fiction.* New York: Twayne Publishers, 1995.

Tetel, Marcel. *Marguerite de Navarre's Heptameron: Themes, Language and Structure.* Durham, N.C.: Duke University Press, 1973.

Thomas. *Les Fragments du Roman de Tristan.* Ed. Bartina Wind. Genève: Droz, 1966.

Thouzellier, Christine. *Livre des deux principes. Introduction, texte critique, traduction, notes et index.* Paris: Le Cerf, 1973.

Thurman, Judith. *Secrets of the Flesh: A Life of Colette.* London: Bloomsbury, 1999.

Topsfield, L. T. *Chrétien de Troyes: A Study of the Arthurian Romances.* Cambridge: Cambridge University Press, 1981.

————. *Troubadours and Love.* Cambridge: Cambridge University Press, 1975.

Tristan et Yseut: premières versions européennes. Ed. Christiane Marchello-Nizia. Paris: Gallimard, Bibliothèque de la Pléiade, 1995.

Urfé, Honoré d'. *L'Astrée.* 5 vols. Lyons: Pierre Masson, 1925–28.

Valéry, Paul. *Oeuvres.* Paris: Gallimard, Bibliothèque de la Pléiade, 1960.

Véran, Jules. *Les poétesses provençales du moyen âge et de nos jours.* Paris: A. Quillet, 1946.

Vidal, Gore. Review of *Lions and Shadows* by Christopher Isherwood. *New York Review of Books.* 9 December 1976.

Wakefield, Walter L. *Heresy, Crusade and Inquisition in Southern France 1100–1250.* Berkeley and Los Angeles: University of California Press, 1981.

Ward-Jouve, Nicole. *Colette*. Brighton: Harvester, 1987.

Waugh, Evelyn. *Brideshead Revisited*. Boston: Little, Brown, 1946.

Wettstein, J. *Mezura: L'Idéal des troubadours*. Zurich: Leeman, 1945.

Whitman, Walt. *"O throat!"* "Out of the Cradle Endlessly Rocking." *Complete Poetry and Collected Prose*. New York: Library of America, 1982. 391.

Whitney, Craig. R. "In Final Adieu, France Gives Pamela Harriman Top Honor," *New York Times,* 9 February 1997.

Wicky-Ouaknine, Lise. "Femmes troubadours: Au jeu de l'amour vrai, quelques strophes d'avance." *Féminin passé* no. 267 (décembre, 1987): 34–37.

Wild, David. *Seinfeld; the totally unauthorized tribute [not that there's anything wrong with that]*. New York: Three Rivers Press, 1998.

Willemart, Philippe. "Les sources de la jouissance et de l'art selon Proust," *Littérature,* no. 89 (février, 1993): 33–43.

Wills, Gary. *John Wayne's America*. New York: Touchstone (Simon & Schuster), 1997.

Wilson, J.J. "Why *Orlando* is Difficult?" *New Feminist Essays on Virginia Woolf.* Ed. Jane Marcus. Lincoln: University of Nebraska Press, 1981. 170–184.

Winegarten, Renée. *The Double Life of George Sand: Woman and Writer.* New York: Basic Books, 1978.

Winn, Colette. "Marguerite de Navarre." in *French Women Writers.* Eds. Eva Martin Sartori and Dorothy Wynne Zimmerman. New York, Westport Ct, London: Greenwood Press, 1991. 313–323.

Wolf, Naomi. *The Beauty Myth*. New York: William Morrow, 1991.

Wolfson, Susan J. "*Lyrical Ballads* and the Language of (Men) Feeling: Wordsworth Writing Women's Voices." *Men in Feminism*. Ed. Thaïs Morgan. Albany: State University of New York Press, 1994. 29–57.

Woolf, Virginia. *Between the Acts.* New York: Harcourt, 1941.

———. *The Diary of Virginia Woolf.* 5 vols. Ed. Anne Oliver Bell. New York: Harcourt Brace Jovanovich, 1977–84.

———. *Moments of Being.* Ed. Jeanne Schulkind. New York: Harcourt Brace Janovanovich, 1976.

———. *Orlando: A Biography.* New York: Harcourt Brace & Company, 1992.

———. *A Room of One's Own.* New York: Harcourt Brace Jovanovich, 1981.

———. *The Waves.* New York: Harcourt, Brace, 1931.

———. *A Writer's Diary.* New York: Harcourt, 1954.

Zufferey, François. "Toward a Delimitation of the Trobairitz Corpus." *The Voice of the Trobairitz.* Ed. William D. Paden, Philadelphia: University of Pennsylvania Press, 1982. 30–43.

FILMOGRAPHY

And God Created Woman (Et Dieu . . . créa la femme). Dir. Roger Vadim. U.C.I.L./ Cocinor, 1956.

Barbarella. Dir. Roger Vadim. Paramount Pictures, 1968.

Being John Malkovich. Dir. Spike Jonze. Grammercy Pictures, 1999.

Bringing Up Baby. Dir. Howard Hawks. Malofilm Distribution, 1938.

Butch Cassidy and the Sundance Kid. Dir. George Roy Hill. Twentieth Century Fox, 1969.

Chasing Amy. Dir. Kevin Smith. Miramax Films, 1997.

Cléo de 5 à 7. Dir. Agnès Varda. Rome Paris Films, 1985.

The Crying Game. Dir. Neil Jordan. Channel Four Films, 1992.

Johnny Guitar. Dir. Nicholas Ray. Republic Pictures, 1954.

Humoresque. Dir. Jean Negulesco. MGM, 1946.

In & Out. Dir. Frank Oz. Paramount Pictures, 1997.

The Kiss of the Spider Woman. Dir. Hector Babenco. Columbia TriStar, 1985.

Love and Death on Long Island. Dir. Richard Kwietniowski. Cinepix Film Properties, Inc., 1997.

La Cage aux folles. Dir. Edouard Molinaro. Les Productions Artistes Associés, 1978.

M. Butterfly. Dir. David Cronenberg. Warner Bros., 1993.

The Malady of Death. Dir. Jeffrey Skoller. Canyon Cinema, 1994.

Men. Dir. Doris Dörrie. Movies Unlimited, 1985.

Philadelphia. Dir. Jonathan Demme. Columbia TriStar, 1993.

Pinky. Dir. Elia Kazan. Twentieth Century Fox, 1949.

Pulp Fiction. Dir. Quentin Tarantino. Miramax Films, 1994.

Odd Couple. Dir. Gene Saks. Paramount Pictures, 1968.

Ridicule. Dir. Patrice Leconte. Miramax Films, 1996.

Sans toit ni loi. Dir. Agnès Varda. Films A2, 1961.

Saturday Night Fever. Dir. John Badham. Paramount Pictures, 1977.

Shampoo. Dir. Hal Ashby. Columbia Pictures Corporation, 1975.

Some Like It Hot. Dir. Billy Wilder. United Artists, 1959.

Thelma & Louise. Dir. Ridley Scott. MGM, 1991.

Tootsie. Dir. Sydney Pollack. Columbia Pictures, 1982.

Trois hommes et un couffin (*Three Men and a Cradle*). Dir. Coline Seveau. Flack Film, Sopro Films, TFI Films, 1985.

Victor/Victoria. Dir. Blake Edwards. MGM, 1982.

Viktor und Viktoria. Dir. Reinhold Schünzel. Universum Film A.G., 1933.

Index

Duras, Marguerite, 7, 8, 17, 71,128,
  180, 182–87, 192; *L'Amant*, 7,
  182–87; *La maladie de la mort*,
  185–86; *La mer écrite*, 182
Duvernoy, Jean, 11

effeminacy, 8, 56, 96, 105, 212
  see also female impersonation;
  feminine; femininity
Eleanor of Aquitaine, 27, 40, 227 n.
  41
Elizabethan age, 6, 169
epic poems: see *Chansons de geste*.
Eros, 33
eroticism, 2, 5, 8, 10, 13, 16, 22, 23,
  26, 29, 31, 36, 38, 43, 45, 63,
  66, 69, 76–78, 81, 84, 87–90,
  94, 96, 133, 45, 149, 153, 164,
  165, 171, 172, 186, 197, 198
  and bliss, 10, 12, 14, 156–57
  homosexual, 2, 12–13, 16, 71, 76,
    203, 210, 213
  heterosexual, 2, 12–13, 26, 31,
    36, 38, 50, 69, 76
  and writing, 58, 68, 85–7,
    159–65, 171
  and troubadours, 2, 26, 34,
    36–37, 38, 106, 195
erotic love, 8, 26, 36, 38, 50
Errante, Guido, 222 n. 12
exchange of hearts, 19, 28, 31,
  36–37, 42, 51–2, 71, 76, 96, 97,
  106
  see also Fin'*Amors*

Farinelli, 16
Faulkner, William, 232 n. 6
Faust, Diana, 228 n. 2
female impersonation, 8, 15, 22, 58,
  77, 79, 113, 149–50, 197–98,
  199, 200, 203

feminine, "the," 3, 12, 19, 22, 42,
  46, 50, 53, 56–7, 83, 89, 109,
  112, 114, 123, 140, 142, 245,
  146, 202, 312 n. 10
  as (self)difference, 111–12, 116,
    123, 124, 169–70, 172, 189
  double feminine, 4, 44, 101, 116,
    118, 145, 153, 173, 181,
    193
  voice, 10, 12, 14, 15
  as writing position, 6, 22–23, 74,
    77, 107, 170, 218 n. 16
femininity, 8, 11, 13, 14, 42, 49, 161,
  169, 204, 205, 218 n. 16
  anti-feminism, 56, 69
  and language, 10, 91
  feminism, 56–57
  performance of (masquerade),
    14–15, 21–24, 58, 114, 120,
    123, 124, 125, 126, 155, 158,
    197–204, 205–07
  and woman writer, 61–62,
    123–29, 190 (*see* vagabondage)
  and writing, 16–20, 21–24,
    61–62, 70, 107, 112, 116, 124,
    129, 172–74, 176–77, 190
femme fatale, 42, 48, 189
Ferrante, Joan, 67
fetishism, 88–90, 91, 130, 231 n.
  27
Fichte, Johann Gottlieb, 17, 97–99,
  100, 112
Fin'Amors, 2, 3, 16, 17, 19, 26, 29,
  31, 32, 38, 40, 41, 42, 43, 44,
  45, 47, 48, 52, 53, 55, 60, 61,
  65–69, 71–72, 74, 75, 80, 82,
  83, 86, 91, 96, 99, 103, 106,
  110, 127, 144, 158, 161, 201,
  207, 208, 221 n. 3, 224 n. 20,
  229 n. 10
  see also courtly love
Fischer, Lucy, 229 n. 1
Fitzgerald, Penelope, 98–99

and heterosexuality; 1–2, 6, 8, 12,
25, 38–39, 106, 148–9, 152–54,
159, 163–65, 172–74, 181, 196,
207
as language, 11, 28–29, 31,
33–34, 39, 53, 57–58, 74, 137,
156–60, 170, 190
masculine, 205
and sexuality, 36, 49, 73–74,
77–78, 89–90, 111–12, 146–51,
154, 160–67, 171, 186, 191,
209, 211
troubadour (*see trobairitz*)
wild woman, 187–94
woman in love, 118, 161, 180, 190
writer, 5–8, 17, 19–20, 21, 55,
62–63, 64, 68–9, 77, 89,

107–08, 123–29, 144–45,
chapter 5 passim
Wolf, Naomi, 224 n. 22
Wolfson, Susan J., 233 n. 15
Woolf, Virginia, 6, 17, 19, 113, 124,
155, 159, 167–74, 177, 180;
Between the Acts, 168; *Orlando*,
6, 17, 124, 155, 159, 167–74,
177, 237 n. 12, 238 n. 14, n.
15, n. 16; *A Room of One's
Own*, 19, 173 238 n. 13, n. 21;
The Waves, 169; *A Writer's
Diary*, 167
Wordsworth, William, 97, 233
n. 15
writing, *see* desire, eroticism,
feminine, woman writer